I0128161

George W. Bush

SUNY series on the
Presidency: Contemporary Issues

John Kenneth White, editor

George W. Bush

Evaluating the President at Midterm

Edited By
Bryan Hilliard, Tom Lansford, Robert P. Watson

State University of New York Press

Published by

State University of New York Press, Albany

© 2004 State University of New York
All rights reserved

Printed in the United States of America

No part of this book may be used or reproduced in any manner
whatsoever without written permission. No part of this
book may be stored in a retrieval system or transmitted in any
form or by any means including electronic, electrostatic,
magnetic tape, mechanical, photocopying, recording,
or otherwise without the prior permission in
writing of the publisher.

For information, address State University of New York Press,
90 State Street, Suite 700, Albany, NY 12207

Production by Michael Haggett
Marketing by Susan M. Petrie

Library of Congress Cataloging-in-Publication Data

George W. Bush: evaluating the president at midterm/edited by Bryan Hilliard,
Tom Lansford, and Robert P. Watson.
  p. cm.
  Includes bibliographical references and index.
  ISBN 0-7914-6133-5 (hardcover: alk. paper—ISBN 0-7914-6134-3
(pbk.: alk. paper)
  1. Bush, George W. (George Walker), 1946– 2. United States—Politics and
government—2001. I. Hilliard, Bryan, 1957– II. Lansford, Tom. III. Watson,
Robert P., 1963–
E903.G465 2005
973.931'092—dc22   2004008538

10 9 8 7 6 5 4 3 2 1

For Brenda, Amber, and Claudia—
With all our love and admiration

Contents

Preface

Evaluating presidents is a compelling and an important exercise. Whether it occurs on political talk shows, among colleagues standing around the office water cooler, by the political cartoonist's pen, or through the act of voting, evaluation is something we all do on a regular basis. The process of rating and evaluating presidents by presidential pollsters or scholars has far-reaching consequences. Presidents and members of Congress watch the presidential approval ratings closely, with an eye to how changes in popularity impact the commander in chief's ability to govern. Such polls are now taken on an almost daily basis, and any change in one direction or the other may have dramatic consequences. Indeed, the news media devotes considerable attention to the opinion polls and the periodic presidential rankings by scholars. It is natural to want to know how the president has performed, and it is unavoidable to compare the performance of presidents. So too do the stakes remain high even after a president leaves office. A president's standing is then subject to frequent reevaluations by historians, whose hindsight benefits from the release of documents, new interpretations of events, and the passing of time.

This book is dedicated to evaluating the presidency of George W. Bush. Presidential assessment is an exciting and a challenging enterprise, made all the more difficult by the fact that, as we write, the president is still in office. The evaluation contained herein was conducted at midpoint in an effort to provide one of the earliest scholarly assessments of President George W. Bush. However, this evaluation does not pretend to provide an exhaustive and a conclusive assessment of Bush's presidency. It only begins what will be a long process. The utility of this early rating is that it provides us with an important analysis of his first two years in office—the time of the key transition to governing and first "100 days," the period of greatest appointment and nomination activity, and his initial attempt to set the legislative agenda—and the momentous events that surrounded Bush's first two years. This early assessment further allows us to begin to ask the kinds of questions that will shape future discussions and that will eventually help evaluate Bush's presidential performance, while producing information for later comparative analysis.

Most ratings of presidents occur long after they leave office. Such ratings are done through ranking polls whereby presidents are placed in categories such as "great" and "failure" or rank-ordered from top to bottom by presidential historians. This book offers an evaluation of George W. Bush that goes beyond such evaluative tools and public approval ratings by employing political, historical, and ethical assessments of the Bush presidency and his leadership, ethical record, domestic policy, foreign policy, national security policy, and team of advisors. The assessments are balanced and probing, and every effort was made by the contributors and the editors to produce scholarly yet highly readable chapters. We believe the book is thus suitable for students—undergraduate and graduate—beginning their study of the presidency. Scholars and researchers from various disciplines should also find the book valuable. The book concludes with a graded "report card" of George W. Bush at midpoint.

This project is the by-product of a scholarly conference convened at the Gulf Coast Campus of the University of Southern Mississippi on November 22 and 23, 2002. Thirty experts on the presidency from around the country and world, with a variety of viewpoints, and representing such fields as history, political science, and philosophy, participated in the conference. The work of fourteen of those participants is included in this book. Of course, without the quality scholarship of these contributors, this book would not be possible, so to our valued colleagues we offer our appreciation for sharing our enthusiasm for evaluating President Bush.

The editors wish to thank the administration of the University of Southern Mississippi-Gulf Coast for hosting the conference, in particular, Dr. Denise von Herrmann for her encouragement and support. Generous financial support was provided by the Center for International Politics and Ethics, and we are in their debt. We would also like to thank Jack Covarrubias and Sharon Meyers for their assistance with the project, and we express our appreciation to James D. Buffett for his assistance with manuscript preparation. Others—the staff at the Library of Congress, the Congressional Research Service, and office of congressman Robert Wexler—provided assistance in collecting data. To Michael Rinella and the staff at State University of New York Press, we extend our sincere appreciation for supporting this project.

Bryan Hilliard
Henniker, NH

Tom Lansford
Long Beach, MS

Robert P. Watson
Boca Raton, FL

Introduction

Robert P. Watson, Bryan Hilliard, and Tom Lansford

Why evaluate the president? It is an endeavor performed at some level and to some degree by countless Americans and individuals around the world. The nightly newscasts, editorial pages, and talk radio shows certainly engage in their share of analysis, coinciding in the modern era with the emergence of the president as the focal point of the American political system and symbol of the nation. As the presidency is the country's most visible office, Americans generally know a great deal about the office and the person occupying it. The country (and a good part of the world) watches presidential inaugurations, follows the annual State of the Union address, and understands the roles presidents play in state affairs, ceremonial events, and times of crisis. From the armchair pundits who assess their president on a regular basis to those of us who perform our civic duty every four years at the polls, the president is routinely evaluated.

With the public, the press, and presidential scholars alike focusing on presidential performance, something of a cottage industry of presidential ratings has emerged. It all began in 1948, when the results of a poll were published in *Life* magazine.[1] The noted historian Arthur Schlesinger surveyed fifty-five historians, asking them to rate the presidents in categories of "great," "near great," "average," "below average," and "failure." Schlesinger was asked to produce another ranking, and he obliged in 1962 by publishing the results of a survey of seventy-five historians in the *New York Times Magazine*.[2]

Since the two Schlesinger polls, several scholars have offered rankings and ratings of the presidents,[3] public approval polls have become a daily feature of presidential politics,[4] a scholarly field of presidential character study has emerged,[5] and the media is vigilant in its watch for even the slightest hint of a presidential stumble or political miscue. Indeed, presidents are the focus of the proverbial poking and prodding of scholars and biographers, and they continue to be long after they leave office. In recent years, scholars have even begun evaluating and ranking the performance of first ladies.[6]

Presidential performance has been assessed in many different ways. Public opinion ratings have been employed, along with numerical rankings beginning with number "1," "best" and "worst" labels, Likert scales, Schlesinger-inspired categories such as "great," "average," and "failure," and even dozens of scientifically weighted criteria such as the number of vetoes sustained and treaties ratified. Presidential scholar Stephen J. Wayne identifies several perspectives used in assessing presidents: use of power (Neustadt); character-based leadership qualities

(Barber, Renshon); leadership style (Burns, Greenstein); democratic leadership (Burns); political leadership (Davis, Milkis); effectiveness in modeling contemporary beliefs about leadership (Burns, Edwards and Wayne, Genovese); how well they overcome the paradoxes that frame the office (Cronin and Genovese); the historic/cyclical periods in which they serve (Skowronek); and the use of rhetoric and ability to motivate the public (Kernell).[7] What remains clear is that both considerable debate on and interest in evaluating the presidents exist.

THE CHALLENGE OF THE PRESIDENCY, AND THE CHALLENGE OF ASSESSING THE PRESIDENT: A COMPLEX, EVOLVING OFFICE

The presidency is the center of American government. In spite of institutionalized checks and balances, the presidency has evolved well beyond the constitutionally weak office envisioned by the framers to become the most dominant institution in government. While still an office shaped by its history and constitutional limitations, it bears little resemblance to the one George Washington forged over 200 years ago. The office has evolved over time in response to crisis, the expanding role of government domestically and of the United States in world affairs, and through the sheer will of its occupants and their expansive view of Article II of the U.S. Constitution. Not surprisingly, questions have been raised both historically and today about how to view or study the presidency. Dating to the nation's founding, Hamilton and others maintained that the presidency was a vital and necessary part of the political system, while others saw it as a potentially dangerous office. So too is the presidency fairly unique as a national office among the nations of the world.

As such, studying the presidents and presidency is a complicated and problematic undertaking, with disagreement on how to assess presidents. For instance, presidential scholars are frustrated by the state of scholarship in the discipline.[8] In general, research on the presidency suffers from a lack of theory building and models by which to test these theories, as well as a lack of systematic approaches to the study of the subject. There is no agreement about a unifying theory in the field by which to view the office, and no one best approach is suitable for all research questions.

Some of the sources available to presidential scholars—and how to use those sources—also present potential problems. While there are some excellent and informative presidential memoirs and biographies of presidents, scholars must be mindful that what the president or a former aide says about the president might be what they want the public to hear about the president. Vested political interests influence the way the story of history is told. Presidents and their former aides have imperfect (and selective) memories in reporting details of their administration, and other biographers and scholars might lack the ideological distance from the subject necessary to offer an objective, neutral, and probing assessment.

A number of other likely and unlikely forces must be considered—or ignored—when assessing presidents. From Thomas Jefferson to Theodore Roosevelt to Ronald Reagan, the presidents and the president's friends pay attention to their standing among historians. Richard Nixon and Bill Clinton in particular were quite concerned with their eventual ranking and courted scholarly goodwill in their post-White House careers. While still in office, Clinton started meeting with scholars to discuss his legacy. In recent years, concerned Washington scholars, in an effort to repair their subject's standing, convened conferences and produced new scholarship after the "Father of His Country" slipped from two to three and then to four in some of the rankings. Suggesting that pollsters have a liberal bias, Ronald Reagan supporters commissioned a presidential ranking poll of "friendly" conservatives. The poll lifted the "Gipper" from twenty-fifth place and the company of Chester A. Arthur to "near-great" status. Whether or not the many books the "statesman" Richard Nixon wrote after leaving office will overcome the Watergate scandal and his resignation, or whether the Nobel Prize-winning work of humanitarian Jimmy Carter will erase the memories of stagflation and the 444 days of the Iranian hostage crisis remains to be seen. When assessing the president's *presidency*, they should not. It is against these challenges and others that we endeavor to assess George W. Bush's performance.

How to Evaluate Presidents?

One of the challenges of evaluating presidents is conflicting public expectation about the office. The American public has for some time had overly high expectations of their presidents, and these expectations are rising.[9] For instance, the expectations people have are not only unrealistic but they eclipse the formal powers of the office needed to meet those expectations. These rising expectations followed the expanding activism of government throughout the twentieth century by liberals and progressives, whereby a role for the White House and national government developed in improving the quality of people's lives and addressing economic and national security crises. This was especially the case during Franklin D. Roosevelt's presidency, when the role, scope, and size of government were greatly expanded. Likewise, national security concerns such as World War II, the Cuban Missile Crisis, and the nuclear threat of the Cold War, as well as the contemporary attacks by terrorists, resulted in a further enlargement of the presidency.

Presidents have contributed to this expansion through the ambitious and exhaustive array of promises they make on the campaign stump, which also generally exceed the limited constitutional powers of the office and generally outdistance presidential actions once in office.[10] In a sense, the level of importance afforded and the centrality in the U.S. political system of presidents are beyond the real power held by presidents. The public routinely believes presidents are responsible—both good and bad—for occurrences and items they may have little power to effect. In the words of President Jimmy Carter: "When things go bad you get entirely too much blame. And I have to admit that when things go good, you get entirely too much credit."[11]

Yet it must be noted that the president does more than promote and implement public policy. The president assumes the symbolic role of leader of the nation, worldwide champion of democracy, and leader of his or her party. To be sure, generations of children are imbued with patriotic stories of presidents. As such, scholars must take into account this symbolic role when assessing presidents and somehow incorporate it into the more "substantive" and direct means of evaluation.

Most recent presidents have been seen by the public, press, and presidential scholars alike as rather mediocre. The question is often asked: where have all the great presidents gone? The answer might be in part due to inherent difficulties and "ungovernability" of the contemporary office, as eluded to at the outset of the Introduction. For instance, leading presidential scholars Thomas Cronin and Michael Genovese have noted several troubling paradoxes of the office.[12] The paradoxes of the American presidency are such that Americans want conflicting and possibly improbable or unrealistic things from their presidents: the public wants presidents to be bold leaders yet sensitive to public opinion; they want their leaders to solve an array of challenges yet do not want or trust the centralized power often necessary to address these same challenges; there is a general preference for bipartisan or nonpartisan presidents, yet supporters of each party want presidents to forward their preferences and agenda. To Cronin and Genovese, these paradoxes produce inconsistent demands that lead to a "damned if you do, damned if you don't" scenario for the occupant of the Oval Office.[13]

Another issue that arises is whether it is the person or the policy that is evaluated. It is generally agreed that the public considers the personality of presidents in their approval or disapproval of performance.[14] Approval is somewhat of a popularity contest where personal characteristics such as warmth, strength, and charisma translate well at the polls. The public has little interest in the details of public policy, but the public certainly knew that Dwight Eisenhower was a war hero. Indeed, the media also focuses more on the personality of presidents than on the specifics of policy. John F. Kennedy benefited from his good looks, just as Ronald Reagan's charm propped up his approval rating. Richard Nixon's scandalous behavior continues to receive more ink than his legislative record. Personality is far easier to understand than, say, the intricacies of atomic energy regulation or anti-inflation policy, and it sells more newspapers. This leads to the challenge of how to determine or measure personality or character.[15] The public has varying views on what they want or admire in a president, and it is difficult for scholars neither trained in psychoanalysis nor possessing intimate and sustained access to their subjects to attempt to measure personality. What one might deem to be strong leadership might be seen by another as being autocratic. Standing firmly by one's convictions might just as well be a case of stubbornness. Prudence is both a virtue and a vice in the presidency.

On the other hand, a case can be made that personality *is* substance, character *is* king, and the personalized nature of the office is such that the presidency is first and foremost about moral character,[16] so it must be incorporated into our analysis of presidents. At the same time, personality certainly does not solely determine presidential standing or approval. There are, after all, great and frequent shifts in presidential standing, while the person in office remains the same. Evaluations must consider both the person and the policies of that person.

Scandal also appears to factor into assessments of a president. Such presidents as Richard Nixon and Warren Harding, both mired in scandal, are routinely ranked poorly compared to their peers. Events such as Watergate, Teapot Dome, and an array of unethical behaviors by the president or his aides negatively impact presidential standing. However, should one blemish—even a large one—as the saying goes, be the tail that wags the whole dog? To what extent is Lyndon B. Johnson's impressive legislative record diminished by Vietnam? Should Ronald Reagan's productive first term be overshadowed by the Iran-Contra scandal and the inactivity of his second term? How does the negative impact of Bill Clinton's improper relationship with an intern compare to the record economic prosperity the country enjoyed during his administration? Similarly, a question exists as to whether one major success should outweigh an otherwise unremarkable presidential record.

Not all scandals are equal, and scholars need to do a better job of thoroughly considering the impact of the scandal—economically, politically, on the standing of the office, and over the long term—when evaluating or ranking presidents. It is difficult to determine the impact on the office and on national policy of scandals, but such a determination needs to be attempted. It would certainly appear that the consequences to U.S. foreign policy were far graver and harmful from Reagan's Iran-Contra scandal than, say, from Clinton's sexual affair with an intern. Yet the Monica Lewinsky ordeal led to impeachment proceedings, contributed to gridlock on Capitol Hill, and resulted in an inability by the president, Congress, the press, and the nation to focus on much else, including pressing policy concerns. By the same account, marital infidelity by other presidents (e.g., Franklin D. Roosevelt, John F. Kennedy) certainly did not diminish their standing, nor did such universally and timelessly inhumane acts as owning slaves keep George Washington, Thomas Jefferson, and Andrew Jackson out of a top-10 ranking. Indeed, it might be argued that such blemishes on a president's character are far worse than, say, Clinton's deceit about his affair, which is widely seen as a revealing glimpse into a larger character problem. By that same criterion, would not George Bush's "deceit" regarding his "no new taxes" pledge be equally problematic or indicative of a character blemish? Or, given the massive budget deficits Bush faced, perhaps his broken pledge might be better viewed as a pragmatic decision than a lie. Judged from the safe distance of history, it might have been both bolder and wiser to break the pledge than honor it.

A number of inappropriate activities were associated with the Grant and Nixon administrations, and both former presidents continue to suffer in the rankings and scholarly evaluations because of them. Yet Grant's mistake was one of *omission*, unlike Nixon's mistake, which was one of *commission*. Grant had the poor judgment to appoint and then fail to supervise a number of unethical individuals. The former Civil War hero would, nonetheless, leave the presidency a popular man and leave the office in better health than when he entered it. It is conceivable that he would have won a third term had he pursued it in 1876. Richard Nixon, on the other hand, was the source of much of the unethical conduct in his administration, and he was forced to resign from an office that he dramatically weakened. Had he not resigned, he most likely would have been removed by Congress. Nixon will most assuredly always be remembered for resigning and for the Watergate scandal. Both events had a significant and negative impact on the office, whereas the same cannot be said for Grant's scandals. But Nixon should also be remembered for his historic China policies. The impeachments of Andrew Johnson and Bill Clinton are also likely to tarnish their legacies well into the future, as well they should. This has certainly been the case for the 135 years or so since Johnson's presidency. Both events had an impact on the office. Yet it appears that the negative impact on the office itself was not lasting and that the impeachment charges were not justified, which might necessitate a reconsideration of the events and standing of the two presidents adversely affected.

Nixon, Reagan, and Clinton—all presidents involved in the most spectacular scandals of the modern era—enjoyed decisive reelection victories, which might be seen as public confirmations of their presidencies and leadership. However, all three went on to become embroiled in scandal during their second term. There must certainly be a role in presidential ratings for public approval, reelection, and scandal, but it is easier said than determined. In hindsight, Gerald Ford and Jimmy Carter appear to have been remarkably ethical, but both were defeated at the polls and left behind marginal presidential records. So one is left to ponder how these events should factor into presidential ratings.

The standing of presidents varies over the course of the term or terms in office. This phenomenon often occurs after the president has left office. After leaving the White House, Eisenhower, for instance, was rated slightly below average in the 1962 Schlesinger poll. The formal general was seen as inactive and too disengaged from his own presidency. However, as new information and documents have become available to scholars, and with the (nearly) "20-20" vantage point of history, Eisenhower's reputation has gradually rebounded to a respectable "near great" in some recent polls. Harry Truman was not popular among the majority of the American public or members of Congress during his presidency. Truman's contemporaries joked that "to err is Truman," and the Speaker of the House of Representatives deemed Truman "the worst president in history."[17] Truman's approval plummeted from almost 90 percent after World War II to 23 percent in late 1951, which remains the all-time lowest rating with the exception of that for Richard Nixon before his resignation in 1974. Despite this, Truman is now widely considered a "near-great" president and is consistently ranked in the top 10 of all presidents. Moreover, Truman has been mentioned as a role model by nearly every presidential candidate of both parties in recent years. The improvement of Truman's reputation took many years, and his impressive achievements and handling of monumental events—the ending of World War II, the Marshall Plan, the establishment of the United Nations (UN) and the North Atlantic Treaty Organization (NATO), desegregation of the military, having the courage and wisdom to fire Gen. Douglas MacArthur, and so on—took many years to be fully understood and appreciated.

Herein lies a cautionary lesson to would-be evaluators of presidents, and one understood by the authors of this book engaged in an early assessment. This assessment of President George W. Bush is not meant to be the final word on his performance. It is still too early to tell how George W. Bush and recent presidents will be rated by historians, and too early to determine the long-term impact of their policies and actions in office. Recent rating polls have reflected some upward movement of Ronald Reagan, as enough years have passed since his presidency to begin to assess his legacy. Apparently, his peace-through-strength military buildup has been given credit by scholars for contributing to the collapse of the Soviet Union, while the large budget deficits, a shrinking industrial base, and the reduction of environmental programs that occurred under his watch have not proven as troubling as had previously been thought. The same might be said of Reagan's lax management style. However, unlike many other presidents, there is considerably less consensus on his standing. Reagan ranks anywhere from "near great" to "below average" in recent polls, although some consensus should soon form with the further passage of time.

It is even more challenging to evaluate Reagan's successors, George Bush and Bill Clinton, because their presidencies are even more recent. Both seem to be especially difficult to assess. Scholars remain divided over whether or not Bush deserves credit for leading an international coalition of nations in the Persian Gulf War or whether, in light of subsequent events, he erred in not removing Saddam Hussein from power when he had the chance. While the war accomplished its objectives in impressive fashion, the oil-based energy policies promoted by President Bush and U.S. support for Iraq in the Iran-Iraq conflict of the 1980s contributed to Hussein's power in the first place. The same sticky questions fog Bush's leadership, as it remains to be seen whether he deserves credit for presiding over the end of the Cold War or whether he squandered the opportunity to act more boldly to shape the post-Cold War order in its aftermath. The president enjoyed a high approval rating, near 90 percent, after the Persian Gulf War, but he saw his popularity erode to roughly 30 percent by mid 1992.

In the initial years after leaving the White House, Bill Clinton's legacy has been tarnished by the scandal involving his intern, Monica Lewinsky. Whether this will change and he will be remembered for eliminating long-running budget deficits and presiding over a period of general peace and unprecedented economic prosperity cannot be determined at this time. Clinton's legislative accomplishments are seen by some as little more than incremental co-optation of Republican plans, while others feel he deserves credit for protecting Medicare, environmental programs, and education from "right-wing extremism." About the only certainties at this point in time are that Bush's military victory will work for him, and his single term in office will work against him, and that Clinton's reelection will work for him, and his impeachment will work against him. Both presidents are likely to remain ranked as "average."

Today, John F. Kennedy and Ronald Reagan remain quite popular among the public and seem likely to remain popular with the passage of time. Yet neither is considered one of the "great" presidents. This example points to the quandary of whether scholars should consider public opinion in rating presidents, a question hotly contested by those that rank presidents. Indeed, there are conceptually two different ways of looking at the issue of presidential standing. One considers popularity or approval ratings as gauged by the American public in the increasingly regular opinion polling industry. These are influenced by public opinion, subject to great and frequent changes, and are determined primarily by average citizens. The other conceptual approach is to consider historical reputation and ranking. This is also subject to changes, although with far less regularity and extent, and is determined largely by experts on the presidency. In the debate between whether to employ popular or scholarly based ratings, one cannot ignore a president's popularity with or approval by the public. Yet the reliability of such measures as anything other than immediate gauges of approval is questionable. Public opinion polls do not permit the respondent time for reflection or comparison, and one cannot assume that respondents have intimate familiarity with, say, Millard Fillmore or Franklin Pierce.

Gallup commissioned presidential ranking polls by the public. The results, even though they are interesting, further point to the unsuitability of opinion polls as the means by which comprehensive presidential assessments are done. For instance, Clinton was rated as the top president by 13 percent and the worst president by 20 percent polled. It is doubtful that a president could be both best *and* worst. Kennedy received more votes for greatness than did Lincoln and Washington, and the first president was rated far below what any serious scholar would consider. Such polls of the public place Kennedy and Reagan at the top of the list, well above where the scholarly polls rate them. Yet one would be hard pressed to find a scholar who would, unlike the general public, rank either president above George Washington, Andrew Jackson, Woodrow Wilson, or Harry Truman.[18]

ASSESSING PRESIDENTIAL PERFORMANCE

The previous discussion points out the challenge of *how* to rate the presidents and what to consider while doing so, but it also raises the question of *when* to evaluate. The Eisenhower and Truman examples also present a challenge to an early assessment such as is found in this book, yet it also invites early, frequent, and continuous assessments, along with the need for new approaches to evaluating presidents. Indeed, shifts in the standing of presidents both during and after their presidencies are not unusual, and scholars remain divided about how best to assess presidents.[19]

It is beneficial to contemplate the advice of leading presidential scholar James MacGregor Burns, who points out four additional anomalies of attempted ratings of presidents. According to Burns, there is a maleness to the rating game, in that presidents are assessed by male traits and qualities and from the perspective of males; the president is evaluated as part of and within the institution of the presidency, yet there is much disagreement about how to view or assess the institution; presidents are evaluated comparatively, but we disagree on what we want in a president and what qualities to use to assess them; and the interaction of situation and agency cannot be ignored, as specific situational opportunities might help or harm a presidency, and, given the nature of the office, some question whether a president (other than the case of Theodore Roosevelt) can achieve greatness without a war or crisis.[20]

RANKING PRESIDENTS

George Washington and Abraham Lincoln loom large as heroic figures, more myth than men. All presidents have benefited from the prestige that these men brought to the office, while simultaneously struggling under their aura. In the modern era, the looming legacy of Franklin D. Roosevelt (FDR) has set the bar quite high, and he both set the standard for contemporary presidents and is credited for establishing the "modern presidency." Perhaps not surprisingly, all those serving subsequent to him have generally had difficulty governing in his shadow. For instance, FDR presided over one of the most critical times in the nation's history—the Great Depression and World War II. He demonstrated bold, visionary leadership and challenged the very way of thinking about the role of government and "approach to governing," charting a new course for governance, taking on powerful business and economic interests, leading his countrymen out of economic crisis, and winning the greatest war. Even Ronald

TABLE 1
Early Rankings of the Presidents

1948 Schlesinger Poll	1962 Schlesinger Poll
GREAT	GREAT
1. Lincoln	1. Lincoln
2. Washington	2. Washington
3. F. Roosevelt	3. F. Roosevelt
4. Wilson	4. Wilson
5. Jefferson	5. Jefferson
6. Jackson	
	NEAR GREAT
NEAR GREAT	6. Jackson
7. T. Roosevelt	7. T. Roosevelt
8. Cleveland	8. Polk
9. J. Adams	9. Truman
10. Polk	10. J. Adams
	11. Cleveland
AVERAGE	
11. J. Q. Adams	AVERAGE
12. Monroe	12. Madison
13. Hayes	13. J. Q. Adams
14. Madison	14. Hayes
15. Van Buren	15. McKinley
16. Taft	16. Taft
17. Arthur	17. Van Buren
18. McKinley	18. Monroe
19. A. Johnson	19. Hoover
20. Hoover	20. B. Harrison
21. B. Harrison	21. Arthur
	22. Eisenhower
BELOW AVERAGE	23. A. Johnson
22. Tyler	
23. Coolidge	BELOW AVERAGE
24. Fillmore	24. Taylor
25. Taylor	25. Tyler
26. Buchanan	26. Fillmore
27. Pierce	27. Coolidge
	28. Pierce
FAILURE	29. Buchanan
28. Grant	
29. Harding	FAILURE
	30. Grant
	31. Harding

Reagan, the president in the modern era whose ideology was most diametrically opposed to FDR's, admired FDR and occasionally cited his words and memory while governing.

As this example demonstrates, the first and most obvious characteristic of presidential ratings is that they are comparative. Presidents are measured against one another, as opposed to being evaluated independent of one another, according to the U.S. Constitution, or against world leaders. Most employ categories such as "great," "near great," and so on—or some derivative of this—in rating presidents, although some assessments simply rank the presidents chronologically from first to last, or best to worst. Most ratings, including the first ratings and the most popular ones, do not use specific criteria in evaluating the presidents. Rather, in the words of Arthur M. Schlesinger Jr., whose father invented the rating game and whose 1996 ranking of presidents is one of the most cited, ratings attempt to evaluate the president from a "holistic" not "mechanistic" approach.[21] Presidents are considered for their overall record. Other, more "mechanistic" efforts have developed a series of criteria—constitutional, quantitative, legislative-based, public opinion-based, and so on—to use in rating presidents.

Most ratings are based on polls of scholars, typically historians, who are asked to evaluate the presidents and place them into the aforementioned categories and best-worst listings. These polls generally survey thirty to seventy scholars, although there are some notable exceptions. While Arthur Schlesinger polled fifty-five and seventy-five historians in 1948 and 1962, respectively, and his son, Arthur Schlesinger Jr., surveyed thirty-two scholars in 1996, Robert K. Murray and Tim H. Blessing used a seventeen-page instrument to poll 953 historians in 1982.[22] William Henry Harrison and James A. Garfield are usually omitted from the ratings because of their abbreviated tenures in office,[23] however, a few efforts included these two presidents.[24]

Table 1 lists the first two ranking polls, conducted by Arthur Schlesinger. Table 2 gives examples of recent, well-known ratings.

CRITICISMS OF THE RANKINGS

It is a challenge to evaluate presidents, much less group leaders into categories. Not surprisingly, the endeavor has been criticized. First and foremost, as methodologists would point out, there is a small "N"—only forty-two individuals have served as president, with George W. Bush serving as the country's forty-third president (Grover Cleveland served two nonconsecutive terms)—and considerable variation in approach and style among them. There also exists the problem of how to evaluate such a multifaceted office (the U.S. Constitution is vague, the office is always evolving, and each president approaches it in a unique, highly personalized way), which criteria to use (a "holistic" versus a "mechanistic"

TABLE 2
Examples of More Recent, Well-Known Polls

1982 Murray-Blessing Poll	*1996 Schlesinger Jr. Poll*	*2000 C-SPAN Historian Poll*
GREAT	GREAT	1. Lincoln
1. Lincoln	1. Lincoln	2. F. Roosevelt
2. F. Roosevelt	2. Washington	3. Washington
3. Washington	3. F. Roosevelt	4. T. Roosevelt
4. Jefferson		5. Truman
	NEAR GREAT	6. Wilson
NEAR GREAT	4. Jefferson	7. Jefferson
5. T. Roosevelt	5. Jackson	8. Kennedy
6. Wilson	6. T. Roosevelt	9. Eisenhower
7. Jackson	7. Wilson	10. L. Johnson
8. Truman	8. Truman	11. Reagan
	9. Polk	12. Polk
ABOVE AVERAGE		13. Jackson
9. J. Adams	HIGH AVERAGE	14. Monroe
10. L. Johnson	10. Eisenhower	15. McKinley
11. Eisenhower	11. J. Adams	16. J. Adams
12. Polk	12. Kennedy	17. Cleveland
13. Kennedy	13. Cleveland	18. Madison
14. Madison	14. L. Johnson	19. J. Q. Adams
15. Monroe	15. Monroe	20. Bush
16. J. Q. Adams	16. McKinley	21. Clinton
17. Cleveland		22. Carter
	LOW AVERAGE	23. Ford
AVERAGE	17. Madison	24. Taft
18. McKinley	18. J. Q. Adams	25. Nixon
19. Taft	19. B. Harrison	26. Hayes
20. Van Buren	20. Clinton	27. Coolidge
21. Hoover	21. Van Buren	28. Taylor
22. Hayes	22. Taft	29. Garfield
23. Arthur	23. Hayes	30. Van Buren
24. Ford	24. Bush	31. B. Harrison
25. Carter	25. Reagan	32. Arthur
26. B. Harrison	26. Arthur	33. Grant
	27. Carter	34. Hoover
BELOW AVERAGE	28. Ford	35. Fillmore
27. Taylor		36. Tyler
28. Tyler	BELOW AVERAGE	37. W. Harrison
29. Fillmore	29. Taylor	38. Harding
30. Coolidge	30. Coolidge	39. Pierce
31. Pierce	31. Fillmore	40. A. Johnson
	32. Tyler	41. Buchanan
FAILURE		
32. A. Johnson	FAILURE	
33. Buchanan	33. Pierce	
34. Nixon	34. Grant	
35. Grant	35. Hoover	
36. Harding	36. Nixon	
	37. A. Johnson	
	38. Buchanan	
	39. Harding	

debate), and how to account for the time in which the president served (times of war might "make the man;" comparing someone who served in 1800 with someone who served in 2000).

The criticism that has generated the most debate has been that of the bias of the ratings because of the partisanship and ideology of those performing the assessment. In what is sometimes deemed the "Harvard yard bias," critics have alleged that most scholars who rate presidents are liberals who are registered Democrats and teach at elite institutions of higher learning. This produces, they allege, a predisposed bias for liberal Democrats, presidents with an active record of government intervention, and a tendency to compare all presidents to FDR.[25] In response to this concern, conservative organizations, such as the Intercollegiate Studies Institute, and conservative scholars have pursued their own ratings.[26] Such ratings have produced some noticeable differences: Woodrow Wilson often drops from "near great" to "below average"; Ronald Reagan, who is usually judged "average," moves to "near great"; Bill Clinton and Lyndon B. Johnson drop from "average" and "high average" to "failure"; and average presidents Jimmy Carter and Dwight Eisenhower become a "failure" and "near great, respectively." However, Richard Pious, a leading presidential scholar, has suggested that if a liberal bias were at work in the polls, then Lyndon Johnson and John Kennedy would be rated higher, while Eisenhower would not be rising in polls.[27] Likewise, perennial bottom dwellers Grant and Nixon are also showing some upward movement in recent polls, and a few conservatives do rate fairly highly. Pious further notes that Democrats might have had the good fortune of serving in more interesting times (World War I, the Great Depression, World War II, the start and peak of the Cold War, etc.), which might explain the generally higher ranking of Democrats. At the same time, some Republicans have suffered "spectacular failures" (Grant, Harding, and Nixon).

Republicans are not the only presidents rated poorly. Joining Harding, Nixon, Grant, Coolidge, and Hoover at or near the bottom, for instance, are Democrats Buchanan, Pierce, Andrew Johnson, and Tyler. Republican Abraham Lincoln tops the ranking, and Republican Theodore Roosevelt is a regular in the top 10. After an exhaustive study of presidential rankings, Tim Blessing concludes that partisanship of the raters is not a major issue in determining presidential standing,[28] and a conference of distinguished presidential scholars on the issue of presidential ratings held at Hofstra University in October 2000 concluded that the effect of rater bias or partisanship was "minimal at best."[29] The rating game has endured. Indeed, it flourishes.

CONCLUSION

Assessing the presidents is a challenging endeavor, especially when done while the president is still in office. The benefits of assessing a president at midpoint are many: it begins the analysis that will continue for years to come; the first two years (some even argue that the first 100 days) are widely considered the most crucial period of the presidency;[30] it generally marks the period of greatest nominating, appointing, and legislative activity; the period typically ends with the party's losses in the midterm elections and a new strategy for the second half of the term; insights about priorities and the president's leadership approach can be gained from assessing the important transition and learning periods of the presidency; and it produces an early picture of the high and low points of the particular president.

This assessment is certainly not a definitive evaluation of George W. Bush. To be sure, as has been discussed in this introductory chapter, a president's standing is subject to the changing whims of public opinion during his term and often changes over time after he leaves office. As more information becomes available when presidential papers are organized and presidential libraries opened, and as events unfold as a result of presidential actions and inactions, scholars are able to reassess their subjects and place them in a new or larger context, as will be the case for George W. Bush. The task before us, then, has been to avoid looking at contemporary political events from the perspective of the headlines but rather with a dispassionate eye to history.

NOTES

1. Arthur M. Schlesinger, "Historians Rate U.S. Presidents," *Life*, November 1, 1948, 65–66, 68, 73–74.

2. Arthur M. Schlesinger, "Our Presidents: A Rating by 75 Historians," *New York Times Magazine*, July 29, 1962, 12–13, 40–41, 43.

3. Some of the more popular polls of presidents include the Schlesinger 1996 poll: see Arthur M. Schlesinger Jr., "The Ultimate Approval Rating," *New York Times Magazine*, December 15, 1996, 46–47; the Murray and Blessing poll, Robert K. Murray and Tim H. Blessing, *Greatness in the White House: Rating the Presidents*, 2nd ed. (University Park: Pennsylvania State University Press, 1994); C-SPAN's "Survey of Presidential Leadership: How Did the Presidents Rate?" February 21, 2000, www. americanpresidents.org/survey/. See also William Pederson and Ann McLaurin, *The Rating Game in American Politics* (New York: Irvington, 1987).

4. A number of organizations such as Gallup take regular polls on presidential approval. See, for instance, www.gallup.com.

5. Among the leading studies of presidential personality and character are James David Barber, *The Presidential Character: Predicting Performance in the White House*, 4th ed. (Englewood Cliffs: Prentice Hall, 1992); Fred I. Greenstein, *The Presidential Difference: Leadership Style from FDR to Clinton* (New York: Free Press, 2000); Fred I. Greenstein, *Leadership in the Modern Presidency* (Cambridge: Harvard University Press, 1988).

6. Ranking polls on the first ladies have been done by the Siena Research Institute at Siena College in New York and Robert P. Watson; see Robert P. Watson, *The Presidents' Wives: Reassessing the Office of First Lady* (Boulder: Lynne Rienner, 2000), 171–98; Robert P. Watson, "Ranking the Presidential Spouses," *The Social Science Journal* 36, no.1 (1999): 117–36.

7. Stephen J. Wayne, "Evaluating the President: The Public's Perspective through the Prism of Pollsters," *White House Studies* 3, no. 1 (2003): 35–40.

8. For a discussion of the approaches to and challenges of studying the presidency, see George C. Edwards III and Stephen J. Wayne, *Presidential Leadership: Politics and Policy Making*, 5th ed. (Boston: Bedford/St. Martin's Press, 1999), 503–13; George C. Edwards III and Stephen J. Wayne, *Studying the Presidency* (Knoxville: University of Tennessee Press, 1983), 17–49.

9. James P. Pfiffner, *The Modern Presidency*, 3rd ed. (Boston: Bedford/ St. Martin's Press, 2000).

10. Ibid.

11. Godfrey Hodgson, *All Things to All Men: The False Promise of the Modern American Presidency* (New York: Simon & Schuster, 1980), 25.

12. Thomas E. Cronin and Michael A. Genovese, *The Paradoxes of the Modern Presidency* (New York: Oxford University Press, 1998).

13. Ibid.

14. See Cronin and Genovese, *The Paradoxes of the Modern Presidency*, Wayne, "Evaluating the President," 35–40.

15. Attempting to assess presidential character is a difficult endeavor. Studies such as those by James David Barber, *The Presidential Character*, have come under severe criticism. For a comprehensive discussion of the criticisms of studying presidential personality see Greenstein, The Presidential Difference.

16. See Robert Shogun, *The Double-Edged Sword: How Character Makes and Ruins Presidents, From Washington to Clinton* (Boulder: Westview Press, 1999).

17. Alan Brinkley, "Work Hard, Trust in God, Have No Fear," *New York Times Book Review*, June 21, 1992, 1.

18. The C-SPAN viewer poll of the public places both John F. Kennedy and Ronald Reagan at the top and well above such presidents as Abraham Lincoln, Franklin D. Roosevelt, and George Washington. See www.americanpresidents.org.

19. Among the challenges of ranking the presidents are shifts that occur as new information comes to light. See, for instance, D. A. Lonnstrom and T. O. Kelly, "Rating the Presidents: A Tracking Study," *Presidential Studies Quarterly* 27, no. 3 (Summer 1997): 591; Arthur B. Murray, "Evaluating the Presidents of the United States," in *The American Presidency*, ed. David C. Kozak and Kenneth N. Ciboski (Chicago: Nelson-Hall, 1985), 437–48.

20. James MacGregor Burns, *The Power to Lead: The Crisis of the American Presidency* (New York: Simon & Schuster, 1984); James MacGregor Burns, *Presidential Government: The Crucible of Leadership*, 2nd ed. (Boston: Houghton Mifflin, 1973).

21. See Arthur M. Schlesinger Jr., "Commentary," *White House Studies* 3, no. 1 (2003): 75–77.

22. See Murray and Blessing, *Greatness in the white House*; Schlesinger, "Commentary." The Intercollegiate Studies Institute (ISI) polled thirty-eight scholars, C-SPAN's survey of presidential historians polled fifty-eight, Porter polled forty-one, and the *Chicago Tribune* polled forty-nine.

23. William Henry Harrison served as president for only one month, dying from complications contracted during his long inaugural address that was delivered in foul weather. James A. Garfield died at the hands of an assassin only months into his term. For a discussion for not including these presidents in rating polls, see Max J. Skidmore, "Presidents after the White House: A Preliminary Study," *White House Studies* 2, no. 3 (2002): 237–50.

24. See C-SPAN, "Survey of Presidential Leadership."

25. Thomas Bailey, *Presidential Greatness* (Stanford: Stanford University Press, 1967), chap. 4.

26. One of the most comprehensive attempts to rank the presidents from George Washington through Ronald Reagan was done by Murray and Blessing, *Greatness in the White House*. The ISI commissioned its own poll with thirty-eight conservative scholars. See James Pierson, "Historians and the Reagan Legacy," *The Weekly Standard* September 29, 1997, 22–24.

27. Felzenberg suggests that presidential raters favor liberal, activist presidents using the standard of FDR. See, for instance, Alvin S. Felzenberg, "Partisan Biases in Presidential Ratings: Ulysses, Woodrow, and Calvin, 'We Hardly Knew Ye,'" *White House Studies* 3, no. 1 (2003); Alvin S. Felzenberg, "There You Go Again: Liberal Historians and the *New York Times* Deny Ronald Reagan His Due," *Policy Review* (March–April 1997). Richard M. Pious, "Reflections of a Presidency Rater," *White House Studies* 3, no. 1 (2003).

28. See Tim H. Blessing, "Presidents and Significance: Partisanship As a Source of Perceived Greatness," *White House Studies* 3, no.1 (2003); Murray and Blessing, *Greatness in the White House.*

29. Meena Bose, "The Leadership Difference: Rating the Presidents," *White House Studies* 3, no. 1 (2003): 3–20.

30. See Schlesinger Jr., "The Ultimate Approval Rating," 46. Arthur M. Schlesinger Jr., "Rating the Presidents: Washington to Clinton," *Political Science Quarterly* 112, no. 2 (1997): 179–90.

Part 1

Leadership and Character

Chapter 1

The Arbiter of Fate

The Presidential Character of George W. Bush

Bill Kirtley

INTRODUCTION

Character counts when a nation chooses its president, and George W. Bush raised character to the level of a campaign issue in 2000. Scholars and partisans agree that character is vitally important; however, they use the word to mean different things. The Greeks coined the word "charakter," meaning "to engrave." Today it refers to moral strength and discipline, an individual's distinctive traits, or even a person considered decidedly different. In his seminal work *The Presidential Character*, James David Barber, a political scientist now retired from Duke University, viewed character as an individual's pattern of behavior or personality.[1] He used this view of character to analyze Richard Nixon and to predict the eventual crises and tragedies of the Nixon administration.

This chapter seeks to use Barber's arguments to illuminate the character of our current president and utilizes a three-part structure for the investigation: Barber's argument in *The Presidential Character* is explained; Barber's ideas are used to structure a biography of George W. Bush's formative years and classify his personality; and the exciting and dangerous activity of predicting how George W. Bush will react to future events is undertaken. In so doing, the criticisms of Barber's work are taken into consideration, and the analysis of George W. Bush's character is mindful of the limitations of such efforts.

Barber's Argument

Barber believed that there were five parts to personality, and that they developed sequentially over time. The first and most important element of personality was character. For this reason, Barber often used the terms interchangeably. *Character*

19

is developed in childhood, and it is the unique aspect of personality that defines who we are and how we relate to our environment. Barber argued that character was the most accurate predictor of behavior in adulthood.[2]

A *worldview* is gained in adolescence. It is the way one perceives social causality, human nature, and the central moral conflicts of one's time.[3] *Style* is acquired in early adulthood. It is the most obvious aspect of personality, as it is a way of acting. Style involves the ability to perform political activities involving *personal relations*, *rhetoric*, and *work ethic*.[4] A president's first political success marked his adoption of a style in early adulthood. Barber believed it was the key to understanding character.[5] Presidential personalities operate in specific political situations that Barber called the "environment." Presidents succeed when they develop strategies to satisfy their needs and the environment has the potential to fulfill them. If their needs are not met, they become frustrated and angry. Barber believed there were two significant environmental factors, the *climate of expectations* and the *power situation* when a president takes office.[6] Taken together, all of these aforementioned factors assist us in understanding presidential character.

Character Types

Barber argued that there were two ways of describing character: presidential activism (active-passive) and whether the president enjoyed politics (positive-negative). These two dimensions yield four types. *Active-positive* types are energetic workers with high self-esteem. They are self-motivated, result oriented, and relate well to the environment. *Active-negative* types also invest a lot of energy in the job, but they do so for different reasons. They are compulsive workers motivated by ambition. *Passive-positive* types seek affirmation. They react to events and the opinions of others. They enjoy their jobs and value their leisure. *Passive-negative* types are withdrawn and exhibit low self-esteem. They work determinedly out of a sense of duty.[7]

Barber classified fifteen American presidents using this typology of character types. He believed that active-positive types generally made the best presidents and active-negative types the worst.[8]

Critique

Barber's arguments are used because they are notable and enjoyed a degree of success in predicting the future. Adherence to them might help avoid the partisanship prevalent in many biographies of Bush. However, criticism of Barber's arguments, as well as his vigorous defense of his work, should be noted before they are applied to Bush.

In an otherwise favorable review in the *New York Times Book Review*, historian Bruce Mazlish charged that the prospect of isolating a few events from the

Active

Thomas Jefferson	Woodrow Wilson
FDR	Richard Nixon

Positive ——————————————————————— **Negative**

Warren Harding	Calvin Coolidge
Ronald Reagan	Dwight Eisenhower

Passive

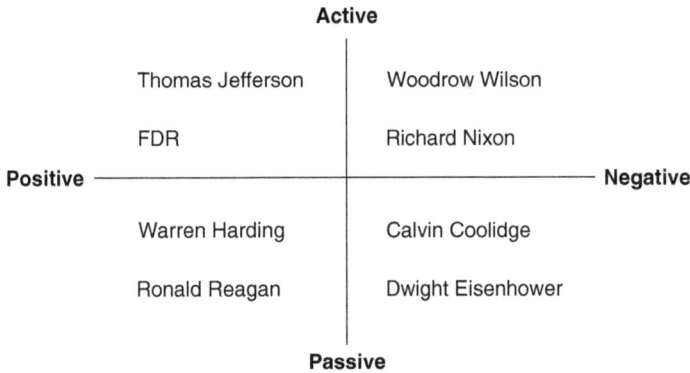

FIGURE 1.1   Barber's Typology of Character types.

entirety of human life and basing predictions upon them seemed doubtful, especially considering the varied nature of Barber's sources. Mazlish also thought that Barber's categories were too narrow and confining.[9] Barber admitted that Nixon added "individual peculiarities" to the active-negative type.[10]

James Qualls, a graduate student in political science at Johns Hopkins University, insisted that predictability alone did not elevate Barber's arguments to the level of scientific theory. He attacked Barber's methodology in an article, "Barber's Typological Analysis of Political Leaders," which appeared in the *American Political Science Review* in 1977. Qualls charged that Barber paid attention to events and situations that corresponded to his typology and ignored those that did not, an error known as "selective observation."[11]

In a blistering reply, Barber insisted that he collected all relevant material, even that which seemed contrary to his arguments. Barber never intended his work as a "mathematical, mechanical, or definitive treatment of the subject."[12] He characterized his work as arguments rather than theory. *The Presidential Character* contained no charts, graphs, or statistical analyses.

Students attempting an assignment based on Barber need a guide through the thickets of *The Presidential Character*. Because of numerous revisions, Barber's work became what he called a "strange book."[13] He varied the formats and arguments in different parts of his book.[14] The lesson for us is to be aware of Barber's limitations and to emphasize the fact that his arguments were intended to be starting points for discussion rather than ready-made conclusions.

BUSH BIOGRAPHY

G. W. Bush is a remarkably positive person, seemingly free of inner conflicts. However, he becomes defensive when reporters probe his relationship with his father; he sees such queries as disparaging his own character. In response to one such query, he observed, "I haven't spent a lot of time psychoanalyzing myself."[15] Bush believes that the roots of his personality are "far more complex than one or two events."[16] However, he credits his mother and father with having a huge influence on his life, and he openly acknowledges their unconditional love.

Character

Barbara Bush gave birth to George Walker Bush on July 6, 1946, in Groton, Connecticut. His father, George Herbert Walker Bush, was a student at Yale. The family called their son Georgie or little George, anything but Junior. His grandmother recalled that he was a happy baby, but that he looked hurt the moment she stopped paying attention to him.[17] After graduation, George W. Bush's father moved the family to Texas and entered the oil business.

An event in 1953 still affects the Bush family. Robin, young George's little sister, died from leukemia. George's parents feared that a seven-year-old boy was too young to live with the knowledge that his sister was dying and so they did not tell him until after Robin died. He recalls: "Minutes before I had a little sister, and now, suddenly, I did not." He repeatedly asked, "Why didn't you tell me?"[18]

Young George attempted to lighten the gloom that settled over the family after the tragedy. His mother recalled how the elder Bush took young George to a football game. Georgie observed that he wished he was Robin. When his father asked him why, he replied, "I bet she can see the game better from up there than we can here."[19] Georgie often stayed home to console his mother rather than going out to play. Cousin Elsie Walker observed: "You look around and see your parents suffering so deeply and try to be cheerful and funny, and you end up becoming a bit of a clown."[20] The death of his sister taught Bush "never to take life for granted" and "to enjoy whatever life might bring, to live each day to its fullest."[21] This event instilled in him a sense of fatalism, but it also taught Bush that an optimistic spirit could overcome many of life's challenges.

Barbara and George H. W. Bush instilled in their son such values as a sense of duty, competitiveness, and the desire to be a "good man." To the Bushes, that meant being a good sport, unpretentious, and, above all, fiercely loyal. Extended family gatherings centered around games and sports. George W. Bush's cousins and siblings looked up to him as the chief instigator and competitor.

Cousin Elsie Walker explained what growing up in the Bush family meant: "There was a lot of pressure on George to develop himself within that family context. That's why it took George a longer time to decide where he was going."[22] Young Bush's behavior often disappointed his parents. He dealt with the fear of disappointment by adopting a nonchalant attitude. However, Bush's frustration at failing to meet expectations led to a certain amount of anger, which surfaced later in life, when he drank alcohol or suspected people of treating his family unfairly.

Worldview

Barbara Bush characterized her relationship with her son in this way: "We fight all the time. We're so alike in that way. He does things to needle me, always."[23] As a teenager, George adopted his mother's outspoken style to express his concern for her. During one of his father's absences, his mother had a miscarriage. George drove her to the hospital. Barbara recalled: "He picked me up the next day.... He talked to me in the car and he said, 'Don't you think we ought to talk about this before you have more children?' "[24]

As an adult, Bush sees the world through the eyes of Midland, Texas, where he was surrounded by "love and friends and sports."[25] Children played in the streets, and people helped each other. When the family moved to Houston in 1959 to be closer to the offshore oil rigs that were his father's business, gregarious George quickly made friends at Kinkaid, a private school. In 1961, Phillips Academy in Andover, Massachusetts, accepted fifteen-year-old George as a student.

Style

George W. Bush refined a leadership style that served him well in the political arena while a student at Phillips, Yale, and Harvard Business School. He developed a unique rhetorical style, established more of a work ethic, and practiced his own wacky, offbeat sense of humor. At first, young George was lonely at Phillips, but he soon found outlets for his buoyant personality. He was always at the center of things—noisy, loud, and irrepressible. He was the head football cheerleader his senior year and a member of the class rock-and-roll band. Gregarious George loved people and quickly learned their names. He sought them out and gave them nicknames. He was an average student and would later remind "C" students during his 2001 commencement address at Yale that they too could become president.[26] People, not books, were his teachers.

Bush's unique relationship with the English language has multiple causes. He can be indirect and elliptical like his father, but more often he is witty and direct like his mother. Add to this a penchant to speak "West Texan" and the result is a president who said that the people have "misunderestimated me," among other unusual uses of the English language.[27] Journalist Gail Sheehy wrote an article, "The Accidental Candidate," for *Vanity Fair* in which she quoted speech expert Nancy LaFever, who said: "the errors you've heard Governor Bush make are consistent with dyslexia."[28] To that claim, Bush replied: "That woman who knew I had dyslexia—I never interviewed her."[29] Dyslexics often compensate for their difficulties with language by developing good memories and people skills. Since left handers, like the president, are more likely to exhibit the signs of dyslexia, perhaps there is a measure of truth in LaFever's assertion.[30]

Bush spent little time studying at Phillips and at Yale. He devoted his energies playing intramural athletics, schmoozing with his fraternity brothers, and socializing with members of Skull and Bones, a secret society at Yale. He occasionally found himself in trouble. Police arrested Bush for stealing a wreath from a hotel and for disorderly conduct after a college football game.

The period of young adulthood dragged on for G. W. Bush. There were political and business successes, a wonderful wife, and twin daughters, but a drinking problem retarded his progress to maturity. He drank heavily in college and abused alcohol even after a drunk-driving arrest in 1976. George W. Bush woke up with a hangover after his fortieth birthday party in 1986 and decided to quit. This decision enabled him to achieve peace and gain a new sense of direction.

Bush's first political success at Phillips was modest. "It was during the spring of my senior year that my political talents first blossomed. I helped organize a stickball league and named myself high commissioner."[31] He organized campus teams into a league that included everyone who wanted to play. He named one team "Nads," delighting in the vulgar double entendre, "Go Nads."[32] The yearbook memorialized this achievement, but Bush's peers never thought of him as a class leader in the traditional sense.

PERSONALITY TYPE

President George W. Bush can be characterized as a "passive-positive." His self-esteem depends on affirmation from others. His election as president was a milestone in his lifetime quest to please his parents. He consults with his father and surrounds himself with father figures. Because approval is such an integral part of his character, he reacts rather than acts. Bush's first reaction to a lockout of West Coast longshoremen was to let the disputants work out the problem themselves. He acted only when his advisors outlined the economic impact of the lockout on the nation's economy.

Bush is an exuberant, positive extrovert. He never was the type of child who could play quietly alone. Bush loves the gregarious nature of politics and is fearless in an interpersonal sense, shaking hands and meeting people. He enjoys being president. Attaining the office gave him a sense of personal fulfillment, and like William Howard Taft and Ronald Reagan, two other passive-positive presidents, Bush does not believe that he has to work hard at it. He craves comfortable and familiar surroundings, takes naps, goes to bed early, and takes long vacations at his ranch.

Bush's Career

G. W. Bush believes that his religious conversion strengthened his character and propelled him to financial and political success. He moved back to Midland, Texas, after earning an MBA from Harvard. He used $15,000 left over from an educational fund to start Arbusto Energy, a company dealing with oil leases. Bush's company prospered in a period characterized by high oil prices and favorable tax laws. In 1977, he ran for Congress, meeting his future wife, Laura, during the unsuccessful campaign. In 1986, Bush traded the assets of his company for stock in Harken Energy and moved his young family to Washington, D.C., to help his father run for the presidency. After his father's inauguration, G. W. Bush returned to Dallas, Texas. He persuaded a group of investors to purchase the Texas Rangers professional baseball team. As a reward for his efforts, the investors made him the managing general partner.

In 1994, G. W. Bush returned to politics, defeating Ann Richards in the race for governor of Texas. After serving two terms as governor, young Bush decided to enter the race for the presidency. He raised more money than any other presidential candidate in history. His initial secret for soliciting funds was using his mother's Christmas card list to solicit donations.

Environment

The mood of the country during and after the disastrous 2000 election was grim. Eric Pooley wrote in a *Time* magazine article "How Can He Govern?" that whoever won the election would enter the "White House more battered and bruised than the man moving out."[33]

Soon after Bush was sworn in on January 20, 2001, he spoke at a luncheon of congressional leaders. He promised them that he would work with Republicans and Democrats to "rise above expectations."[34] Even so, many Americans believed that Bush, with his less than cerebral approach to governing and laid-back manner, would not succeed. In addition to a cynical and divided electorate, the newly elected president faced a Congress characterized by gridlock. The Senate was split 50-50, and the Republicans clung to a small majority in the House. Bush's optimism, self-discipline, and ability to work in a bipartisan manner were assets in his successful effort to implement his limited agenda. He persuaded Congress to enact tax cuts and education reform during a short honeymoon period.

Bush exceeded expectations after the attack on the World Trade Center towers on September 11, 2001. He turned out to be a forceful commander in chief. His message was direct, sincere, and compassionate. There were tears in his eyes when he asked for prayers for all those who grieved. Americans understood his description of the war as one between good and evil. Bush received high popularity ratings and unqualified support during the war in Afghanistan.

Barber's arguments help us understand the strengths and weaknesses of Bush as a person, but what do they tell us about the future?

The Future

The Oracle of Delphi's predictions were successful because they were ambiguous enough that they came true no matter what happened. The accuracy of scholarly predictions, however, must depend more on what does happen. The following five predictions all depend on whether the *environment* satisfies or frustrates the needs of a passive-positive president.

First, Bush will continue to seek advice and comfort from "good men," including his father. He finds men of stature and delegates responsibility to them. Bush's penchant for loyalty makes it difficult for him to discipline his appointees. Similar problems brought disgrace to the administration of another passive-positive president, Warren G. Harding.

Second, the passive nature of Bush's character leads one to believe that he is more apt to accomplish projects narrow in scope and limited in objective. His political successes during the first "100 days" of his administration are more like his *independent political success*, modest in nature and accomplished by selling the program to a diverse group of people. Bush seems uncomfortable with programs such as Homeland Security, a project that a more active president would appreciate for its transformational potential.

Third, Bush's conflicted *worldview* is both fatalistic and idealistic. Bush sees the world as a place where war is inevitable. President Bush will expand military operations in Iraq as long as he has the support of people whose opinion he considers important. Bush believes that Midland, Texas, is a microcosm of how the world ought to work. His fundamental Protestant religious outlook reinforces these nostalgic memories and leads him naturally to a belief in a bipolar world of good versus evil. This notion may help him lead in a wartime situation but makes it difficult for him to understand complex problems of peace and security.

Fourth, Bush's positive and determined *style* will prove both a help and a hindrance. It enhanced his role as leader in the war against terrorism and in the war against Iraq. Bush connects with people and enlists them in support of his team. On the other hand, his bluntness and bravado may needlessly antagonize our allies.

Fifth, Bush's undoing may very well be domestic events. Assets that are valuable in wartime can be liabilities in tackling complex domestic issues such as the economy. The elder Bush enjoyed tremendous popularity during the Gulf War, but he lost his bid for reelection because he misread the concern of many Americans over the economy. Bush may follow in his father's footsteps.

CONCLUSION

One of the interesting components of doing research on Bush was looking at the pictures of him as a youngster. My favorite is of eight-year-old Georgie in a baseball uniform. He has a tight-jawed look of determination that says he will do his best to catch his father's blazing fast ball. Look carefully at the future president's face the next time you see a picture of him talking tough about a regime change in Iraq. You will see that same expression and further proof of our analysis using the arguments of James David Barber. Here is a man whose self-esteem depends on defending and pleasing his father.

Bush eschews self-analysis of this sort, but he proudly declares that family, unconditional love, the death of his sister, and growing up in Midland, Texas, had a powerful influence on the development of his character. He admits that he achieved maturity after a long and difficult struggle. Bush and his parents can finally see him now for the person he really is. The fate of the nation, and perhaps the world, depends on his continued growth. He is more direct and decisive than his father and thus has the potential to be a better president. At the same time, his passiveness can lead to lethargy and his positiveness can blind him to the consequences of the agonizingly difficult decisions he must make as leader of the world's most powerful nation.

NOTES

1. James David Barber, *The Presidential Character* (Englewood Cliffs: Prentice Hall, 1972).

2. James David Barber, "President Nixon and Richard Nixon: Character Trap," *Psychology Today*, October 1974, 114.

3. Barber, *Presidential Character*, 5.

4. Ibid.

5. Ibid., 7.

6. Barber, "President Nixon and Richard Nixon: Character Trap," 114.

7. Based on chart by Paul R. Edelman, Sauk Valley Community College, //svcc.il.us/academics/classes.ediemap/gov163/chapter12Presidency.

8. Barber, "President Nixon," 114.

9. Bruce Mazlish, "Review of Presidential Character by James David Barber," *New York Times Book Review*, October 8, 1972, 30. How can you categorize both Lyndon Johnson and Richard Nixon as active-negative? Johnson's negativism arose from the circumstances of the Vietnam War and Nixon's from his own personal demons.

10. James David Barber, "Nonsensical Analysis of Nonexistent Works," *American Political Science Review* 71 (1977): 215.

11.　James H. Qualls, "Barber's Typological Analysis of Political Leaders," *American Political Science Review* 71 (1977): 182.

12.　Barber, "Nonsensical Analysis," 215.

13.　Barber, *Presidential Character*, xiv, 484.

14.　Barber analyzes presidents in several different ways, as individuals and grouped by type. His predictions are placed at the beginning, middle, or end of a chapter. He classifies George Herbert Walker Bush as active-positive. He views the senior Bush as "a man in search of a mission" because of his failure to develop a worldview during adolescence See Ibid., 458.

15.　Quoted in Nicholas Kristof, "The 2000 Campaign," *New York Times*, September 11, 2000, 1.

16.　Quoted in George Lardner Jr. and Luis Romano, "Tragedy Created Bush Mother-Son Bond," *Washington Post*, July 26, 1999, A1.

17.　Barbara Bush, *A Memoir* (New York: Scribner, 1994), 27.

18.　Lardner Jr. and Romano, "Tragedy," A1.

19.　George W. Bush, *A Charge to Keep* (New York: Morrow and Co., 1999), 15.

20.　Lardner Jr. and Romano, "Tragedy," A1.

21.　Bush, *A Charge to Keep*, 15.

22.　George Lardner Jr. and Luis Romano, "Bush: So-So Student but a Campus Mover," *Washington Post*, July 27, 1999, A1.

23.　Lawrence I. Barrett, "Junior Is His Own Bush Now," *Time*, July 31, 1989, 60.

24.　Lardner Jr. and Romano, "Tragedy," A1.

25.　Bush, *A Charge to Keep*, 18.

26.　Frank Bruni, *Ambling into History* (New York: Harper Collins, 2002), 226.

27.　Jacob Weisberg, *Bushisms* (New York: Fireside, 2001), 22, from a speech in Bentonville, Arkansas, November 6, 2000.

28.　Gail Sheehy, "The Accidental Candidate," *Vanity Fair*, October 2000, 164.

29.　Weisberg (speech, Orange County, California, September 15, 2000).

30.　"Bush Denies Dyslexia," *ABC News Web*, September 12, 2000, http://abcnews.go.com/sections/politics/Daily/News/Bush_dyslexia.

31.　Bush, *A Charge to Keep*, 21.

32.　Bruni, Ambling into History, 19.

33.　Eric Pooley, "How can He Govern?," *Time*, November 20, 2000, A1.

34.　Quoted by Heron Marquez, *George Bush* (Minneapolis: Learner, 2002), 101.

Chapter 2

Compassionate Conservatism Meets Communitarianism

W. W. Riggs

INTRODUCTION

George W. Bush captured the Republican Party presidential nomination in 2000, then the presidency itself with the defeat of Al Gore, a "New Democrat," by campaigning as a "different kind of Republican."[1] Bush identified himself as a compassionate conservative, one who was opposed to the liberalism of the Democratic Party and the traditional conservatism of the Republican Party, by emphasizing decidedly centrist themes and policy proposals.[2]

At midpoint of Bush's first term in office, assessments were collected regarding his performance as president and the performance of his administration. However, little scholarly attention was ever devoted to understanding the meaning of "compassionate conservatism," let alone its theoretical roots.[3] A search of the scholarly databases JSTOR and PROQUEST DIRECT returned no entries for "compassionate conservatism." What is compassionate conservatism, and what are its theoretical roots? I contend that the communitarian critique of liberalism provided the Republican Party with the normative foundation from which to critique the liberalism of the Democratic Party and to justify their more centrist policy proposals in the name of compassionate conservatism.

Political movements must present a coherent message, or at least one perceived to be coherent, in order to sway a sufficient number of adherents and to avoid the damaging charge that the movement is without principle. The normative groundwork on which compassionate conservatives stand is in contrast to traditional Republican Party membership. However, it is necessary for compassionate conservatives to adhere to a normative political theory that provides a principled justification for their centrist policies, allowing them to claim moral authority over not only traditional liberal thought and practice but traditional Republican thought and practice as well. This moral authority allows compassionate conservatives to claim that their political path is not only the prudent one to take, it is also the morally correct path. The ability to make this moral claim is an important source of strength for any movement, particularly in terms of its potential for success over a long period of time. Therefore, it is essential to examine the normative theoretical claims on which compassionate conservatives ground their policy proposals, because the strength of these normative claims is a significant factor, among many others, for an explanation of the shape and success of the movement and the reasons underlying the policy proposals.

Furthermore, in order to evaluate the merits of any public policy, it is necessary to understand the strongest arguments available for and against them. Candidate Bush adopted compassionate conservatism as his mantra when running for president, so it was anticipated that this new Republican ideology would undergird his policy proposals if elected. Even if one could claim that Bush operated for strictly pragmatic political considerations, that alone is not enough to credit or discredit his policy proposals, because there are normative arguments available to justify these proposals. Since normative arguments can and do strengthen policy proposals, scholars need to better understand the overall meaning and the potential viability of the movement's policy proposals. Bush, regardless of whether or not he acts from pragmatic or genuinely moral considerations, has adopted some sort of normative beliefs. It would seem that these normative beliefs let Republicans establish a political message that draws heavily on communitarian ideas and theories.

The purpose of this chapter is to discuss the theoretical underpinnings of Republican compassionate conservatism. In their attempt to distance themselves from the more traditionally conservative wing of the Republican Party, it is suggested that compassionate conservatives have developed a political message within the nexus of the liberal-communitarian philosophical debate.[4] These communitarian critiques of liberalism provide Republicans the normative foundation from which to critique the Democratic Party with a compassionate conservative alternative that in turn justifies their own more centrist policy proposals.

This argument is defended by first reviewing the compassionate conservative literature and then by examining the Republican Party platform. It was first hypothesized that an examination of the party platform would identify the presence or absence of particular themes that can be associated with the normative ideology of compassionate conservatism, thereby strengthening its viability as a normative grounding for future policy proposals. The themes of opportunity and community were identified within the Republican Party platform and provided a means for comparison with similar themes in communitarian literature.

THE SEARCH FOR AN IDEOLOGY

The literature dealing with "who is" George W. Bush, although far from definitive, seems to suggest that he may actually be three people; first Bush is similar to former president Bill Clinton in some ways;[5] second, Bush is to the right of Ronald Reagan ideologically;[6] and third, Bush is really a compassionate conservative offering new leadership ideology to the Republican Party.[7]

The Making of Compassionate Conservatism

Bush's political philosophy of compassionate conservatism has its initial roots in the work of Marvin Olasky, who has been identified as the "godfather" of this political ideology. As a sometime advisor to Bush (he served as chair of Bush's campaign subcommittee on religion), he has provided an active voice in the welfare reform and social policy development of the president.[8] Olasky is a professor of journalism at the University of Texas and a senior fellow of the Acton Institute for the Study of Religion and Liberty, a nonprofit group advocating religious liberty, economic freedom, and personal responsibility.[9]

Olasky's enhanced stature among American conservatives evolved from a series of books written during the past decade that introduced compassionate conservatism to Republicans, including Newt Gingrich and Charles Murray, the latter of "bell curve" infamy.[10] His groundbreaking and most notable work prior to compassionate conservatism, which became the theme for the 2000 Republican presidential campaign, was *The Tragedy of American Compassion*, published in 1992.[11] The book chronicled the history of American volunteer aid societies and charitable organizations. Olasky identified these community volunteer efforts as the "Early American Model of Compassion" and noted that these organizations tended to require some sort of work in exchange for food and shelter. Olasky's research revealed that inherent in this early American model of compassion was the inclusion of the "prescriptive" twin beliefs of assisting the needy primarily through faith-based private-sector programs (instead of relying upon government's traditional welfare services) and the "transforming power of faith." The early model also called for a distinction between the deserving and undeserving poor and the coupling of the receiving of charity with shame and an obligation to remedy the individual failings that led to poverty and degradation.

Olasky contrasts this early model that advocated work in exchange for food and shelter with a more contemporary social policy. This latter policy began with President Franklin D. Roosevelt's New Deal and became institutionalized with the "War on Poverty" programs of the 1960s, whereby compassion came to mean just merely giving to the needy without concern for their self-sufficiency. Philanthropy gradually became as cold as paying taxes, while undermining the adage that able-bodied individuals should work.[12] The result was the transformation of thought that "taught the poor to regard public assistance as an entitlement rather than a confession of moral failure and a down payment on reformation."[13] Olasky writes: "it became better to accept welfare than to take in laundry."[14]

Olasky's recent book (with President Bush penning the foreword), *Compassionate Conservatism: What It Is, What It Does, and How It Can Transform America*, published in 2000, provides answers to the questions raised in *The Tragedy of American Compassion*. He provides examples of success stories illustrating that economic redistribution by itself cannot effectively fight poverty, because such programs neglect the attitudes that frequently undergird poverty. Olasky writes:

> Governments can do certain things very well, but it cannot put hope in our hearts or a sense of purpose in our lives. That requires churches and synagogues and mosques and charities . . . compassion means suffering with a person in distress and developing close personal ties. More people are understanding that the problem with the welfare state is not its cost but its stinginess in providing help that is patient; help that is kind; help that protects, trusts, and perseveres; help that goes beyond good intentions into gritty, street-level reality.[15]

Westbrook notes in this latest book that Olasky has moderated his view regarding the elimination of government entirely from its welfare responsibility.[16] Olasky is now in agreement with President Bush that government cannot be completely replaced by charities. Instead, the two must become partners with government fulfilling the role of the "subsidiarist," whereby the state funds and monitors social policy but contracts it out to civil institutions. Although this is considered to be closely identified with Catholic social thought, Democrats Bill Bradley and Benjamin Barber share the same idea.[17] In sum, Olasky claims that in order for changes to be effective in combating the culture of poverty they must be personal, challenging, and spiritual, which are requirements that government cannot meet.

Intellectual Roots

Newt Gingrich identifies four realities that make such change even more difficult. First is that individuals within a dysfunctional culture must transfer their loyalties. The second reality is that to do so is very difficult. A third reality is that such cultural change is best done outside of government, because governments are not set up as agents of acculturation. We would strongly resist any call for a cultural change by government. The fourth reality is that cultural change cannot be legislated by government. The solution is one of more citizen responsibility.[18]

The call for more citizen responsibility is at the core of compassionate conservatism and, as Gerber effectively argues, it establishes a Kantian ethical theory that provides an implicit moral framework in which individuals are ends in themselves, to be responsible free agents accountable for their personal

actions, and voluntary faith-based associations should develop a public conscious-
ness and commitment to engage in good works to promote the public good.[19]
President Bush sums it up by saying: "let's change your heart first, and the good
results will follow." Thus, the goals of teaching the needy to help themselves
and develope a sense of self-reliance are achieved and, if some souls are saved
along the way, so much the better.[20]

Bush seems to be in agreement with Olasky's premise that the poor and
needy require spiritual guidance in addition to economic relief in order to
develop the moral and character traits that produce good citizens. The addition
of a spiritual element is an anathema to liberal pundits, because it violates the element of moral neutrality traditionally established as the cornerstone of contemporary liberalism. It was the requirement for the state to remain morally neutral
that initiated the liberal-communitarian debate. Do compassionate conservatives
and communitarians have more in common?

COMMUNITARIANISM AND COMPASSIONATE CONSERVATISM

What follows is a discussion of the themes of equality and opportunity as identified in the 2000 Republican Party platform compared with the same topics as
set forth in the 1999 communitarian publication, *The Responsive Communitarian
Platform*.[21]

Opportunity

The 2000 Republican Party platform emphasized equality of opportunity as a
cornerstone of the party while exhorting all to a rejection of hatred and bigotry
and the denouncement of all who practice or promote racism, anti-Semitism,
ethnic prejudice, and religious intolerance. It supports faith-based organizations. The plank continues with a litany of traditional Republican ideology that
includes support of the First Amendment right of free association exemplified
in the Boy Scouts as a private organization, who propose disallowing gays in
their organization. (One may discern that this support could also be interpreted
as a "code words" regarding an anti-gay position.) Affirmative action quotas are
rejected in favor of "treatment as individuals and not as groups." Second
Amendment prerogatives are supported regarding the right to keep and bear
arms. The platform states support (through the Fourteenth Amendment) for
the rights of unborn children, no public funds for abortion, the appointment of
pro-life judges, and ending the involuntary use of union dues for political purposes. What do communitarians say regarding equality of opportunity?

The communitarian position dealing with equality is contained in *The
Responsive Communitarian Platform: Rights and Responsibilities*. This platform

emerged from the efforts of a group of scholars led by Amatai Etzioni, a professor of sociology at Georgetown University during the 1980s, who challenged the liberal individualism set forth in John Rawls's 1971 work, *A Theory of Justice*.[22] Other members of the group included Charles Taylor, Alisdaire MacIntyre, Daniel E. Bell, Phillip Selznick, Robert Bellah, Michael Walzer, and Michael Sandel. What united these scholars was their agreement that liberal individualism, and its preoccupation with rights claims, ignores the importance of communal relationships to personal identity, to moral and political thinking, and to judgments about human well-being.

Communitarians view equality of opportunity as a principle of social justice. For communitarians, equality of opportunity incorporates it as a value within a moral community of open competition for self-regarding ends. Similar to the Republican Party platform, communitarians feel that whatever opportunities exist should be open to all without regard to social origins, including race, creed, ethnicity, or gender. By doing so, communitarians feel that equality of opportunity vindicates moral equality by recognizing the need to overcome prejudice and systematic subordination while maintaining the legitimacy of differential rewards. It could be argued that George W. Bush, in his "The Duty of Hope" speech, acknowledges this view by stating that the "invisible hand works many miracles, but it does not touch the human heart."[23] There is the suggestion that some sort of obligation may be incurred within the community that can only be exercised through lending a helping hand.

Like compassionate conservatives, communitarians advocate an energetic sense of civic responsibility in order to master the skills of self-government. The communitarian perspective also recognizes that communities have the duty to be responsive to their members and to foster participation and deliberation in the social and political life of the community. This seems to be in keeping with the intended goals of the volunteerism emphasized by the compassionate conservatism ideology.

The compassionate conservative emphasis on shared relations through volunteerism suggests a communitarian understanding of *essentially* shared relations between persons as opposed to *contingent* relations between individuals. These different ways of viewing a shared relationship each presupposes a different conception of self-identity. The difference can be illustrated by looking at the example of marriage. A view of marriage as an essentially shared relationship would see marriage as a sacred bond, the redefinition of two separate selves into a union. An alternative view of marriage is as a contingently shared relationship similar to a commercial contract entered into for a mutual benefit. While this marriage example may seem to be an idealized image of communitarian bonds when transferred to larger groups, the point is that communitarians and compassionate conservatives both call attention to the social side of nature, to the responsibilities that must be borne by citizens, individually and collectively, in a regime that also must respect rights.

Community

The Republican Party platform acknowledges the role of individual rights and the responsibilities that go with them as the foundation of free society. Americans are to be united by a common good and common goals while also acknowledging the strength found in diversity. Our commitment to one another is to resolve differences with civility, trust, and mutual respect.

At the core of community is the family, and strengthening the family improves the quality of life for all. The Republican Party platform supports marriage as the legal union of one man and one woman, while encouraging the courts not to recognize other alternative conceptions of family and denouncing the glorification of violence and the abuse of women and children through pornography. In general, the Republican Party platform endorses and is supportive of individuals and organizations that want to advance this cultural renewal.

Compassionate conservatives are very much aware that individuals thrive when they are rooted in a strong value system that is imparted through family, church, and other civic-oriented institutions. The prevailing problems of drugs, out-of-wedlock births, crime, and abuse arise out of weaknesses in the culture.[24] Getting control of one's life requires support from family, church, and community.

The communitarian perspective begins with the rejection that a liberal state cannot act to advance human excellence. Selznick argues: "it is a parody of democracy to say that democratic institutions are mainly geared to manage diversity; and that the main evil to be considered is moral coercion, that is, the burden of accepting, as legitimate, conclusions that offend one's moral convictions. . . . Democracy looks to substance as well as to procedure."[25] Barber's literature on democracy adds that the substance of democracy and its substantive commitments are provided by the community.[26] This perspective seems to suggest that the compassionate conservative idea of volunteer organizations becoming partners with government merits consideration.

Communitarians note that social order rests on strong families. However, as Olasky has written, it was widely assumed in industrial America that public institutions could and should fill the breach created by failing families and communities.[27] Even the Clinton-led "New Democrats" acknowledged that the liberal egalitarian remedies that supported the professionalization and bureaucratization of social workers and led to the replacement of volunteers with trained "experts" contributed to the unforeseen result of the displacement of many traditional community-based efforts to provide needy people with spiritual as well as material aid. In time, the government's social safety net became a snare for many poor citizens, a final destination rather than a way station back to family, work, and self-reliance. Recalling the 1992 Democratic Party plank that included the infamous sound bite, "governments don't raise children, people do," communitarians recognize that in order to build a better society, we must begin with the family, and that includes efforts to slow down divorce rates.[28]

Communitarians recognize that if citizens follow a purely private life in pursuit of self-interest, then their social, political, economic, and moral order will suffer. Consequently, some measure of caring, sharing, and being our brother's keeper is essential if we are not to fall back on an even more expansive government, bureaucratized welfare agencies, and swollen regulations, police, courts, and jails. Much as do compassionate conservatives, communitarians propose programs of national and local service and volunteer work to bring people closer together while fostering mutual respect and tolerance.

CONCLUSION

Republicans have long suggested that traditional Democratic Party politics will foster an absence of civic identity and responsibility that ignores the individual in his or her capacity as a citizen and community member in favor of rights-based individualism. Compassionate conservative rhetoric suggests an alternative to that erosion of civic responsibility.

The normative groundwork on which compassionate conservatism rests is in contrast to the traditional Republican Party membership. It is obvious that the recent political successes of the Republican Party can by no means be explained entirely through an examination of the normative theory of compassionate conservatism. Undoubtedly, the pragmatic political goals of gaining power and winning elections was and is the driving force of the political actors of any political movement. But these political actors require an ideology, a stated set of principled beliefs, on which to ground their actions, even if they only adopt such grounds for political purposes.

If compassionate conservatives are to convince the electorate that they are a different, better alternative to their fellow Republicans, and to the opposition, the Democratic Party, then they must present a message that differs markedly from traditional Republican conservatism while simultaneously avoiding the perception that they are merely compromising their beliefs to gain political power. The normative ideology of compassionate conservatism suggests an alternative to that erosion of civic responsibility. Compassionate conservatism wants to turn taxpayers into citizens. However, communitarian literature also provides a normative emphasis on renewing civic identity and responsibility that is neither liberal nor conservative. Communitarianism suggests that among the many proper roles of government are the restoration of community and the tempering of individual rights with a commensurate social responsibility. The normative ideology of compassionate conservatism echoes this communitarian theory, which may help us in evaluating the roots of George W. Bush's political beliefs and his claim to act as a compassionate conservative.

NOTES

1. See Thomas Edsall, "Changing Attitudes towards Hard-line Conservatism," *Washington Post*, June 27, 2000; Richard Lowry, "The Limits of Compassion," *The National Review*, April 3, 2000; Dana Millbank, "What 'W' Stands For," *The New Republic*, April 8, 1999; John O'Sullivan, "Compassion Play," *National Review*, February 22, 1999.

2. Paul Burka, "Grading George W," *Texas Monthly*, March 1999; GOP, Republican Party Platform, 2000, www.rnc.org/GOPInfo/Platform/2000platform1.htm.

3. Mitchel Gerber, "The Inherent Kantian Ethical Implications of Bush's Compassionate Conservatism" (paper presented at the Presidential Election Series Forum, Southeast Missouri University, February 2, 2000).

4. To explore the debate, please see: Ellen Buchanan, "Assessing the Communitarian Critique of Liberalism," *Ethics* 99 (July 1989); Amatai Etzioni, *A Responsive Society* (San Francisco: Josie-Bass, 1991), and *Rights and the Common Good: The Communitarian Perspective* (New York: St. Martin's Press, 1995); Charles Taylor, *Sources of the Self: The Making of Modern Identity* (Cambridge: Cambridge University Press, 1989); Philip Selznick, *The Moral Commonwealth: Social Theory and the Promise of Community* (Berkeley: University of California Press, 1987).

5. See Douglas Alexander, "Compassion Is the New Politics," *New Statesman*, September 20, 1999, or Stuart M. Powell, "Bush Seen Copying Clinton's Centrist Tactic," *San Antonio Express*, May 5, 2002.

6. See Giles Marshall, "What Can George W. Bush Teach the Conservatives," *Reformer Magazine* (Autumn 1999), or Ed Crane, "The Dangers of Compassionate Conservatism," Cato Policy Report (May–June 2001).

7. See E. J. Dionne Jr., "Conservatism Recast: Why This President's Reach Could Be Monumental," *Washington Post*, January 27, 2002.

8. Marvin Olasky, *Compassionate Conservatism: What It Is, What It Does, and How It Can Transform America* (New York: Free Press, 2000).

9. Melanie Perren, "Olasky Commends Compassion," *Washington Witness*, October 10, 2002.

10. Marvin Olasky, *Renewing American Compassion* (New York: Free Press, 1996).

11. Marvin Olasky, *The Tragedy of American Compassion* (New York: Free Press, 1992).

12. Olasky, *Renewing American Compassion*, 15–17.

13. Robert Westbrook, "Compassionate Conservatism: What It Is, What It Does, and How It Can Transform America," *Christian Century*, September 13, 2000, 1–4.

14. Olasky, *Compassionate Conservatism*, 22.

15. Ibid., 35.

16. Westbrook, "Compassionate Conservatism," 3.

17. Ibid., 2.

18. Newt Gingrich, quoted in the foreword to Olasky, *Renewing American Compassion*, vi.

19. Gerber, "The Inherent Kantian," 1–14.

20. George W. Bush, "The Duty of Hope" (speech, Indianapolis, July 22, 1999).

21. Communitarian Network, *The Responsive Communitarian Platform: Rights and Responsibilities*, February 26, 1999, http://www.gwu.edu/~ccps/RCP.html.

22. John Rawls, *A Theory of Justice* (Cambridge: Harvard University Press, 1971).

23. Bush, "The Duty of Hope."

24. Stephen Goldsmith, "What Compassionate Conservatism Is—and Is Not," *Hoover Digest*, April 30, 2000.

25. Phillip Selznick, quoted in *The Essential Communitarian Reader*, ed. Amatai Etzioni, (Oxford: Rowan & Littlefield, 1998), 75.

26. See the following Barber works: Benjamin Barber, *The Conquest of Politics: Liberal Philosophy in Democratic Politics* (Princeton: Princeton University Press, 1989); *A Passion for Democracy* (Princeton: Princeton University Press 1988); *A Strong Democracy: Participatory Politics for a New Age* (Berkeley: University of California Press, 1984).

27. Olasky, *Renewing American Compassion*, 28.

28. See William Galston, "A Liberal-Democratic Case for the Two-Parent Family," in *The Essential Communitarian Reader*, ed. Amatai Etzioni (Oxford: Rowan & Littlefield, 1998), 145–155.

Chapter 3

The Embryonic Stem Cell Debate and the Battle between Politics and Ethics

Bryan Hilliard

INTRODUCTION

On August 9, 2001, less than seven months after taking office, President George W. Bush gave a nationally televised speech in which he set forth the administration's policy regarding federal funding of human embryonic stem cell research. In broad outline, the policy allows, within certain ethical guidelines, federal funds to be used for research on existing stem cell lines but no federal money to be used to support the destruction of embryos or for research on stem cells derived from embryos destroyed after the August decree.[1] This policy statement was the culmination of months of public debate and was considered by many an "artful political compromise."[2] Some observers in the media opined that the debate and the resulting policy, whatever it would be, would define the rest of Bush's presidency.[3] Indeed, within the context of evaluating the first two years of Bush's term, the administration's policy is quite instructive. That is, the handling of the stem cell debate provides answers to such admittedly esoteric questions as: Is President Bush acting with integrity? Do he and his administration understand and appreciate the complexities of moral reasoning and the connections between that reasoning and politics in setting public policy? Is he able and willing to separate the political from the ethical? Both the policy itself and the manner in which Bush formulated the policy provide insight into the moral leadership of George W. Bush.

POLITICS AND ETHICS

The events that transpired during the summer of 2001 constitute the quintessential example of what can be seen as a battle between politics and ethics.

In its simplest form, this notion represents the struggle between doing what is politically expedient, on the one hand, and only doing what one can provide good and sufficient ethical justification for, on the other hand. Implicit in this struggle is the contention that ethics, as a practical manifestation of philosophy, insists on clear, careful, and precise justifications. Politics, in contrast, uses sloppy language and often clings to the flimsiest of justifications. Where the professional ethicist relies on conceptual clarity and solid reasoning, the career politician relies on eloquence and persuasion. The ethicist purports to eschew the opinions of others; politicians, often for their very survival, must take account of and honor the various opinions and special interests of others.[4] No doubt this struggle is influenced by the fact that we live in a democratic society with many different ethical views and moral convictions. Acknowledging this moral pluralism and developing consensus are challenges faced by all national leaders.[5] At its core, then, the battle between politics and ethics can best be characterized by the question, "How should a politician mesh what is ethically desirable with what is politically viable?"[6] To do well in this battle, to engage successfully the demands of both politics and ethics, a political leader will set the public agenda, promote social discourse, and implement policies that are effective, that meet the needs of various constituencies and stakeholders, and that sustain the rigors of ethical justification.

Rarely has it been more important for political leaders to engage in this assessment and evaluation than in the area of human embryonic stem (HES) cell research and the government's role in such research. At stake are such concerns as how the nation will view the moral status of human life at its very beginning and what limitations, if any, the nation will place on scientific and medical research in pursuit of alleviating or curing some of our most serious illnesses and injuries. Two points are argued: first, Bush's policy lacks sufficient ethical justification; second, Bush's approach to stem cell research and to other issues involving the value of life constitutes a conceptual confusion over derivative and detached interests. These two problems have plagued and will continue to plague the Bush administration. In the battle between politics and ethics—in pursuit of framing public policy that respects moral pluralism—it seems that adequate moral justification and clarity are the first casualties.

At first glance, of course, it might be asserted that the Bush policy on HES cell research is a success—a prime example of setting public policy and respecting moral pluralism at the same time—in that it satisfied everyone to some extent and yet made absolutely no one happy. As one observer noted:

> It upset abortion foes, who saw in it a retreat from a campaign promise they thought Bush had made to view embryonic and fetal life as sacred and morally equivalent to the lives of children and adults. It upset research supporters, who saw in it an implicit position that no form of human life, no matter how rudimentary, could be sacrificed in

the future, even if that would condemn hundreds of thousands of patients to suffering and death. And it upset segments of the academic community, which viewed the policy as analytically flawed and internally inconsistent.[7]

But is the policy that Bush articulated really an example of meshing political expediency with rigorous ethical reflection? The above concerns, or disappointments, on the part of various constituencies echo, at least in part, concerns over the moral permissibility of stem cell research itself. The catalogue of moral questions is extensive: Is there a morally relevant distinction between funding the destruction of embryos and funding research only on cells taken from destroyed embryos? How should informed consent of donors of embryos be promoted and protected? Should we revisit the issue of the moral permissibility of in vitro fertilization (IVF) and other reproductive technologies? If we were to decide that HES cell research were morally allowable, what are the implications for cloning? Given that millions of Americans face obstacles in obtaining and paying for health care, is it morally defensible to devote so much private and public resources to HES cell research? What guidelines should be implemented to monitor and control corporate profits stemming from the future therapeutic uses of such technology?

Answering these and other questions constitutes an intricate part of the debate surrounding embryo research. More importantly perhaps, these questions form the foundation of a policy that itself may help shape the scientific agenda for the first decade of the twenty-first century. In the context of bioethics, science, and public policy, a great deal is at stake. One commentator notes:

> [N]o previous century has produced such a high level of apprehension about the future. Perhaps the reason for this is that as science generates a larger set of opportunities for us all, it simultaneously raises the level of moral responsibility that falls on our shoulders, and it is this moral or ethical challenge about which we are so uncertain.[8]

No doubt trying to formulate and justify a public policy that involves so many scientific and bioethical issues will be difficult. Such a task makes clarity and consistency all the more important. The moral responsibility of the Bush administration to be clear and consistent is one it cannot dismiss. The argument can be made that Bush fulfilled his responsibilities. In the weeks leading up to the statement, Bush and his staff met with all sides in the debate—evangelical Christians, scientists, and patient advocates. He was lobbied by the pope to oppose funding, and by Orrin Hatch and Nancy Reagan to support it.[9] That political calculations were a part of the decision process is clear,[10] but Bush seemed to be genuinely concerned with understanding and evaluating ethical justifications used by all sides in the stem cell debate.

Ethical Confusion

Prior to the announced policy, some degree of rigorous ethical thinking on stem cell research and government's proper role in the research had taken place. The House and Senate had debated this and related issues for at least five years. In addition, certainly Bush was aware of and considered the work of the National Institutes of Health (NIH) and the National Bioethics Advisory Commission (NBAC);[11] both agencies had devoted a great deal of time and effort to formulating recommendations for a national policy on HES cell research.[12] Bush, however, ignored the recommendations of these two entities. The NIH recommended using federal funds for research on cell lines derived (using nonfederal funds) from embryos, earlier or in the future, within certain guidelines. The NBAC recommended the use of federal funds for both the derivation of and research on embryonic stem cells within certain ethical guidelines. The administration's policy designates use of federal money for conducting research on cell lines derived (not using federal funds) from embryos before August 9, 2001.[13]

One is left to wonder why this date has such importance, and certainly it is difficult to find ethical significance for it. One commentator has noted: "it should also be ethically acceptable to provide federal funds for research on stem cell lines derived in the future, after August 9 as well as before, with nonfederal funds and within the same ethical guidelines."[14] Too, it is not quite clear why the administration makes the distinction between not using federal funds for derivation and allowing the use of federal funds for research. As the same commentator notes:

> One argument for this option is that a strict separation between derivation and use would adversely affect the development of scientific knowledge. For instance, the methods for deriving embryonic stem cells may affect their properties, and scientists may increase their understanding of the nature of such cells in the process of deriving them.[15]

Other concerns lead one to conclude that Bush neither provided sufficient ethical justification for, nor anticipated relevant ethical consequences of, his policy. These consequences include inadequate informed consent guidelines for embryo donors;[16] complex legal issues, including patent law problems, with the new policy;[17] and problems associated with private corporations getting involved in stem cell research.[18] For many, the most significant lapse in ethical reflection for which Bush bears some responsibility concerns the lack of a thorough analysis of the costs and benefits of HES cell research. Are the sacrifices of early human life worth the possible benefits in medical therapy? What value will these therapies have if there are millions of Americans who cannot afford them?[19] Raising these concerns need not imply a substantive view on the morality of HES cell research. The point is rather that there is little evidence to suggest that these concerns were raised in an effective way. That these concerns seem not to have been addressed naturally leads one to conclude that the public debate taking place around the country in the summer of 2001 may not have been as enlightened and in depth as one would have desired. But of course one might still conclude that the policy is "good enough," is at least acceptable.

Rights and Intrinsic Value

However, a more insidious problem exists within Bush's policy, and this goes straight to the issue of the battle between politics and ethics. The problem is one that few have noticed, yet it is all around us in political and ethical discourse. Bush has not shared the specifics of his view regarding the intrinsic value of human life, especially very early human life. We have public statements—from the presidential campaign, from speeches to various interest groups, and even from the stem cell policy itself—but these statements are either unclear or inconsistent on the issue of what Bush means when he asserts that early human life is sacred. Underlying almost all of the bioethical, religious, and political concerns surrounding stem cell research is one central issue: determining the moral status of embryos and deciding what weight, if any, to accord this moral status. This issue also appears to provide the underpinning, both ethical and political, of the Bush administration's policy toward destruction and subsequent research on embryos. It is to this issue that we now turn.

Debate and discussion over the moral status of the human embryo is a purely philosophical and ethical concern, and it is a concern that has engendered much argument and conceptual analysis.[20] The facts of human development, biology, and genetics are important, but they are not determinative of the normative issue at hand. Americans—ethicists, scientists, jurists, religious leaders, politicians, and the lay public—are certainly not new to this debate. For more than thirty years the United States has engaged in a conversation (admittedly on occasion devolving into a shouting match and even violence) regarding the moral status of fetuses, most notably in the context of abortion and fetal-tissue research. And indeed, there are certainly similarities, if not a kind of symmetry, between the two discussions. Those more likely to attribute great moral significance to fetuses, especially early fetuses, are more likely to assign profound moral status to embryos, even preimplantation embryos. Those hesitant to call fetuses "persons" are more likely to resist attributing great moral weight to embryos, especially very early embryos. Obviously this is not an all-or-nothing issue. Beings for whom we do not assign full moral status may still be deserving of some degree of moral consideration and respect, while beings who do enjoy full personhood may under certain circumstances have their rights and interests violated.

Customarily, one can take any of three positions regarding the moral status of embryos: some regard the embryo as possessing full personhood with all the rights and interests of other full-fledged persons such as children and adults; others admit that embryos possess some moral status and are deserving of some degree of moral respect (perhaps as potential persons), but they certainly do not enjoy the same rights as other members of the moral community; and there are still others who hold that embryos are deserving of no moral consideration at all.[21] These various positions involve making and defending boundary decisions[22] regarding the point at which human life begins and the point at which the moral category of personhood is established.

A perfect example of the debate over the moral status or personhood of embryos occurred in the U.S. Senate in an exchange between Senators Sam Brownback (R-KS) and Arlen Specter (R-PA) in April 2000.[23] Brownback wanted to draw an analogy to Nazi atrocities committed before and during World War II in his condemnation of the practice of extracting stem cells from embryos, even embryos already destined to be destroyed. Specter replied that the Nazis were killing living people, and that embryos were not living people. Brownback's reply was that embryos are also living.[24] Not withstanding the fact that raising the specter of crimes against humanity is somewhat morally disingenuous, both senators were locked in a fundamental and an important disagreement over what significance to attribute to early embryos. This disagreement has been a continuing theme in House and Senate discussions not only over HES cell research but also over therapeutic and reproductive cloning. Some of the most heated exchanges over personhood occurred during deliberations in April and May 2002 over a bill (S. 1899) sponsored by Brownback that would criminalize all forms of cloning, even the cloning of cells for research. Brownback's bill would impose fines of up to $1 million and prison sentences of up to ten years for researchers who engaged in cloning.[25] Obviously there is a great deal at stake for everyone involved.

MAKING DISTINCTIONS

That the Bush administration believes that early embryos are worthy of protection is quite obvious. During the presidential campaign, Bush was quite clear that he opposed federal funding on stem cell research. He told the U.S. Conference of Catholic Bishops: "Taxpayer funds should not underwrite research that involves the destruction of live human embryos."[26] This stance certainly gratified those on the right and helped alleviate their concerns regarding Bush's position on abortion; that is, that abortion is morally wrong, except in cases of rape and incest. Bush's position does seem to be that fetuses and even embryos are just as much deserving of protection as children and adults. One need only recall one of Bush's first actions after taking office. In a reversal of Clinton administration policy, he issued an executive order cutting off federal funding to overseas agencies that support women seeking an abortion. And in another move indicative of the administration's view on the moral status of fetuses, in September 2002, the Department of Health and Human Services announced that it would consider fetuses unborn children so that states could extend health insurance benefits to pregnant women and their fetuses.

Whatever one thinks of the moral justification of such policies, no doubt they are the consequence, at least in part, of a particular stance regarding the personhood of embryos and fetuses. The exact specifics of Bush's moral convictions remain unclear, however. To claim, as Bush seems to do, that embryos and fetuses are similar to children is to imply that they have rights, the first position outlined earlier. Certainly many on the right—Bush's most ardent supporters—take this position. Perhaps, however, Bush considers life in its early development as extremely important—perhaps even sacred—but does not mean to claim that these forms of early life actually have the rights and interests of children and adults, the second position outlined earlier. Which position is Bush's? The answer has implications not only for the HES cell debate but also for any policy directly or indirectly involving embryos and fetuses.

Therapies resulting from research on human embryos hold great potential to revolutionize health care. These therapies can only be developed if early human life is destroyed. One's position on the morality of destroying early embryos does not rely so much on whether life is sacred but rather on how the phrase "life is sacred" is interpreted. In his book *Life's Dominion: An Argument about Abortion, Euthanasia, and Individual Freedom*, Ronald Dworkin sets forth and defends a distinction with respect to the view that life is sacred.[27] While Dworkin's focus is on fetuses specifically and legislation regarding health care in general, his distinction, and the employment of that distinction, is quite instructive here. Dworkin first observes that such phrases as "life begins at conception" and "human life is sacred" can be understood to have two different meanings. On the one hand, such phrases might be taken to mean that preimplantation embryos, embryos, and fetuses have rights and interests equivalent to children and adults. Persons holding such a view will maintain that the government should do everything within its power to protect these rights and interests. Dworkin calls such a claim a "derivative claim." Brownback appears to hold such a view. On the other hand, the view that life is sacred might be taken to mean that human life is intrinsically valuable in and of itself, independent of whether a particular life has rights or interests. Based on this view, killing human life at any stage of development is a sort of "cosmic shame"—not because of any supposed rights or interests that the life may possess, but because life, even early life, has intrinsic value.[28] Dworkin calls this the "detached claim." Specter might be sympathetic to this view. Dworkin continues by discussing the political, ethical, and legal implications of this distinction.

Dworkin's contention is that there is a significant difference in believing that life is sacred, because beings, even ones at very early stages of development, have rights and interests, and believing that life is sacred just because it is human life. The former view is considered by most extremely difficult to defend, because rights, especially absolute rights, do not automatically flow from moral status. The latter view holds "that human life is sacred just in itself; and that the sacred nature of a human life begins when its biological life begins, even before the creature whose life it is has movement or sensation or interests or rights of its own."[29] This detached view of the importance of human life is one that almost all of us share: the atheist and the theist, the Republican and the Democrat, the conservative and the liberal. Most all of us are willing to grant that human life, at whatever stage of development, is extremely important, and we grant this whatever our particular backgrounds or worldviews. What people holding the detached view do not grant is that embryos have the same rights as other members of the moral community.

Dworkin is convinced that this confusion over derivative and detached claims is what makes public policy regarding abortion and even euthanasia so polarizing and filled with derision. He notes:

> The scolding rhetoric of the "pro-life" movement seems to presuppose the derivative claim that a fetus is from the moment of its conception a full moral person with rights and interests equal in importance to those of any other member of the moral community. But very few people—even those who belong to the most vehemently anti-abortion groups—actually believe that, whatever they say. The disagreement that actually divides people is a markedly less polar disagreement about how best to respect a fundamental idea we almost all share in some form: that individual human life is sacred. . . . [W]e must be careful to distinguish the public rhetoric in which people frame their opinions from the opinions themselves, which sometimes can be recovered only by a more careful examination than polls and demonstrations provide. . . . Many people who are asked to state their views in a general and abstract way find it natural to use the strident and heated rhetoric that leaders of various interest groups have made prominent, whether or not it fits their actual instincts and convictions. They may act very differently from what their rhetoric suggests when making actual decisions in concrete situations involving their own family or friends or themselves.[30]

One last aspect of Dworkin's observations seems especially relevant to this issue, and this concerns the act of criminalizing certain behaviors. If indeed, as does seem the case, our sympathies lie with detached claims, then how free are we to actualize those claims into law and public policy? With detached claims, it can be argued that the lives of fetuses or early embryos are sacred, and that killing them would therefore be wicked or evil. Or one could argue that the lives of fetuses or early embryos are sacred, and that killing them would therefore be very sad or unfortunate but not wicked or evil. In either case, one begins from the same place but ends with a very different conclusion. This demonstrates that views about the sacredness, the intrinsic value, of life are quite personal and a matter of conscience. Dworkin cautions against trying to craft public policy or advocate for the passage of new laws and prohibitions based on matters of conscience. In a democratic society with many competing and justifiable ethical beliefs and positions, it seems dangerous indeed for one political institution, one agency, even one person, to dictate what will and what will not be permitted based on a personal worldview.[31]

Dworkin's analysis allows Bush's policy on stem cell research and his meaning behind the claim that early embryos have intrinsic value to be examined in a new light. If Bush is making a derivative claim, then he needs to put forth arguments supporting his belief that early embryos have the same rights as adults. If Bush is making a detached claim, then he is obligated to admit as much and then address the issue of why public policy should be framed in accordance with his conscience. Either task is momentous and carries with it tremendous political and ethical risks. To claim that the federal government has a derivative interest in protecting early embryos would ignore the moral importance of making cost-benefit analysis and runs counter to the imperative that the right to life is not absolute. To mandate the protection of embryos based on a detached interest is to force one particular worldview on a pluralistic society. Bush and his administration may possess a well-formed view of the meaning of intrinsic value of human life but, for various reasons, may have chosen not to share this view with the American public.

INTEGRITY AND CONSCIENTIOUSNESS

At this point, the issue of integrity becomes relevant. Charges that someone lacks integrity are serious and should not be made lightly. At a minimum, the person making such a charge should be as clear as possible regarding the meaning of integrity and how that conception has been violated. Bush's policy on HES cell research suggests a lack of integrity. Because such research deals specifically with health care, the definition of integrity used in Beauchamp's and Childress's seminal work in bioethics, *Principles of Biomedical Ethics*, might be adapted and useful. In that work, they define "integrity" as:

> . . . soundness, reliability, wholeness, and integration of moral character. In a more restricted sense, moral integrity means fidelity in adherence to moral norms. Accordingly, the virtue of integrity represents

two aspects of a person's character. The first is a coherent integration of aspects of the self—emotions, aspirations, knowledge, and so on—so that each complements and does not frustrate the others. The second is the character trait of being faithful to moral values and standing up in their defense when necessary.[32]

Related to integrity is the virtue of conscientiousness; indeed, the two are inseparable. To act conscientiously is to "do what is right because it is right, to try with due diligence to determine what is right, to intend to do what is right, and to exert an appropriate level of effort to do so."[33] A person of integrity will strive for coherence and balance as well as possess a set of moral values and principles to which she or he can be faithful. But integrity also demands careful and thoughtful attention to the possibility that some values may change, and that some moral commitments may have to be altered, focused in another direction, or abandoned altogether. A person of integrity, especially a person with power over others, will avoid "moral tyranny."[34] Integrity and conscientiousness demand that people responsible for formulating and implementing public policy exercise due diligence and devote appropriate effort to what is right. With public policy in the context of stem cell research and other biotechnologies, we see the impact that integrity and conscientiousness have. This impact can be stated succinctly:

> It is inevitable that the rapid pace of development of new knowledge and, therefore, of new opportunities—that is, applications—is certain to generate new issues and new anxieties in the ethical arena. We can anticipate, therefore, a continued search for those social processes or controls, possibly public policies of one type or another, that will improve our chances of selecting the most ethically acceptable applications of our expanding knowledge base. As a result, just as we expect that new science will gain its moral relevance from the nature of the uses we make of new knowledge, we should understand that our moral propositions—old and new—are themselves about to be tested and retested in their application to our evolving social, cultural, and historical circumstances and the changing technological context.[35]

This brief discussion of integrity and conscientiousness, and their relationship to public policy, affords us insight into Bush's deliberations. That he has political concerns—keeping conservatives happy, working with Congress, reaching out to as many in the electorate as possible—is not the problem. The problem is that Bush may not be aware of his own motivations. Or, what would be worse, he is aware of his convictions and ethical values but is unwilling (unable?) to examine and reevaluate them within the context of new technological developments.

Bush's Integrity

At this point, the public has every right to question Bush's integrity on this issue. In defending his position, Bush noted that his policy "allows us to explore the promise and potential of stem cell research without crossing a fundamental moral line by providing taxpayer funding that would sanction or encourage further destruction of human embryos that have at least the potential for life."[36] But this defense still leaves people guessing as to Bush's real view regarding moral status and its implications. For many, the phrase "fundamental moral line" implies that embryos have rights and interests. On the other hand, the phrase "potential for life" might be interpreted to mean that embryos are sacred and should only be destroyed after great moral consideration. Integrity and conscientiousness demand that Bush make known to the American public his moral convictions.

If Bush genuinely believes that all human life, at whatever stage of development, is sacred and has intrinsic value and therefore has the same rights as children and adults, then he needs to give reasons, preferably good and sufficient reasons, for this position. If, on the other hand, he holds the view that life is sacred and has intrinsic value just because it is human life, then he needs to be straightforward about this and explain the reasons his worldview should dominate in the debate over the federal government's role in supporting stem cell research. It makes a difference whether one genuinely believes that preimplantation embryos are intrinsically valuable and thus have rights and interests equal in importance to adults, or whether one believes that preimplantation embryos are intrinsically valuable, and that their destruction should only take place after serious moral reflection.

Bush's stem cell policy is ethically confused, but at bottom the problem with the policy is that it indicates a lack of integrity. After Clinton's National Bioethics Commission disbanded, Bush put into place the Council on Bioethics. Will Bush dissuade the council from seriously considering the ethical issues in stem cell research as some already fear?[37] During the remainder of Bush's presidency, other legal and public policy issues surrounding the moral status and the legal rights of individuals will come to the fore. With the victories in the midterm elections, Bush will have an easier time getting his judicial nominees through Congress. As such, in the remainder of his presidency we are likely to witness the Justice Department working to repeal Oregon's Death with Dignity Act. And, of course, there will be opportunities to revisit and formulate additional policies on HES cell research. All of these policies directly involve moral commitments to the sacredness of human life. From these commitments certain implications for public policy and law flow. Bush must demonstrate that he is dedicated to paying attention to his personal commitments and values, that he is dedicated to doing what is right only after a careful and thorough examination of his values and commitments in light of relevant facts. Not only must

Bush be clear and precise with the American public, he must be clear and precise in his own mind. Integrity demands nothing less.

NOTES

1. R. A. Charo, "Bush's Stem Cell Compromise: A Few Mirrors?," *Hastings Center Report* 31, no. 6 (2001): 6–7.

2. D. Rosenberg, "Stem Cells Show Progress," *Newsweek*, August 12, 2002, 8.

3. J. Cloud, "Bush's No-Win Choice," *Time*, July 23, 2002, 22–26.

4. S. R. Latham, "Ethics and Politics," *American Journal of Bioethics* 2, no. 1 (2002): 46–47.

5. C. Strong, "Those Divisive Stem Cells: Dealing with Our Most Contentious Issues," *American Journal of Bioethics* 2, no. 1 (2002): 39–40.

6. G. Outka, "The Ethics of Human Stem Cell Research," *Kennedy Institute of Ethics Journal* 12, no. 2 (2002): 175–213.

7. Charo, "Bush's Stem Cell Compromise," 6.

8. H. T. Shapiro, "Reflections on the Interface of Bioethics, Public Policy, and Science," in *The Cloning Sourcebook*, ed. R. J. Klotzko (New York: Oxford University Press, 2001), 221.

9. J. Spike, "Bush and Stem Cell Research: An Ethically Confused Policy," *American Journal of Bioethics* 2, no. 1 (2002): 45–46.

10. Cloud, "Bush's No-Win Choice," 22–26.

11. K. E. Hanna, "Stem Cell Politics: Difficult Choices for the White House and Congress," *Hastings Center Report* 31, no. 4 (2001): 9.

12. E. M. Meslin and H. T. Shapiro, "Some Initial Reflections on NBAC," *Kennedy Institute of Ethics Journal* 12, no. 1 (2002): 95–102.

13. J. F. Childress, "Federal Policy toward Human Embryonic Stem Cell Research," *American Journal of Bioethics* 2, no. 1 (2002): 34–35.

14. Ibid., 34.

15. Ibid., 35.

16. J. J. Fins and M. Schachter, "Patently Controversial: Markets, Morals, and the President's Proposal for Embryonic Stem Cell Research," *Kennedy Institute of Ethics Journal* 12, no. 3 (2002): 265–78.

17. Ibid., 265–78.

18. C. MacDonald, "Stem Cell Ethics and the Forgotten Corporate Context," *American Journal of Bioethics* 2, no. 1 (2002): 54–55.

19. R. Dresser, "Embryonic Stem Cells: Expanding the Circle," *American Journal of Bioethics* 2, no. 1 (2002): 40–41.

20. R. M. Green, "Determining Moral Status," *American Journal of Bioethics* 2, no. 1 (2002): 20–30. For a much more detailed analysis of these and other issues, see Andrea L. Bonnicksen, *Crafting a Cloning Policy* (Washington, D.C.: Georgetown University Press, 2002).

21. Ibid., 20.

22. Green, "Determining Moral Status," 22.

23. Bonnicksen, *Crafting a Cloning Policy*, 19–20.

24. Ibid.

25. J. Brainard, "Celebrities, Scientists, and Politicians Try to Shape the Debate over Cloning," *Chronicle of Higher Education*, May 17, 2002, A27–A30.

26. C. B. Cohen, "Stem Cell Research and the Role of the New President's Council on Bioethics," *American Journal of Bioethics* 2, no. 1 (2002): 43–44.

27. R. Dworkin, *Life's Dominion: An Argument about Abortion, Euthanasia, and Individual Freedom* (New York: Knopf, 1993). All of the material used in the notes section for this chapter is from Dworkin's first chapter.

28. Ibid., 13.

29. Ibid., 11.

30. Ibid., 11, 20.

31. Ibid., 20–22.

32. T. Beauchamp and J. Childress, *Principles of Biomedical Ethics*, 5th ed. (New York: Oxford University Press, 2001), 35–36.

33. Ibid., 37.

34. Shapiro, "Reflections on the Interface of Bioethics," 220.

35. Ibid., 221.

36. Childress, "Federal Policy," 34.

37. Ibid., 35.

Part 2

Domestic Policy

Chapter 4

An Early Assessment of President George W. Bush and the Environment

Glen Sussman and Byron W. Daynes

INTRODUCTION

Throughout the twentieth century, the environment has been an issue in presidential campaigns and administrations. At the beginning of the twentieth century, a national conservation policy was first established by Theodore Roosevelt. In the 1930s, Franklin D. Roosevelt's presidency was characterized as the "age of conservation." During the 1960s, Lyndon Johnson spoke about beautification, while Richard Nixon declared the 1970s the "decade of the environment." Theodore Roosevelt set aside millions of acres of public land as national forests and national parks, and Franklin Roosevelt used the Civilian Conservation Corps to both employ young men and to promote conservation. Nixon established the Environmental Protection Agency (EPA) and signed into law the landmark National Environmental Policy Act.[1] In his run for the presidency in 1988, George H. W. Bush declared that he would be an "environmental president." Four years later, Bill Clinton became the "great green hope" for environmentalists.

In contrast, Dwight Eisenhower viewed the environment as a state and local problem. Ronald Reagan exhibited a distinct environmental attitude: "Reagan's environmental views oscillated in a narrow band between indifference and hostility. His appointments often reflected this hostility and his desire to deregulate environmental agencies."[2] Reagan's successor, George H. W. Bush, used the power resources of the presidency to ensure the passage of the Clean Air Act of 1990.[3] However, he backed off his commitment to environmental goals due to pressure from business and industry. For example, at the 1992 Earth Summit in Rio, he signed the Convention on Climate Change only after

We would like to thank our research assistant, Brooke Ollerton, Brigham Young University, for her helpful contributions to this chapter.

mandatory obligations were replaced by voluntary guidelines, and he stood alone in his refusal to sign the Convention on Biodiversity.

Subsequent to the terrorist attacks on September 11, 2001, President George W. Bush used "security" as a framework for public discourse. He frequently talked about economic security, national security, and homeland security. However, to what extent has *environmental security* assumed a prominent place in his administration's agenda?

FRAMEWORK FOR THE STUDY

In order to offer an early assessment of the Bush administration's environmental policy, this chapter uses *presidential roles* as a methodological approach. This framework, initially developed by Tatalovich and Daynes in their study of presidential power, identified presidential roles as a "set of expectations by other political elites and the citizenry which defines the scope of presidential responsibilities within a given sphere of action."[4] As *commander in chief*, the president must balance the competing needs of national security and the environment. As *chief* diplomat, the president conducts foreign policy. This includes diplomatic efforts regarding international environmental policy. The *chief executive* role concerns presidential domestic policy making. Presidents, for instance, make important appointments, including the Secretary of the Interior and head of the Environmental Protection Agency. The role of *legislative leader* involves the president's relationship with the Congress. This can include signing, vetoing, or proposing environmental legislation. As *opinion/party leader*, the president can reach out to the public through a variety of media outlets and the political party.

George W. Bush ran for the presidency in 2000 as a "compassionate conservative" and talked about bringing civility and humility back to the White House. To what extent did the Bush administration include the environment in its political agenda, and in what ways did it support or oppose environmental initiatives?

Opinion/Party Leader

The president can reach out to the American public through a variety of major outlets, including the Inaugural Address and State of the Union messages as well as through radio addresses to the American people. In five major national broadcasts to the American public, President Bush made a total of 103 references to ten major issues.[5] Not surprisingly, almost three out of ten references were made to terrorism. As far as the other issues were concerned, Bush made the most references to the economy, Social Security and Medicare, defense, and education. To a much lesser degree, he referred to health care, civil rights, energy, the environment, and campaign finance reform.

If one makes the assumption that presidents talk about their priorities in their major speeches to American citizens, the environment was not a top priority for this president. In the first two years of his presidency, only 3 percent of all references to major issues made by Bush concerned the environment as an important public policy area, while 4 percent involved energy policy.

Another outlet the president can use to communicate with the public and talk about important issues of the day is the weekly national radio address. Each week the radio address focuses on one primary issue, while some include more than one issue. Although terrorism was a major concern for the president, over 30 percent of the radio addresses focused on economic issues, including the budget, taxes, and unemployment. Besides education and defense, few other issues received attention, while campaign finance reform was virtually nonexistent. About 5 percent of the president's radio addresses to the nation concerned the environment or energy policy.

The limited attention to the environment in national addresses to the American public (both televised and on the radio) suggests that the environment was not a top priority for the Bush administration. An alternative explanation is that rather than "going public,"[6] the president chose to remain relatively "silent" on this issue. For instance, Eshbaugh-Soha argues that it is difficult for presidents to speak out and take a contrary position on valence issues, or issues that have majority support, for example, clean air.[7] He concludes that presidents can influence policy by "staying private" and choosing other methods.

Although Bush's public discourse on the environment was negligible compared to other issues, his public position on oil drilling in Alaska's Arctic National Wildlife Refuge (ANWR) might be considered a tactical effort to help him (and his party) in his 2004 reelection campaign in energy-producing states.

Legislative Leader

As a legislative leader, the president must use personal influence and individual skills as a negotiator in order to persuade. The president can support or oppose legislation, but Congress has substantial resources vis-à-vis the president regarding their relationship. Sometimes a president gains visibility through bill signing or vetoing a bill. Other times, publicity focuses on the president's budget and whether—or to what extent—the policy areas are winners or losers in budget battles.

Early in his first year in office, Bush had to respond to Congress and the media regarding several environmental initiatives, including the administration's budget priorities (lack of funding for environmental issues), oil drilling in the ANWR, and the level of arsenic in drinking water. When he presented his initial budget in April 2001, Bush was met with opposition by congressional

Democrats, who criticized what they saw as unnecessary cuts in social services, environmental programs, and other areas.

Congressional Democrats, backed by public opinion, opposed Bush's efforts to open up the ANWR to oil exploration, although Alaskan officials supported it. President Bush responded that if Congress refused to support his position on the ANWR, then he would direct Secretary of the Interior Norton to pursue oil exploration on other federal lands that were not protected.[8]

Congressional Democrats were angry with the administration over its approach to energy policy, which included the blatantly pro-oil industry actions of its Energy Task Force, headed by Vice President Dick Cheney, a former oil executive. Allegations were made that the vice president and the task force had met with representatives of business and industry in shaping energy policy, while environmentalists were excluded from the meetings.[9] A potential constitutional conflict ensued after the administration refused to release the records of the energy task force meetings to the General Accounting Office.[10]

Bush also had to respond to Congress over his plan to suspend the standard imposed by President Bill Clinton regarding arsenic levels in drinking water. After considerable congressional and public opposition over the relaxed standard, the White House announced in April 2001 that it would postpone the decision until February 2002, and it promised that it would reduce the amount of arsenic in drinking water by 60 percent.[11] Subsequent to a House vote that required the administration to maintain the Clinton standard, the EPA reversed its decision in November and indicated that it would adopt the previous standard.[12]

Chief Executive

As chief executive, the president can make important contributions to domestic policy making through the power of appointment and by issuing executive orders and proclamations. Bush used his appointment power to influence environmental policy, but in a way unfavorable to the natural environment. Only two of his appointments could be characterized as "green"—Fran Mainella, director of the National Park Service, was considered to have a "strong and proven track record" by the National Parks Conservation Association; and former New Jersey governor, Christie Todd Whitman, was appointed to head the EPA.[13] She was confirmed 99–0 by the U.S. Senate. As governor, she was considered a moderate Republican with a mixed record on the environment.

While Mainella and Whitman constituted the marginally "green" component of Bush's environmental appointees, other key appointments reflected a decidedly pro-industry orientation, beginning with former Wyoming senator and petroleum entrepreneur, Dick Cheney, as Bush's vice-presidential running mate. Key environmental appointments, then, included individuals with interests that favored economic growth and development as opposed to conservation

and the employment of alternative sources of energy. The interests represented
by George W. Bush's appointments included the fossil fuel industry, mining,
ranching, and timber. As heads of agencies, Bush's appointees were in a position to use their power to appoint lower-level officials and staff that would
most likely share the Bush environmental philosophy.

Executive orders and proclamations—another resource of presidential
executive power—if taken together, provide the president with the ability to
shape domestic policy. By midterm in office, Bush had issued seventy-four
executive orders and 212 proclamations. Environmental executive orders represented only 6.8 percent of all executive orders, while environmental proclamations constituted about 10 percent of all proclamations issued. The number
of environmental executive orders issued by Bush was substantially lower than
the number issued by his predecessors, Franklin Roosevelt through Bill
Clinton, and were often measures *opposed* to environmental protection.

Chief Diplomat

In international affairs, the president is the country's chief diplomat who represents the United States at world conferences and engages in diplomatic
efforts involving the treaty process. Global climate change represented the
major global diplomatic concern during the first two years of the Bush administration. The human impact on the global climate was documented by scientists in the 1930s and the 1950s as they saw increasing temperatures arising
from a buildup of carbon dioxide in the atmosphere.[14] Over the intervening
years, the scientific community continued to produce studies showing the relationship between carbon dioxide concentrations in the atmosphere and the
potential for global warming. By 1990, the United Nations' sponsored Intergovernmental Panel on Climate Change (IPCC) announced that "human
activities are substantially increasing the atmospheric concentrations of greenhouse gases" (carbon dioxide, nitrous oxide, sulfur dioxide, methane) that will
most likely result in "an additional warming of the Earth's surface."[15] The
IPCC produced two more reports that confirmed its original findings, and in
2001 the United States National Academy of Sciences publicly stated that,
despite some scientific uncertainties, there was a relationship between atmospheric greenhouse gas emissions and global warming.[16]

Internationally the global climate change issue was framed within two
major agreements—namely, the 1992 Earth Summit's Convention on Global
Climate Change and the 1997 Kyoto Protocol. While the former included
voluntary targets and guidelines, the latter demanded mandatory reductions
in greenhouse gas emissions. President George H. W. Bush signed the
Convention on Global Climate Change only after the "voluntary" components
of the agreement were in place. President Bill Clinton signed the Kyoto

Protocol that required that greenhouse emissions would be reduced to 1990 levels by 2008–2012. This would require different reduction levels by different countries with an average 5.2 percent cut in greenhouse gas emissions by protocol signatories. However, the Republican-controlled U.S. Senate made it quite clear that it would not ratify the treaty in light of the heavy lobbying coming from the fossil fuel industry that challenged the science and threatened senators and workers by arguing that the protocol would be harmful to the U.S. economy.[17]

Once in office, President Bush responded to the Kyoto Protocol by labeling it "fatally flawed," and he renounced it in March 2001. Organized interests were clearly divided on the administration's policy. While environmentalists were critical of Bush's approach to the Kyoto Protocol, the Global Climate Coalition, a U.S. fossil fuels group, announced that "It's sort of irrelevant for the United States," and the actions of the Bush administration supported that idea.[18] At the same time, mounting scientific evidence confirmed that human activities were contributing to global warming.[19]

In August 2001, international delegates met in Morocco to build on the success achieved earlier in the year in Bonn. The United States stood alone in its opposition to the Kyoto Protocol, as it did when the previous Bush administration rejected the Biodiversity Convention a decade earlier at the Earth Summit in Rio. While opposing the Kyoto Protocol, the George W. Bush administration promoted an energy production and consumption policy instead of focusing on conservation.[20] At the same time, automobile fuel efficiency standards in the United States continued to decline.[21]

To his credit, the president declared his support for the Stockholm Convention on Persistent Organic Chemicals that would restrict the use of twelve lethal chemicals.[22] The president also supported and authorized through 2004 the "debt-for-nature swaps" of the Tropical Forest Conservation Act.

Commander in Chief

In the international arena, the president also serves as the country's chief military leader. As such, the president must "balance the requirements of national security with other important international interests such as public health, environmental quality, human rights among others."[23]

When addressing defense policy, President Bush favored national security over the environment. For instance, he promoted his plan to open up ANWR as "energy security," saying that

> diversity is important, not only for energy security but also for national security. Overdependence on any one source of energy, especially a foreign source, leaves us vulnerable to price shocks, supply interruptions, and in the worst case, blackmail.[24]

Bush ran afoul of Puerto Rico and environmentalists over bombing practices on the island of Vieques. After much criticism about navy bombing practices, the administration agreed to halt all military exercises and bombing runs by May 2003.[25] Environmental groups filed a lawsuit against the navy alleging that the island was contaminated with toxic substances from bombs and other explosives and the use of Agent Orange, napalm, and depleted uranium.[26]

After the September 11, 2001 terrorist attacks on the United States, the EPA dropped its opposition to the use of Halon 1301 (a fire suppressant harmful to the ozone) used by the air force, and whose F-16s are the single, largest emitter of the gas. Its production was banned at Montreal in 1994 (the United States was a signatory to the agreement). Although the air force suspended the use of this fire suppressant in peacetime operations, it continued to use it in combat and reconnaissance missions. A senior EPA official stated that after September 11, "it is not an issue worth worrying about."[27]

CONCLUSION: AN "ENVIRONMENTAL" PRESIDENT?

"The president has become the primary focus of national political attention," states Mary Stuckey, "and the president's talk has become the primary focus of the presidency."[28] Bush began his presidency with an emphasis on reducing federal regulations while promoting economic growth and development with less attention to conservation and alternative sources of energy (see Table 4.1).[29] He employed symbolic politics to deal with environmental concerns. In other words, he would talk favorably about the environment or support environmental initiatives as long as he did not see any negative impact on the American economy or natural resource interests. Many of his political appointments reflected his anti-environmental orientation.

On February 14, 2002, near the beginning of the second year of his presidency, the Bush administration announced its new *Clear Skies* and *Global Climate Change Initiatives*.[30] This consisted of increased funding for research to address climate change as well as adding additional funding for clean energy tax incentives. The theme of the initiative, however, was a slow process underlined by voluntary measures.

Although environmentalists and many congressional Democrats remained displeased with Bush's approach to the global climate change issue, some Republicans were also unhappy with the proposals. According to the communications director of the grassroots organization, Republicans for Environmental Protection (REP America), "The good news is that the president is finally talking about the need to reduce greenhouse gas emissions that are altering the world's climate. The bad news is that his proposal won't accomplish much."[31] Moreover, Bush may be "pushed aside" as some corporations already see "green"

TABLE 4.1
A Midterm Evaluation of President George W. Bush and the Environment

	Evaluation
Election	Compassionate conservative; less reliance on federal government; reduce regulations
Environmental Philosophy	Pro-development/economic growth
Influence on the President	Vice president; business and industry, especially fossil fuel interests; conservative Republicans
Attitude toward Global Climate Change (Global Warming)	Support for voluntary guidelines and targets; sees flaws in existing global climate change agreements
Methods	Speeches; appointments; market-based approach; energy task force; budget reductions; reduced reliance on diplomacy; unilateral action by the United States; observer rather than participatory status among global partners
Energy Policy	Focus on production and consumption and downplay conservation and energy efficiency; support oil drilling in Alaska's Arctic National Wildlife Refuge and in other sensitive/fragile public lands
Presidential Leadership on the Environment	Administration and supporters argue that Bush (43) plays a leadership role; environmentalists and congressional Democrats criticize the president for failing to show leadership
U.S. Leadership on Global Climate Change	Abandoned opportunity to demonstrate leadership on global climate change; rejected Kyoto Protocol; successful international environmental cooperation uncertain without participation and leadership by the United States
Environmental Security	Bush (43) emphasis on national, economic, and homeland security—"environmental security" not on administration's agenda

in promoting green. According to a recent news report:

> Car giants Toyota and Honda have invested heavily in producing hybrid cars that will significantly reduce greenhouse gas emissions, and corporations like IBM, Johnson & Johnson, and Polaroid have all committed to reducing their carbon dioxide emissions well below the Kyoto target.[32]

On February 23, 2002, Bush announced a shift in the Superfund policy, a fund that was established in 1980 to support the cleanup of hazardous waste sites around the country. The act employed a "polluter pays" principle, and it was to be financed by a tax on industry.[33] The administration stated that fewer sites would be identified, and that taxpayers would now bear the brunt of paying the cleanup costs. (On March 13, 2002, EPA administrator Christie Todd Whitman defended the new policy, while both Democratic and Republican members of Congress expressed concern about the shift in the cost burden to taxpayers and the reduction by half in the number of serious cleanup sites.)

On February 24, 2002, the president renewed his call for opening up ANWR to oil drilling.[34] Although he would face stiff resistance from environmentalists and members of the U.S. Senate, he renewed his argument that "America is already using more energy than our domestic resources can provide and unless we act to increase our energy independence, our reliance on foreign sources of energy will only increase."[35] Environmentalists countered by arguing that ANWR oil resources were small, that wildlife and the pristine region would be threatened, and that more emphasis should be placed on conservation measures. On April 18, 2002, partisan conflict over ANWR resulted in a major defeat for the president's energy program. In a 54–46 vote, the Senate rejected proposed oil and gas drilling in ANWR.[36] Over 80 percent of Democratic senators voted against drilling, while a comparable proportion of Republicans supported it. The outcome of the vote reflected public opinion where a majority of Americans opposed drilling for oil in ANWR. However, the Republican takeover of Congress in the fall 2002 elections prompted the administration to again propose drilling in ANWR.

In her assessment of Bush's first 100 days in office, reporter Margot Higgins stated that "while Bush barely mentioned the environment in his campaign, the environment is clearly an area where he may have the most impact."[37] This midterm analysis of the Bush administration generally confirms her assessment. It is apparent that although the environment did not receive high *public* visibility in his presidential speeches, the president employed alternative methods to pursue his (anti) environmental agenda. In this way, he attempted to avoid public scrutiny of his actions. Finally, while increasing the frequency of references to national security, economic security, and homeland security, "environmental security" has all but been ignored in President Bush's public discourse and political agenda.

NOTES

1. Andrea K. Gerlak and Patrick J. McGovern, "The Twentieth Century: Progressivism, Prosperity, and Crisis," in *The Environmental Presidency*, ed. Dennis L. Suden (Albany: State University of New York Press, 1999), (pg 41–76); J. Brooks Flippen, *Nixon and the Environment* (Albuquerque: University of New Mexico Press, 2000).

2. Benjamin Kline, *First Along the River: A Brief History of the U.S. Environmental Movement*, 2nd ed. (San Francisco: Acada Books, 2000), 102.

3. Glen Sussman and Mark Andrew Kelso, "Environmental Priorities and the President As Legislative Leader," in *The Environmental Presidency*, ed. Dennis L. Soden, (Albany: State University of New York Press, 1999), 119–25.

4.   Raymond Tatalovich and Byron W. Daynes, *Presidential Power in the United States* (Monterey, Calif.: Brooks/Cole, 1984), chap. 1. Several factors provide the strength for each of these roles and can affect presidential action. These factors include the *authoritative basis* of the presidency found in the Constitution, federal statutes, and court decisions; *decision making* that can be constrained by the number of political actors putting pressure on the president; *public opinion and/or organized interests* that can support or oppose presidential action; *expertise* that involves available information, quality of advice, and the personal capacity of the president to understand complex issues; and *crisis situations* that can enhance presidential discretion or power.

5.   The ten issues are campaign finance reform, civil rights, defense, the economy, education, energy, the environment, health care, Social Security and Medicare, and terrorism.

6.   Samuel Kernell, *Going Public: New Strategies of Presidential Leadership*, 3rd ed. (New York: Congressional Quarterly, 1997).

7.   Matthew Eshbaugh-Soha, "'Staying Private' in the Administrative Presidency," *PRG Report* (newsletter of the Presidency Research Group of the American Political Science Association, Fall 2001, 11).

8.   George W. Bush, "The President's News Conference, March 29, 2001," American Reference Library's *Weekly Compilation of Presidential Documents*, www.sourcedocuments.com (accessed November 19, 2001); see also Christopher Doering, "Gas, Oil Estimates in U.S. West Too High, Says Green Group," www.enn.com/extras/printer-friendly.asp?storyid = 48828 (accessed October 30, 2002).

9.   According to the League of Conservation Voters:

The Bush administration's 63-member energy advisory team, which is charged with helping chart the new administration's energy policies, has 62 members with ties to oil, nuclear, coal, or other polluting interests. Between 1999 and 2000, 58 of these members gave $8 million in campaign contributions to the Republicans. Companies and associations affiliated with these members—including the National Mining Association, American Petroleum Association, Edison Electric Institute, Southern Company, American Gas Association, Enron Corp.—would benefit in various ways from Bush administration proposals to invest billions of dollars in coal research and drill for oil and gas in Alaska's National Wildlife Refuge and other public lands. Most would benefit from the Bush administration's decision not to regulate carbon dioxide emissions from power plants and to back out of the Kyoto climate treaty.

See League of Conservation Voters, "Bush and the Environment: A Citizen's Guide to the First 100 Days," www.lcv.org/pdfs/Bush_and_the_environment_text.pdf (accessed April 30, 2001).

10.   Jeff Gerth, "Accounting Office Demands Energy Task Force Records," *New York Times*, June 19, 2001, www.nytimes.com (accessed November 19, 2001).

11.   Douglas Jehl, "EPA to Abandon Arsenic Limits for Water Supply," *New York Times*, March 21, 2001, Proquest (accessed November 8, 2001).

12. A study released by the National Academy of Sciences argued that even Clinton's standards were not sufficient. See, for instance, Douglas Jehl, "House Demanding Strict Guidelines on Arsenic Levels," *New York Times*, July 28, 2001, Proquest (accessed November 12, 2002); Katharine Q. Seelye, "E.P.A. to Adopt Clinton Arsenic Standard," *New York Times*, November 1, 2002, Proquest (accessed November 12, 2001); "Arsenic Standard for Water Is Too Lax, Study Concludes," *New York Times*, September 11, 2001, Proquest (accessed November 16, 2001).

13. John Cushman, "An Environmental Appointee Bush Critics Seem to Like," *New York Times*, August 27, 2001, Proquest (accessed November 16, 2001).

14. As early as 1896, Swedish chemist Svante Arrhenius noted that an increase in atmospheric carbon dioxide and increasing global temperatures result from industrialization. See Gordon J. MacDonald, "Scientific Basis for the Greenhouse Effect," *Journal of Policy Analysis and Management 7* (1988): 427.

15. J. T. Houghton, G. J. Jenkins, J. J. Ephraums, eds., *Climate Change: The IPCC Scientific Assessment* (Cambridge: Cambridge University Press, 1990).

16. Eric Pianin, "A Second Opinion on Global Warming," *Washington Post National Weekly*, June 11–17, 2001, 31.

17. Sebastian Oberthur and Herman E. Ott, *The Kyoto Protocol: International Climate Policy for the 21st Century* (Berlin and New York: Springer Verlag, 1999), 69.

18. "U.S. Quiet in Climate Talks," www.enn.com/2001/TECH/science/11/10/climate.talks.ap/index.html (accessed November 10, 2001).

19. See, for instance, a summary of the findings of the Intergovernmental Panel on Climate Change, in "New Evidence Confirms Rapid Global Warming, Say Scientists," United Nations Environment Programme News Release 2001/5, www.enn.com/extras/printer-friendly.asp?>storyid=3176&pr=html (accessed November 6, 2002).

20. Bush worked with Mexico, Canada, and Russia to find new sources of oil. He and other leaders also created a North American Energy Working Group and engaged in a Western Hemisphere energy plan. See, for instance, George W. Bush, "The President's News Conference with Summit of the America's Leaders in Quebec," *Weekly Compilation of Presidential Documents*, April 27, 2001; "The President's News Conference with President Putin in Kranj," *Weekly Compilation of Presidential Documents*, June 16, 2001; "Remarks on Accepting a Bush of Winston Churchill and an Exchange with Reporters," *Weekly Compilation of Presidential Documents*, July 16, 2001; "North American Leaders' Statement," *Weekly Compilation of Presidential Documents*, April 22, 2001.

21. John Heilprin, "New 2003 Model Cars Headed for Showrooms Show Steady Decline in Fuel Economy," www.enn.com/extras/printer-friendly.asp?storyid=48840 (accessed October 30, 2002).

22. George W. Bush, "Remarks Announcing Support for the Stockholm Convention on Persistent Organic Pollutants," *Weekly Compilation of Presidential Documents*, April 19, 2001.

23. Byron W. Daynes and Glen Sussman, *The American Presidency and the Social Agenda* (Upper Saddle River: Prentice Hall, 2001), 120.

24. George W. Bush, "Remarks Announcing the Energy Plan in St. Paul, Minnesota, May 17, 2001," *Weekly Compilation of Presidential Documents*, American Reference Library, May 17, 2001, www.access.gpo.gov/nara/pdbrowse.html www.gpoaccess.gov/wcomp/v37no19.html (accessed October 10, 2001).

25. David E. Sanger and Christopher Marquis, "U.S. Said to Plan Halt to Exercises on Vieques Island," *New York Times*, June 14, 2001, Proquest (accessed November 8, 2001).

26. Bob Herbert, "When the Bombing Ends," *New York Times*, June 18, 2001, Proquest (accessed November 8, 2001).

27. Eric Pianin, "War Effort Pushes 'Green' Issues Aside; Environmental Groups Rethink Agenda As Nation Focuses on Anti-Terror Fight," *Washington Post*, October 21, 2001, Proquest (accessed October 31, 2001).

28. Mary Stuckey, *The President As Interpreter-in-Chief* (Chatham, N.J.: Chatham House, 1991), 134.

29. Table 4.1 is adapted from Glen Sussman, "International Cooperation, the American Presidency, and Global Climate Change," in *Proceedings of the 2001 Berlin Conference on the Human Dimensions of Global Environmental Change: Global Environmental Change and the Nation-State*, ed. Frank Biermann, Rainer Brohm, and Klaus Dingwerth (Potsdam: Potsdam Institute for Climate Impact Research, 2002), 75–76.

30. The proposal was an effort by the Bush administration to demonstrate that it was making progress in terms of air quality and global climate change issues. See George W. Bush, "President Announces Clear Skies and Global Climate Change Initiatives," www.whitehouse.gov/news/release/2002/02/print/20020214-5.html (accessed February 15, 2002).

On Earth Day 2002, former vice president Al Gore referred to the president's proposal as a "dirty skies initiative." See Dan Balz and Dana Milbank, "On Earth Day, Bush v. Gore," *Washington Post*, April 23, 2002, A1.

31. Although Democrats and Republicans have been divided on environmental issues, moderate Republicans at the national and local levels have expressed concern about environmental policies emanating from the White House. See "Bush Climate Plan Only a Baby Step, Green GOP Group Says," www.enn.com/direct/display-release.asp?id = 6239 (accessed February 15, 2002).

32. Suzanne Elston, "Human Impact: How We Trigger Global Warming and What Each Individual Can Do About It," www.enn.com/indepth/warming/overview.asp (accessed January 30, 2002).

33. Michael E. Kraft, *Environmental Policy and Politics*, 2nd ed. (New York: Longman, 2001), 18.

34. John Heilprin, "EPA Chief Defends Halving Toxic Waste Cleanups As Superfund Money Near Depletion," www.enn.com/news/wire-stories/2002/03/03132002/ap_46657.asp (accessed March 13, 2002).

35. In his second year in office, the president continued to promote a fossil fuel development energy policy. See "Bush Renews Campaign for Arctic Oil," *New York Times*, www.nytimes.com/apon...onal/AP-Bush-Energy.html (accessed February 24, 2002).

36. Helen Dewar, "Senate Vote Blocks Drilling in Refuge," www.washingtonpost.com/wp-dyn/articles/A12079-2002Apr18.html (accessed April 20, 2002).

37. Margot Higgins, "100 Days of Bush: Disaster Zone for the Environment?," www.enn.com/news/enn...ries/2001/04/04032001/bushover_43213.asp (accessed June 6, 2001).

Chapter 5

Vigor and Vacillation

An Early Assessment of Bush's Economic Policy

Chris J. Dolan

INTRODUCTION

Upon ascending to the presidency in January 2001, George W. Bush put domestic and international economic issues at the center of his legislative proposals, actively seeking to distance himself from his predecessor by endorsing moderately conservative economic reform, including: a $1.6 trillion income tax cut; a partial privatization of Social Security; delinking labor and environmental considerations in free trade policies; abandoning the use and threat of import fees and quotas to protect U.S. businesses; a free-trade zone of the Americas and restructuring relations with Mexico and Japan; and expanded trade promotion powers from Congress.

Although some of his initiatives were controversial and his election questioned, President Bush was vigorous in his pursuit of these goals. Following a shortened transition, Bush assembled what he believed would be an economic team that would advance his so-called "compassionate" economic objectives. Senior members of the Bush economic team recognized this and set relatively pragmatic economic goals and held realistic expectations. As a result, Congress responded to Bush's initiatives with relatively sizeable Democratic support.

Shortly after the September 11, 2001 (9/11) terrorist attacks, Bush's economic focus eroded as his administration became consumed with the war on terrorism and embroiled in a much publicized debate on the impending U.S. invasion of Iraq. The president also mishandled several high-profile issues, which tarnished Bush's bipartisan image. Among Bush's post-9/11 troubles were his inability to pass an economic stimulus to shore up the crippled post-9/11 economy; failure to adequately respond to financial crises in Latin America; hesitation to respond to a series of corporate accounting scandals; and pursuit of a threatening policy of trade protectionism on steel.

Therefore, in examining President Bush's economic policy at midterm, one witnesses two different approaches toward the economy: a pre-9/11 approach that engaged in a vigorous campaign to attain clearly articulated economic initiatives, and a post-9/11 approach that has vacillated on all things economic.

Since the end of the Cold War, presidents have struggled to adapt to the rise of greater complexity in U.S. and world politics. Throughout the Cold War, economic issues were low policy matters and subordinated to security demands; in the post-Cold War, economics and security are both high policy, demanding significant attention from presidents. The challenge for President Bush is acknowledging that although 9/11 reaffirmed security issues as high policy, it has not relegated economic issues to the back burner.[1]

PRE-9/11 VIGOR

With his moderately conservative economic program clearly articulated, President Bush created an economic team that was vigorous and focused in its pursuit of his policy objectives. The administration pursued a program that would be acceptable to members of Congress on both sides of the aisle. Bush's economic team included key members of the National Economic Council (NEC) Principals Committee—especially National Economic Advisor Dr. Lawrence Lindsey and the NEC staff—Treasury Secretary Paul O'Neill, Commerce Secretary Donald Evans, Director of the Office of Management and Budget (OMB) Mitch Daniels, Chair of the Council of Economic Advisors Glenn Hubbard, and U.S. Trade Representative Robert Zoellick. Other key players were Bush's closest political advisors, namely, senior advisor Karl Rove, White House Chief of Staff Andrew Card, and Counselor to the President Karen Hughes.[2] Although the team was a victory for the business community and was committed to free-market principles, it never endorsed such positions as dismantling cabinet departments and agencies or terminating particular social programs, which had been the case at the outset of previous Republican administrations and suggested at the close 2000 presidential election.

Overall, the economic team reflected the new president's desire for a tightly knit and centralized economic policy-making arrangement. Bush relied mainly on Lindsey's NEC due to its central location in the Executive Office of the President (EOP) and because of its relative success in coordinating the economic bureaucracy during the Clinton administration, especially during Robert Rubin's tenure as National Economic Advisor.[3] It was also an interesting mix, with Lindsey bringing government experience as a former governor of the Federal Reserve Board and Harvard professor, with O'Neill as a former head of the Alcoa Corporation, with Card as a former transportation secretary, and with Rove and Hughes as close friends of the Bush family.[4]

The most pressing issue confronting Bush was the slowing U.S. economy. While America had not yet experienced two consecutive quarters of economic shrinkage that technically constitute a recession, the plummeting stock markets of 2000, rising oil prices, and declining consumer confidence left everyone feeling the slump. A decade of roaring growth made the downturn feel more painful than it might have in less successful economic times. Shopping for the Christmas holiday seasons in 2001 and 2002 was depressed as buyers tightened their belts. In the upheaval, over 36,000 dot.com jobs were lost amid cuts in traditional industries. For instance, General Motors shed 15,000 jobs, while Montgomery Ward ended 128 years of retailing, leaving 37,000 employees jobless.[5]

The specter of a looming recession provided President Bush with much of the firepower he needed to attain his number one campaign promise: the passage of a $1.6 trillion income tax rate cut. The tax cut was the brainchild of Lawrence Lindsey, who served as Bush's economic advisor on the 2000 campaign, and OMB Director Mitch Daniels.[6] To build momentum, Lindsey convened a two-day economic forum in Austin, Texas, on January 2, 2001, to thrash out an economic program constructed around the tax cut proposal. The thirty-six participants included Daniels and some marquee names, such as former Republican presidential candidate Steve Forbes, Jack Welch of General Electric, and the CEOs of Boeing, Cisco Systems, Eastman Kodak, General Motors, Union Pacific, and Wal-Mart. Some critics suggested that the meeting was little more than symbolism, while others noted that it was pro-industry in its composition.[7]

During the campaign, on the advice of Lindsey, Bush and Cheney spoke often about underlying perils to the U.S. economy, in an attempt to neutralize Democratic campaign boasts about the country's healthy finances. In December 2000, while the presidency was being decided in court, Cheney stated: "America may well be on the front edge of a recession that legitimizes an across-the-board tax cut to jumpstart the economy and put people's money back in their pockets."[8] Even Bush frequently referred to "the impending slowdown in the U.S. economy . . . a tax-relief plan for everybody serves as an insurance policy against a potential economic downturn."[9] Bill Clinton's parting message to Bush, articulated through outgoing Treasury Secretary Larry Summers, was to advocate cutting the national debt before cutting taxes. Even more important was the advice of Alan Greenspan, an advocate of debt reduction over tax cutting.[10]

The pressure on Bush to deal with the recession was made more acute by the fact that his father's presidency was undone by Bill Clinton's relentless focus on the recession of 1990–1991. Bush's Austin summit echoed one held by Clinton during the 1992–1993 transition. The styles of the summits, however, could not be more different. Whereas Clinton held an open forum of 300 economists and business and labor leaders at which he and Hillary Clinton presided and took notes in front of a national television audience, which was encouraged to call in with questions, George W. Bush's meeting consisted of mostly corporate leaders and a preference for discussing policy behind closed doors.

With vigor and determination, Bush called on Congress to enact his tax cut, reemphasizing gloomy portrayals of a troubled economy that were delivered to him by business leaders. Bush contended: "A lot of folks in this room have brought some pretty bad news—that their sales are slowing, that they're having to trim back their work force. We are looking at recessionary numbers."[11] Giving Bush and Lindsey delight was word that the Fed would lower interest rates, a surprise move that delighted everyone in the room but left most calling for additional rate reductions. Bush added, however, that a rate cut alone cannot do the job, saying that his tax cut remains an "integral part of economic recovery."[12]

Was Bush crying wolf on all matters economic? Lindsey's plan of overemphasizing the degree of a possible recession—cutting marginal rates regardless of the macroeconomic and global circumstances—ignores two hard lessons of the presidency: that the first policy impulse of the incoming president is usually wrong on economic issues, since campaign politics not substantive economic issues drive most of legislative proposals; and, second, that some bold economic initiatives fail. Upon Gerald Ford's assumption of the presidency in 1974, and with the inflation rate stratospheric, the president's economic team confronted ruinous price increases with absurd "Whip Inflation Now" buttons and hard times with Draconian budget policies. Many of them (then chief of staff Dick Cheney, then defense secretary Don Rumsfeld, and then deputy OMB director Paul O'Neill) pushed Ford to embrace these practices. One member of the Ford administration who appeared in early 2001 to have learned that fiscal fine-tuning of the economy is tenuous was Alan Greenspan.

President Jimmy Carter also faced an economic crisis and proposed a fiscal stimulus to give every individual a miniscule $50 rebate. Eventually he gave up; in one of his few good lines as president, Carter joked that since economists said most people had already spent the rebate ahead of receiving it, he did not have to actually give it to them. Bush's father also led with his mouth, pointlessly expending much of his political capital on a capital gains rate cut.[13] Bill Clinton made the mistake of clinging to his campaign's emphasis on the still-stagnant economy and proposed a stimulus that went down in defeat and withdrew a promised middle-class tax cut.[14]

When Congress passed a compromise package of $1.35 trillion in cuts, Bush won his first major legislative triumph. However, the potentially fatal issue yet to be addressed was the possibility of running budget deficits following the tax cuts. Determined not to repeat his father's political misstep on taxes, Bush may have repeated Reagan's fiscal folly instead by embracing a "tax cut and spend" fiscal policy.[15] When George H. W. Bush broke his famous "read-my-lips,no-new-taxes" pledge by raising taxes, the right wing never forgave him. George W. Bush made tax cuts the centerpiece of his campaign and was unwavering in his drive to deliver. Unfortunately, in his zeal, Bush is revisiting the Reagan formula that pushed the nation into the red, as big tax cuts in the absence of spending cuts produce large deficits.[16] After finally enjoying budget surpluses at the close of the Clinton administration, the country was now plunged back into huge deficits at the midterm of Bush's presidency.

Clinton-era foreign economic policies, many of them supported by Republicans, also appeared in the Bush administration's pursuit of expansive free-trade policies. Bush sought to complete bilateral trade deals with Jordan, Singapore, Vietnam, and Australia and to finalize the thirty-four nation Free Trade Agreement of the Americas (FTAA), which would transform most of the Western hemisphere into the world's largest free-trade zone.[17] In pursuing these measures, Bush sought to emancipate free trade from labor and environmental restrictions with presidential Trade Promotion Authority (TPA), which would make fast-track negotiating powers permanent.

President Bush also sought to strengthen bilateral cooperation with Mexico, especially on immigration and the war on drugs. In fact, Bush's first foreign trip of his presidency was to Mexico to meet with President Vicente Fox on these issues. Reversing what he believed were eight years of tension, Bush directed the joint committee of the National Economic Council and the National Security Council to draft a legislative proposal that would create an open-borders policy to allow U.S. and Mexican workers to move freely across the U.S.–Mexico border.[18] Bush also signaled his support for permanently certifying Mexico as an ally in the war against illegal drugs. In addition, in a move designed to expand the Republican Party's base and against the wishes of Lindsey, O'Neill, and Commerce Secretary Evans, Bush indicated his support for an amnesty to the roughly 3 million Mexican citizens working illegally in the United States.[19]

POST-9/11 VACILLATION

Clearly, the U.S. economy was devastated by the 9/11 terrorist attacks. In response, the Federal Reserve Board and the White House launched a powerful, double-barreled effort to revive the economy. The Federal Reserve cut its short-term interest rate target by half a percentage point to 2.5 percent, the lowest in four decades. At the White House, Bush, O'Neill, Lindsey, Daniels, Hubbard, and Greenspan met to shape a $100 billion package of tax cuts and spending initiatives (mostly financial bailouts of the airlines and businesses with ties to the World Trade Center), forming what Bush called an "economic security package."[20] At the time, Bush's famous rhetorical line was: "the best way to stimulate demand is to give people money so they can spend it."[21] The problem was that it was likely to consume the $52 billion surplus.

Bush's economic security package was not well received in Congress. How could a $100 billion stimulus revive a $10 trillion economy that Bush said was already in a recession? Earlier in the year, Congress approved $38 billion in tax rebates, which had already been delivered. O'Neill and Evans faced the sharpest criticism from Republican senators, who contended that the Bush administration should concentrate on tax breaks. Even Senator Don Nickles (R-Ok) criticized Bush for considering a minimum-wage increase, which O'Neill and Evans said remained an option.

By late October, it appeared that the bipartisan unity in the war on terrorism clearly did not spark a love fest on the economy. Democrats balked at additional support for big business, pointing out that Congress already approved $40 billion for cleanup and $15 billion in aid and loan guarantees for the aviation industry. Although the House passed $100 billion in additional tax cuts and new spending, the 216–214 vote followed an angry debate and marked a sharp departure from the bipartisan comity that prevailed in Congress during the previous weeks, with Democrats charging that it favored special interests at the expense of workers and the unemployed.[22] The Senate Finance Committee also bid farewell to bipartisanship when it approved in an 11–10 vote an economic stimulus package totaling only $70 billion. The attacks of 9/11 only exacerbated tensions between congressional Democrats and the Bush White House.

President Bush himself was also not above the political fray. By the time he delivered his second State of the Union address in 2002, the economic stimulus measure was still stalled in Congress, with the White House and Senate only agreeing to extend unemployment benefits to workers by thirteen weeks. The president used his weekly radio addresses to turn up the heat on the Senate's one-vote Democratic majority. On December 15, he stated: "the Senate has failed to act. And while the Senate has failed to do its work, more and more Americans have been thrown out of work."[23]

Even the politically gratifying military victories in Afghanistan did not entirely put to rest unsettling questions about the administration's conduct of economic policy. The most distressing problem is Bush's failure to define America's economic interests after 9/11. The administration's economic priorities before 9/11 consisted of tax cuts and free trade, which led some moderate Democrats and think tanks to support the White House.[24] Bush's inability to redefine economic priorities with the stimulus measure began the process of questioning his presidential leadership.

Part of the problem rested in the hands of President Bush, who declined to define the size and content of the stimulus plan. Instead, he and his economic team allowed the House Budget Committee to start, literally, with a blank piece of paper. In doing so, Bush put the Republican Party in a tenuous position on other issues. The NEC's failure to adequately shape an economic stimulus derailed Bush's desire for a new energy policy. Bush's goal of expanded oil drilling in Alaska died when environmental groups launched a successful and aggressive campaign to sever the nexus between drilling in Alaska and 9/11. If the White House were interested in liberating the nation's energy policy from pre-9/11 problems, it would have responded by immediately seizing the post-9/11 moment instead of hesitating.

As the fight over the stimulus package was playing out in the media, a series of corporate scandals surfaced, threatening to undermine the Bush White House. Executives of the Houston-based Enron Corporation first sent passions flying after revealing that the company used partnerships with Arthur Andersen, its top accountant and consultant, to hide losses and sell millions in company stock while prohibiting its own employees from unloading their 401(k) shares. While Enron spread its campaign donations to both Republicans and Democrats in Congress, it funneled millions to Bush's 2000 presidential campaign and had close personal ties with the Bush family. Questions were raised over Bush's knowledge of the company's schemes, including Oval Office meetings between the president, Rove, and disgraced Enron CEO Kenneth Lay.[25]

After the Enron scandal came a rash of other corporate misdeeds. Arthur Andersen, which made millions both in auditing Enron's accounts and while serving as its consultant, was found guilty of obstructing justice after it revealed that its accountants shredded documents related to Enron's accounting misdeeds. WorldCom/MCI announced the largest bankruptcy in U.S. history after CEO Bernard Ebbers "borrowed" millions of dollars in company stock to finance his lavish lifestyle. Adelphia Communications founder John Rigas was arrested in July on federal charges that he and his sons defrauded investors by using the company as a "personal piggy bank."[26] Then, on August 21, 2002, Enron financial chief Michael Kopper pled guilty to conspiracy to commit wire fraud and money laundering, keeping the scandal fresh in people's minds.

As the number of corporations under investigation increased, top administration officials persuaded the president to distance himself from the issue, even as disgruntled Enron employees publicly disclosed their devastating losses. In response, O'Neill and Evans cautioned Bush against any new government program that would regulate corporate auditing and consulting. Lindsey and the NEC staff advised the president to avoid making public statements or holding press conferences on the issue for fear that it would anger business groups.

However, the initial White House policy of silence only made matters worse. After the Rigas arrest, the Justice Department announced a joint investigation with the Securities and Exchange Commission (SEC) of Bush's tenure as head of Harken Inc. and Vice President Cheney's term as CEO of Haliburton, two Texas energy firms. After investigators turned up the heat on Bush and Cheney, the White House decided that it was time to act. Senior political advisor and top spin doctor Karl Rove pressed the president to sign a corporate reform measure that overhauled accounting practices and consulting standards. He also held a series of Clinton-style economic forums between his NEC/Principals Committee and business leaders at the University of Alabama and

TABLE 5.1

The Dow Jones and unemployment

Significant points in the Dow Jones industrial average, 1994–2002

Average on week of	Dow	Event
November 23, 1994	3,674	Start of the 1990s Bull Market
March 29, 1999	10,006	First Dow Close above 10,000
January 14, 2000	11,723	The All-Time High
March 20, 2001	9,720	Dow Closes below Previous Year Low
September 11–14, 2001	9,605	Terrorist Attacks Close Dow for Four Days
September 17, 2001	8,920	Biggest One-Day Fall in Dow History (685 Points)
September 21, 2001	8,235	Dow's Second Worst Week Ever (−14.26%)
December 31, 2001	10,021	Dow up 21.7% from September 21 low
July 23, 2002	7,702	Post-9/11 Low following Bankruptcy of World Com/MCI and the rest of John Rigas of Adelphia
August 21, 2002	8,962	Michael of Enron Pleads Guilty to Conspiracy
October 7, 2002	8,423	Increased War Talk with Iraq Keeps Markets Down

Source: http://www.djindexes.com/jsp/industrrialAverages.jsp?sideMenu=true.html.

TABLE 5.2

Total Percentage of Unemployed Persons, 2000–2002

	2000	*2001*	*2002*
January	4.0	4.2	5.6
March	4.0	4.3	5.7
October	4.2	5.0	5.9
December	4.1	5.8	Yet to be released

Source: "Labor Force Statistics for Current Population Survey," Bureau of Labor Statistics, U.S. Department of Labor. Washington, D.C.: U.S. Government Printing Office, October 2002.

Baylor University.[27] As for Vice President Cheney, with Haliburton under SEC investigation, the White House sent him on submarine inspections and to North Dakota and Idaho to stump for Republican candidates.

Moreover, throughout 2002, Wall Street confidence slipped as the Dow Jones posted record losses, sending fears in some circles of a protracted recession. The airline industry, which Bush had "bailed out," continued to struggle and post losses. Not helping the volatile markets was the administration's continued focus on Iraq, which was unsettling for Wall Street investors. Confounding the economic situation was the unemployment rate, which by October 2002 edged up to 5.9 percent.

The state of the post-9/11 political landscape demonstrated that Bush's political strength was on prosecuting the war against the Taliban and Al-Qaeda. So why should he not pursue a similar approach to the economy? It was clear for Rove that the easiest way to improve the ethics of corporate America was for

President Bush to prosecute as many CEOs as possible and throw just enough of them in prison to get into the headlines. This fits Bush's image as being tough on crime and terrorism; as governor of Texas, he aggressively administered the death penalty, and as president, he unleashed America's military might on Afghanistan. The inattentiveness and volatility of American public opinion helped him. Moreover, if the business cycle holds, as it usually does, the president will weather the storm as Ronald Reagan did in his first term. Bush also remembers how the recession of 1992 peaked long enough so Clinton could turn his father out of office. However, the state of the budget is worrisome for the president. Bush's OMB released a mid-year report posting a $106 billion deficit for 2002—the first since 1997—and projecting deficits until 2005.

Bush has also vacillated in his post-9/11 foreign economic policy. While he successfully lobbied Congress for permanent trade promotion authority, his administration mishandled an array of international economic issues. President Bush's response to emerging currency crises in Latin America provides a useful illustration. When the financial crisis hit Argentina in mid 2001, Lindsey and the NEC staff first denied that it was serious and persuaded the president to let the currency markets work out the instability. Lindsey then denied that the United States or the International Monetary Fund (IMF) could do anything about it, arguing that any multilateral response would be problematic. O'Neill made matters worse when he stated that Argentina's dire predicament was "entirely its own doing."[28] When leaders in Buenos Aires threatened to default on foreign loans, Lindsey and O'Neill ignored the threats.[29] Instead of advising those leaders to abandon nineteenth-century currency arrangements that U.S.-trained economists imposed, the NEC insisted that Argentina slash social spending as a condition of international aid. When the government eliminated 28,000 jobs, people rioted and Argentina's government collapsed, rattling many on Wall Street.

The situation worsened after the crisis quickly spread to Uruguay and Brazil. In early August, the Bush administration shifted course and announced a temporary loan of $1.5 billion to Uruguay from the Treasury Department's Exchange Stabilization Fund (ESF).[30] Two problems remained, however. First, Bush's response may have been too late, since it appeared that the Argentine crisis had already spread to Uruguay. Second, he put Paul O'Neill—who acquired a famous reputation for making public gaffes—in charge of enforcing the new policy. His visit to Latin America on August 4, 2002, is a case in point. As O'Neill left Washington, the Bush administration announced that it would provide Uruguay with a temporary loan of $1.5 billion to enable the government to reopen the country's banks on August 5, despite the fact that just one day earlier O'Neill indicated that no U.S. help would be offered.[31]

Politically, Lindsey and O'Neill were concerned with issuing so-called "financial bailouts" in response to currency crises. This was key to their desire to set Bush apart from Clinton, who acquired the image of a financial traffic cop with Robert Rubin as his deputy.[32] Bush officials asserted that Clinton's financial assistance to Mexico in 1995, the IMF, and East Asia in 1998 made little sense because these countries already faced unsustainable debts.

Bush also vacillated in his foreign economic policy toward Europe, for instance, the issue of fair competition between the U.S. steel industry and its European counterparts. For years, American steel companies based largely in key political battleground states such as West Virginia, Pennsylvania, and Ohio complained that high import fees and tariffs levied on U.S. steel by Europe stymied U.S. steel production. In an effort to win these important states in 2000, candidate Bush promised to retaliate against the European Union. Once elected, Bush found it difficult to distance himself from his campaign promises.[33] In October, the International Trade Commission reported that U.S. steel had indeed been injured by European tariffs. In response, Bush imposed three years of quotas ranging from 8 percent to 30 percent on a variety of imported steel products. Critics, mostly conservatives, contended that the move was a tax increase from a president who promised that taxes would be raised "over my dead body."[34]

Bush's decision was made over the objections of Lindsey and his NEC staff, which protested that the move would tarnish the president's image as a free trader.[35] Politics naturally played a role in the decision—getting an edge for Republicans in steel states was crucial for the midterm elections and beyond. Karl Rove understood all too well that busting up the Democratic coalition and building an enduring conservative majority required that Bush build alliances with ideological opposites on economic issues.[36]

The larger issue involves Bush's disregard for the global context. National Security Advisor Condoleezza Rice and Secretary of State Colin Powell worried that a "trade war" with Europe might compromise U.S. anti-terrorism efforts and any hope of building a United Nations coalition against Iraq.[37] The United Kingdom, which would be a key ally in the war on terrorism, stood to lose over 5,000 jobs from Bush's action.[38] Bush's decision did not help Tony Blair persuade restless Labor Party members to back the United States against Saddam Hussein.

THE BUSH ECONOMY

Bush's vacillation in the face of economic stagnation, a volatile stock market, and a seemingly endless sequence of corporate scandals is understandable. However, his failed economic security package, his mismanagement of international financial crises, his steel tariffs, and the corporate accounting scandals are illustrations of a vacillating post-9/11 economic policy. Bush might pay a price for his missteps in the 2004 election. As economic indicators continued to fluctuate in mid 2003, Democrats have referred to the bleak period between

2001 and 2003 as the "Bush Economy," and they are likely to do so in upcoming elections. While the verdict is out on whether the 2001 tax cuts were a serious mistake, the fact remains that the deficit is now expected to rise in the "Bush Economy."

A major component contributing to the post-9/11 vacillation was the Bush economic team. Paul O'Neill's leadership as treasury secretary was anything but astute. He lacked the appropriate experience and knowledge to serve in this position and was unable to send the kind of signals that might have reassured markets at crucial moments. While Lawrence Lindsey enjoyed a successful career as an economist and as a former Fed governor, his partisanship, unbending belief in free-market principles, and devotion to tax cuts as a universal cure have limited President Bush's political options. By the end of 2002, Bush made major changes as he forced the resignations of O'Neill, Lindsey, and embattled SEC Chair Harvey Pitt—Pitt's came coincidentally on election night in November in an effort to minimize his controversial tenure—and William Webster as the head of a new accounting oversight board. These moves reflected Bush's desire to eliminate the weakest economic policy links in his administration.

In reality, many of Bush's economic problems were out of his direct control, and if the 2002 midterm elections were an illustration, he has convinced the voting public that this is the case (however, polls taken at the two-year anniversary of his presidency show a public increasingly worried about the direction of the economy and Bush's handling of it). Yes, the nation will eventually move out of recession. Left to its own devices, it will undoubtedly right itself, because U.S. economic institutions are strong. However, the bursting of the dot.com bubble left investors uncertain about where the economy's future prospects lie. The revelation that a few major corporations have spectacularly overstated their income made financial reporting suspect. The terrorist attacks and the fear of more to come elevated America's vulnerability. Under these circumstances, it became more important than ever for Bush to have a clear, compelling set of economic policies and to demonstrate a steady hand at the wheel.

Although most of the blame should rest on President Bush's own shoulders, the timing of these events will largely absolve him of carrying the full burden. Too much has gone wrong too quickly for it to affect him solely. The same might be true for the Republican Party in upcoming elections. If Al Gore were in the White House and if Larry Summers or Robert Rubin were still at the helm of the U.S. Treasury, then most of the troubles that happened on Bush's watch would have happened on theirs.

However, there is the question of Bush's economic leadership. His "down-home" manner and imprecision during economic hard times appeared not to bode well for his presidency, although it was not a factor for voters in the 2002 midterm elections when Democrats failed to effectively challenge Bush on a number of economic issues and present an economic policy alternative. However, it does not help politically when Bush touts the untapped values in stocks after admitting that "I'm not a stockbroker or a stock picker," or when he joked at Baylor University that he found it hard to grasp government accounting practices.[39] This is not to say that Bush has not attained some of his goals. He won expanded Trade Promotion Authority from Congress and was victorious on the tax cut. What he needs for the remainder of his presidency is an economic team that can adapt his tax-cutting passion to a broader economic vision; a team that sees the fiscal necessity of reining in deficits and the political value of appealing to a wider constituency.

In the end, however, President Bush's post-9/11 economic policy is far more problematic than his economic team. Unlike his pre-9/11 course, the president has opted to stake his political future on a tax cut and spend economic program even as he governs with a Republican Congress. In February 2003, Bush proposed a plan to eliminate the dividend tax to win the support of what he says is a fast-growing, newly decisive shareholder electorate. In April, the president requested an additional $80 billion in supplementary defense spending following the cessation of hostilities in Iraq. Given how the market has performed over the past two years, one would think the potential for higher deficits and additional debt would have warned the president that tax cuts in the absence of spending cuts are not the most effective prescription for the economy. Moreover, the political fallout of the plan could be devastating, as key moderate Republicans, namely, Senators George Voinovich (Ohio) and Olympia Snowe (Maine), have publicly opposed the dividend tax cut measure.

It is apparent that President Bush is attempting to reshape the prevailing economic order at a premature point in his presidency. The only presidents in the twentieth century who came close to successfully redirecting the economic order—Franklin Roosevelt and Ronald Reagan—did so because the old orders were collapsing. Roosevelt's New Deal made government a permanent fixture in the economy, and Reagan's supply side program reminded us that the private sector still matters. Circumstances are not ripe at the current time to merit a restructure of the economic order. Worse yet, what Bush is proposing is to erect a new economy by giving more power to the national security establishment and ignoring the political consequences of mounting deficits and debt.

In the years since FDR galvanized the nation during the Great Depression and Second World War, Americans have expected their presidents to shepherd them through crises. For instance, FDR knew that he could not tame the Depression with the New Deal, but he realized that he could at least lead the nation through it with some action. Ronald Reagan reasserted the image of strong U.S. global leadership in the wake of Watergate and Vietnam. For a man who stood so tall after 9/11, President Bush has been slow and wobbly in tackling the economy since 9/11. Bush's post-9/11 economic vacillation should draw comparisons to Herbert Hoover and Jimmy Carter. In an administration that possessed an exquisite sense of the public mood prior to 9/11, it has been deaf in answering questions about the economy and too beholden to tax cut and spend policies that do not address long-term economic implications.[40]

NOTES

1. See Chris J. Dolan, "Presidential Coordination Efforts in Economic Policymaking, *White House Studies*, 3, no. 2 (2003); Jerel A., Rosati, *The Politics of United States Foreign Policy* (Fort Worth: Harcourt Brace, 1999); Daniel Yergin, *Shattered Peace: The Origins of the Cold War and the National Security State* (Boston: Houghton Mifflin, 1977).

2. The NEC, which was created by President Clinton in Executive Order 12835, is charged with integrating domestic and international economic issues, coordinating the economic policy-making process, and pursuing the president's policy objectives. The national economic advisor (assistant to the president for economic affairs) has three major roles: to advise the president on economic issues in both foreign and domestic policy; to coordinate and manage all aspects of the economic policy-making process; and to chair the NEC/Principals Committee (NEC/PC).

3. Bush's goal was to replicate the success of Clinton's initial economic team, led primarily by Robert Rubin and Lloyd Bentsen. At the beginning of his first term, Clinton named Rubin to head the NEC and Lloyd Bentsen to lead the Treasury Department. Bentsen, who was chair of the Senate Finance Committee, had political smarts to burn, and Rubin, who ran the Wall Street firm, Goldman Sachs, knew market psychology and international finance. See Bob Woodward, *The Agenda* (New York: Simon & Schuster, 1996). Rubin and Bentsen even knew one another, with Rubin having managed the Bentsen family portfolio while at Goldman Sachs. See Elizabeth Drew, *On the Edge: The Clinton Presidency* (New York: Simon & Schuster, 1995).

4. George W. Bush, *A Charge to Keep: My Journey to the White House* (New York: Harper Trade, 2001); Frank Bruni, *Ambling into History: The Unlikely Odyssey of George W. Bush* (New York: HarperCollins, 2002).

5. Seth Borenstein, "Top Prospects Draw Criticism from Groups," *Pittsburgh-Post Gazette*, December 21, 2001, 12.

6. Sue Kirchhoff, "Lindsey, Bush Economic Planner," *Boston Globe*, January 4, 2001, A16.

7. Jonathan Weisman, "Economic Session to be Private, No Showcase," *USA Today*, January 3, 2001, 5A.

8. Philip Delves, "Threat of Recession Forces Bush to Reconsider Tax Cuts," *Daily Telegraph*, January 2, 2001, 16.

9. Ibid.

10. Philip Delves, "Dollar in the Hand Is Worth Two in the Bush," *Daily Telegraph*, December 16, 2000, 29; Mary Dejevsky, "Bush Reaches 100th Day with Little to Proclaim," *The Independent*, April 30, 2001, 12.

11.   Edwin Chen, "Economic Meeting Validates Bush's Warnings of a Recession," *Los Angeles Times*, January 4, 2001, A12.

12.   Ibid.

13.   Jonathan Alter and Howard Fineman, "A Dynasty's Dilemma," *Newsweek*, July 29, 2002, 16–20. This article also provides a detailed assessment of what they describe as vast similarities between Bush Sr. and Bush Jr. For example, Alter and Fineman contend that both presidencies were strong on war but weak on the economy. This assessment of the Bush presidency's pre- and post-9/11 handling of economic issues suggests that Bush was hi ghly effective in coordinating economic policy making and was vigorous in the pursuit of economic goals until September 11.

14.   Even though the tax cut was Bush's largest proposal, he failed to distinguish himself from previous Republican presidents by avoiding to publicly support any real spending cuts. In his first State of the Union address to Congress in February, the president told lawmakers that we could have it all: protect Social Security, fix Medicare, build a missile defense system, pump up education, add a prescription drug program for seniors, improve national parks, and pay down the federal debt. It was a constantly upbeat performance by the new president.

15.   Mary Dejevsky, "One Win, the Bush Juggernaut Halts," *The Independent*, May 27, 2002, 19.

16.   Alter and Fineman, "A Dynasty's Dilemma," 17–19.

17.   Catherine Ong, "Bush's Expanding Free Trade," *Business Times of Singapore*, June 11, 2001, 1–2.

18.   Eric Schmitt, "Open Door, Open Questions," *New York Times*, July 22, 2001, 10.

19.   Lynda Goyov, "Wooed with Hope of Amnesty Warms Mexicans to Bush," *Boston Globe*, July 28, 2001, A1.

20.   Ann Kornblut, "Bush Plans to Aid the Economy," *Boston Globe*, October 5, 2001, A1.

21.   Jeff Toedtman, "America's Ordeal, Healing the Economy," *Newsday*, October 3, 2001, A3.

22.   Jeff Toedtman, "Bush Pushes Plan for the Economy," *Newsday*, October 4, 2001, A3; Jeff Toedtman, "House Passes Tax Cut Bill," *Newsday*, October 25, 2001, A13.

23.   Timothy J. Burger, "Bush Blames Senate for Stalled Economic Plan," *New York Daily News*, December 16, 2001, 14.

24.   Michael S. Greve, "Questions Linger on Bush's Goals," *Los Angeles Times*, November 19, 2001, A28.

25.   Robert Scheer, "Enron, Symbolic of Bush Blunders," *Newsday*, December 27, 2001, A31.

26.   Howard Fineman and Michael Isikoff, "Laying Down the Law," *Newsweek*, August 5, 2002, 20–25.

27.   Elisabeth Bummiler, "Bush Forum on Economy: More Than the Usual Crowd," *New York Times*, August 12, 2002, 2.

28. Thomas Catan, Mark Mulligan, and Gwen Robinson, "Bush Pledges to Work with Argentina's Government?," *Financial Times*, December 29, 2001, 11.

29. Anthony Faiola, "Despair in Once Proud Argentina," *Washington Post*, August 6, 2002, A1.

30. The ESF was first established by the Gold Reserve Act of 1934 and was funded by the sale of gold until 1971, when President Nixon removed the United States from the gold standard. The ESF statute gives the president and the treasury secretary the authority to utilize a broad range of loans and credits, including swaps of dollars for foreign currencies, and guarantees, securities, gold, and foreign exchange. The United States has entered into over fifty swap arrangements and bridge loans with foreign governments since 1934—most in the last twenty years.

31. See Richard Oppel, "Easing Its Stance, US Offer Loans to Uruguay," *New York Times*, August 4, 2002, 4; Tony Smith, "World Watches Anxiously As Brazilian Economy Totters," *New York Times*, August 6, 2002, 3.

32. Kevin Smith, "The Economist Global Policy Agenda: South America's Dominoes," *Economist*, August 5, 2002, 16–18.

33. Jeffery Frankel, "The Crusade for Free Trade," *Foreign Affairs*, March–April 2001, 155.

34. Paul Magnusson, "Bush's Steely Pragmatism," *Business Week*, March 18, 2002, 44.

35. Rammesh Ponnuru, "A Free Trade President?," *National Review*, May 20, 2002, 9.

36. See Gloria Borger, "You Just Can't Win," *US News and World Report*, April 15, 2002, 28; Harold Meyerson, "Karl Rove's Wedges," *The American Prospect*, April 8, 2002, 2.

37. Following the imposition of new steel tariffs, the WTO approved $4 billion in EU sanctions against U.S. businesses. See Rich Thomas, "Bush Is No Hypocrite," *Newsweek*, March 18, 2002, 67; "WTO Allows Europe to Impose Record Sanctions against the US," *New York Times*, August 30, 2002, 1.

38. Jamie Dettmer, "Steel Strikes a Blow against Free Trade," *Insight*, April 1, 2002, 47.

39. Bummiler, "Bush Forum on Economy," 2.

40. Fineman and Isikoff, "Laying Down the Law," 20–25.

Chapter 6

Ironing Out Reelection

George W. Bush and the Politics of Steel

Douglas M. Brattebo

Introduction

In March 2002, President George W. Bush imposed tariffs ranging from 8 percent to 30 percent on steel imports for three years. The decision, which came on the heels of a closely contested recommendation by the six-member United States International Trade Commission (ITC), had been the subject of intense debate. The steel industry, organized labor, and members of Congress from steel states had demanded that Bush put in place some protection for Big Steel, but a coalition of steel-utilizing manufacturing companies, consumer groups, and free traders also had lobbied his ear to the contrary. The president's inner circle had been equally divided. When the president put the tariffs in place, he gave the industry much, but not all, of what it had sought, and he put American steel producers on notice that the measures were designed to provide them with a three-year respite to restructure the industry.

Bush's new steel tariff policy caused a political firestorm. Domestic reactions were predictably and sharply divided. The international reaction, however, was uniformly and harshly negative. The European Union (EU), Russia, and countries in Asia and Latin America condemned Bush's decision and declared the tariffs a harbinger of a looming global trade war. The EU filed a complaint with the World Trade Organization (WTO) and went so far as to compose a list of U.S. products, manufactured in states of particular political importance to the president, for possible tariff retaliation. The EU's reaction was so intense because the president's steel tariffs not only exacerbated ongoing U.S.-EU trade spats but also because the tariffs were emblematic of what many nations in the world perceive to be Bush's penchant for unilateralism. For several months it appeared that the steel tariff decision even had the potential to affect the international coalition in the War on Terror.

What has been too easy to forget in all of this is the fact that presidents and steel tariffs have a long and storied history, and Bush was merely writing the most recent chapter. There is no denying that Bush defended the steel industry, despite his free-trade inner compass, because he wanted to help Republican representatives and senators in the 2002 midterm elections and because he wants to win Ohio and West Virginia in 2004. Beyond the political calculation that it is possible to create blue-collar "Bush Democrats" in swing states in time for reelection, however, there towered a central strategic policy calculation: offering protection to Big Steel, despite the thorny politics and mixed economic effects, would help pave the way for both the congressional renewal of Trade Promotion Authority (TPA) and the eventual creation of the Free Trade Area of the Americas (FTAA).

The president's protection of the steel industry has begotten a host of demands for the protection of other sectors of the U.S. economy, ranging from agriculture to forest products and textiles, and he may have to indulge these calls in a similar way to move his global free-trade agenda forward on the home front. None of this, though, has the power to alter the fate of Big Steel. The aging behemoths of the U.S. steel industry that remain wedded to old-fashioned methods of production are going to die out in the next two decades. In fact, in December 2003, Bush lifted the tariffs. In a drive to reduce the world glut of low-priced steel and to cement the FTAA, Bush will tell domestic steel producers that they have not used their breathing space wisely enough and now must navigate the unchecked currents of the international marketplace. However strange it may seem to those who have listened to the domestic political din surrounding the steel tariff decision, when the president runs for reelection in 2004, his fate will hinge on larger factors, and not the tariff issue.

PRESIDENTS AND STEEL: HISTORICAL PERSPECTIVE

The relationship between presidents and steel is not much younger than the presidency itself. Presidents, premodern and modern, most often have dealt with steel in the context of tariffs. Presidential assent to protection of the steel industry, in varying ways and degrees, has been the rule. Post-FDR presidents of both parties have usually found the political motives and methods to aid the steel industry, even after its decline commenced in earnest in the late 1960s. Indeed, George Melloan has called steel tariffs the "oldest and most frequently repeated mistake of American presidents."[1] But, perhaps no modern president has found himself confronting the politics of steel so directly and purposefully as Bush.

President Bill Clinton was no stranger to heavy lobbying by the steel industry to set tariffs on imported steel, and the pressure was particularly acute during his second term. The Clinton administration had helped the industry with import quotas on a handful of steel products, but the Clinton team did not urge an investigation by the ITC under Section 201 of the 1974 Trade Act. Clinton, who had begun his first term with the enactment of the North American Free Trade Agreement (NAFTA), did not want to leave office labeled a "protectionist." Perhaps more to the point, Clinton and his advisors did not believe a convincing legal case could be made that steel imports were undermining the domestic steel sector enough to warrant safeguard measures. Gene Sperling, Clinton's head of the National Economic Council, noted that steel imports peaked at 30 percent in 1998 but receded to 27 percent of domestic consumption in 2000. Given such data, the Federal Trade Commission (FTC) was unlikely to find the requisite damage.[2]

This was a formidable show of fealty to market economics by Clinton, who as a presidential candidate had visited a steel plant in Weirton, West Virginia, in 1992 and vowed to stop the flood of cheap foreign steel into the United States. Eight years later, many steelworkers in West Virginia and elsewhere who had witnessed firsthand the further demise of the steel industry were enraged at Clinton for not throwing them a lifeline. Ralph Nader's spoiler campaign was fueled in large part by a backlash against Clinton's pursuit of free trade.[3] Candidate Bush and his advisors sensed an opportunity, and in October 2000, his running mate, Dick Cheney, came to the same city to make a pledge: "If our trading partners violate trade laws, we will respond swiftly and firmly and enforce our laws."[4] The votes of steelworkers and their families and neighbors may well have provided the 40,000-vote margin by which Bush carried West Virginia, and thus won the presidency.[5] It was no accident that in President Bush's steel tariffs package, announced in early March 2002, foreign imports destined to compete with a tin steel mill in West Virginia were subjected to the highest possible tariff of 30 percent.[6]

The Decline of Big Steel

The United States' steel industry is declining in economic importance, although it still wields disproportionate political clout. The industry's decline began in the 1960s, when foreign steel industries posed stiff competition.[7] The trends accelerated in the period 1997–1998, when the Asian financial crisis led to a surge of cheap steel imports.[8] In 1953, the steel sector employed 650,000 people.[9] Today, it employs approximately 160,000, and the steel-using sector of the economy, with more than 8 million employees, dwarfs the steel sector.[10] Wal-Mart, with its nearly 1 million employees, employs more people than the entire United States steel industry.[11] "Steel users represent 13.1 percent of the gross domestic product, while steel producers account for 0.5 percent."[12]

The steel sector, however, is concentrated in swing states that are important in presidential elections.[13] Steelworkers are located predominantly in

Michigan, New York, Ohio, Pennsylvania, and West Virginia—and fully 300,000 retired steelworkers call Florida home.[14] It is hard to imagine that legislators and presidents would be so responsive to this constituency if its members lived in states that consistently tipped to one party or the other in presidential elections.[15] In 2000, Gore won Michigan, New York, and Pennsylvania; Bush won Ohio, West Virginia, and Florida.

There are now 600,000 retired steelworkers, nearly four times the number of current steelworkers, and they rely on the rickety industry for their retirement and health care benefits.[16] At Bethlehem Steel Corporation, for example, there are 74,000 retirees, a figure five times greater than the number of current employees, and Bethlehem currently records $2 billion in unfunded pension liabilities and $3 billion in expected health claims.[17] These "legacy" costs, stemming from extremely generous benefit packages unwisely granted in fatter times, now sit like millstones around the necks of many steel companies.

Since the end of 1997, thirty-one U.S. steel companies have filed for bankruptcy, and 20,000 jobs have been lost.[18] For inefficient steel plants, the handwriting is on the wall, no matter what the government does. In the case of ailing companies, bankruptcy might offer a chance at new life. Those with efficient productive facilities would be sold off through bankruptcy court to domestic or foreign firms, and their purchasers would be free of legacy costs.[19] At the very least, more mergers will be necessary so that the legacy costs can be assumed by solvent parent companies.[20] Nonbankruptcy mergers, however, have become problematic; as the legacy costs of the sick firms have mounted, and government assumption of them has not been forthcoming, U.S. steelmakers have been less willing and able to combine to stand up against larger foreign competitors.[21]

In 2001, the United States imported about 22.2 million tons of steel, roughly 20 percent of its total demand.[22] Domestic production capacity remains nearly the same as it was in 1977, but production is made with less capital and labor than before.[23] The industry has transformed into two distinct industries: "One employs about 100,000 people and has failed to modernize its large, increasingly unprofitable blast furnaces. The other is composed of modern 'minimills,' smaller plants with high-tech electric furnaces."[24] In 1977, the minimills produced only 10 percent of the steel consumed in the United States, but today they make nearly half of it, and they can compete against foreign producers even when steel prices are very low.[25] Minimills produce a ton of steel with one-seventh the number of worker hours, and they pay lower wages.[26] Steelworkers at traditional facilities make $17 more than the average laborer and $14 more than the average manufacturing employee.[27] Old steel mills are truly profitable only in periods of high demand and high prices.[28] Some traditional domestic producers may still exist in the future, but they will be partnered with minimills so that the former can finish the hot- and cold-rolled products of the latter.[29] The traditional firms, then, "look much like Remington trying to protect its manual typewriters from the onslaught of Dell computers loaded with Microsoft software."[30]

Bush's Decision to Protect the Steel Industry

In February 2001, the ITC announced that it would go forward with an investigation of the effects of steel imports on the domestic steel industry.[31] Steel companies had petitioned for the investigation under Section 201 of the 1974 Trade Act, which permits "industries seriously injured or threatened with serious injury by increased imports" to request action.[32] The WTO recognizes the legality of such "safeguard" measures.[33] Safeguard inquiries by the ITC, of which there were only two in 1995, have become much more common and numbered fifty-three in 2001.[34]

Legislators from steel states had been pressuring the president to get on with the Section 201 investigation, and they were hearing from Robert Zoellick, the U.S. trade representative, that stern actions in defense of the steel industry, including quotas and tariffs, were on the table.[35] By early June 2001, Bush formally requested that the ITC carry out its investigation, siding with the arguments of steel companies and labor unions that their industry was under siege from imports, a finding that would serve as grounds for the ITC to recommend remedies to the president, who would have latitude in modifying them.[36] Bush's final remedy, according to trade law, would have to "provide greater economic and social benefits than costs."[37] The president's formal call for an ITC investigation was "only the fourth made by the White House since the Trade Act of 1974 was created."[38]

In August 2001, steel state representatives introduced the Steel Revitalization Act (H.R. 808), which proposed the limitation of steel imports, increased government lending to steel companies, and government coverage of the steel industry's legacy costs.[39] The House Steel Caucus, consisting of 117 representatives, was making its weight felt.[40] Bush also had to contend with the Senate Steel Caucus, made up of thirty senators.[41]

The ITC ruled in late October that imports had caused serious injury to twelve of thirty-three lines of domestic steel products, and it commenced hearings to decide what specific remedies to recommend to the president by December.[42] Steelmakers requested tariffs of up to 50 percent for four years.[43] A coalition of manufacturing companies (the Consuming Industries Trade Action Committee, or CITAC[44]) and other large steel users lobbied against the tariffs with equal fervor.[45] Also opposed were ports, longshoremen, and farmers.[46] Foreign steelmakers also advertised and lobbied to counteract the efforts of domestic steel producers.[47] As the date for the president's decision neared, the lobbying went into overdrive on both sides, with steelworkers rallying outside of the White House, while opponents visited the nation's capital to argue that tariffs would choke off port traffic and inadvertently hurt agricultural exports.[48]

Bush sang the praises of free trade in a speech in February: "Those who shut down trade aren't confident ... in the American worker. They're not confident in the American entrepreneur. They're not confident in American products."[49]

Nonetheless, on March 4, 2002, the president announced that he would slap tariffs of 8 percent to 30 percent on most steel imports.[50] Bush called the tariffs "temporary safeguards" that would give the domestic steel industry time to restructure.[51] Critics of the president did not understand that he and his inner circles had come to see helping Big Steel as a means to a larger end: persuading members of the House and Senate to support his international free-trade agenda.[52]

One member of the ITC had hinted to the press that the panel's October 2001 ruling had been intended to provide Bush with "leverage" in international trade negotiations aimed at curtailing surplus world steel production.[53] At the urging of Zoellick, the president had made the most of that leeway, taking measured steps to show laborers and legislators alike that "trade laws could work to the advantage of American workers as well as consumers."[54] As Zoellick confessed to Brazilian business leaders on March 13, 2002: "We are committed to moving forward with free trade, but, like Brazil, we have to manage political support for free trade at home. We have to create coalitions."[55]

The ITC presented President Bush with a wide array of potential remedies.[56] The core of the ITC's proposals was that tariffs should start fairly high and decline until expiring at the end of four years, and that steelmakers should be put on notice that this window was only a respite.[57] The percentage benchmarks for the proposed tariffs varied across sixteen product categories.[58]

The Dynamics of the Steel Decision within the Bush Administration

Different discussions within the administration involved Bush, Cheney, Zoellick, Commerce Secretary Donald Evans, Treasury Secretary Paul O'Neill, Secretary of State Colin Powell, National Security Adviser Condoleezza Rice, Labor Secretary Elaine Chao, Attorney General John Ashcroft, and Karl Rove, the president's political advisor.[59] O'Neill, Evans, and Zoellick were at the heart of the deliberations.[60] Two members of this triumvirate had strong personal connections to the steel industry. O'Neill retired in 2000 as head of Alcoa, the nation's largest aluminum company, and Evans used to work for Armco Steel.[61] At the end of February 2002, the president's inner circle on the steel tariff issue met to hash out the final policy. In his role as moderator of the meeting, Lawrence Lindsey, head of the National Economic Council, was mum about his well-known stance that no protection should be offered to the steel industry. R. Glenn Hubbard, chairman of the Council of Economic Advisors, shared Lindsey's view but was not silent and argued that a tariff is effectively a tax on consumers.[62] Rove did not speak up at the meeting, but his desire to protect steel industry jobs, and thus to enhance the GOP's fortunes in the 2002 midterm and 2004 presidential elections, was already manifest to all.[63] Evans also spoke out in favor of tariffs, sounding "very much like the steel industry executives," according to one observer.[64] Additionally, Mitchell Daniels, director of the Office of Management and Budget, thought ill of the tariffs.[65] And Alan Greenspan, testifying before Congress on the health of the economy, commented on what he considered the illogic of steel tariffs.[66]

The electoral considerations of steel policy aside, some arguments coming from inside and outside the administration concerning the need to protect Big Steel centered on the notion that the industry is essential for national defense.[67] The president himself had told steelworkers in Pittsburgh in late August 2001 that the health of their industry was a matter of national security.[68] However, two large domestic producers could meet the total needs of the U.S. military.[69] "Airplanes are now made of aluminum and composites, tanks are made with spent uranium, and GI helmets are made with Kevlar."[70] Moreover, the view that steel production capacity equals national power is antiquated. As Loren Thompson, analyst at the Lexington Institute, explains, "Security isn't about basic metals. It's about photons and electrons."[71] More compelling were arguments that a shriveled domestic steel production capacity could, in times of peak demand, lead to delays for manufacturers in obtaining supplies from abroad, thus necessitating the maintenance of large, expensive inventories.[72] There also are some experts who believe that the presence of an adequate domestic steel industry helps the country maintain its edge in developing "new alloys and new production techniques" of particular importance in the machine tools industry.[73]

It ultimately fell to Zoellick to bridge the gap between the protectionists and the free traders. O'Neill later groused publicly about the outcome, saying that he still believed steel tariffs were a bad idea, a view that many administration members held strongly.[74] In fact, most policy-making officials were unhappy with the result, but with a regime of three-year declining tariffs not set to expire until after the 2004 presidential election, Rove and his political staffers had gotten much of what they wanted.[75] One little-mentioned provision of the new steel tariffs package, however, would allow the president to review it in total after just eighteen months.[76]

The Economic and Political Aftermath

There was no shortage of estimates about the damage that a new steel tariffs regime would wreak on the economy. *Newsday* was not unique in positing that the result would be added expenses of over $1 billion per year to steel-using companies, and that for every steel job saved, four would be lost in other areas of the economy.[77] The Institute for International Economics initially had estimated that a tariff of 20 percent would cost consumers $2.4 billion in its first year, with a price tag cost of over $7 billion over the life of the tariffs, and consumers ultimately paying $326,000 for each one of the 7,300 steel jobs likely to be saved.[78] Of the plan finally approved by President Bush, the Institute for International Economics predicted a total bill to consumers of up to $12 billion and lost sales by foreign steel producers of up to $22 billion.[79] Estimates pegged increases in the price of domestic steel at 6 percent to 8 percent, part of which would be passed along to consumers of goods made in part or in full from steel.[80] Robert Crandall, an economist and a senior fellow at the Brookings Institution, stated that the tariffs would prevent the economy from emerging from recession.[81]

The president's own annual economic report to Congress had earlier offered the following prediction: "Imposing trade restrictions in an effort to save those jobs [threatened by trade] will only destroy, or prevent the creation of, jobs in other sectors."[82] Bush might later have come to wish that he had heeded this warning more fully as major ports such as New Orleans suffered a marked downturn in shipping because of the tariffs.[83] Advisors to the president admitted shock at how rapidly the effects rippled through the economy.[84] The price of hot-rolled steel, buoyed by a falling dollar and slightly faster economic growth, went from $210 per ton at the end of 2001 to over $300 per ton in early June 2002, and steel suppliers broke contracts and held out for extra money from manufacturers.[85] Lead times for steel orders by manufacturers soon increased by 60 percent.[86] Honda Motor Corporation, encountering just such a conundrum in June 2002, announced that it had made preparations to airlift 2,000 tons of foreign steel to its production facilities in the United States and Canada in case domestic sources could not meet demand at reasonable prices by July.[87] Domestic steel manufacturers increased the price of steel by 80 percent to 90 percent, as opposed to the 8 percent to 9 percent they had estimated to the Bush administration before the tariffs were imposed.[88]

A political backlash against the tariffs was taking shape as a result of these trends. The newfound opposition to the tariffs was fanned further by the realization that old-style steel companies, which had promised to consolidate and retrench while tariffs were in place, were instead expanding traditional production methods to take advantage of higher market prices.[89] The president found a way to lift the tariffs by granting case-by-case tariff exemptions on specific steel imports.[90] By early September, the administration had effectively lifted one-third of the steel tariffs it had imposed in March.[91] By late September 2002, the House Small Business Committee urged Bush to "lift these tariffs as soon as possible."[92] This was quite a departure from early May, when the House had defeated, by a vote of 386–30, a bill that would have scaled the tariffs back to 20 percent.[93] Most significantly, the president had granted tariff exemptions to 60 percent of originally affected imports from Europe, and 70 percent of British imports.[94] Bush had not yet come full circle on steel tariffs, but he was on his way.

The International Reaction

In a word, the international reaction to Bush's imposition of steel tariffs was *angry.* The EU had started fighting against the possibility of tariffs well before the ITC concluded its Section 201 investigation. Pascal Lamy, the EU's trade commissioner, stated as early as July 2001: "We do not believe the problems of the U.S. steel industry lie with the rest of the world. The U.S. steel industry needs to restructure itself."[95] Lamy sought to head off the tariffs, stating that the EU would complain to the WTO if they were imposed, and warning that such a move would send the wrong signal about U.S. leadership.[96] The world's top steel-producing countries convened in Paris in December 2001 in an effort to reduce the overproduction of steel.[97] These cuts were contingent upon the nonimposition of tariffs by the United States,[98] and they were a response to Bush's insistence that the world's major steel producers form a de facto cartel to reduce the global steel glut.[99] The countries agreed to cut production by 10 percent over ten years, but because 20 percent of the world's capacity is super-fluous, the Bush team was unimpressed by the plan.[100]

Virtually every major ally of the United States—Canada, Mexico, Japan, Germany, Britain, France, Italy, Belgium, the Netherlands, Turkey, China, Russia, and Brazil—stood to lose significantly.[101] These nations arranged for a second round of talks aimed at increasing the voluntary reductions they had agreed to in December. The EU nations volunteered to double their commit-ment to reduce steel overproduction, but the United States still considered the cuts inadequate and asked for monitoring to enforce the agreement.[102] The total commitment of these countries was set at 120 million tons over ten years, but current world overcapacity stood at 200 million tons in 2002.[103] It soon became clear that the United States would not accept the plan. The EU pledged to protest to the WTO in the event of U.S. tariffs.[104]

As NAFTA partners, Canada and Mexico would be entitled to full com-pensation against tariffs on their steel, so Bush opted to exempt them from the tariffs. China, Japan, Germany, Taiwan, and South Korea would bear the brunt of the tariffs, but many countries (such as South Africa), whose support was crucial in global trade talks, might be exempted.[105] Countries whose steel ship-ments to the United States constitute less than 3 percent of total imports also would be exempted.[106] By manipulating import figures, Bush found a way to extend exemptions to Argentina, Romania, Thailand, and the Czech Republic.[107] Still, the outcry was deafening.

Perhaps most ominously, trade experts outside of the White House gener-ally agreed that the WTO would likely rule in favor of the EU. The United States had already lost three similar cases in the WTO.[108] The administration's action came at an awkward time for U.S.–European relations, due to "Mr. Bush's rejection of the Kyoto protocol on global warming; his withdrawal from the 1972 Anti-Ballistic Missile Treaty with Russia; and his description of Iraq, Iran, and North Korea as an 'axis of evil.'"[109] Lamy sniffed: "The international market isn't the Wild West, where everyone can act as he pleases."[110] *The Guardian* stated: "Such disregard for the rest of the world is the leitmotiv of the Bush administration."[111]

The full response of the EU consisted of three parts: the filing of its formal complaint; a request to the United States for a compensatory lowering of
tariffs on EU nonsteel imports; and, in the event that the Bush White House
would not grant such relief, the drawing up of a list of U.S. products on which
the EU reserved the right to impose immediate retaliatory safeguard tariffs.[112]
It was not hard to detect in the vehemence of the EU's reaction the organization's desire to take on the United States after years of trade disputes over lesser
things such as bananas, hush kits for aircraft, and beef.[113] Lindsey responded
that he "found there to be a bit of a glasshouse problem" in Europeans' tendency
to assume that their hands were clean on the subject of trade.[114] However,
China also filed a complaint with the WTO, and Australia, Japan, and South
Korea announced that they likely would do the same.[115]

The list of U.S. goods that the EU drew up for possible retaliation was the
most blatant example of European discontent: it contained over 300 products,
many of which were targeted because they were produced in certain states
likely to be important to the Republican Party in the upcoming elections.[116] It
was a bold step, and it was indicative of Lamy's determination that the EU
assume its ostensibly rightful place as the new arbiter of global trade rules.[117]
Both the EU and the United States were aware that their acrimony over the
steel tariffs had reached unsettling levels, but it was not until May 2002 that
they found a way to back away from the scuffle. Leaders of the EU met with
Bush in Washington that month, and the president told Lamy that he would
seek, during the next Congress, to reform the current system of tax breaks for
its companies exporting goods overseas.[118] In return, the EU stated that it would
not unilaterally impose retaliatory tariffs on American goods but would wait
until a verdict from its pending complaint with the WTO.[119] Soon, Japan and
Norway, which also had been pondering unilateral tariffs to strike back at the
United States, announced that they too would wait for a ruling from the WTO.[120]

At a meeting of thirty-nine member states of the Organization for
European Cooperation and Development (OECD) in Paris in mid September
2002, the Bush administration proposed the abolition of "subsidies, tariffs and
tax preferences for the world steel industry," seeking to do away with the more
than 200 million tons of excess world steel production.[121] The nations did not
reach consensus but instead adjourned until December, when they will seek to
agree on a definition for "subsidy."[122] The Americans and Europeans had not
kissed yet, but it was evident that they were in the process of forgiving each
other—something that had not been a foregone conclusion in the tense months
after Bush had imposed the steel tariffs. Before the end of September 2002, the
EU went the final step and announced that since the United States had dis-
mantled a large share of its steel tariff regime through the granting of exemptions, no tit-for-tat sanctions would be forthcoming.[123] This development, borne
of the president's willingness to shoot holes through his own system of tariffs,
was a sign that things were coming full circle.

The Political and Policy Road Ahead

Bush knows that steelworkers, as much or more than any other single constituency, put him in the White House by a whisker and may be crucial to keeping him there in 2004. Republican strategists were concerned that if the steel issue backfired on the president before the 2002 midterm elections, the GOP could have lost its majority in the House,[124] but the party actually gained seats. Most competitive House races were outside of the Rust Belt. It is possible that Bush's protection of the steel industry prevented more competitive races from emerging in Michigan, Ohio, Indiana, Illinois, and Kentucky.[125]

The White House political team is planning for another squeaker in 2004. West Virginia's five electoral votes could once again determine the winner of the presidency. After all, the margin of victory for the president in the Electoral College in 2000 was four electoral votes, and it appears that due to Bush's handling of the Yucca Mountain nuclear waste repository issue, Nevada's four electoral votes will be off the table.[126] Bush was the first nonincumbent Republican to carry West Virginia since 1928,[127] and as a former Clinton aide has said, "You only need one steel plant to close in West Virginia to turn that state around for us."[128] The president is banking on his handling of the steel tariffs issue to turn large numbers of steelworkers into Bush Democrats, just as many of them for a time voted for Ronald Reagan in the 1980s. Even with further declines in the steel industry, Bush may have a shot at doing this. Steelworkers remember Clinton's hollow 1992 pledges to help them and give Bush high marks for appearing to look out for them so far.[129] If Bush opts to scrap the whole system of steel tariffs in mid 2003, it will be especially interesting to see what the implications are for the political leanings of steelworkers when they vote for president more than a year later.[130]

Fascinating and gritty though the electoral calculus of the steel industry may be, one must not forget that there is more at stake than control of the White House. From his first days in office, Bush has had his eyes fixed on regaining TPA from Congress and guarding the steel industry was a crucial element in getting representatives and senators to renew that power.[131] Plenty of representatives had warned Bush in the spring of 2001 that they would vote against TPA if the president did not look out for their steel constituents back home.[132] Periodic congressional renewal of TPA was pro forma during the cold war, but Congress let it lapse in 1994 in protest against what many legislators perceived to be Clinton's heavy-handed pursuit of votes for free-trade measures.[133] The great advantage of TPA to presidents, of course, is that it allows them to negotiate trade agreements that Congress then must take or leave as complete packages not subject to amendment.

Steel protection, the president hopes, also will pave the way for ultimate congressional approval of the lower global trade barriers coming from the latest round of WTO talks inaugurated in November 2001 in Qatar.[134] In Bush's view, the final culmination of congressional support for open markets would be the FTAA, to be phased in in stages starting in 2005. C. Fred Bergsten, one of America's foremost experts on international trade, has predicted that Bush's small backward steps to secure congressional support for TPA will be vindicated when Congress approves the FTAA.[135] Getting there, however, requires traveling a road along which every free-trade measure is bought by offering sops to one special interest or another.

Nowhere is the protection of economic sectors more noticeable than in agriculture. After heaping $5.5 billion in extra aid to farmers in 2001 on top of the $25 billion in supplemental spending on agriculture during the three previous years, the total supplemental tab for agriculture is slated to top $79 billion over the next ten years, and the total annual tab for agriculture is running at more than $25 billion.[136] The forest products sector also has received the protection for which it has clamored. When the Canadian government proved not to be amenable to taxing its timber producers, the United States imposed a 27 percent tariff on Canadian two-by-fours and other softwood products.[137]

Bush succeeded in getting TPA through the House in November 2001 by a single vote, something that would not have been possible had the White House not telegraphed the steel industry about its intentions about tariffs.[138] The moves to protect lumber producers proved even more crucial for greasing the skids for TPA in the Senate. Democratic Senator Max Baucus of montana, chairman of the Senate Finance Committee, which had jurisdiction over TPA, took a strong personal interest in protecting the timber industry; so did Republican Senate Minority Leader Trent Lott of Mississippi.[139] One aide to the Senate Finance Committee remarked: "It would have been tough to get fast track to the floor at all if something hadn't been done on lumber. These things like lumber and steel are much more intensely felt by members than airy-fairy things like NAFTA and the WTO, which they just see as academic and long-term."[140] Congress finally delivered TPA to the president in August 2002. To reach that milestone, however, Bush had to make further concessions concerning the education and training of American workers displaced by freer global trade.[141] The president also had to throw a few bones to the textile industry, concentrated in swing states such as Georgia, and the timing clearly was propitious for the 2002 midterm elections.[142]

CONCLUSION

When steel magnate Andrew Carnegie was called to testify before a Senate committee in 1908 about the possibility that steel tariffs might spark a trade war with Europe, he unburdened himself: "Take back your protection; we are now men, and we can beat the world at the manufacture of steel."[143] Alas, such a sentiment is not likely to touch the ears of future presidents. Globalization may foster economic growth, interdependence, and even peace, but its benefits are not evenly distributed, and it deals harsh blows to certain economic sectors and the workers employed therein. In the years ahead, United States presidents—like the executives of many other countries—will find themselves spending an increasing portion of their time attempting to manage the process of globalization so it remains tenable to vocal domestic constituencies.

Bush lifted his steel tariffs—roughly on schedule—in December 2003, but there will be no shortage of calls by the steel industry, and other industries, for such protection in the years to come. At the time of this writing, the administration is marching forward with a panoply of bilateral free-trade agreements, with Australia and Singapore high on the list; also in the making are regional pacts for Central Africa and, of course, the Western Hemisphere.[144] Along the way, domestic constituencies will have to be pacified, and it should come as no surprise that Bush and other presidents will have to resort to occasional bouts of protectionism, no matter what their ideological lights may tell them. Such policy shifts and feints have become *de rigueur*, and there is a healthy touch of old-fashioned democracy in them.

Could Bush's decision on steel tariffs make all the difference for him—positively or negatively—in 2004? Perhaps, but it is not likely. The president's political fortunes will rise or fall on larger matters such as the state of the economy at home and progress (or the lack thereof) in the War on Terror abroad. The very free-trade agenda that his efforts on behalf of steel have enabled him to promote may well become part of an enduring overall economic policy achievement, but not by 2004. As such, this trade offensive may appeal to many voters in many states someday, but this fact is more likely to provide succor to Bush's successors than to him. If the economic picture does not brighten soon enough, the president knows that he will be held accountable, no matter how grateful some steelworkers in a few key states might be for any fleeting protection he afforded them. Bush's firing of Treasury Secretary O'Neill and National Economic Council Chairman Lindsey on December 6, 2002, was consistent with that realization.[145] "In 2004, Bush will win or lose for reasons entirely unconnected with an irrelevant, dying industry."[146]

NOTES

1. George Melloan, "Caving in to 'Big Steel' Tarnished Bush's Image," *Wall Street Journal*, March 12, 2002, A27.

2. J. Kahn, "Bush Moves against Steel Imports," *New York Times*, June 6, 2001, A1.

3. Paul Krugman, "Testing His Metal," *New York Times*, March 8, 2002, A21.

4. Mick Anderson, "Steel Decision Could Firm Up GOP Political Foundation," *Los Angeles Times*, March 6, 2002, A1.

5. Ibid.

6. Leon Hadar, "Bush Slaps Tariffs of Up to 30% on Imported Steel," *Singapore Business Times*, March 7, 2002, accessed on LexisNexis Academic in November 2002.

7. Liz Marlantes, "Bush Weighing Steel Industry Protection," *Christian Science Monitor*, February 28, 2002, 2.

8. Ibid.

9. R. Samuelson, "Steel—Just a Symptom," *Washington Post*, March 13, 2002, A29.

10. Kahn, "Bush Moves against Steel Imports," A1.

11. Samuelson, "Steel," A29.

12. Mark Niquette, "Steel Tariffs' Effects Expected to Take Time," *Columbus Dispatch*, March 6, 2002, 1B.

13. "Mr. Bush's Steel Test," *Washington Post*, December 26, 2001, A30.

14. Elaine Lafferty, "Bush Steel Tariff Gamble Could Spark Trade War," *Irish Times*, March 7, 2002, 19.

15. Samuelson, "Steel," A29.

16. J. Kahn, "Trade Panel Backs Steel Makers," *New York Times*, October 23, 2001, C1.

17. Steven Pearlstein, "Doubts Arise about Need to Save All U.S. Steelmakers," *Washington Post*, December 8, 2001, E1.

18. Sid Maher, "Metal Fatigue," *Courier Mail*, March 2, 2002, 31.

19. Pearlstein, "Doubts Arise," E1.

20. Ibid.

21. Gregory Cancelada and Philip Dine, "Granite City Steel Might Benefit From New Tariffs," *St. Louis Post-Dispatch*, March 6, 2002, C1.

22. Clayton Hirst, "18,000 More Jobs at Risk, Corus Warns," *Independent on Sunday*, July 22, 2001, 1.

23. Robert Crandall, "Win for Big Steel Would Cost Jobs," *Chicago Sun-Times*, February 2, 2002, 18.

24. "Import Tariffs' True Costs," *Los Angeles Times*, February 7, 2002, 16.

25. Ibid.

26. James Cox, "Bush Slaps Tariffs on Steel Imports," *USA Today*, March 6, 2002, 1B.

27. Carolyn Lochhead, "Bush's Sop to Union Voters," *San Francisco Chronicle*, March 11, 2002, B5.

28. Samuelson, "Steel," A29.

29. Lynne McKenna Frazier, "Critics Say Bush's Steel Tariffs and Loopholes Won't Fix Industry Crisis," *News-Sentinel*, September 3, 2002, accessed on LexisNexis Academic in November 2002.

30. Crandall, "Win for Big Steel," 18.

31. Blair Pethel, "Steel Import Probe Restarted by Bush," *Pittsburgh Post-Gazette*, February 6, 2001, B2.

32. David Smith, "Steeling Away," *London Sunday Times*, March 10, 2002, accessed on LexisNexis Academic in November 2002.

33. David Friedman, "Why Excuse Some Steel Dumpers?," *Los Angeles Times*, March 24, 2002, M1.

34. Elizabeth Olson, "W.T.O. Loophole Allows a Surge in Protectionism," *New York Times*, June 13, 2002, W1.

35. Jonathan Riskind, "Tariffs Considered to Ease Steel Crisis, Ney Says," *Columbus Dispatch*, April 1, 2002, 14A.

36. Kahn, "Bush Moves against Steel Imports," A1.

37. "Import Tariffs' True Costs," LA Times February 7, 2002, B16.

38. K. Henry, "Steel Hurt by Imports, Panel Finds," *Baltimore Sun*, October 23, 2001, 1C.

39. P. Krouse, "Steel Bill Awaits Study of Imports," *Plain Dealer*, August 1, 2001, C2.

40. Bill Walsh, "U.S. Steel Makes Appeals for Help from Capitol Hill," *Times-Picayune*, December 29, 2001, 1.

41. I. Stelzer, "Bush Concedes a Battle to Win Free-Trade War," *London Sunday Times*, March 10, 2002, accessed on LexisNexis Academic in November 2002.

42. "Steel Industry Hurt by Imports," *Chicago Sun-Times*, October 22, 2001, 4.

43. Blair Pethel, "Steelmakers Seek Import Tariff Relief of $12 Billion," *Pittsburgh Post-Gazette*, November 28, 2001, B10.

44. Marilyn Geeway, "Steelworkers Hoping Bush Enacts 40% Tariff," *Atlanta Journal and Constitution*, March 5, 2002, 6D.

45. Joseph Kahn, "Steel Users Campaigning against Curbs on Imports," *New York Times*, January 23, 2002, C2.

46. "Washington Wire," *Wall Street Journal*, February 1, 2002, A1.

47. Elizabeth Marchak, "Steel Campaign Heats Up As Federal Action Nears," *Plain Dealer*, February 14, 2002, C1.

48. Bill Walsh, "Bush Prepared on Steel Tariffs Issue," *Times-Picayune*, February 28, 2002, 5.

49. Edward Alden and Guy De Jonquieres, "Bush Move Marks U.S. Trade Policy Turning Point," *Financial Times*, March 6, 2002, 12.

50. Mike Allen and Steven Pearlstein, "Bush Settles on Tariff for Steel Imports," *Washington Post*, March 5, 2002, A1.

51. Catherine McLeod, "U.S. Risks Trade War with 30% Tariff on Steel," *Glasgow Herald*, March 6, 2002, 1.

52. Kahn, "Trade Panel Backs Steel Makers," C1.

53. "Import Tariffs' True Costs," 16.

54.   Allen and Pearlstein, "Bush Settles," A1.

55.   Jennifer L. Rich, "U.S. Admits That Politics Was behind Steel Tariffs," *New York Times*, March 14, 2002, W1.

56.   Len Boselovic, "Steel Import Tariffs Remedy Draws Fire," *Pittsburgh Post-Gazette*, December 8, 2001, A9.

57.   "U.S. Steel Tariffs a Grave Concern," *Australian Financial Review*, December 11, 2001, 54.

58.   David Feldman, "Why Risk Alliances to Bail Out Big Steel?" *Baltimore Sun*, January 28, 2002, 9A.

59.   James Gerstenzang, "Team Signals Help Is on the Way for Steel Industry," *Los Angeles Times*, March 1, 2002, A1.

60.   Kahn, "Bush Moves against Steel Imports," A1.

61.   Walsh, "U.S. Steel Makes Appeals," 1.

62.   Joseph Kahn and David E. Sanger, "Bush Officials Meet to Seek a Compromise on Steel Tariffs," *New York Times*, March 1, 2002, C1.

63.   Ibid.

64.   Ibid.

65.   "Washington Wire," *Wall Street Journal*, March 1, 2002, A1.

66.   Richard Stevenson, "Recovery Near, But Its Vigor Is in Doubt," *New York Times*, February 28, 2002, C1.

67.   George Will, "Bending for Steel," *Washington Post*, March 7, 2002, A21.

68.   George Will, "Steel Tariffs Would Shame Finance Bills," *Chicago Sun-Times*, February 14, 2002, C1.

69.   Pearlstein, "Doubts Arise," E1.

70.   Ibid.

71.   S. Greenhouse, "Beyond Tariffs: Why Steel Isn't Dead," *New York Times*, March 10, 2002, 5.

72.   Ibid.

73.   Ibid.

74.   Joseph Kahn and Richard W. Stevenson, "Treasury's Chief Is Said to Fault Steel Tariff Move," *New York Times*, March 16, 2002, A1.

75.   Robert Novak, "Harsh Reaction to Tariffs Stuns Bush," *Chicago Sun-Times*, March 17, 2002, 39.

76.   Steven Pearlstein, "Bush Sets Tariffs on Steel Imports," *Washington Post*, March 6, 2002, E1.

77.   "Steel Tariffs Okay if They Help Bush Sell Free Trade," *Newsday*, June 8, 2001, A50.

78. Joseph Kahn, "U.S. Trade Panel Backs Putting Hefty Duties on Imported Steel," *New York Times*, December 8, 2001, C1.

79. Joseph Kahn, "Steel Users Campaigning against Curbs on Imports," *New York Times*, January 23, 2002, C2.

80. Pearlstein, "Bush Sets Tariffs on Steel Imports," E1.

81. Crandall, "Win for Big Steel," 18.

82. "Bush Goes Astray on Steel," *Boston Herald*, March 6, 2002, 22.

83. K. Darce, "Steel Tariffs Might Not Be Ironclad," *Times Picayune*, May 21, 2002, 1.

84. N. King, "America Feels Pain of Tariffs on Steel Imports," *Wall Street Journal*, May 31, 2002, A2.

85. "Next Steps on Steel," *Washington Post*, June 5, 2002, A22.

86. "CITAC Steel Consumers Testify," *PR Newswire*, September 25, 2002.

87. "Honda Considers Airlift of Steel," *New York Times*, June 29, 2002, C4.

88. R. G. Edmundson, "Unsettled Market," *Journal of Commerce*, September 2, 2002, 32.

89. Carter Dougherty, "Steel Mill Renewal," *Washington Times*, September 11, 2002, C8.

90. Oliver Morgan, "States of Uncertainty," *London Observer*, September 15, 2002, 6.

91. John Hall, "Steel Tariffs Tossed Aside, Bush Renews Trade Vision," *Richmond Times-Dispatch*, September 1, 2002, B2.

92. "CITAC Steel Consumers Testify."

93. Bruce Alpert, "House Doesn't Bend on Steel Tariffs," *Times Picayune*, May 9, 2002, 1.

94. David Wastell, "Trade War Averted after U.S. Concessions," *Sunday Telegraph*, September 29, 2002, 32.

95. Clayton Hirst, "18,000 More Jobs at Risk, Corus Warns," *London Independent on Sunday*, July 22, 2001, 1.

96. Paul Meller, "Opposition to Steel Plan," *New York Times*, December 11, 2001, W1.

97. Guy Matthews, "The U.S. Won't Take 'No' for an Answer at Paris Steel Summit," *Wall Street Journal*, December 14, 2001, A1.

98. James Cox, "Steelmaking Nations Favor Capacity Cuts," *USA Today*, December 19, 2001, 6B.

99. Matthews, "The U.S. Won't Take 'No,'" A1.

100. Edmund Andrews, "Pact to Cut Steel Production Doesn't End Risk of Trade War," *New York Times*, December 19, 2001, C8; Cox, "Steelmaking Nations," 6B.

101. Feldman, "Why Risk Alliances?," 9A.

102. "EU Increases Steel Cuts to Avert U.S. Action," *Australian Financial Review*, February 9, 2002, 11.

103. "Bush to Mull Over Steel Compromise, *Australian Financial Review*, February 11, 2002, 9.

104. Roland Watson, "U.S. Steel Dispute with Europe May Spark Trade War," *London Times*, March 2, 2002, A8.

105. Kahn and Sanger, "Bush Officials meet to seek compromise on Steel Tarrifs," A1.

106. Allen and Pearlstein, "Bush Settles," A1.

107. Elizabeth A. Marchak and Stephen Koff, "Nations Get Special Break on Tariffs," *Plain Dealer*, March 24, 2002, A1.

108. Edmund Andrews, "Angry Europeans to Challenge U.S. Steel Tariffs at W.T.O.," *New York Times*, March 6, 2002, C12.

109. David Sanger, "Bush Puts Tariffs of As Much As 30% on Steel Imports," *New York Times*, March 6, 2002, A1.

110. Steven Pearlstein and Clay Chandler, "Reaction Abroad on Steel Is Harsh," *Washington Post*, March 7, 2002, E1.

111. "Steeling for a Fight: Europe must combat U.S. Protectionism," *The Guardian*, March 6, 2002, 21.

112. Martin Fletcher, "EU Condemns Bush's 'Wild West' Steel Tariffs," *London Times*, March 7, 2002, A6.

113. Michael Brown, "Take No Notice of the EU's Crocodile Tears Over Mr. Bush's Steel Tariffs," *London Independent*, March 8, 2002, 4.

114. David Smith, "Steeling Away," *London Sunday Times*, March 10, 2002, accessed on LexisNexis Academic in November 2002.

115. "China Files Complaint to W.T.O. on Steel Tariffs," *New York Times*, March 15, 2002, 4.

116. Martin Fletcher, "Tights and Corsets May Feel Pinch in Trade War with U.S.," *London Times*, March 23, 2002, (money) 10.

117. S. Rickter, "Is This Europe's Hour to Lead on Free Trade?," *New York Times*, April 1, 2002, A19.

118. Edward Alden and Richard Wolffe, "Bush Seeks to Defuse EU Trade Row," *Financial Times*, May 3, 2002, 10. This was fortunate, because at the end of August 2002, the WTO would rule that the EU has the right to impose up to $4 billion in penalties on the United States unless it redresses this feature of its tax laws; see Edmund L. Andrews, "U.S. Rebuked," *New York Times*, September 1, 2002, 4.

119. Warren Vieth, "Bush Vows to Fix Trade Spat," *Los Angeles Times*, May 3, 2002, A1.

120. Michael Mann and Francis Williams, "Japan to Protest against U.S. Steel Tariffs," *Financial Times*, May 18, 2002, 8.

121. Dale McFeatters, "Free Trade in Steel," *Scripps Howard News Service*, September 10, 2002.

122. "EU/US: Steel Dialogue Stilted," *European Report*, September 18, 2002.

123. David Wastell, "Trade War Averted after U.S. Concessions," *Sunday Telegraph*, September 29, 2002, 32.

124. Sid Maher, "Metal Fatigue," *Courier Mail*, March 2, 2002, 31.

125. Nick Anderson, "Steel Decision Could Firm Up GOP Political Foundation," *Los Angeles Times*, March 6, 2002, A1; Tom Skotnicki, "But It Could Bring Freer Trade," *Business Weekly Review*, March 14, 2002, 10.

126. Susan Page, "Bush Policies Follow Politics of States Needed in 2004," *USA Today*, June 17, 2002, 1A; "No Steel Tariffs," *San Diego Union-Tribune*, March 5, 2002, B8.

127. Luke Collins, "Bush Buys Votes in Crucial States," *Australian Financial Review*, March 7, 2002, 9.

128. Mike Allen, "Politics a Key Force in Forging Policy," *Washington Post*, April 6, 2002, E1.

129. Francis X. Clines, "In Grateful Big Steel States, the Bush Democrat May Be Born," *New York Times*, March 10, 2002, 39.

130. Jim Ostroff, "Bush's Steel Tariffs Slated for Meltdown," *Kiplinger Business Forecasts*, September 5, 2002, XXX.

131. "Bush Steels Himself for Trade Spat," *Tampa Tribune*, June 9, 2001, 16.

132. Anne E. Kornblut and Sue Kirchhoff, "Bush Slaps Tariffs on Steel Imports," *Boston Globe*, March 6, 2001, F1.

133. Guy Jonquie and Edward Alden, "Cold Steel," *Financial Times*, March 7, 2002, 18.

134. Evelyn Iritani, "Imports Hurt Steel Industry, Panel Rules," *Los Angeles Times*, October 23, 2001, 1.

135. T. Roeser, "Bush Plays Steel Card Cleverly," *Chicago Sun-Times*, March 9, 2002, 20.

136. Holger Jensen, "Bush's Chances on Trade No Better Than Clinton's," *Rocky Mountain News*, May 10, 2001, 36A.

137. Warren Vieth, "Bush Vows to Fix Trade Spat," *Los Angeles Times*, May 3, 2002, A1.

138. The final House vote in July 2002 provided a margin of only three votes; see Edmund Andrews, "U.S. Rebuked," *New York Times*, September 1, 2002, 4; Paul Blustein, "A Free-Trade Gamble by the US," *Washington Post*, March 29, 2002, E1.

139. Andrews, "U.S. Rebuked"

140. Ibid.

141.   Mike Allen, "Bush Hopes to Temper Steel Tariffs With Free-Trade Measures," *Washington Post*, April 4, 2002, A7.

142.   Lee Siew Hua, "U.S. Textile Lobby Makes Pitch for Protectionism," *Singapore Straits Times*, April 5, 2002, accessed on LexisNexis Academic in November 2002.

143.   Leo Lewis, "Bush, the Man of Steel, Is Humbled by a $4 Billion Battering from the WTO," *Independent on Sunday (London)*, September 1, 2002, 6.

144.   Paul Blustein, "U.S., Singapore Near Pact on Trade," *Washington Post*, November 20, 2002, E3.

145.   Dana Milbank, "With '04 in Mind, Bush Team Saw Economic, Political Peril," *Washington Post*, December 7, 2002, A1.

146.   Mark Steyn, "Sorry, Mr. Bush, You've Lost Your Biggest Fan," *London Sunday Telegraph*, March 10, 2002, 22.

Chapter 7

The Politics behind Bush's No Child Left Behind Initiative

Ideas, Elections, and Top-Down Education Reform

Robert Maranto, with Laura Coppeto

INTRODUCTION

On January 8, 2002, after nearly a year of negotiations in Congress, President George W. Bush signed into law the "No Child Left Behind Act of 2001," a six-year reauthorization of the Elementary and Secondary Education Act (ESEA), first passed in 1965. The act won high praise. No less than David Broder, the dean of the Washington press corps, wrote that the law "may well be the most important piece of federal education legislation in thirty-five years." Perhaps more accurately, Clinton Education Secretary Richard Riley recalled of the 1994 reauthorization: "We called ours sweeping. . . . Whoever passes the next reauthorization will call it sweeping."[1]

In fact, the 681-page No Child Left Behind (NCLB) Act leaves intact the highly complex structure of federal education policy, with its fifty-four odd elementary and secondary programs and hundreds of provisions—each with its own congressional, bureaucratic, or interest group constituency.[2] Yet NCLB does break new ground by pushing states to stress school-level accountability. The act requires annual proficiency testing in reading and math for grades 3–8 using state tests, which the U.S. Department of Education must approve, forces states to publish results of school-level testing broken down by subgroup (ethnicity, special education, free lunch status, and Limited English Proficiency [LEP] status), encourages reconstitution of failing schools, and allows parents in failing schools to attend other public schools and use Title I money for tutoring. The act also experiments with alternative teacher certification and provides money for more phonics-based reading approaches.[3]

Why did President George W. Bush make education reform the highlight of his domestic agenda, with NCLB the first bill introduced in the 107th

Congress? What explains the president's willingness (to the dismay of many conservative and neoliberal intellectuals) to jettison most school choice provisions from the original NCLB plan? Why did Bush seek a centrist solution garnering an overwhelming majority in Congress rather than a more thoroughgoing but partisan reform? Can NCLB succeed? These questions will be explored in a discussion of President Bush's goals in education reform and the policy process and outcomes of NCLB. Bush emphasized education reform in part because he cares about education, particularly for immigrants, and in part for electoral reasons. Second, it appears that the president's relatively quick compromise—one informant called it a "precompromise" on school choice—reflected both political goals and Bush's beliefs that government institutions can work if driven by standards. It seems likely that NCLB will somewhat improve the academic performance of low-achieving students, though we doubt more thoroughgoing effects.

NOBLESSE OBLIGE TEXAS STYLE: BUSH AND CORPORATE/COMPASSIONATE CONSERVATISM

President Bush's interest in education is both personal and political. Personally, Bush suffered a traumatic transition on moving from a mediocre Texas public high school to the prestigious Phillips Academy in Andover. Days after arriving, the normally ebullient Bush asked friends, "how am I going to last here a week?"[4] He fell on the margins academically, "terrified of flunking out of Andover and the embarrassment it would cause himself and his family."[5] While inferior preparation handicapped Bush, eventually he "worked hard, buckled down, and learned a lot."[6] In the end, he recalled, "the high standards lifted me up."[7] Bush holds his personal success as evidence that any student can meet academic standards. Former school librarian Laura Bush focuses her husband on education. Even critics admit that, unlike the previous Texas governor, Ann Richards, Bush risked substantial political capital trying to equalize Texas school funding, facing opposition from his GOP base.[8]

Both personally and politically, Bush's support for public education complements his goal to welcome immigrants—including illegals—into American society. Unlike Republican leaders such as California Governor Pete Wilson, Texas Governor Bush refused to attack Mexican immigration, even after immigrant-bashing Pat Buchanan was endorsed by twenty-five of the sixty-two members of the Texas State Republican Executive Committee in the 1996 GOP presidential primaries. When Buchanan criticized Mexican immigrants in Dallas in 1995, Bush countered: "It is easy for some to pick on our friends from the South . . . and I don't like it." Bush opposed English-only laws and proposals to expel the children of illegal immigrants from school.[9] In part, this reflected the needs of businesses dependent on cheap labor, free trade, and cross-cultural understanding. As Soskis writes: Texas's "supposedly reactionary business elite . . . has largely accepted multiculturalism as a way of life."[10] Bush backs business politically, but Reed also sees a personal element:

> The desire to provide will never be squelched. . . . I understand why these people are here . . . there are a lot of jobs people in Texas won't do—laying tar in August or chopping cedars. People argue that if we don't educate [immigrants] they'll go home, and that's not true. If we educate them, at least they can become more productive members of society. This is good public policy. I would be willing to defend this position as the best position not only for Texas, but for the nation. According to a friend, young George's "deputy mom" was an immigrant housekeeper, and the issue "is almost Biblical with him.[11]

Of course, Republican outreach to Hispanic voters makes political sense.[12] Even so, Bush took risks. *New York Times* reporter Nicholas Kristof saw the presidential candidate repeatedly remind white, conservative audiences in a must-win primary state of the nexus between education and upward mobility for minorities:

> [Bush] almost never talked about the importance of improving education without noting the strides that he said Hispanic and black students in Texas had made. He answered every question he received about illegal immigration—a source of intense vexation for some South Carolinians—by reminding voters that many Mexicans streamed into the United States simply to seek a better life for their children.[13]

Bush's views on immigration and poverty may stem from his Christianity and his seeming embrace of "compassionate conservatism," as devised by occasional Bush advisor and University of Texas Professor Marvin Olasky. A saved Christian, Olasky argues that traditional welfare state programs fail by providing material goods without the spiritual and intellectual empowerment for independence: welfare produces clients rather than citizens, fostering self-destructive behavior. In contrast, religious social services both feed people and build their character.[14]

Bush seemingly feels a religious and class-based obligation to help the poor help themselves, but unlike Olasky, he also has faith in large secular institutions, particularly corporations and public schools. In this respect he is a traditional Texas conservative: "The [Texas] conservative ideology does not reject all government . . . it opposes those government policies that are not designed to promote economic growth and development. The business of Texas government, therefore, is business."[15]

Such corporate conservatism was increasingly under attack by liberals as Texas became more like the rest of America.[16] More importantly for a GOP governor seeking the presidency, corporate "country club" conservatives increasingly faced attack by religious conservatives skeptical of free trade, internationalization, and large institutions. These populist conservatives wanted education run by religious schools or by local government rather than state or national government.[17] Peter Beinart's 1998 *New Republic* cover story, "The Big Debate: George W. Bush Battles the Republican Right," notes that increasingly strident Texas GOP activists "fear large and distant concentrations of power," whether governmental or corporate:

> It is over this issue of bigness that George W. Bush has defined himself as governor. Time and time again, his state party's belief in the illegitimacy of centralized authority has collided with his belief in its responsible and energetic management. And thus Bush, the frontrunner for his party's presidential nomination in 2000, has found himself at the vanguard of a debate that preoccupies American conservatism: how to harness the anti-Washington and anti-Wall Street populism unleashed by the end of the Cold War so that it doesn't slam up against the Republican Party establishment . . . [Bush supports] something like "national-greatness conservatism," an emerging brand of conservatism that tries, against the currents pushing the American right toward the worship of localism, to justify the exercise of concentrated power. . . . The three things about which Bush shows real passion are immigration, free trade, and his testing program to make sure that no child graduates third grade without being able to read. What they have in common is managed bigness—Bush believes in international engagement, as opposed to the growing conservative obsession with national sovereignty, and in government's ability to enforce common principles rather than letting each community set its own.[18]

Not surprisingly, particularly on education, Bush had better relations with Texas's pro-business Democratic state legislative leaders than with the often hard-Right state GOP.[19]

Texas Education Reform: Standards Trump Choice

Though most studies suggest that school choice improves schooling,[20] the education policy community has for years fought over whether top-down standards forced on schools by central bureaucracies or parental choice and free markets can best improve education.[21] Bush's faith in large institutions, including traditional public schools, explains why in both Texas and Washington he

supported public school standards rather than school choice. As Ivins and
Dubose detail, Bush gave little more than rhetorical support to a school voucher
initiative backed by one of his major fund-raisers.[22] In contrast, as Ivins and
Dubose admit, and as Bush boasts, the governor expended tremendous time,
energy, and political capital improving Texas public schools.[23]

Bush pursued three distinct strategies in school reform, with varying degrees
of vigor and success. Most important, in his first big education initiative during his first legislative session, he shepherded through the legislature the first
complete overhaul of the Texas education code in almost fifty years. The new
code delegated decisions about how to run schools to local education authorities (LEAs) but also required district- and school-level reporting of the Texas
Assessment of Academic Skills (TAAS), the standardized test devised by previous gubernatorial administrations. (Ivins and Dubose report that Bush had been
expected to end the experimental TAAS; instead, he embraced it.) Widespread
reporting of TAAS results led both the state legislature and school districts to
devote more resources to after school and summer school programs to improve
the achievement of low-performing students, most of them minorities. Similarly,
in the 1999 state legislative session, Bush pushed through a measure requiring
students to pass TAAS before advancing to the next grade, pushing LEAs to
enforce existing state policies banning social promotion. Still, as Gorman writes,
Bush's reforms were less novel than his supporters suggest:

> Building on the work of one's predecessors can produce success stories.
> That's just what Bush did as governor of Texas. His reforms expanded
> those of former governor Ann Richards, whose reforms built on those
> in places like Dallas and previous statewide efforts led by, of all peo-
> ple, Ross Perot. Dallas, as it happens, is where then-school board
> president Sandy Kress initiated accountability—using standardized
> test scores to reward and sanction schools. "This is our theme," Kress
> said. "We may not know a lot of music in Texas, but we can sing the
> song we know well."[24]

One education analyst suggested that TAAS' longevity made it part of the
culture of Texas public schooling. Bush's main contribution was to reemphasize
TAAS rather than end it as governors typically dispatch their predecessors' inno-
vations. Rudalevige notes that Texas "teachers and administrators saw their
own careers tied to student performance."[25] On the 2000 campaign trail, presidential candidate Bush often attacked "the soft bigotry of low expectations"—
the tendency of traditional public schools to expect little of African-American
and Hispanic students. In fact, standards-based reforms may prove particularly
helpful for minorities, who are often warehoused by traditional public schools.[26]

Bush's Texas reforms combining state standards and accountability with
local control match ideas from the Progressive Policy Institute and the New

Democratic think tank, and with some Clinton administration proposals.[27] As Beinart writes: Bush policies "stem from the neoliberal premise that government should give localities enough authority so they can fairly be held accountable for educating their students to a uniform standard . . . localism as a means to a common end."[28]

Bush's second reform, a limited foray into school choice, seemed less successful. Bush did not initially push charter schools, independent public schools of choice,[29] though he did sign a 1995 bill allowing charters. In 1997, however, at his urging, the Texas Education Agency approved a plethora of new charters, increasing the statewide number from seventeen to 168 in just six months. Unfortunately, this rapid expansion weakened quality control and state oversight. The resulting scandals tarnished the charter movement in Texas, and Bush backtracked.[30] As noted earlier, Bush was even less supportive of vouchers allowing low-income parents to choose private schools.[31] Seemingly, he trusts education elites operating under the right incentives to make better decisions than parents.

Finally, in the 1997 state legislative session, Bush sought to solve a decades-old problem by revolutionizing education finance. Bush proposed increasing the state share of education funding from 45 percent to 63 percent, thus equalizing funding and reducing property tax burdens on poor communities. Bush would pay for this mainly by replacing local property taxes with increased state sales taxes and by closing tax loopholes. As in his earlier policy initiatives, Bush forged close relationships with Democratic leaders in the state legislature, particularly House Education Committee Chair Paul Sadler and Lieutenant Governor Bob Bullock. He met with each on a weekly or even daily basis, and he had great affection for them.[32] Ultimately, however, Bush's plan failed because of opposition from Republican state legislators fearing a state takeover of local schools.[33] Bush critics Ivins and Dubose laud Bush's progressive efforts, contrasted with former governor Richards's reluctance to tackle the issue.[34] Bush himself takes pride in his failed battle, devoting nine pages of his autobiography to it, more than for other policy discussions.[35]

Bush paid no political price for this failure; indeed, it cemented his relationships with centrist Texas Democrats, some of whom endorsed him for president. Political leaders are most influenced by past political successes and failures,[36] thus Texas experiences might lead President G. W. Bush to support school standards rather than school choice, as indeed he did.

Bush's Texas education reforms show elements of his leadership style. In particular, as the Bush psychological profiles developed by Immelman, Greenstein, and Renshon suggest, Bush combines principle-driven leadership and risk acceptance with a pragmatic willingness to compromise for results.[37] He is also notably willing to delegate the details of policy to trusted subordinates. As Barnes notes, while his father "regarded public service as a civic duty . . . George W. views it as a way to accomplish things."[38] As a highly active extrovert, Bush enjoys charming would-be opponents onto his team. For example, Reed notes that while Governor Bush did not develop revolutionary ideas, he was able to "turn issues into concrete proposals that get passed into law . . . so far he has worked the legislature like a seasoned pro, staying out of the spotlight and making allies of the Democrats who run committees."[39] Each tendency was to recur as President Bush managed NCLB.

Impact: From TAAS to NCLB

With the possible exception of charter schooling, Bush's education policies seemingly worked. As Rand Education reports, controlling for socioeconomic status, Texas students scored first in the nation on the highly respected National Assessment of Education Progress (NAEP) tests by the late 1990s, with African-American and Hispanic students doing particularly well.[40] While some fear that TAAS encouraged teaching to the test, NAEP results are less subject to manipulation.[41] Moreover, even critics of standardized testing admit that TAAS pass rates and graduation rates increased more for minority than for white students in the Bush years.[42] In short, the Texas reforms fostered educational equity by helping low-performing students. They did not, however, bring more thoroughgoing reform.

Whatever the educational impacts, Bush's policies paid off politically. As Keen reported during the 2000 presidential primaries: "Bush's emphasis on compassionate conservatism and education are designed to appeal to women. . . . Bush won more of their votes than McCain did in the primary elections."[43] Among those who ranked education as their most important concern in the 2000 presidential election, Gore won a modest 52 percent to 44 percent majority compared to Clinton's 82 percent to 12 percent margin over Bob Dole; thus Bush neutralized a traditionally Democratic issue. Bush did better than Dole among female and Hispanic voters.[44]

Similarly, an analyst from a Right-leaning think tank noted that NCLB "clearly got the GOP on the side of educational improvement." Yet in some ways this was a bold move. After all, education is a traditional state and local function and is highly controversial.[45] Only about 7 percent of total public K–12 education expenditures come from the federal government, mainly through dozens of highly specific ESEA categorical programs aimed at social equity, each with their own champions on Capitol Hill. Presidents Clinton and G. H. W. Bush had tried to make the programs more flexible, and each failed. Indeed, Clinton tried to block grant a number of ESEA programs to increase state and local flexibility, but congressional Democrats opposed "Edflex" moves empowering state and local officials, so the 1994 Clinton reauthorization of ESEA required only that states develop standards and assessments, with undefined "Adequate Yearly Progress" (AYP). In the 1997 and 1998 State of the Union addresses, Clinton urged national tests to benchmark state standards. While the business community supported national standards, Congress did not.[46] As education analyst Chester Finn joked at the time: "Republicans don't like 'national'; Democrats don't like 'test.'"[47] When ESEA reauthorization came due in 2000, Congress left it for the next administration. Given these failures, President Bush showed boldness in sending his NCLB blueprint to Congress days after taking office.

Along with modest increases in funding, Rudalevige reports that the original Bush plan included six main components: annual student testing (developed by states but approved by the U.S. Department of Education) in math and reading in grades 3–8, with reporting broken down by school, and within schools by ethnicity, income (free and reduced lunch), special education status, and LEP status; requirements that AYP be made by "disadvantaged" students for schools to keep Title I funds; consolidation of sixty ESEA grant programs to five, to allow states flexibility to achieve educational goals (Edflex); funding bonuses for schools closing the gap between mainstream and disadvantaged students, with failing schools eventually losing funding; "exit vouchers" allowing Title I students in failing schools to exit to other public or private schools by taking Title I money with them; and state progress benchmarked by NAEP tests, as a check on state standards.[48]

As has been noted,[49] Bush seemingly learned from the failure of Clinton's health care plan and thus sent Congress a broad blueprint early in his administration rather than a more detailed plan later. Further, as Rudalevige notes, much of Bush's plan was cribbed from earlier New Democratic proposals, especially Rotherham's.[50] Bush's key White House education aid, former Dallas school board president Sandy Kress, was in fact a New Democrat who backed school standards but showed some skepticism toward school choice.

In late December, President-elect Bush met with key congressional education leaders of both parties. In these meetings and later, Bush signaled willingness to drop school voucher provisions of NCLB to reach an agreement for standards and testing. As one of our informants put it, Bush "pre-compromised" on school choice. All informants agreed that dropping vouchers reflected both policy goals and political realities. Three with connections to the administration recalled:

> The Bush administration sent very clear signals early on to Miller and Kennedy that they wanted this to be a bipartisan bill, in effect giving liberal Democrats the power to veto school choice and super Edflex. It was a pre-compromise. They did that for two reasons. First, in terms of macro political strategy, the tax cut was aimed more at the Republican base while the education bill was aimed at the moldable middle, suburban soccer moms, swing voters, those sorts of folks. The other reason is that the people advising Bush are only moderately in favor of

school vouchers, charter schools, and other forms of choice. They favor more traditional top-down reform. They really believe that a standardized test-based reform plan can be made to work nationally the way it worked in Texas. They're not against vouchers, they just think that choice is an interesting sideshow, not the center ring. The center ring for them is testing.

Even in the Republican House caucus you probably can't get seventy people who really believe in school choice per se. Mostly they want to show that they are doing something on education and outside of that seventy they are pretty agnostic about how they go about it. I think most of the GOP are conservatives who wanted to focus on tax issues and budget issues and law and order and national security and they really didn't feel like getting up to their elbows in this controversial education debate. Plus Bush is taking great pride in his ability to get the AFT [teachers' union] on board on some of these things and they really didn't need that kind of grief, and among mainstream Republicans there is minimal support for school choice.

Early on [Bush] told me that there's no chance for vouchers because the politics are all against them. People who live in rural areas don't have many choices. People in inner cities are minorities who don't vote for Republicans, and Democrats are not willing to budge on this issue, and the people who live in the suburbs are happy with their schools. So he started off with the view that it's a lost cause because the politics were against it. He didn't do too much for [school] choice in Texas. I think his reasoning in Texas was the same as his reasoning was in Washington. There's no political constituency for it. He didn't consider it a touchstone issue. He considered the touchstone issue to be testing from grades 3–8 and disaggregating into the various groups, so he got what he wanted.

As Table 7.1 shows, voucher provisions were stripped from NCLB by the Senate Health, Education, Labor and Pensions (HELP) Committee in March and by the House Education and the Workforce Committee in May, with no complaint by the White House. Similarly, Edflex provisions were watered down in the House Education and Workforce Committee in April and later further weakened in the Senate. At the same time, Kress worked with moderate Democratic senators and, with President Bush's help, wooed Senator Ted Kennedy, who became a key ally. Breaking with liberals, Kennedy agreed to testing and some funding flexibility in exchange for dropping vouchers to private schools, and simply to join the process.[51]

With support from moderate Democrats and from Kennedy, the likelihood of passage increased, though challenging issues remained. In particular, until the end of the conference committee, Democrats held serious debates

TABLE 7.1
Synopsis of Key Events

Late December 2000	President-elect Bush meets with key congressional education leaders, including Republicans Boehner, Jefford, and Gregg, and Democrats Bayh, Miller, and Roemer.
January 23, 2001	Bush sends thirty-page legislative blueprint to Congress.
February	Representative John Boehner (R, Ohio) announces the creation of a new subcommittee on education reform.
February 15	Senate HELP Committee holds hearings with Education Secretary Rod Paige.
February–March	White House aid Sandy Kress and Gregg bring moderate Democrats and Ted Kennedy into negotiating process.
March 8	HELP Committee approves 20–0 S.1, the "Better Education for Students and Teachers (BEST) Act of 2001, without vouchers, nor large funding increases.
March 22	Boehner introduced his draft of H.R. 1, which includes annual testing, block grants, vouchers, and aid to faith-based organizations.
April	Miller and Boehner compromise on Edflex, giving additional grant flexibility to localities who could transfer some funds across categories, but not to states.
May 2	Miller amendment to strip the vouchers passed House committee 27–20.
May 3	Bill reaches Senate floor.
May 9	H.R. 1 sent to the floor by a 41–7 committee vote.
May 14	Rules Committee keeps tight rein: twenty eight amendments and seven hours of debate.
May 23	House passes the bill 384–45. Most no votes are Republicans against federal intrusion, or the lack of vouchers; some Democrats oppose testing.
May 24	Jim Jeffords leaves GOP, but this has little effect on NCLB, since Gregg and Kennedy drove the process in the Senate.
June 14	S.1 adopted by a 91 to 8 vote. Six Republicans and two Democrats opposed. Accountability provisions resembled those in the House, but on a slower time line.
July 7–9	President Bush pushes NCLB in radio and Rose Garden addresses.
July 10	The Senate named twenty five conferees. One week later the House names fourteen.
September 11	Terrorist attacks raise concerns that NCLB is no longer a priority.
September 25	Boehner announces that "terrorism will not derail America's domestic policy agenda."
October 2001	The Big Four conferees: Boehner, Miller, Kennedy, and Gregg—met consistently for final negotiations.
December 11	Conference committee approves its report but wrangles over final language until December 13.
December 18	House adopted the conference report by a 381–41 margin, and the Senate passes with 87–10. The process "brought the middle together, and held it," said Tim Roemer (D, Ind.).
January 4, 2002	Bill presented to President Bush.
January 8	NCLB, a six-year reauthorization of the Elementary and Secondary Education Act, signed into law.

Source: Rudalevige 2002.

about the meaning of AYP on standardized tests, with Republican governors also arguing for relatively lax standards. Supporters of traditional public schools feared that demanding, European-style standards would in fact find most American schools wanting. In the end, a complex formula was agreed to, with actual implementation by the U.S. Department of Education uncertain.

The president's pre-compromise on school choice and extreme flexibility on Edflex angered conservative supporters of school reform. President Bush could have fought for a stronger bill, but unlike tax cuts and the recent Homeland Security legislation, many Republicans had serious qualms about a larger *federal* role in education reform, not to mention additional federal dollars promised by the legislation,[52] thus a partisan bill may have failed. Further, regarding tax reform and homeland security, Bush's goals were partisan, and thus not easy to compromise. In sharp contrast, Bush's true goals in education reform more resembled those of standards-seeking New Democrats than market-seeking Republicans. Seemingly, the president got what we wanted: tests and standards. And as Rudalevige notes, key to the legislative process was the role of President Bush himself, who brought the key congressional leaders together in part by "embracing Democratic positions and leaders."[53]

IMPACTS? RAISING THE FLOOR

The NCLB Act was unlikely to directly push school reform by removing funding from low-performing schools, since, as one put it, "the hammer provisions are a mess." Further, while local school districts are required to tell parents in failing schools about other public school options, they are in practice unlikely to do so. Finn found that districts were already sabotaging this provision.[54] Moreover, as the informants quoted earlier suggest, standards and testing have not dramatically raised academic achievement for average- to high-achieving students, thus we doubt NCLB can raise American K–12 achievement to "world-class" levels. Indeed, when New York State required the demanding Regents exam for high school graduation, authorities eased the exam rather than face the political consequences of failing large numbers of students.[55] To a lesser degree the same watering down occurred when Virginia imposed its Standards of Learning (SOL) exams, though SOLs did produce some academic gains.[56] Accounts of insiders[57] suggest that contrasting most states, Texas culture is relatively amenable to the top-down quality of standards-based reform: what worked in Texas might not play out in Peoria.

On the other hand, even with its compromised accountability mechanisms, NCLB has already labeled 8,600 schools as failing, roughly 10 percent of American public schools.[58] Several informants commented that by forcing local school systems to test students and report the results, NCLB may improve schools indirectly "in the locally generated discontent it engenders rather than in the top-down reform it triggers." In particular, reporting data by race may push school districts to work to close interracial achievement gaps, rather than hide them. As one education analyst put it:

> Disaggregating results by race will focus increased attention on the worst served kids. It will clarify that. It will force the whole community to look at the data that only the superintendent's office did previously, so it could mobilize the Urban League or the NAACP.

While standardized tests may or may not measure high-level achievement, they do divine basic literacy and numeracy—skills that not all public schools teach black and Hispanic young people.

CONCLUSION: "COMPROMISE" IS EASY WHEN YOU GET YOUR WAY

In purpose, process, and policy, NCLB parallels the education reforms of then Texas governor George W. Bush. In both Texas and Washington, Bush showed interest in and comfort with education policy. Bush's personal history as a struggling student provoked his interest. Ideologically, education reforms aimed at helping poor and minority students comport well with both compassionate conservativism and with Bush's "New Democrat" style attachment to large institutions. Further, Bush's education reforms seemingly earned political support from swing voters, particularly women and Hispanics.

Regarding process, in both Texas and Washington, G. W. Bush worked more with Democrats than with Republicans, and he showed patience through a long policy process. He compromised early, eschewing school choice in favor of standards-based reforms: standardized testing with results reported disaggregated by race. Of course, this "compromise" in fact produced exactly the centrist, standards- and accountability-based policy outcomes that Bush favored. Finally, it seems likely that as in Texas, NCLB will have few impacts on most students but will improve the performance of currently low-performing students. In short, while NCLB may not help most kids, it may help those who need it most. If we can take him at his word, that is in fact what President Bush intended all along.

NOTES

1.   Andrew Rudalevige, "Accountability and Avoidance in the Bush Education Plan," in *Taking Account of Accountability*, ed. Paul Peterson and Martin West (Washington, D.C.: Brookings Institution, 2002), Siobhan Gorman, "Bipartisan Schoolmates," *Education Next* 2, no. 2 (2002): 36–43, 68–88.

2. Chester Finn Jr., "A New Year For Education?," *The Education Gadfly,* January 10, 2002, 1, www.fordhamfoundation.org/gadfly/v02/gadfly02.html. P.1; Krista Kafer, "A Small but Costly Step toward Reform: The Conference Education Bill, www. usatoday.com/news/e98/e1382.html; Rudalevige, "Accountability," 45.

3. Center for Education Reform, CER Newswire [April 1 2002].

4. In an often-told story, Bush used his thesaurus to diversify word choice in an emotional essay about the death of his sister. He wrote "the lacerates ran down my cheeks"—receiving an F on the paper and suffering a humiliating rebuke from his teacher; see Bill Minutaglio, *First Son: George W. Bush and the Bush Family Dynasty* (New York: Random House, 1999), 63–64.

5. J. H. Hatfield, *Fortunate Son: George W. Bush and the Making of an American President* (New York: Soft Skull Press, 2000).

6. George W. Bush, *A Charge to Keep: My Journey to the White House* (New York: HarperCollins, 1999), 20.

7. Hatfield, *Fortunate Son,* 29.

8. Molly Ivins and Lou Debose, *Shrub: The Short but Happy Political Life of George W. Bush* (New York: Random House 2000), 123, 136–40.

9. Peter Beinart, "The Big Debate: George W. Bush Battles the Republican Right," *The New Republic,* March 16, 1999, www.tnr.archive/031698/html.

10. Benjamin Soskis, "Lone Star Joining: Why Texas Looks like America," *The New Republic,* September 11, 2000, www.tnr.com/091800/soskis091800.html (accessed on November 11, 2002).

11. Paul Burka, "Has Governor Bush Monkeyed around with Business?" *Texas Monthly,* June 1999, www.texasmonthly.com/biz/1999/jun/Monkey.2.php; Julia Reed, "The Son Also Rises," *The Weekly Standard,* February 10, 1997, 26.

12. Robert Bryce, "Key Bush Advisor Back in Control," *Salon,* March 8, 2000, www.archive.salon.com/politics2000/feature/2000/03/08/rove/print.html; Judy Keen, "Bush Team Plans for Upcoming Battle," *USA Today,* March 28, 2000, www.usatoday.com/news/e98/e1382.html.

13. Nicholas Kristof, "Political Memo: Rival Makes Bush Better Campaigner," *New York Times,* March 3, 2000, A23.

14. Marvin Olasky, *The Tragedy of American Compassion* (Washington, D.C.: Regnary, 1992); Marvin Olasky, "Compassionate Conservatism," *Veritas,* Fall 2000, 6–11.

15. Kenneth Mladenka and Kim Quaile Hill, *Texas Government* (Monterey, Calif.: Brooks/Cole, 1986), ix.

16. Burka "Has Governor Bush" [see website]; Soskis, "Lone Star Joining". [see website]

17. Ivins and Debose, *Shrub,* 77–80.

18. David Brooks, "A Return to National Greatness: A Manifesto for a Lost Creed," *The Weekly Standard,* March 3, 1997, 16–21.

19.   Fred Barnes, "The Heavyweight: George W. Bush Battles the Republican Right," *The Weekly Standard*, September 14, 1998, 19–23; Beinart, "The Big Debate"; Burka, "Has Governor Bush"; Bush, *A Charge to Keep*; Ivins and Dubose, *Shrub*, 32.

20.   Clyde Belfield and Henry M. Levin, "The Effects of Competition between Schools on Educational Outcomes: A Review for the United States," *Review of Educational Research* 72, no. 2 (2002): 279–341.

21.   Robert Maranto, "The Death of One Best Way: Charter Schools As Reinventing Government," *School Choice in the Real World: Lessons from Arizona Public Schools*, ed. Margaret C. Wang and Herbert J. Walberg (Boulder: Westview, 2001), 39–57.

22.   Ivins and Dubose, *Shrub*, 76–81.

23.   Ibid., 136–39; also see Bush, *A Charge to Keep*, 119–20, 123–30.

24.   Siobhan Gorman, "Bipartisan Schoolmates," *Education Next* 2, no. 2 (2002): 40.

25.   Rudalevige, "Accountability," 16.

26.   Christopher Jencks and Meredith Phillips, eds., *The Black and White Test Score Gap* (Washington, D.C.: Brookings Institution, 1998); Diane Ravitch, *Left Back: A Century of Failed School Reforms* (New York: Simon & Schuster, 2000); William G. Howell and Paul E. Peterson, *The Education Gap* (Washington, D.C.: Brookings Institution, 2002).

27.   Andrew Rotherham, *Toward Performance-Based Federal Education Funding* (Washington, D.C.: Progressive Policy Institute, 1999).

28.   Beinart, "The Big Debate," (see www.tnr.archive/031698.html).

29.   Maranto, "The Death of One Best Way," 39–57.

30.   Ivins and Dubose, *Shrub*, 126–29.

31.   Recent research strongly indicates that vouchers greatly improve the performance of African-American students but have few academic impacts for Hispanics; see Howell and Peterson, *The Education Gap*.

32.   Bush, *A Charge to Keep*, 110–31; Reed, "The Son Also Rises," 25.

33.   Beinart, "The Big Debate," (see website).

34.   Ivins and Dubose, *Shrub*, 135.

35.   Bush, *A Charge to Keep*, 122–30.

36.   Robert Jervis, *Perception and Misperception in International Politics* (Princeton: Princeton University Press, 1976).

37.   Aubrey Immelman, "The Political Personality of U.S. President George W. Bush," in *Political Leadership for the New Century*, ed. Linda O. Valenty and Ofer Feldman (Westport: Praeger, 2002), 81–104; Fred I. Greenstein, "Afterward on George W. Bush," in *The Presidential Difference*, ed. Fred I. Greenstein (Princeton: Princeton University Press, 2001), 273–82; Stanley A. Renshon, "The World According to George W. Bush: Good Judgement or Cowboy Politics," *Good Judgement in Foreign Policy: Theory and Application*, ed. S. A. Renshon and D. Larson (Boulder: Rowman & Littlefield, 2003), 298–320.

38. Barnes, "The Heavy weight," 21.

39. Reed, "The Son Also Rises," 25.

40. David Grissmer, Ann Flanigan, Jennifer Kawata, and Stephanie Williamson, *Improving Student Achievement: What State NAEP Test Scores Tell Us* (Santa Monica: RAND, 2001), 70–73.

41. Ivins and Dubose, *Shrub*, 125; Linda McNeil and Angela Valenzuala, "The Harmful Impact of the TAAS System of Testing in Texas: Beneath the Accountability Rhetoric," in *Raising Standards or Raising Barriers?*, ed. Gary Orfield and Mindy L. Kornhaber (New York: Century Foundation Press, 2002), 127–50.

42. Gary Natriello and Aaron M. Palla, "The Development and Impact of High Stakes," in *Raising Standards or Raising Barriers?*, ed. Gary Orfield and Mindy L. Kornhaber (New York: Century Foundation Press, 2002), 25.

43. Keen, "Bush Team Plans," (www.usatoday.com/news/e98/e1382.html).

44. James W. Ceasar and Andrew E. Busch, *The Perfect Tie: The True Story of the 2000 Presidential Election* (Lanham: Rowman & Littlefield, 2001), 36.

45. Stephen Arons, *Short Route to Chaos: Conscience, Community, and the Re-Constitution of American Schooling* (Amherst: University of Massachusetts Press, 1997); Maranto, "The Death of One Best Way," 39–57.

46. Kenneth K. Wong, *Funding Public Schools* (Lawrence: University Press of Kansas, 1999), 19–30, 45–46.

47. Rudalevige, "Accountability," 9.

48. Ibid, 17–18.

49. Ibid.

50. Ibid, 8–19; also see Rotherham, *Toward Performance-Based Federal Education Funding*, 9–15.

51. Rudalevige, "Accountability," (www.usatoday.com/news/e98/e1382.html) 9.

52. Kafer, (see N.2) Krista Kafer, "A small but costly step toward Reform: The conference Education Bill, "Heritage Foundation, see www.heritage.org/research/education/wm66.cfrr (accessed November 20, 2002).

53. Rudalevige, "Accountability," 31, 68–88.

54. Chester E. Finn Jr., "Leaving Many Children Behind," *The Weekly Standard* 7, no. 47 (August 2002): 26.

55. Diane Ravitch, "The Knowledge Deficit," *Weekly Essays*, the Hoover Institution, September 25, 2002, www-hoover.Stanford.edu/pubaaffairs/we/current/ravitch_0900.html.

56. Frederick Hess, "Reform, Resistance, Retreat? The Predictable Politics of Accountability in Virginia," in *Brookings Papers on Education Policy 2002*, ed. Diane Ravitch (Washington, D.C.: Brookings Institution, 2002), 51–89.

57. Donald R. McAdams, *Fighting to Save Our Urban Schools . . . And Winning!* (New York: Teachers College Press, 2000); Soskis, "Lone Star Joining," 7.

58. Finn, "Leaving Many Children Behind," 8–12.

Part 3

Foreign Policy and the War on Terror

Chapter 8

The Bush Doctrine

Redefining the U.S. Role in World Politics for the Twenty-first Century?

Cameron G. Thies

INTRODUCTION

Many observers find the recently formulated Bush Doctrine a provocative, shocking, and perhaps ill-conceived reaction to a unique set of circumstances facing a relatively inexperienced president. However, when placed in historical context, the Bush Doctrine presents only minor adjustments to the long-standing foreign policy traditions of the United States. This point can be argued by comparing George W. Bush's foreign policy doctrine to that of an earlier Republican president, Dwight D. Eisenhower. Although these men share little in common as individuals, their doctrinal responses to the major threats of their time are very similar. The comparison highlights some of the potential pitfalls of the most recent presidential doctrine, as well as the prospects for its successful enactment.

EISENHOWER AND BUSH

In terms of their experiences prior to becoming president, Bush and Eisenhower could not be more different. Bush grew up in an affluent family with strong East Coast roots, despite experiencing most of his formative years in Texas. Eisenhower had more humble beginnings in small Kansas towns. Bush received his education at Yale and Harvard, while Eisenhower attended West Point. Bush attempted to make it in the oil business in Texas but ended up buying and managing the Texas Rangers baseball team. His political career began with a failed bid for a Texas congressional seat, but he was ultimately elected to the state's governorship, and reelected to the same office just prior to winning the presidency. Eisenhower pursued a professional career in the military, rising rapidly through the ranks to become a five-star general by the end of World War II. He served as the supreme commander of the Allied Expeditionary Force that liberated Europe from Nazi Germany, and he was later appointed by President Harry Truman to command the newly formed North Atlantic Treaty Organization (NATO). Bush served in the Texas Air National Guard in lieu of Vietnam, and he was not widely traveled outside of the United States before becoming president. Eisenhower had lived all over the world, and he knew many of the leaders he would be dealing with from his war and postwar experiences when he assumed his first elective office, the presidency.

Despite these differences in background, Eisenhower and Bush had similar personalities and dispositions. No one thought of either as intellectual giants of their day. Rather, as Stephen Ambrose has said of Eisenhower (but might have easily said of Bush too), "his beliefs were those of Main Street; his personality that of the outgoing, affable American writ large. Almost everyone liked him." Both men saw the world in simple moral terms, as a struggle between good and evil. In both cases, friends and critics worried about how well prepared these men were for the presidency. In Eisenhower's case, the concern was for his inexperience in domestic politics, while in Bush's case, the concern was for inexperience in international affairs.

Bush and Eisenhower had both cultivated an active dislike of the Democratic presidents they were replacing. According to Ambrose, Eisenhower thought that Truman "was guilty of extreme partisanship, poor judgment, inept leadership and management, bad taste, and undignified behavior. Worst of all, in Eisenhower's view Truman had diminished the prestige of the office of the President of the United States."[1] Again, Ambrose might have just as easily been describing Bush's view of Clinton.

This dislike of the previous occupant of the office did not prevent either Eisenhower or Bush from continuing the main foreign policy goals of Truman and Clinton, respectively. Secretary of State Dulles cited the Truman Doctrine as precedent for the Eisenhower Doctrine, essentially declaring it an application of the principle of containment to the Middle East.[2] Eisenhower had approved of all of Truman's major foreign policy decisions, including containment, the Berlin airlift, the involvement in Korea, and the treaty that formed NATO. Bush ran his presidential campaign on a theme of disengagement from world affairs by criticizing Clinton's interventions and attempts at nation building in places such as Haiti and the Balkans. He also advocated scaling back U.S. military commitments around the world, including a reevaluation of NATO's relevance in the post-Cold War era. However, Bush's recently unveiled national security strategy exhibits a surprising degree of continuity from the Clinton administration, including the familiar goals of championing human rights, free markets, free trade, and democracy around the world.[3] Even the goal of maintaining a preponderance of power and the justifications for unilateral preemptive action are notable mainly as changes in rhetoric rather than practice or belief.[4]

FOREIGN POLICIES

This similarity is the result of recurrent themes in U.S. foreign policy rooted in American national identity, such as exceptionalism, moralism, unilateralism, and the swing between isolationism and internationalism that produces a penchant for crusading.[5] These common themes ensure continuity not only from one administration to the next but across longer spans of time. As will be suggested in this chapter, there is a remarkable degree of continuity in U.S. foreign policy between the Eisenhower and Bush administrations, despite the fact that the international environments faced by the two were very different. Eisenhower led one of the competing blocs comprising the bipolar international system. Bush became president of a country unsure if it was the preponderant power in the post-Cold War world, or if its relative power would erode to produce some form of multipolarity. In both cases, the foreign policy doctrines they authored helped construct the international system that they would negotiate through the remainders of their presidencies. The doctrines each formulated to deal with threats to or emanating from the Middle East very much reflected American identity, interests, and power, hence, the remarkable similarity across the years. Given that similarity, the purpose of this chapter is to distill some lessons from the formation and application of the Eisenhower Doctrine that may help us understand the formation and future prospects of the Bush Doctrine.

THE EISENHOWER DOCTRINE

In 1957, Eisenhower was starting his second term as president, having recently weathered the two major foreign policy crises that would help shape his approach to the Middle East—the Soviet invasion of Hungary and the Suez Canal Crisis, both having occurred in 1956. The former reinforced his fear of Soviet intervention to support, maintain, and promote international communism. The latter had a similar effect, and when combined with the rise of Nasserism, and the power vacuum left in the Middle East as a result of the withdrawal of the British and French, Eisenhower and Dulles were prompted to formulate a new strategy for dealing with the region.

The original aim of Eisenhower's foreign policy in the region was to isolate and then reorient Egypt to a pro-Western position, so that Egypt might assist in preventing the spread of Soviet influence throughout the Middle East. The Omega Plan, designed to accomplish these goals through economic, diplomatic, and military cooperation, was derailed after one of its provisions, a delay in funding for the Aswan High Dam, set in motion a chain of events leading to the Suez Crisis.[6] Eisenhower next considered the Baghdad Pact as a possible means of containing the Soviets in the region.[7] Eisenhower thought that the multilateral security organization comprised of the United States and pro-Western states in the region would be the key to containment, yet congressional approval to join the organization appeared unlikely as it was viewed by the U.S. Jewish lobby as an anti-Israeli alliance. It then became clear to Eisenhower that a new policy orientation with the same goal was necessary to visibly aid the states of the region who might be willing to construct an anti-Nasser and anti-Communist coalition of their own. This foreign policy orientation was known as the Eisenhower Doctrine.[8] It was largely a doctrine of Dulles's crafting, as was much of foreign policy until his death in 1959, however, as with every decision emanating from the White House, it reflected Eisenhower's own personal dispositions.

On January 5, 1957, Eisenhower addressed a joint session of Congress to ask for its approval of his foreign policy doctrine for the Middle East. He asked for economic aid programs to strengthen the states of the region, the ability to extend military aid to those states requesting it, and most provocatively, authority to employ "the armed forces of the United States to secure and protect the territorial integrity and political independence of such [Middle Eastern] nations, requesting such aid, against overt armed aggression from any nation controlled by International Communism." As Eisenhower later stated, the resolution he requested from Congress "confers on the President discretion to determine what action should be taken by the United States in any given circumstances."[9] As Crabb noted in his seminal study of U.S. foreign policy doctrines, the ambiguity surrounding the identification of "armed aggression" became the focus of controversy in the new doctrine.[10]

Policy Goals

The two forms of aggression the policy was designed to deal with were external and internal (subversive) aggression. The external dimension gave the president the authority to intervene to prevent interstate aggression, thereby reflecting the desire to prevent "another Hungary" in the Middle East. However, most observers, including Eisenhower, believed that the more likely scenario was subversion from within a country as a result of revolutionary activities, terrorism, propaganda, and military or economic aid.[11] As a result, the Eisenhower Doctrine was interpreted by many, including the House Foreign Affairs Committee, as an assumption of the right for the United States to intervene in the internal affairs of the countries of the region.[12] Further, the criterion used to determine the source of the threat to these countries was acknowledged by Dulles to lack a "precise formula," as judgments would have to be made on a case-by-case basis.[13] The Senate reacted negatively against the perceived "blank check" it was being asked to provide to the president. As Senator Fulbright of Arkansas stated, the president "asks for a blank grant of power over our funds and Armed Forces, to be used in a blank way, for a blank length of time, under blank conditions with respect to blank nations in a blank area.... Who will fill in all these blanks?"[14] Many senators also saw the doctrine as a simple reflection of both Eisenhower's and Dulles's anti-Communist phobia, and as leaving some of the main causes of conflict in the Middle East, such as the Arab-Israeli conflict, unresolved. Others worried that this unilateral policy statement by the United States would undermine both the purpose and prestige of the United Nations.

Despite these reservations, both houses passed the Middle East Resolution (as it was known) in March 1957, providing a legislative seal of approval on the executive branch's foreign policy doctrine. Reception of the doctrine was lukewarm in Europe, as the sting of the Suez Crisis was still fresh in Britain and France. Several pro-Western governments in the Middle East expressed some initial support for the doctrine, including Iraq, Iran, Lebanon, Pakistan, and Turkey, as they expected to be the beneficiaries of the military and economic aid it promised. Public opinion in the region—the "Arab Street," as it is now called—was overwhelmingly opposed to the doctrine, since it seemed to promise renewed Western hegemony in the region, with the United States replacing Britain as the main imperial power.

Implementing the Doctrine

Regardless of world opinion, the Eisenhower Doctrine was applied, or considered, in three instances: Jordan, Syria, and Lebanon. In the spring of 1957, King Hussein of Jordan faced internal unrest among the large population of displaced Palestinians in the country who were opposed to his monarchy. This internal dissent had strong support from the leaders of Egypt and Syria, who viewed Hussein as being far too moderate on the existence of Israel. Eisenhower concluded that this internal aggression was a result of the forces of international communism, and he ordered the U.S. Sixth Fleet to the region to restore order. The crisis subsided quickly, and Jordan received $10 million in economic aid, which King Hussein would later deny was a result of the Eisenhower Doctrine. Jordan was thereafter viewed by the states of the region as a U.S. client, with all of the negative implications that relationship brought for its inter-Arab relations.

By the middle of 1957, Syria was facing another in a series of its own internal political crises. After several U.S. officials were expelled from the country, Eisenhower became concerned about the growing influence of Marxist groups in Syria and the government's increasing dependence upon the Soviet

Union for economic and military aid. Judging a communist takeover to be imminent, Eisenhower and Dulles considered invoking the doctrine but ultimately decided against it as it appeared that preemptive U.S. military intervention might ignite conflict across the region and bring the Soviets into direct confrontation with U.S. supporters such as Turkey. The discussion about intervention ended in February 1958, when Egypt and Syria merged to form the United Arab Republic (UAR). Eisenhower actually misinterpreted the formation of the UAR as an attempt to expand Nasserism in the region, which he equated with communism, when the real impetus for the union came from the anti-Communist Syrian Ba'ath Party. It appears that only the constraints imposed by bipolarity prevented U.S. intervention in Syria given Eisenhower's clear sense that international communism was behind the UAR. The unwillingness to apply the doctrine in the Syrian case led some critics to challenge the consistency of Eisenhower's policy in the Middle East. This foreign policy crisis served mainly to inflame Arab public opinion against the United States.

The most serious test of the Eisenhower Doctrine began in April 1958, when Lebanon's pro-Western President Chamoun announced that he would be a candidate for reelection, something that most observers believed violated the country's constitution. Chamoun's announcement was followed by uprisings throughout Lebanon, which he claimed were fostered by Egypt and Syria. Chamoun asked the United States to invoke the Eisenhower Doctrine, which initially was received favorably, as the claim of Syrian and Egyptian involvement conjured up the specter of international communism for Eisenhower. The situation worsened with the revolution in Iraq that occurred on July 14, which toppled the pro-Western monarchy (many say as a result of its initial support for the Eisenhower Doctrine). After consultation with friendly states in the region, and congressional leaders at home, Eisenhower ordered marines from the U.S. Sixth Fleet to land in Lebanon on July 15. The U.S. occupation was unopposed, yet it further fanned the flames of pro-Nasserism and anti-American imperialism in the region. Order was restored in Lebanon, President Chamoun was persuaded not to seek reelection, and the country resumed its official constitutional stance of neutrality in foreign affairs, thus removing it from being under the auspices of the Eisenhower Doctrine. Once U.S. forces left Lebanon, the Eisenhower Doctrine was effectively defunct as policy for the Middle East.

In hindsight, it appears that there were several major problems plaguing the Eisenhower Doctrine that ultimately led to its short life span. First, the doctrine was perceived as being excessively vague, both in terms of criteria for identifying "armed aggression" as well as the source of the threat. Second, it was applied in an inconsistent manner, with economic aid and troops arriving in Jordan and Lebanon, respectively, but no intervention in Syria, despite the fact that of the three cases, Syria probably represented the country facing the greatest threat from international communism. The dictates of bipolarity seemed to override concerns about consistent application in this case. Third, both at home and abroad, the doctrine was seen as a unilateral policy stance that was incompatible with international law. Many observers felt that the United Nations and the Arab League should deal with security issues in the region. Preemptive intervention by the United States was also seen as hypocritical in the aftermath of the Suez Crisis, something that did figure in Eisenhower's decision not to intervene in Syria. Finally, the doctrine was not well received in terms of official or public opinion around the world, including the very states it was supposed to protect. The states of the Middle East did not fear international communism like Eisenhower did; in fact, their concerns were more with the competing visions of Nasserism and nationalism. If we move forward in time almost half a century, we find President George W. Bush attempting to develop a foreign policy doctrine in response to another ideology plaguing the same region that has been criticized on exactly the same grounds as the Eisenhower Doctrine.

THE BUSH DOCTRINE

Bush had been president for less than a year when he faced his first major crisis in the attacks on the World Trade Center and the Pentagon. These events helped his administration to develop a foreign policy orientation that had seemingly lacked vision prior to September 11, 2001. In a series of remarks and speeches that ultimately crystallized in *The National Security Strategy of the United States*, Bush and his advisors formulated the Bush Doctrine. Although there has been considerable speculation as to the decision-making process that produced the doctrine, recent evidence indicates that Bush is in command of foreign policy.[15] It is clear, however, that the hawks in his administration, led by Secretary of Defense Donald Rumsfeld and Vice President Dick Cheney, in combination with National Security Advisor Condoleezza Rice, provide advice that is more consistent with the underlying disposition of the president.[16]

Just hours after the attacks, Bush appeared at Barksdale Air Force Base in Louisiana to assure the American people that "the United States will hunt down and punish those responsible for these cowardly acts." It was clear from this statement that he intended to use force to strike at those who had murdered so many, but given that the actual perpetrators were dead, it remained to be determined exactly who the United States would hunt down. On September 13, Bush stated that "justice demands that those who helped or harbored the terrorists be punished—and punished severely. The enormity of their evil demands it." Thus the terrorists responsible for September 11 as well as the regimes that harbored them would be held accountable.

In his radio address on September 15, Bush stated that we were preparing for "a different kind of conflict against a different kind of enemy," one that would involve a "comprehensive assault on terrorism . . . without battlefields or beachheads." The previously specific response to the attacks broadened considerably, and by September 17 he remarked to employees at the Pentagon that "our mission is not just Osama bin Laden, the Al Qaeda organization. Our mission is to battle terrorism and to join with freedom-loving people."

Policy Goals

On September 20, before a joint session of Congress, Bush summarized the evolution of his reasoning over the last nine days by identifying Al Qaeda as the perpetrator of the attacks and laying out a course of action that would involve eliminating that terrorist organization throughout the world. Further, the governing Taliban in Afghanistan was ordered to cooperate fully in the search for the perpetrators and the elimination of their training camps, or risk removal from power. And finally, he stated: "Our war on terror begins with Al Qaeda, but it does not end there. It will not end until every terrorist group of global reach has been found, stopped, and defeated." The qualifier "of global reach" had the effect of narrowing the list of groups that the United States would attempt to eliminate, perhaps representing a sober second thought concerning the more open-ended commitment to battle all forms of terrorism, including terrorism of a primarily domestic nature.

At the State of the Union address in January, the targets of the Bush Doctrine changed once again:

> Our nation will continue to be steadfast and patient and persistent in the pursuit of two great objectives. First, we will shut down terrorist camps, disrupt terrorist plans, and bring terrorists to justice. And, second, we must prevent the terrorists and regimes who seek chemical, biological, or nuclear weapons from threatening the United States and the world. . . . States like these [Iran, Iraq, and North Korea], and their terrorist allies, constitute an axis of evil, arming to threaten the peace of the world.

This statement broadened the targets of U.S. action to include not only international terrorist organizations and the governments who harbor them but governments who seek weapons of mass destruction (WMD), seemingly regardless of their connection to Al Qaeda or the specific events of September 11, 2001.

The means by which Bush intended to pursue these regimes developed in three speeches given at military universities: the Citadel, the Virginia Military Institute, and most notably at West Point in June 2002. At West Point, Bush said that the "Cold War doctrines of deterrence and containment" were outmoded, and in the future "we must take the battle to the enemy, disrupt his plans, and confront the worst threats before they emerge." Bush made it clear that in the "war on terror" the United States would engage in the preemptive, unilateral use of force if necessary. This was justified in Bush's mind by his previous classification of the world into states that are with us or against us: "Every nation, in every region, now has a decision to make. Either you are with us or you are with the terrorists." In this "conflict between good and evil," Bush likened the struggle against terror to the Cold War, when "moral clarity was essential to our victory."[17]

Implementing the Doctrine

The Bush Doctrine has come under considerable attack as it has evolved and been applied in specific instances, much like the Eisenhower Doctrine before it. Criticism has come from both the Left and the Right on the domestic political spectrum, as well as from both liberal and realist scholars of international relations and foreign policy. While criticisms from the Left and liberal scholars of foreign policy might be anticipated, perhaps the most telling critique of the Bush Doctrine comes from realist scholars.[18] As with Eisenhower's "armed aggression," many questioned the lack of specificity about the targets of the doctrine, or, more specifically, how regimes who purportedly seek WMD are connected to the War on Terror broadly, or the events of September 11 and Al Qaeda specifically. While most realists supported the specific response to the attacks that involved the pursuit of Al Qaeda and the Taliban regime that supported them in Afghanistan, few agreed with expanding the military response to a general war on terror. Realists such as George Kennan, Barry Posen, Stephen Van Evera, Stephen Walt, and Kenneth Waltz all favor a limited military campaign to finish the hunt for Al Qaeda in Afghanistan. None recommended extending the military campaign to a war with Iraq, which began on March 21, 2003, with a decapitation strike against a location where Saddam Hussein was suspected of staying. Despite a relatively quick battlefield victory over Hussein's armed forces, little evidence has surfaced to substantiate claims of Iraqi possession of WMD or strong ties to Al Qaeda. While continuing to claim that the application of the Bush Doctrine was justified in Iraq, and that evidence would ultimately be uncovered to back this up, the administration has largely emphasized the liberation of the Iraqi people from their dictator as a worthwhile end in itself.

Eisenhower's restraint in intervening in Syria due to the pressures of bipolarity left him open to the charge of inconsistency in the application of his doctrine. Conversely, Bush's lack of constraint in the post-Cold War world has left him open to the same charge. The U.S. base of operations prior to the war in Afghanistan was Pakistan, a nondemocratic state that is probably home to many Al Qaeda who fled Afghanistan once the war had begun. Al Qaeda and Islamic fundamentalist movements are strong in Pakistan, which has nuclear weapons and continues research on chemical and biological weapons, yet Pakistan is not a target of the Bush Doctrine. Saudi Arabia produced the majority of the terrorists who were on the planes that were used to attack the United States, yet it is not a target of the Bush Doctrine. Many critics of the Bush administration's inattention to the Middle East peace process and the particularly brutal tactics of Prime Minister Sharon have argued that Israel, which has all forms of WMD and repeatedly ignores UN resolutions, should be on the list of targets too.[19]

The list of possible targets that qualify for intervention under the Bush Doctrine is indeed long, but given the unrivaled position of the preponderant power of the United States, President Bush has great freedom in his choices. Near the end of the battlefield operations in Iraq, Bush administration officials began to openly warn Syria that its covert assistance to Hussein's regime during the war and its own possession of WMD could bring potential diplomatic, economic, and other unspecified types of sanctions. The administration has also publicized claims that Iran's civilian nuclear program may be contributing to the development of nuclear weapons. While this may be part of a strategy to put neighboring states that the United States dislikes on edge while it has such a large military presence in the region, it also raises the question of why Iraq, and why not Syria or Iran? Why not North Korea for that matter, which also appears to actually possess nuclear weapons and intercontinental ballistic missile capability?

Eisenhower was also criticized for his unilateralism and disregard for existing international law and international organizations when considering preemptive intervention in the Middle East. While realists believe that multilateralism can be a useful tool in the pursuit of U.S. national interest, liberals argue that the United States should lead by example to pursue the War on Terror through international organizations in order to demonstrate that states need not act unilaterally to guarantee their security.[20] The action in Afghanistan was plausibly interpreted as self-defense and raised no objection in the UN. The collective defense clauses of NATO, the Australia-New Zealand-United States alliance (ANZUS), and the Organization of American States (OAS) were even invoked in response to the September 11 attacks. Bush put together an impressive coalition of states for the action in Afghanistan and the initial stages of the War on Terror. However, as he expanded the range of possible targets, as well as the means he intended to use to pursue them, multilateral support started to weaken.

Bush had to be pressured to seek UN approval for his actions with regard to Iraq, largely due to domestic rather than international political considerations. On November 13, 2002, Iraq complied with the UN resolution requiring the placement of weapons inspectors back in the country for the first time since 1998. However, Bush was not satisfied with their activities, and he argued that

Hussein was still hiding weapons that would never be found by the UN teams. Bush then began to push for a second UN resolution that would authorize the use of force if Hussein failed to declare WMD. This round of "diplomacy" served to widen the differences between France, Russia, China, and the United States and United Kingdom (UK). Secretary of Defense Rumsfeld dismissed Germany and France as part of the "old Europe," due to their vocal opposition to U.S. Iraqi policy. After a last-minute summit on the weekend of March 15, 2003, between the United States, United Kingdom, and Spain in the Azores, the United States withdrew its request for a second resolution. By March 17, Secretary of State Powell declared that the time for diplomacy had passed. The UN weapons inspected were ordered out of Iraq by Secretary General Annan that same day, and that evening Bush gave Saddam Hussein an ultimatum to leave Iraq within forty eight hours or the United States would commence military hostilities, which it did without UN authorization.

Much has also been made of the shift from a defensive strategy based on containment and deterrence to a more offensive strategy based on preemption. While the UN charter, and the bulk of international law, sides with the use of force only in self-defense, the United States has long considered preemptive intervention a necessary tool of statecraft. Eisenhower's application of his doctrine in Lebanon, while rhetorically supporting the containment of the Soviet Union, is plausibly interpreted as a preemptive use of force designed to thwart Egyptian and Syrian plans to control the state on behalf of international communism. What is different in the present situation is Bush's rhetoric. The language of the Bush Doctrine is much more aggressively unilateralist and overtly committed to preemptive action. The war in Iraq should serve as a demonstration that Bush will back up that aggressive rhetoric with force. On the other hand, the North Korean situation is a case where aggressive rhetoric has not yet taken U.S. policy beyond containment.

This antagonistic quality of Bush's words and deeds has no doubt contributed to the poor reception of the doctrine around the world. Although the initial reaction to the Eisenhower Doctrine was mildly supportive in Europe and in some states in the Middle East that sought the economic and military benefits it promised, the reaction to the Bush Doctrine has been overwhelmingly negative. The only staunch supporter of the doctrine has been Prime Minister Blair of the United Kingdom. The official reaction in the Middle East has been much the same as during the Eisenhower crusade, except there are fewer pro-Western regimes in the region now. The "Arab Street" also seems opposed to U.S. unilateral intervention in the region. While many Iraqis seem genuinely glad that Hussein has been toppled, they also are eager to have U.S. forces leave quickly. The imposition of an acceptable postwar Iraqi government still smacks of colonialism to the Iraqis and the other states of the region. Recent anti-American protests in Iraq have also resulted in civilian bloodshed. No matter who was ultimately responsible for starting the gunfire in those incidents, they simply do not assist in winning the hearts and minds of the Iraqi people.

CONCLUSION: THE LESSONS OF HISTORY

Eisenhower formulated his foreign policy for the Middle East based on a fear of the spread of international communism. Bush's policy for the Middle East is based on a fear of the spread of international terrorism. In both cases, doctrines were formulated to counter these ideologies, but as Kennan has critically said of doctrines, "they purport to define one's behavior in future situations where it may or may not be suitable."[21] Perhaps presidential doctrines are necessarily vague, designed primarily to evince a sense of preparedness and resolve in the face of crisis. This ambiguity reinforces a sense of inconsistent application of these doctrines as well. Bush says as much in his National Security Strategy. "No doctrine can anticipate every circumstance in which U.S. action—direct or indirect—is warranted."[22] Whether a doctrine is a formal statement approved by Congress, as in Eisenhower's case, or whether it emerges over time through a series of remarks and speeches, as in Bush's, most presidents actually prefer maximum flexibility in their action. Ambiguity guarantees that flexibility, and inconsistency in application is a criticism that most are willing to live with.

Unilateralism and the preemptive use of force are not unusual strategies for the president of the United States, and the rest of the world will never appreciate a country of overwhelming power that intends to pursue these approaches.[23] Most every U.S. presidential doctrine has reserved the right to act unilaterally and preemptively if necessary. The strategy of containing the spread of communism outlined in the Truman Doctrine was made possible through unilateral and often preemptive intervention. This policy stance was reinforced by applications of the Truman Doctrine through the Eisenhower Doctrine for the Middle East, the First Johnson Doctrine for Southeast Asia, the Second Johnson Doctrine for Latin America, the Carter Doctrine for the Middle East, and, in an aggressively global way, by the Reagan Doctrine. Containment and preemption were not mutually exclusive strategies, especially in terms of U.S. policy in the oil-rich Middle East. The post-cold war presidential doctrines of George H. W. Bush and William Jefferson Clinton were also applied in unilateral ways, despite their seeming endorsement of multilateral action. In most ways, the Bush Doctrine differs little from its predecessors due to the American way of crafting foreign policy as a projection of its own national identity, interests, and power.

Initially, it appeared that the main difference with previous doctrines would be that the Bush Doctrine targeted nonstate actors—international terrorist organizations—however, that was quickly changed to include regimes supporting terrorism or pursuing WMD. This shift effectively brought the threat of terrorism back within the familiar realm of sovereign, territorial state interaction. What *is* different with the Bush Doctrine is the lack of any counterweight to the preponderance of power held by the United States at this moment in history. Previous presidents have always operated within a balance of power system, either multipolar, or bipolar, as in Eisenhower's case, or under some uncertainty about the distribution of power, as in the George H. W. Bush and Clinton cases, which constrained the application of their foreign policy doctrines. Despite Bush's aggressive rhetoric, a balance has yet to form against the United States, although the push for the second UN resolution prior to Operation Iraqi Freedom seemed to move Russia and China closer together with continental Europe. The major constraint on the application of the Bush Doctrine in the near future is likely to be domestic public opinion. After the Republican victories in the midterm elections, it seems unlikely that Bush will feel any check on his activities until the race for the next presidential election heats up. Even so, only one Democratic presidential candidate, Howard Dean, has opposed the war in Iraq and the type of unilateral, preemptive action that President Bush favors in his doctrine.

If Bush is unconstrained at home and abroad, then what does the future of the Bush Doctrine look like? Afghanistan has long been declared a victory, yet questions remain about the security of the country outside of Kabul, and the whereabouts of Osama bin Laden and other key Al Qaeda officials. Iraq has been declared a battlefield victory since President Bush's elaborately staged speech to the nation on May 1, 2003, from the aircraft carrier U.S.S. *Lincoln* on its way home from the Persian Gulf. However, Iraq could be Bush's Lebanon. Bush's intervention in Afghanistan, like Eisenhower's in Jordan, garnered little controversy. However, neither improved their respective doctrine's reception in the Middle East. Eisenhower passed over intervening in Syria, which met the conditions for application of the doctrine. Bush certainly has a range of choices available for intervention, even if one limits the application of the doctrine to states that harbor Al Qaeda—Pakistan comes to mind. Eisenhower's decision to send troops to Lebanon, a stretch in terms of preventing international communism, effectively ended his doctrine's usefulness in the region.

Bush may encounter the same problem due to the circumstances of Operation Iraqi Freedom. Bush unilaterally intervened in Iraq over strong international opposition, and over substantial domestic opposition, which may emerge again after the rally around the flag effect diminishes. The U.S. troops may be bogged down in Iraq for quite some time trying to ensure public order, defend the new government, and train a new military for the government to secure its borders with potentially meddlesome neighbors such as Iran. The occupation may also continue to produce civilian casualties; U.S. forces may never know Saddam Hussein's fate, and they may be unable to uncover evidence of WMD. Domestic and international opinion may then prevent the Bush Doctrine from being enacted elsewhere in such a scenario. Bush's doctrine, much like Eisenhower's, has the quality of a "blank check" commitment of U.S. blood and treasure. If the comparison to the Eisenhower Doctrine holds true, a short life span for the Bush Doctrine may be a likely outcome.

If the comparison does not hold, then we may witness more unilateral interventions by the United States, designed to topple regimes that support terrorists or have WMD. The consequences of such activities could lead to the perception of the United States as an aggressive hegemon set on remaking the world in its image, or, even worse, colonizing it. This could prompt balancing against the United States as realists would expect, or the United States may end up in a situation of imperial overstretch, whereby the commitment of resources abroad saps the political and economic health of the country at home. Either scenario may have the effect of leaving the United States more vulnerable to future terrorist attacks. If the states of the Middle East view continued U.S. unilateral intervention as anti-Islamic, for example, if Syria or Iran were targeted, then the United States may find itself facing the worst of the threats that the Bush Doctrine was supposed to counter—states that both have WMD and support international terrorism. In this ironic, but not implausible, outcome, the aggressive rhetoric and behavior of the Bush Doctrine would simply prompt more aggression and result in a spiral of conflict.

NOTES

1. Stephen E. Ambrose, *Eisenhower: The President*, vol. 2 (New York: Simon & Schuster, 1984), 13.

2. See Dulles's testimony in U.S. Congress, House, Committee on Foreign Affairs, *Hearings on Economic and Military Cooperation with Nations in the General Area of the Middle East*, 85th Cong., 1st sess. (January 7–22, 1957), 1–6, 149, and in the Senate, Committees on Foreign Relations and Armed Services, *Hearings on the President's Proposal on the Middle East*, 85th Cong., 1st sess. (January 14–February 4, 1957), 6, 75–76, 133–34.

3. George W. Bush, *The National Security Strategy of the United States of America* see white House at www.whitehouse.gov/response/index.html (Washington, D.C.: 2002). Also see Fareed Zakaria, "Our Way: The Trouble with Being the World's Only Superpower," *The New Yorker*, October 14, 2002, for an argument that Bush's rhetoric, like that of most every U.S. president since World War II, espouses Wilsonian idealism.

4. See Richard K. Betts, "The First-Year Foreign Policy of Bush the Younger," *The Forum*, 1, no. 1 (2002): Gary Schmitt, "A Case of Continuity," *The National Interest* 69 (Fall 2002): 11–13.

5. For an overview of these themes, see Steven W. Hook and John Spanier, *American Foreign Policy Since World War II*, 15th ed. (Washington, D.C.: CQ Press, 2000); Henry R. Nau, *At Home Abroad: Identity and Power in American Foreign Policy* (Ithaca: Cornell University Press, 2002).

6. Ray Takeyh, *The Origins of the Eisenhower Doctrine: The U.S., Britain, and Nasser's Egypt, 1953–57* (New York: St. Martin's Press, 2000), 105–23.

7. The Baghdad Pact included Turkey, Iraq, the United Kingdom, the United States, Pakistan, and Iran and was viewed as the "northern tier" defense zone against communist penetration by Washington.

8. The following description of the Eisenhower Doctrine relies heavily on Cecil V. Crabb Jr., *The Doctrines of American Foreign Policy: Their Meaning, Role, and Future* (Baton Rouge: Louisiana State University Press, 1982); Ambrose, *Eisenhower: The President*; Takeyh, *The Origins of the Eisenhower Doctrine.*

9. Eisenhower, statement made on August 5, 1957, in Department of State, *American Foreign Policy: Current Documents, 1957* (Washington, D.C.: GPO, 1961), 863.

10. Crabb, *The Doctrines of American Foreign Policy*, 156.

11. Dwight D. Eisenhower, *Waging Peace, 1956–1961* (Garden City: Doubleday, 1965), 178.

12. House Report No. 2, 85th Congress, January 25, 1957, in Department of State, *American Foreign Policy: Current Documents* 1957 (Washington, D.C.: GPO, Government Printing Office 1957), 813.

13. Senate, *Hearings on the President's Proposal,* 29.

14. See J. William Fulbright's speech of January 24, 1957, in the *Congressional Record*, 85th Cong., 1st sess., Pt. 2, 1855–57.

15. Bob Woodward, *Bush at War* (New York: Simon & Schuster, 2002).

16. See Nicholas Lemann, "The Next World Order," *The New Yorker,* April 1, 2002, 42–48; Nicholas Lehmann, "The War on What? The White House and the Debate about Whom to Fight Next," *The New Yorker,* September 16, 2002, 36–44.

17. The Bush Doctrine appears in its most complete form to date in *The National Security Strategy of the United States of America*, which declares that "our immediate focus will be those terrorist organizations of global reach and any terrorist or state sponsor of terrorism which attempts to gain or use weapons of mass destruction (WMD) or their precursors." Further, "The United States has long maintained the option of preemptive actions to counter a sufficient threat to our national security. The greater the threat, the greater is the risk of inaction—and the more compelling the case for taking anticipatory action to defend ourselves, even if uncertainty remains as to the time and place of the enemy's attack. To forestall or prevent such hostile acts by our adversaries, the United States will, if necessary, act preemptively."

18. See Lehmann, "The War on What?" John Mearsheimer and Stephen Walt authored an ad opposing the war with Iraq placed in the September 26, 2002, issue of the *New York Times* that was signed by thirty three prominent international relations scholars, most of whom are realists. For some of the controversy that this ad generated, see Robert J. Lieber, "Foreign Policy 'Realists' Are Unrealistic on Iraq," *The Chronicle of Higher Education,* October 18, 2002, B15-16, and the response from John J. Mearsheimer and Stephen M. Walt, " 'Realists' Are Not Alone in Opposing War with Iraq," *The Chronicle of Higher Education,* November 15, 2002, B19.

19.   See "Double Standards," *The Economist* October 12, 2002, 22–24.

20.   On realism and multilateralism, see Kori Schake and Klaus Becher, "How America Should Lead," *Policy Review* 114 (August–September 2002): For a discussion of an alternative doctrine along these lines that might have come from within the administration—Richard Haas's doctrine of integration—see Lehmann, "The War on What?". On the liberal argument on behalf of multilateralism, see Richard Falk, "The New Bush Doctrine," *The Nation,* July 15, 2002.

21.   Jane Mayer, "A Doctrine Passes," *The New Yorker,* October 14 and 21, 2002, 70.

22.   See *The National Security Strategy of the United States of America,* 9.

23.   See the infamous article by Robert Kagan for an argument that the United States and Europe disagree on most issues and approaches to international politics primarily due to their differences in power. Robert Kagan, "Power and Weakness," *Policy Review* 113 (June–July 2002): See www.policyreview.org/jun02/kagan.html 3–28.

Chapter 9

A United Front?

The Bush Administration, Coalition Diplomacy, and the Military Campaign in Afghanistan

Tom Lansford

INTRODUCTION

During Operation Enduring Freedom, the military campaign in Afghanistan, the United States sought a global coalition of potential military partners and engaged in an intensive diplomatic effort to develop a broad-based and multi-lateral alliance. The strategy of the administration of George W. Bush echoed the actions of the first Bush administration during the Persian Gulf War. By the start of the military campaign, the United States had broad international support and pledges of specific military aid and assets from dozens of nations. However, during the military operations, the administration deliberately chose to utilize only a small portion of the proffered assistance, and the bulk of the combat missions was undertaken by U.S. military resources. While the buildup to hostilities paralleled the Gulf War, the actual onset of operations revealed that the Bush administration was determined to retain unilateral control over missions and avoid a number of perceived or potential coalition problems encountered by U.S. forces during the variety of actions during the 1990s, including the Gulf War and the various operations in the former Yugoslavia.

COALITIONS AND COALITION WARFARE

Coalitions and alliances are the most common and the oldest forms of security arrangements in international relations. These formations may be defined as "a formal or informal arrangement for security cooperation between two or more sovereign states."[1] An alliance involves a more formal and long-term structure, while coalitions are often ad hoc and temporary responses to specific threats.[2] Coalitions also commonly have less formal or defined command structures and less rigid objectives.[3] The North Atlantic Treaty Organization NATO is an alliance, while the group of nations brought together during the Persian Gulf War was a coalition. Both alliances and coalitions are formed in response to an external security threat. The total resources and capabilities of the potential enemy faced by the coalition is called the "threat quotient."[4] The cohesiveness and endurance of a coalition are often directly proportional to the threat quotient faced by the collection of states. In other words, the stronger the adversary, the more likely the coalition will act with unity of purpose and resolve. Coalitions that confront weak opponents often face internal rivalries for primacy or a diminution of commitment.[5]

As coalitions form, national governments strive to maximize their security by joining the side they perceive will provide the greatest benefits. Hence, coalitions may be the result of states endeavoring to "*balance* (ally in opposition to the principal source of danger) or *bandwagon* (ally with the state that poses the major threat)."[6] Balancing usually means allying with the weaker side in order to overcome a perceived threat to the regional or international order, while bandwagoning entails joining or supporting the more powerful side to preserve that order.[7] For example, small- and medium-sized powers often form coalitions, or balance, to prevent a major state from gaining regional or global hegemony or primacy.[8] Concurrently, if states perceive that the status quo is beneficial, then they may bandwagon with primary or hegemonic actors in order to increase or ensure relative gains.[9]

The potential for bandwagoning with the more powerful state is increased by a variety of factors. For instance, ideology may prompt states to ally with those coalitions that promote similar political or cultural values, even if it means accepting the primacy of a larger power.[10] John Ikenberry and Charles Kupchan contend that "rightful rule emerges if the hegemon is able to induce smaller powers to buy into its vision of international order and to accept as their own—in short, to internalize and embrace—the principles and norms espoused by the hegemon."[11] In addition, even states concerned about the potential hegemony of rival actors will not balance on the side of weak threats—those that are clearly unable to overturn the status quo of the international system. As David Lake notes, the key to the success of such a security system dominated by one state is the ability of the superpower to "build loyalty and compliance by credibly committing not to exploit their subordinates."[12]

States may also perceive that a superpower is a benign or beneficial hegemon or primary actor. As such, a powerful state may act to preserve an international system that is beneficial to its coalition partners. Such a system may be "deliberately established by dominant actors who succeed in getting others to conform to the requirements of these orders through some combination of coercion, co-option, and the manipulation of incentives."[13] Such a superpower serves to set and enforce the rules of the international system.[14] Coalitions likewise serve the interests of these great powers through burden sharing and institutionalizing cooperation.[15]

In the United States, John Gerard Ruggie contends that the proliferation of multinational institutions such as the UN or NATO or the EU in the post-World War II era was the result of American preferences for "world order."[16] Over time, the habits of cooperation and collaboration in security matters would become institutionalized on both sides of the Atlantic, creating an environment conducive for the continuation of formal and informal security interaction, even in the absence of a major threat along the lines of the Soviet Union.[17] As such, transatlantic security cooperation has become a security policy in and of itself instead of simply a mechanism to achieve broader policy objectives.[18]

American Preferences and Coalitions

One enduring feature of U.S. security policy in the post-World War II era has been a marked preference for the use of alliances and coalitions during military operations. Historian John Lewis Gaddis concludes that the Eisenhower administration realized that U.S. power alone might not be sufficient to counter the Soviets; instead, "the U.S. would also need the manpower reserves and economic resources of the major industrialized non-communist states."[19] Specific examples of U.S.-led coalition warfare included a range of operations from the cold war era through the Persian Gulf War and the Balkan missions of the post-cold war era.[20]

Coalition Lessons

Often the military coalitions deployed by successive U.S. administrations were "coalitions of the willing." In other words, instead of utilizing the full range of assets and resources of formal alliances, the United States would develop an informal coalition of those nations willing to bandwagon on a particular issue. This minimized potential leadership or mission problems and increased the effectiveness of the coalitions, although not all problems were eliminated.[21] The Persian Gulf War is usually cited as one of the foremost examples of the utility of a broad military coalition.[22] During the conflict, the United States employed an informal coalition of the willing. The first Bush administration did not seek military assets and resources from each of its alliance partners and allies. Instead, it relied upon those states that had the capabilities that Washington found useful. At the core of the coalition were states that contributed military resources and assets. These states participated at two levels. The "inner core" consisted of states that contributed significant resources and whose withdrawal from the coalition would have substantially raised both the physical and fiscal costs of the campaign. The "outer core" consisted of states that contributed token forces or whose contributions created problems in planning or operations. Included in this category were states such as Syria or other "fire alarm" states that consistently threatened to withdraw from the coalition if actions were deemed to violate the consensus around which the coalition was based.[23] The outer band of the coalition included states that did not contribute military assets but offered financial or diplomatic support. In spite of the varying levels of support, the U.S.-led effort was still the "largest and most capable international military coalition in a generation."[24]

During the Gulf operations, a number of problems emerged that highlighted the problems inherent in coalition warfare. There was resistance to a unified command and control structure. Nations such as France and Italy sought separate roles for the European forces to enhance their status and expand the autonomy of European security structures. One British officer noted that "political games were going on which had less to do with efficient execution of the blockade and rather more to do with eroding American domination of NATO and the newly formed Coalition."[25]

The later experiences in Bosnia and Kosovo reinforced these problems. For instance, U.S. military planners encountered problems trying to achieve consensus on target identification and missions planning.[26] In addition, U.S. officials perceived that the Europeans exerted an unreasonable degree of political interference in the day-to-day operations.[27] In an executive summary of a National Defense University symposium, one of the conclusions was that "National (parochial) decisions constrained Allied Operations," and that "the constraints imposed on the planning process were the inhibitions of those nations doing the planning."[28] Most significantly, the operations in the Balkans revealed a significant gap between U.S. and allied military capabilities, especially in regard to precision-guided munitions.[29] A Defense Science Board report pointed out: "U.S. and allied military commanders and other officials have expressed concern that with the USA's unmatched ability to invest in next-generation military technologies, it runs the risk of outpacing NATO and other allies to the point where they are incapable of operating effectively with U.S. forces on future battlefields."[30]

THE COALITION AGAINST INTERNATIONAL TERRORISM

Following the September 11, 2001, attacks, the Bush administration embarked upon a broad diplomatic initiative to develop a coalition that paralleled the U.S.-led formation of the Gulf War. The administration also indicated its preference for a coalition of the willing that would allow states to contribute those assets and resources that were politically feasible for a military campaign in

Afghanistan. For instance, Deputy Secretary of State Richard Armitage told the European nations that "in this coalition building there is a continuum from, on the one hand, rhetorical or political support for activities . . . and at the far end of the continuum is the possibility of some military activity either together or unilaterally."[31]

The ultimate goal of the administration was to achieve the proverbial best of both worlds. The administration sought to "pick and choose among its allies, fashioning the moral authority of an international coalition without having to deal with the problems of the whole alliance."[32] At the core of the administration's strategy were three factors. First, both Secretary of State Powell and Secretary of Defense Donald Rumsfeld joined with National Security Advisor Condoleezza Rice in advocating a policy whereby the majority of combat operations were undertaken by U.S. forces. This would ensure Pentagon control of military missions and avoid the problems in command and control experienced during the Persian Gulf War and the Balkan operations. Second, there was a strategic imperative as well, since only the United States had an extensive arsenal of precision-guided munitions and quantities of the various unique warfighting capabilities that the campaign in Afghanistan would require. Hence, while a variety of nations would deploy small contingents of special operations forces, the major ground operations would be undertaken by U.S. conventional and special operations assets. Third, and finally, there was the recognition that many states could provide more nonmilitary assistance than combat aid. The administration did not want to "push" too strenuously for military aid at the expense of cooperation on intelligence and criminal justice issues, including efforts to freeze financial assets and close money trails. In the end, the Bush administration pursued policies designed to produce a global counterterrorism coalition that "would assign different tasks to different countries, with many of the players involved in intelligence-gathering, police work, and bushwacking on money trails—but perhaps few actually joining in the military phase."[33]

A Coalition of the Willing

The nature of the terrorist attacks and the subsequent diplomatic offensive undertaken by Bush combined to produce various levels of support for the United States very quickly. States from around the world signaled their intention to bandwagon with the United States against the real and potential threats posed by Al Qaeda and their Taliban hosts. In the month between the attacks and the onset of the U.S.-led military campaign, all of the world's major international and regional organizations and a wide range of individual states pledged various levels of support for the United States. Nations tended to join the U.S. coalition for three broad, and essentially interrelated, reasons. First, a number of states faced threats from Islamic extremist groups, many of which had ties to Al Qaeda, including the Abu Sayeef group in the Philippines and a variety of Al Qaeda splinter cells throughout Western Europe. Second, states such as Pakistan perceived the potential to reap dramatic security benefits from bandwagoning with the United States. For instance, following the September 11 attacks, Bush issued Presidential Determination 2001-28, which ended arms sanctions on Pakistan and India "in the interest of the national security of the U.S."[34] In Pakistan, military aid was supplemented by a $1 billion aid package, including economic assistance and debt relief (making Pakistan the second-largest recipient of foreign aid after Israel).[35] Third, the administration signaled its desire to accept a variety of nonmilitary aid, especially in the realm of law enforcement, intelligence cooperation, and financial oversight. Specifically, the administration called upon nations to freeze the assets of suspected terrorist groups and increased the number of organizations on the official terrorism lists. Rice summarized the nonmilitary components of the campaign in the following manner: "This is a broad coalition in which people are contributing on very different and very many fronts. The key to the broad coalition is to remember that, while everybody understandably wants to focus on military contributions, this is not the Gulf War."[36] In fact, the administration went to great lengths to get the message out about the nonmilitary aspects of the coalition. Besides Rice, a number of other administration officials made the case for the broad-based nature of the coalition. Deputy Defense Secretary Paul Wolfowitz characterized the campaign as a combination of coalition efforts along a variety of fronts.[37]

From the perspective of core allies, there were two major concerns about the coalition that the administration was endeavoring to build: first, that the United States would not limit its response to Afghanistan and Al Qaeda, but that it would use the opportunity to expand the War on Terror and take action against states such as Iraq and Iran; second, that military aid and assistance to the United States would leave the Western allies unable to continue other security missions, such as those in Bosnia and Kosovo.[38] Then French foreign minister Hubert Vedrine insisted that NATO's invocation of Article 5 did not "abolish the freedom of action of each ally."[39] German Foreign Minister Joschka Fischer echoed the sentiments of his French colleague and publicly warned the United States against a "hasty reaction" to the attacks.[40] Meanwhile, then French prime minister Lionel Jospin publicly noted that there could be no "war against Islam or the Arab-Muslim world."[41]

However, there was also a strong imperative for the allies to act. For instance, among the NATO allies, it was quickly decided that inaction, or even the impression of it, would be the worst policy, for "NATO would be accused of being divided over combating terrorism . . . we must close ranks. There is no other option."[42] In addition, the administration signaled its intent to confine the initial phase of the campaign to Afghanistan and Al Qaeda and to consult with the allies before any expansion of combat missions.[43] Furthermore, allies who were reluctant to contribute forces to the military operation in Afghanistan pledged to provide the forces necessary to ensure the continuation of NATO missions in the Balkans. Significantly, U.S. tactics gained the support of both China and Russia, which both had experienced a variety of tensions with the Bush administration. In the aftermath of the September 11 attacks, a new closeness emerged between Bush and Russian President Vladimir Putin. Some manifestations of this newfound closeness included a Russian agreement to supply weapons to the anti-Taliban Northern Alliance.[44] Putin, in fact, would refer to the campaign against Al Qaeda as a "joint effort" that required the United States and Russia to "pull together."[45]

Coalition Benefits

Within three weeks, the Bush administration had assembled a broad-based, multifaceted coalition and obtained concrete diplomatic and security pledges from a number of states. By September 30, there were forty-six specific declarations of support from multilateral organizations. The administration also gained a variety of forms of bilateral cooperation. More than 100 nations increased intelligence cooperation and collaboration to some degree in response to the attacks, and the United States increased counterterrorism operations with 200 different national intelligence or security services around the world. Finally, the administration obtained the close cooperation of key regional actors, including Pakistan as well as the major moderate Arab states.[46]

Even before the military campaign began, the administration gained notable benefits from its coalition of coalitions. For instance, the Treasury Department succeeded in securing permission to freeze twenty Al Qaeda accounts in overseas banks. There were approximately 200 arrests of persons suspected to have ties to Al Qaeda outside of the United States. The United States also gained permission to utilize air bases in a variety of states, and ultimately Washington would even be granted base rights in the former Soviet Republics of Tajikistan and Uzbekistan.

Much of the noncombat military support during Operation Enduring Freedom came from the NATO allies. In fact, Bush would call NATO "the cornerstone" of the military coalition."[47] The alliance shared intelligence on matters related to terrorism and counterterrorism and "increased exchanges of information and intelligence."[48] NATO allies also pledged to increase their aid and assistance to key states in Central and South Asia to support the U.S. effort.[49] In addition, NATO states pledged to backfill in operations where U.S. troops had to be redeployed for the Afghan campaign. For instance, Greece offered to supply troops to offset planned withdrawals of American forces from NATO missions in the Balkans.[50] Finally, NATO agreed to station naval task forces in the Mediterranean and Red Sea in order to interdict Al Qaeda ships and to deploy the alliance's airborne warning and control system (AWACS) to protect U.S. airspace.[51]

OPERATION ENDURING FREEDOM

For the actual military campaign in Afghanistan, Bush sought to avoid the problems of previous coalition operations. Specifically, the administration wanted to establish a clear chain of command and ensure unity of command under U.S. Central Command, led by Army General Tommy Franks. Philip Gordon summarized the broad U.S. sentiment, which perceived multilateral

> support as politically useful but not particularly significant militarily. In this case it was reinforced by what many Americans saw as a key "lesson" of Kosovo. Whereas many in Europe saw the Kosovo air campaign as excessively dominated by the U.S. and American gener- als, most Americans—particularly within the military—saw just the opposite: excessive European meddling, with French politicians and European lawyers interfering with efficient targeting and bombing runs, and compromising operational security. This time, the Bush team determined, would be different.[52]

Combat operations began on October 7, 2001. While both U.S. and British forces conducted air and cruise missile attacks during the first days of the cam- paign and a number of other countries later contributed forces, the overwhelm- ing majority of missions were undertaken by the U.S. military.[53] Since the majority of the air and missile attacks were carried out with precision-guided weaponry, only the United States had the capability to undertake the majority of the missions.[54] By month's end, the coalition had conducted some 2,000 combat sorties and dropped more than 1 million humanitarian ration packets to the Afghan people.[55]

At the core of the U.S. strategy was the effort to utilize the Northern Alliance to conduct the majority of ground combat operations. Special forces units from a variety of coalition nations, including the United States, Australia, Canada, France, Norway, and the United Kingdom, operated with the Northern Alliance forces and coordinated close-air support and aerial bombardments. The month-long bombing campaign significantly weakened and demoralized the Taliban and Al Qaeda forces. Following the surrender of Mazar-e-Sharif on November 9, 2001, the Taliban and Al Qaeda forces quickly collapsed, and Kabul fell four days later. The U.S. strategy and the support of coalition partners allowed the administration to minimize U.S. deployments and reserve mobi- lizations. Still, the main lesson for the administration and the Pentagon seemed to be the utility of U.S. domination of command and missions during combat operations. The U.S. commanders perceived that Operation Enduring Freedom could have easily been conducted solely with U.S. assets.

For the administration, the results of Operation Enduring Freedom confirmed the utility of its approach. After the fall of the Taliban, one of the main lessons that U.S. officials touted was that "a military hub-and-spoke command operation has worked far better for Washington than the consensus decision making on which it had to rely during the NATO air campaign over Kosovo and Serbia in 1999, which left many in the U.S. Defense Department deeply frustrated."[56] The coalition partners had contributed to the victory in Afghanistan, but to the United States, their support was more symbolic than significant.

Aftereffects

The main U.S. requests for troop deployments from the coalition came after the fall of the Taliban. On December 20, 2001, the UN Security Council authorized the deployment of a peacekeeping force to provide stability for the Afghan interim government. While the coalition had only provided minimal troops for the combat operations, they would ultimately provide the bulk of the UN-sponsored peace mission. After lobbying by Bush and Powell, the British agreed to initially lead the UN mission and provide the core of the 5,000-member force. Under the terms of the mission, the UN troops would actually remain under the overall operational command of the United States. British Ministry of Defense officials stated that the missions of the peacekeeping force would be carried out "in cooperation with the Americans, they are the big brother."[57] Hence, the United States would continue to have the best of both worlds. Although the administration gained British consent for this arrangement, other coalition allies were less than pleased with the arrangement. Germany officially objected to U.S. command of the UN mission.[58] Berlin requested that any UN-sponsored peace mission have an autonomous command.[59] A compromise was brokered, whereby the lead nation of the UN mission would have operational command, but the United States would retain overall area command in order to coordinate operations and deployments.[60]

Paris also signaled its displeasure with the overall division of labor of the Afghan campaign. The French had sought a greater role in the military operations, but only on the condition that they have greater influence in the planning and command of the missions. French policy makers were concerned with issues of their nation's international rank and its global status. Consequently, they objected to the perception of having to "clean up" after the U.S.' actions by manning and funding the UN mission. To Paris, the word from Washington seemed to be: "We'll do the cooking and prepare what people are going to eat, then you will wash the dirty dishes."[61]

In the end, UN forces were deployed mainly around Kabul and a few major cities, while U.S. and other coalition combat forces had freedom of movement throughout Afghanistan to conduct search-and-destroy operations against remaining Al Qaeda and Taliban forces. The UN mission was headquartered in the Afghan capital and tasked to support the interim government of Hamid Karzai.[62] Some sixteen nations contributed troops to the mission. The largest contingent came from the United Kingdom, with 1,800 soldiers. Other troops were provided by a range of coalition allies, including Germany, France, Italy, New Zealand, Norway, Portugal, and the Netherlands. After a six-month rotation, the British turned command over to the Turks, with Germany scheduled to take command next.[63]

While the administration accomplished its short-term goals in regard to Afghanistan, the manner in which the coalition operated may create future problems for U.S. foreign policy. The reluctance to allow allies significant influence within the coalition may limit the capability to draw states into future bandwagoning. Resistance to an expansion of the war on terror to include Iraq was one manifestation of this trend. In addition, the common notion among the core allies of the United States, that the superpower is benign and promotes multilateral cooperation and collaboration, was eroded.

The diplomatic wranglings over military intervention in Iraq demonstrated the potential negative ramifications of the administration's strategy. While states such as Germany, France and Russia each had considerable domestic interests that prompted opposition to Operation Iraqi Freedom, at the core of the efforts of the countries was the attempt to practice constrained balancing against U.S. primacy. None of the major states ever seriously contemplated providing overt military aid to Iraq, but France, Germany, and Russia and other states did endeavor to constrain the policy options of the United States in order to influence American strategy and to reaffirm their own global importance or power. This effort failed as the Bush administration developed an alternative coalition which, while much weaker in pure power or diplomatic terms, actually confirmed the inability of those balancing states to restrain American actions. In choosing whether to balance or bandwagon, the states that bandwagoned with the United States came out as the victors. These states received new or renewed U.S. aid, attention, and various other carrots, while the states that opposed U.S. action have faced various forms of official and unofficial retaliation from the United States (this retaliation ranges from Bush's cancelled meeting with Canadian Prime Minister Jean Chretien to the limited U.S. boycotts of French consumer goods).

For the Bush administration, the conflict in Iraq was fought with another form of coalition of coalitions (or coalition of the willing). For the administration, the American military power success further undermined the value of broad-based international coalitions. The U.S. military was able to operate unencumbered by the problems often encountered with multilateral operations.

Far from acting as a warning against future actions of a unilateral nature the machinations surrounding the conflict in Iraq have most likely encouraged the tendency for limited coalition actions by the Bush administration. This is especially true since multilateral cooperation in the War on Terror, in terms of law enforcement and financial cooperation, has continued unabated.

CONCLUSION

Following the September 11 terrorist attacks, the Bush administration had two interconnected, but not necessarily complementary, short-term goals. First, it sought to develop a broad-based coalition that would underscore global support for the United States and add legitimacy to potential U.S. actions against the Taliban and Al Qaeda. In this regard, the administration sought to parallel the success of the coalition formed during the Persian Gulf War in terms of the number and diversity of members. The second goal was to avoid the perceived mistakes of past coalition experiences during the Persian Gulf War and the NATO-sponsored missions in the Balkans. Specifically, the administration wanted to ensure unity of command and maintain its ability to identify targets and undertake operations with minimal political interference.

The Bush administration was successful in its pursuit of both goals. It was able to bring together a wide number of states, including nations with which it had various levels of diplomatic tension, such as China and Russia, into a coalition of coalitions. International support ranged from tacit diplomatic endorsement of, and consent for, U.S. policies to improvements in multilateral counterterrorism efforts to offers of military assets and resources. The administration found itself in the comfortable position of being able to pick and choose from among the proffered aid. Concurrently, by limiting both the number and influence of the coalition partners, the United States was able to conduct Operation Enduring Freedom on its terms.

While successful in the short run, the long-term ramifications of the administration's polices are much more problematic. The use of limited coalitions, or small coalitions of the willing, has devalued the imperative to build large, multifaceted coalitions that enjoy widespread international support. Instead, the administration will likely continue to cobble together small groups of nations to support specific, issue-oriented goals. This will likely undermine the notion of the United States as a benign superpower and reinforce notions of American unilateralism. Nonetheless, the multilayered form of coalition, or the coalition of coalitions, will likely remain the preferred arrangement for future U.S.-led multinational security operations because of the immediate benefits to the United States and the degree of choice offered to the nation's allies and potential partner states.

NOTES

1. Stephan M. Walt, *The Origins of Alliances* (Ithaca: Cornell University Press, 1987), 12.

2. For a broader explanation of the differences, see Glenn H. Snyder, "Alliance Theory: A Neorealist First Cut," *International Affairs* 44 (Spring 1990): 103–24.

3. See Wayne A. Skillet, "Alliance and Coalition Warfare," *Parameters* 23 (Summer 1993): 74–85.

4. Michael W. Doyle, "Balancing Power Classically: An Alternative to Collective Security?" in *Collective Security beyond the Cold War*, ed. George Downs (Ann Arbor: University of Michigan Press, 1994), 158.

5. For examples, see Keith Neilson and Roy A. Prete, eds., *Coalition Warfare: An Uneasy Accord* (Waterloo, Ont.: Wilfrid Laurier University Press, 1983); Jehuda Wallach, *Uneasy Coalition: The Entente Experience in World War I* (Westport: Greenwood Press, 1993).

6. Stephan M. Walt, "Alliance Formation and the Balance of Power," *International Security* 9, no. 4 (Spring 1985): 4.

7. The seminal work on balance of power systems remains Kenneth Waltz, *Theory of International Politics* (Reading, Mass.: Addison-Wesley, 1979), especially chap. 6.

8. Edward Vose Gulick, *Europe's Classical Balance of Power* (Washington, D.C.: AHA, 1955), 61.

9. Walt, American Historical Association, "Alliance Formation," 8.

10. Robert L. Rothstein, *Alliances and Small Powers* (New York: Columbia University Press, 1968), 178.

11. John G. Ikenberry and Charles A. Kupchan, "Socialization and Hegemonic Power," *International Organization* 44 (Summer 1990): 151.

12. David A. Lake, "Beyond Anarchy: The Importance of Security Institutions," *International Security* 26, no. 1 (Summer 2001): 140.

13. Oran R. Young, "Regime Dynamics: The Rise and Fall of International Regimes" in *International Regimes*, ed. Stephen Krasner (Ithaca: Cornell University, 1983), 100.

14. On this notion of "leadership theory," see David A. Lake, "Leadership, Hegemony, and the International Economy: Naked Emperor or Tattered Monarch with Potential?" *International Studies Quarterly* 37, no. 4 (December 1993): 459–89.

15. For a more thorough discussion, see Robert O. Keohane and Joseph S. Nye, *Power and Interdependence*, 2nd ed. (New York: HarperCollins, 1989).

16. See John Gerard Ruggie, "Third Try at World Order? America and Multilateralism after the Cold War," *Political Science Quarterly* 109 (Fall 1994): 553–70.

17. For an expansion of these four points, see Robert J. Lieber, "No Transatlantic Divorce in the Offing," *Orbis* 44, no. 4 (Fall 2000): 571–85.

18. Gunther Hellmann and Reinhard Wolf, "Neorealism, Neoliberal Institutionalism, and the Future of NATO," *Security Studies* 3, no. 1 (Autumn 1993): 20.

19. John Lewis Gaddis, *Strategies of Containment: A Critical Appraisal of Postwar American National Security Policy* (New York: Oxford University Press, 1982), 152.

20. For a brief overview, see John D. Becker, "Combined and Coalition Warfighting: The American Experience," *Military Review* 73 (November 1993): 25–29.

21. Mark Schissler, *Coalition Warfare: More Power or More Problems?* (Newport, RI (Rhode Island): U.S. Naval War College, 1993).

22. See Mashhud H. Choudhry, *Coalition Warfare: Can the Gulf War-91 Be the Model for Future?* (Carlisle Barracks, Pennsylvania: U.S. Army War College, 1992); James P. Dunnigan, and Austin Bay, *From Shield to Storm: High-Tech Weapons, Military Strategy, and Coalition Warfare in the Persian Gulf* (New York: Morrow, 1992).

23. Lake, "Beyond Anarchy," 152.

24. Gary G. Sick and Lawrence G. Potter, "Introduction," in *The Persian Gulf at the Millennium: Essays in Politics, Economy, Security, and Religion*, ed. Gary G. Sick and Lawrence G. Potter (New York: St. Martin's Press, 1997), 1.

25. Theodore Craig, *Call for Fire: Sea Combat in the Falklands and the Gulf War* (London: John Murray, 1995), 168.

26. Suzanne Daley, "NATO Quickly Gives the U.S. All the Help That It Asked," *New York Times*, October 5, 2001, 6.

27. Wesley Clark, *Waging Modern War: Bosnia, Kosovo, and the Future of Combat* (Washington, D.C.: Public Affairs, 2001).

28. Institute for Strategic Studies, "After Kosovo: Implications for U.S. and Coalition Warfare—Executive Summary" (Fort McNair, D.C. National Defense University: NDU, 1999).

29. During the Kosovo operation, such capabilities were almost entirely limited to the United Kingdom and France.

30. As reported by Bryan Bender, "U.S. Worried by Coalition 'Technology-Gap'," *Jane's Defense Weekly*, July 29, 1998, 8.

31. NATO, "Press Availability: U.S. Deputy Secretary of State Armitage and NATO Secretary General Lord Robertson," Brussels, September 20, 2001.

32. Ibid.

33. Howard LaFranchi, "Despite Talk of Coalition, U.S. Mostly Goes It Alone, *The Christian Science Monitor*, October 29, 2001.

34. U.S., White House, "Presidential Determination 2001–28," September 22, 2001.

35. Rory McCarthy, "U.S. to Reward Pakistan with Billions in Aid," *The Guardian*, September 20, 2001, www.quardian.co.uk/international/story/0,3604, 554814,00.html

36. Condeleezza Rice, Press Briefing, Washington, D.C., November 8, 2001.

37.   Paul D. Wolfowitz and Joschka Fischer, Press Briefing, Pentagon, September 19, 2001.

38.   Joseph Fitchett, "NATO Unity, but What Next," *International Herald Tribune*, September 14, 2001.

39.   Judy Dempsey, "Use of Article 5 Marks Policy Shift for Europe," *Financial Times*, September 16, 2001.

40.   Ibid.

41.   Quoted in Suzanne Daley, "After the Attacks: In Europe; A Pause to Ponder Washington's Tough Talk," *New York Times*, September 16, 2001, 4.

42.   Judy Dempsey, "NATO Quick to Set Historic Precedent," *Financial Times*, September 14, 2001.

43.   Wolfowitz and Fischer, Press Briefing.

44.   The United States provided Russia with $45 million to give the Northern Alliance military equipment; see Bill Gertz, "Russia Supplies Tanks," *Washington Times*, October 25, 2001, Kevin O'Flynn, "Russia in Multi-Million Arms Deal with Northern Alliance," *The Guardian*, October 23, 2001.

45.   Quoted in Michael Wines, "Putin Urges a 'New Level' of Trust with America," *New York Times*, November 11, 2001, 9.

46.   U.S., White House, "Operation Enduring Freedom Overview: Campaign against Terrorism Results, Period Covered 14–30 September 2001," Fact Sheet, October 1, 2001.

47.   George W. Bush, Press Briefing, Washington, D.C., September 20, 2001.

48.   NATO, "Statement on Combating Terrorism: Adapting the Alliance's Defense Capabilities, Issued at the Meeting of the North Atlantic Council in Defense Ministers Session Held in Brussels," Press Communique PR/CP (2001), 173, December 18, 2001.

49.   Ibid.

50.   "Greek Troops to Serve in Afghanistan," *International Herald Tribune*, December 19, 2001.

51.   NATO, "Statement to the Press by NATO Secretary General Lord Robertson on the North Atlantic Council Decision on Implementation of Article 5 of the Washington Treaty Following the 11 September Attacks against the U.S.," Brussels, October 4, 2001.

52.   Philip H. Gordon, "NATO after 11 September," *Survival* 43, no. 4 (Winter 2001–2002): 4.

53.   The first strikes included fifteen land-based bombers and twenty five carrier-based U.S. aircraft. In addition, British and American naval units fired fifty cruise missiles; U.S. Department of Defense, Central Command, "Operation Enduring Freedom Update," October 8, 2001, http://www.centcom.mil/operations/Enduring_Freedom.

54.   More than 70 percent of the aerial ordnance used in the Afghan campaign was precision guided. In contrast, 30 percent of the munitions used in Kosovo were

precision guided, while only 10 percent of the ordnance in the Gulf War was precision guided; see Joseph Fitchett, "High-Tech Weapons Change the Dynamics and the Scope of Battle," *International Herald Tribune*, December 28, 2001, 1.

55. U.S. Department of Defense, "Statement of the Secretary of Defense," No. 560–01, November 1, 2001.

56. David M. Malone, "When America Banged the Table and the Others Fell Silent," *International Herald Tribune*, December 11, 2001, 17.

57. James Meek, Richard Norton-Taylor, and Michael White, "No. 10 Retreats on Plan to Send More Troops," *The Guardian*, November 20, 2001, 1.

58. Carola Hoyos and Gwen Robinson, "Multinational Peacekeeping Force Approved," *Financial Times*, December 21, 2001, 1.

59. Carola Hoyos, Andrew Parker, and Hugh Williamson, "Antiterrorist Coalition Threatened with Split," *Financial Times*, December 20, 2001, 1.

60. Germany, Bundesregierung, "Schröder on Germany's Involvement in UN-Approved International Security Assistance Force," press release, December 22, 2001.

61. Joseph Fitchett, "U.S. Allies Chafe at 'Cleanup' Role," *International Herald Tribune*, November 26, 2001.

62. Alexander Nicoll, "Troops' Role Is to Help Interim Rulers," *Financial Times*, January 11, 2002.

63. Ibid; also see "UK Outlines Plans for Afghan Troop Deployment," *Financial Times*, January 10, 2002.

Chapter 10

The Bush Military Tribunal

Relying on the Nazi Saboteur Case

Louis Fisher

INTRODUCTION

On November 13, 2001, President George W. Bush authorized the creation of a military tribunal to try those who assisted in the September 11 terrorist attacks on the World Trade Center and the Pentagon. He relied extensively on a military tribunal established by President Franklin D. Roosevelt in 1942, after the capture of eight German saboteurs. The U.S. Supreme Court later upheld the jurisdiction of the tribunal in *Ex parte Quirin* (1942). Those who support the Bush tribunal refer to *Quirin* as the "most apt precedent."[1]

Serious questions were raised in 1942 about the wisdom and legality of the military tribunal. Interdepartmental conflicts within the Roosevelt administration were so great that when Germany sent a second team of saboteurs to the United States in 1944, leading to yet another military tribunal, a collision between the Justice Department and the War Department forced significant modifications in the organization and conduct of military tribunals. Both administratively and legally, the 1942 precedent is unreliable.

THE 1942 MILITARY TRIBUNAL

After receiving training in Germany, eight saboteurs came to the United States in 1942 in two submarines, one U-boat landing off the coast of Long Island and the second near Jacksonville, Florida. The first group, headed by

---

This chapter draws from the author's forthcoming book, *Nazi Saboteurs on Trial: A Military Tribunal and American Law*, to be published in 2003 by the University Press of Kansas.

Edward John Kerling, left on May 27 for Florida. The second group, with George John Dasch as leader, left two days later for Long Island. Because Dasch decided to turn himself in, the Federal Bureau of Investigation (FBI) was able to round up the others with little difficulty.

Initially the government planned to try the men publicly in civil court. During the interrogation of the eight Germans, FBI agents assumed that the men would be arraigned before a district judge and tried in civil court. They encouraged Dasch to go before a judge and plead guilty, and they said that if he agreed to plead guilty, then they would set in motion a presidential pardon. At the military trial, Dasch's attorney asked an FBI agent: "Was it stated as a part of that proposal that after his plea of guilty he should be sentenced, and that during the trial he should not divulge anything with respect to the agreement that was made, and that after the case had died down and for about, say, three to six months, the FBI would get a Presidential pardon for him?" The agent replied: "That, in substance, is true."[2]

On June 27, the FBI told Dasch that he would be indicted and tried before a federal court. Dasch testified that he agreed to plead guilty with the understanding that everything would be kept quiet. Yet from his cell the following morning, he saw an agent reading the Sunday newspaper. Dasch's photo was "in front."[3] Believing that he had been betrayed, Dasch withdrew his offer to plead guilty. He now wanted to go into civil court and make a full explanation.[4] This turn of events helped convince the administration to choose a secret military trial and prohibit any appeal to civil courts. The public had the impression that superior FBI investigative skills had quickly uncovered the plot. FBI Director J. Edward Hoover, having received credit for discovering the saboteurs, did not want it known that Dasch had turned himself in and helped apprehend the others. Also, the government did not want to broadcast how easily German U-boats had reached American shores undetected. By sending a message that the executive branch had vast capacity to intercept enemy saboteurs, the United States might discourage future attempts by Germany.

There was a third reason for a secret military trial. The statute on sabotage carried a maximum thirty-year penalty. The government was not even sure that it would prevail on that charge. The men had not actually committed an act of sabotage. In his memoirs, Attorney General Francis Biddle concluded that an indictment for attempted sabotage probably would not have been sustained in a civil court "on the ground that the preparations and landings were not close enough to the planned act of sabotage to constitute attempt."[5] The federal law on conspiracy to commit crimes was available, but the maximum penalty was only three years.[6] The Judge Advocate General of the Army, Maj. Gen. Myron C. Cramer, had reached the same conclusion. A district court could not impose "an adequate sentence."[7]

On June 29, Biddle met with Secretary of War Henry L. Stimson to let him know that the Justice Department preferred trial by military court. To Stimson's surprise, Biddle, "instead of straining every nerve to retain civil jurisdiction of these saboteurs, was quite ready to turn them over to a military court." [8] By the next day, journalists learned that the basic decision of proceeding by military trial had been made. Newspaper stories revealed that Roosevelt would appoint a seven-member military commission to try the eight men, and that Biddle would share prosecutorial duties with Cramer.[9] Stimson saw little reason why an Attorney General should commit the time and energy to a case "of such little national importance." He thought that Biddle, with more important duties in running the Justice Department, could find people with the requisite competence and experience to conduct the prosecution. However, as Stimson noted in his diary, Biddle "seemed to have the bug of publicity in his mind." [10]

Roosevelt's Proclamation and Order

On July 2, less than a week after the eight men had been apprehended, President Roosevelt issued Proclamation 2561 to create a military tribunal. The proclamation denied "Certain Enemies Access to the Courts of the United States," [11] and stated that U.S. safety demanded that all enemies who entered U.S. territory for invasion, sabotage, espionage, "or other hostile or warlike acts should be promptly tried in accordance with the law of war." Referring to the "law of war" was important. Had Roosevelt cited the "Articles of War," he would have triggered the statutory procedures established by Congress for courts-martial. The category "law of war," undefined by statute, represents a collection of principles and customs developed in the field of international law.

The second paragraph of the proclamation describes Roosevelt as acting as commander in chief, "by virtue of the authority vested in me by the Constitution and statutes of the United States." Thus he did not claim inherent or exclusive constitutional authority. He acted under a mix of constitutional authority accorded to the president and statutory authority granted by Congress. The second paragraph denied the eight men access to any civil court. Roosevelt felt strongly about denying judicial review to the saboteurs. He told Biddle: "I won't give them up . . . I won't hand them over to any United States marshal armed with a writ of habeas corpus. Understand?" [12]

On the same day, Roosevelt issued a military order appointing the members of the military commissions, the prosecutors, and the defense counsel.[13] Acting under the 38th Article of War, he appointed Maj. Gen. Frank R. McCoy to serve as president of the commission, and he appointed six other generals to complete the seven-man commission. The military order directed Biddle and Cramer to conduct the prosecution and assigned Col. Cassius M. Dowell and Col. Kenneth Royall to serve as defense counsel. On July 7, Col. Carl L. Ristine was appointed to represent Dasch, leaving Dowell and Royall to defend the other seven.

Roosevelt's order clearly liberated the commission from some of the restrictions established by Congress in the Articles of War. The commission would "have power to and shall, as occasion requires, make such rules for the conduct of the proceeding, consistent with the powers of military commissions under the Articles of War, as it shall deem necessary for a full and fair trial of the matters before it." The power to "make such rules" freed the commission from procedures enacted by Congress and the *Manual for Courts-Martial.*

The military order also departed from the Articles of War with regard to the votes needed for sentencing. The order states that the concurrence of "at least two-thirds of the members of the Commission present shall be necessary for a conviction or sentence." Two-thirds of the commission could convict and sentence the men to death. Under a court-martial, a death penalty required a unanimous vote. Finally, the order directed that the trial record, including any judgment or sentence, be transmitted "directly to me for my action thereon." This too marked a shift from military trials. Under Articles of War 46 and 50 1/2, any conviction or sentence by a military court was subject to review within the military system, including the Judge Advocate General's office. The July 2 order vested the "final reviewing authority" in President Roosevelt.

The Military Trial

The trial took place in the west wing of the fifth floor of the Justice Department building, with the public and the press excluded. Biddle and Cramer drafted a statement on the reasons for a secret military commission. It was "of the utmost importance that no information be permitted to reach the enemy on any of these matters," followed by seven items, the first of which read: "How the saboteurs were so swiftly apprehended." [14] The Biddle-Cramer statement further notes: "We do not propose to tell our enemies the answers to the questions which are puzzling them." Certainly one of the "puzzles" in the minds of Nazi authorities was how the American government could round up the eight men so quickly. To top U.S. officials, the reason was obvious: Dasch turned himself (and others) in. Biddle did not want that information made public.

On July 7, the day before the trial began, the tribunal adopted a three-and-a-half page, double-spaced statement of rules, dealing primarily with secret sessions, the taking of oaths of secrecy, the identification of counsel for the defendants and the prosecution, and the keeping of a record. Only eight lines referred to rules of procedure: peremptory challenges would not be allowed, there would be one challenge for cause, and the language stated that the commission "shall be governed by the Articles of War, but the Commission shall determine the application of such Articles to any particular question." [15] The commission could thus discard procedures from the Articles of War or the

Manual for Courts-Martial whenever it wanted. As General Cramer advised the Commission: "Of course, if the Commission pleases, the Commission has discretion to do anything it pleases; there is no dispute about that."[16]

The government charged the eight Germans with four crimes: one against the "law of war," two against the Articles of War (81st and 82nd), and one involving conspiracy. The prosecutors thus combined a mix of offenses that were nonstatutory (law of war) and statutory (Articles of War). The distinction was fundamental. In American law, the creation of criminal offenses is reserved to the legislative branch, not to the president. The U.S. Constitution vests in Congress the power to "define and punish Piracies and Felonies committed on the high Seas, and Offenses on Land and Water."[17] The ability to charge individuals with violations of the "law of war" shifted the balance of power from Congress to the President.

Charge I ("("Violation of the Law of War")") consisted of two specifications, drawing from general principles of international law. The first specification charged that Kerling and his seven colleagues, being enemies of the United States and acting on behalf of Nazi Germany, had "secretly and covertly passed, in civilian dress, contrary to the law of war" through U.S. military and naval lines and defenses. They went behind those lines and defenses to commit acts of sabotage, espionage, "and other hostile acts" to destroy certain war industries, war utilities, and war materials within the United States. Specification 2 of Charge I repeated much of this language but added that the eight men assembled explosives, money, and other supplies, and that in addition to "committing acts," they *attempted* to commit them.

The next two charges drew from the Articles of War enacted by Congress. Charge II ("Violation of the 81st Article of War") goes beyond sabotage efforts to the communicating of intelligence with each other and to enemies of the United States. Charge III ("Violation of the 82nd Article of War") focused on spying and attempts to communicate information to Germany. Charge IV ("Conspiracy to Commit All of the Above Acts") claimed that the eight men "did plot, plan, and conspire with each other, with the German Reich, and with other enemies of the United States, to commit each and every one of the above-enumerated charges and specifications."

Even before the commission could swear itself in, defense counsel Royall took the floor to state that Roosevelt's order creating the commission "is invalid and unconstitutional." Drawing upon the principles established by the Supreme Court in *Ex parte Milligan* (1866), he said that the civil courts in the District of Columbia were open and operating. He questioned the jurisdiction of any court except a civil court. Moreover, he charged that Roosevelt's order "violates in several specific particulars congressional enactments as reflected in the Articles of War."[18] Biddle rebutted Royall, arguing, "this is not a trial of offenses of law of the civil courts but is a trial of the offenses of the law of war, which is not cognizable to the civil courts."[19]

Going to Civil Court

Royall had several times indicated to the commission that he might go to civil court to test the constitutionality of Roosevelt's proclamation and order. On the afternoon of July 21, he told the commission that as defense counsel he had an obligation to take the case to civil court. He began contacting justices of the Supreme Court to see if they were willing to meet in special session in the middle of the summer to take up the question. He first met with Hugo Black at the justice's home in Alexandria, Virginia, and on July 23, he met with Black at Justice Owen Roberts's farm outside of Philadelphia. Dowell, Biddle, and Cramer joined them. After Roberts talked with Chief Justice Harlan Fiske Stone by phone, it was agreed that the Court would hear oral arguments on Wednesday, July 29.[20]

All of this had been agreed to without any action by a lower federal court. Royall started the process by filing a petition for a writ of habeas corpus for the seven defendants he represented. On July 28, District Judge James W. Morris issued a brief statement denying permission, stating that under Roosevelt's proclamation, they were not privileged to seek any remedy or maintain any proceeding in civil courts.[21]

Oral argument before the Supreme Court began at noon on July 29 and continued for nine hours over a two-day period. Without waiting for an appeal from the district court to the appellate court (the D.C. Circuit), the Court allowed oral argument to begin. Justice Frankfurter asked both Royall and Biddle on what grounds the Court could take the case directly from Judge Morris, and why Royall had not appealed Morris's decision to the D.C. Circuit. Royall promised to take whatever procedural steps were necessary to get the paperwork to the D.C. Circuit.

Another problem was the number of justices who could have recused themselves. Frank Murphy, who thought his status as an officer in the military reserves made it inappropriate for him to sit on the case, refused to participate. Chief Justice Stone's son, Lauson, had been part of the defense team. Biddle assured Stone that his son, although a part of the defense at the military tribunal, did not participate in the habeas corpus proceedings, and that distinction satisfied both Stone and Royall. There were grounds for two others to disqualify themselves. Felix Frankfurter had already advised Stimson that the Germans should be tried by a military commission, and that the commission should be composed entirely of soldiers.[22] James F. Byrnes had been serving as a de facto member of the Roosevelt administration for the previous seven months, giving advice on draft executive orders, a draft of the Second War Powers bill, and other administration proposals.[23]

In oral argument, Dowell and Royall flagged several issues, including the *Ex Post Facto* Clause. The Constitution prohibits Congress from passing a law that inflicts punishment on a person for an act which, at the time committed, was not illegal, or increasing the penalty for a crime committed in the past. Yet Roosevelt's proclamation had been issued after the commission of the acts charged against the defendants. Without the proclamation, the maximum penalty for sabotage in time of war could not exceed thirty years. In espionage, the death penalty was not mandatory. Roosevelt's proclamation allowed the death penalty if two-thirds of the tribunal so voted, even though Article of War 43 required a unanimous vote for a death sentence. On July 2, Congress could not have passed legislation increasing the penalty for the acts already committed. How could the president so act?[24]

Royall insisted that Congress possessed the constitutional authority to legislate on military courts and military tribunals, and that any action by the president contrary to statutory standards would be invalid. Instead of complying with Article of War 38, which directed the *president* to prescribe the rules of procedure, Roosevelt transferred that function to the military commission. The articles required unanimity for a death penalty; Roosevelt's proclamation allowed a two-thirds majority. Under Article 46, the trial record of a general court-martial or a military commission would first go to a staff judge advocate or the Judge Advocate General for review. Article 50½ provided for examination by a board of review. Roosevelt's proclamation provided that the trial record of the military commission would come directly to him as the final reviewing authority. Instead of having the judge advocate general function in an independent capacity to review the adequacy of a military trial, Roosevelt placed him in the role of prosecutor with the Attorney General.[25]

At noon on July 31, Chief Justice Stone read a short per curiam opinion that upheld the military tribunal. Defense lawyers carried the papers from the D.C. Circuit to the Supreme Court only a few minutes before Stone spoke. The petition for certiorari was not filed in the Court until 11:59 A.M. One minute later, the Court convened, granted cert, and announced its per curiam decision.[26] In announcing its decision, the Court said that it was acting "in advance of the preparation of a full opinion which necessarily will require a considerable period of time for its preparation and which, when prepared, will be filed with the Clerk."

The full decision would not appear until October 29, but the per curiam gave the military commission the authority it needed to complete its work. The trial moved to its final day. Two days later, the tribunal decided that all eight men were guilty and deserved the death penalty. After review by President Roosevelt, six men were electrocuted on the morning of August 8, 1942. Dasch received a sentence of thirty years, and Burger was given life.

The Full Opinion

It would be almost three months before Chief Justice Stone completed the decision giving legal and constitutional reasons for the *per curiam*. With six of the Germans executed, clearly nothing in the Court's opinion could cast doubt on the per curiam. Neither did Stone want the Court's reputation damaged by concurrences and dissents.

Stone knew that the full opinion would have to deal with the issue of whether Roosevelt had acted consistently with the Articles of War, and that the full opinion would have a "a sour look" if the men had been executed "without the kind of review required by 50½."[27] He wrote to Frankfurter on September 10, revealing that he found it "very difficult to support the Government's construction of the articles [of war]." He said it "seems almost brutal to announce this ground of decision for the first time after six of the petitioners have been executed, and it is too late for them to raise the question if in fact the articles as they construe them have been violated." Only after the war, he said, would the facts be known, because the trial transcript and other documents would be released to the public. By that time, Dasch and Burger could raise the question successfully, which "would not place the present Court in a very happy light."[28]

Looking down the road, Stone saw great risks for the Court: "Whenever the facts do become known, as they ultimately will, the survivors, if still in prison, will be in a position to raise the question. If the decision should be in their favor it would leave the present Court in the unenviable position of having stood by and allowed six to go to their death without making it plain to all concerned—including the president—that it had left undecided a question on which counsel strongly relied to secure petitioners' liberty."[29]

In order to present the issues fully to the justices, Stone prepared a memo opinion with alternative endings designated "Memorandum A" and "Memorandum B". The first declined to pass upon the construction of the articles; the second ventured a construction. He acknowledged that Memorandum B troubled him, because he could find no basis in the record to write an opinion on the subject, and he was "reluctant" to see the Court write an advisory opinion.[30]

The Court decided to avoid the pitfalls of Memorandum B. The full decision released on October 29 concluded that the secrecy surrounding the trial made it impossible for the Court to judge whether Roosevelt's proclamation and order violated, or were in conflict with, the Articles of War.[31] Having issued the per curiam, the justices were in no position to look too closely at whether Roosevelt acted inconsistently with the Articles of War. In the words of Alpheus Thomas Mason: "Their own involvement in the trial through their decision in the July hearing practically compelled them to cover up or excuse the President's departures from customary practice."[32]

Stone wanted a unanimous opinion without any concurrences that might raise doubts about the per curiam, the full opinion, or the execution of six men. Stone did what he could to keep daylight from shining through vulnerable spots in the decision and discouraged his colleagues from offering supplemental views. He did not want them wandering down unnecessary alleyways that might embarrass the Court. Nevertheless, Robert Jackson worked on several drafts of a concurrence. Constantly nudged by his colleagues, he withdrew it.

Jackson was not the only justice who penned individual views. Frankfurter had a "memorandum" in page proofs, agreeing with Stone's position as to why Memorandum B was defective. On the first page of this memo, Frankfurter spoke with assurance that "there can be no doubt that the President did *not* follow" Articles of War 46–53. On page three, he states that he had "not a shadow of doubt" that Roosevelt "did not comply with Article 46 *et seq.*" Yet he then fudges the issue by saying that "either he did comply or he did not." Years later, Douglas said that it was "unfortunate the court took the case." While it was "easy to agree on the original *per curiam*, we almost fell apart when it came time to write out the views." [33]

At some point in October, when it looked like the Court might fragment with separate statements, Frankfurter wrote a peculiar document he called "F. F.'s Soliloquy." The memo is especially bizarre because it represents a conversation between Frankfurter and the saboteurs, six of whom were dead. Moreover, the memo abandons any pretense of judicial objectivity and balance. After listening to their argument for a writ of *habeas corpus*, he calls them "damned scoundrels" who had a "helluva cheek" asking for a writ. They were "just low-down, ordinary, enemy spies who had done "enough mischief already without leaving the seeds of a bitter conflict involving the President, the courts, and Congress after your bodies will be rotting in lime." [34]

The Court's full opinion touched on one of the motives for hearing the case in an extraordinary summer session: "In view of the public importance of the questions raised by their petitions and of the duty which rests on the courts, in time of war as well as in time of peace, to preserve unimpaired the constitutional safeguards of civil liberty." [35] Yet there was never a likelihood that the Court would exercise judicial review in any but the most limited sense. It would not scrutinize the record of the tribunal, attempt to take the case away and transfer it to a civil court, or reverse President Roosevelt. The Court was going through the motions.

Could the president act independently under his interpretation of inherent or implied power, even to the extent of acting contrary to congressional policy as expressed in statute? The Court decided not to go there: "It is unnecessary for present purposes to determine to what extent the President as Commander in Chief has constitutional power to create military commissions without the support of Congressional legislation." [36]

Did the president's proclamation and order conflict with Articles of War 38, 43, 46, 50½, and 70? The Court held that the secrecy surrounding the trial and proceedings before the tribunal "will preclude a later opportunity to test the lawfulness of the detention." [37] So much for the Court's earlier claim that it was there in time of war or peace "to preserve unimpaired the constitutional safeguards of civil liberty."

SCHOLARLY EVALUATIONS OF *QUIRIN*

The Court received great credit for meeting in special session to consider the legal rights of the Nazi saboteurs. The haste with which the Court moved, however, left doubts whether justice had been served. Were nine hours of oral arguments an impressive display of judicial independence and the "American Way," or largely for show?

Justice Frankfurter was sufficiently troubled by the decision to ask Frederick Bernays Wiener, an expert on military justice, to offer his views on *Quirin*. Wiener prepared three analyses: the first on November 5, 1942, the next on January 13, 1943, and the final on August 1, 1943. Each letter found serious problems with the Court's work. He criticized the Court for creating a "good deal of confusion as to the proper scope of the Articles of War insofar as they relate to military commissions." Weaknesses in the decision flowed "in large measure" from the administration's disregard for "almost every precedent in the books" when it established the military tribunal.[38]

A particularly potent section of Wiener's critique centered on Article of War 46, requiring the trial record of a general court-martial or military commission to be referred to the staff judge advocate or the Judge Advocate General. It seemed "too plain for argument" that AW 46 required "legal review of a record of trial by military commission before action thereon by the reviewing authority; that the president's power to prescribe rules of procedure did not permit him to waive or override this requirement; that he did in fact do so; and that he disabled his principal legal advisers by assigning to them the task of prosecution."[39] It would be difficult to craft a more sweeping condemnation.

Wiener flagged other problems. Military commissions were normally appointed by War Department Special Orders, not by presidential proclamation or military order. He cited only one precedent of using the Judge Advocate General of the Army as prosecutor, and it was one "that no self-respecting military lawyer will look straight in the eye: the trial of the Lincoln conspirators." Even in that sorry precedent, "the Attorney General did not assume to assist the prosecution."[40]

These letters from Wiener must have hit home with Frankfurter. In 1953, when the Court was considering whether to sit in summer session to hear the espionage case of Ethel and Julius Rosenberg, one of the justices recalled that the Court had sat in summer session in 1942 to hear the sabotage case. Frankfurter wrote: "We then discussed whether, as in *Ex parte Quirin*, 317 U.S. 1, we might not announce our judgment shortly after the argument, and file opinions later, in the fall. Jackson opposed this suggestion also, and I added that the *Quirin* experience was not a happy precedent."[41]

Recent studies of *Quirin* are quite critical of the Court. To Michal Belknap, Stone went to "such lengths to justify Roosevelt's proclamation" that he preserved the "form" of judicial review while "gutt[ing] it of substance."[42] As long as justices marched to the beat of war drums, the Court "remained an unreliable guardian of the Bill of Rights."[43] In a separate article, Belknap describes Frankfurter in his "Soliloquy" essay as a "judge openly hostile to the accused and manifestly unwilling to afford them procedural safeguards."[44] David J. Danelski regards the full opinion in *Quirin* as "a rush to judgment, an agonizing effort to justify a *fait accompli*."[45] The opinion represented a victory for the executive branch but for the Court "an institutional defeat."[46]

Two Saboteurs in 1944–1945

Germany made a second attempt to send saboteurs to the United States by submarine. William Colepaugh and Erich Gimpel, trained in sabotage and espionage, left Germany on U-boat 1230 and entered Frenchman's Bay on the coast of Maine on November 29, 1944, where the two men came ashore in a rubber boat.[47] Colepaugh, age twenty-six, was a Connecticut-born U.S. citizen. Gimpel, thirty-five, was a native of Germany. After making their way to New York City, they had a falling out and were picked up by the FBI.

Initially, they were to be tried in the same manner as the eight Nazi agents in 1942: by a military tribunal sitting on the fifth floor of the Justice Department in Washington, D.C. Biddle and Cramer would conduct the prosecution. However, this time Stimson intervened forcefully to block their participation. Writing to President Roosevelt on January 7, 1945, Stimson argued that a repeat of the 1942 procedure "is likely to have unfortunate results." Another military tribunal appointed by the President, with Biddle and Cramer serving as prosecutors, "would certainly be attended by headlines and worldwide publicity. This would almost certainly lead to charges in Germany that innocent Germans were being tried and condemned by an extraordinary legal proceeding." Such a trial, he feared, would likely lead to German mistreatment of American Prisoners of War (POW). Stimson wanted the men tried either by court-martial or military commission, with the appointment authority placed in the army commander in Boston or in New York.[48]

In his diary, Stimson expressed contempt for Biddle's grandstanding. He records that at a cabinet meeting, he told Roosevelt that he "wouldn't favor any high ranking officers as members of the tribunal and did not propose to have the Judge Advocate General personally try it." Stimson, indicating that Roosevelt apparently agreed with him "fully," noted that Biddle continued to press his position. After returning from the meeting, Stimson spoke to a colleague in the War Department about Biddle's attitude: "It is a petty thing. That little man is such a small little man and so anxious for publicity that he is trying to make an enormous show out of this performance—the trial of two miserable spies. The President was all on my side but he may be pulled over."[49]

On January 12, President Roosevelt released a military order that empowered the commanding generals, under the supervision of the Secretary of War, to appoint military commissions to try Colepaugh and Gimpel. The trial record would not go directly to the President, as in 1942. The review would be processed within the Judge Advocate General's office under Article 50½.[50] Roosevelt did not appoint the seven-man tribunal. That was done by Maj. Gen. Thomas A. Terry, commander of the Second Service Command, who also selected the officers to serve as prosecutors and defense counsel. Two members from the Justice Department assisted with the prosecution.[51] Biddle had no role as prosecutor, while Cramer was limited to his review function within the Judge Advocate General's office. The trial took place not in Washington, D.C., but at Governor's Island, New York City.[52]

On February 14, 1945, the tribunal sentenced Colepaugh and Gimpel to die by hanging. President Roosevelt died on April 12, before the executions could be carried out. On May 8, President Harry Truman announced the end of the war in Europe. The following month, he commuted the death sentences for the two men to life imprisonment.[53] In 1955, Gimpel was released from prison and deported to Germany, while Colepaugh was paroled in 1960.

THE BUSH MILITARY ORDER

By 2001, the issue of military tribunals seemed quaint if not antiquated. Few people could recall *Ex parte Quirin* or what happened to the eight German saboteurs. All that changed rapidly on November 13, 2001, when President George W. Bush issued a military order authorizing the creation of a military commission to try those who provided assistance for the terrorist attacks of September 11. In many respects, his order tracks the Roosevelt proclamation and military order of 1942. The Bush order allows any evidence that would have "probative value to a reasonable person." The Roosevelt order spoke of "probative value to a reasonable man." The Bush order directs the Secretary of Defense to issue orders and regulations to provide for "a full and fair trial." The same phrase appears in Roosevelt's 1942 order. The Bush order permits conviction and sentencing by two-thirds of the members of the military commission, the same fraction used in the Roosevelt order.

The Bush order also prohibits judicial review: "The individual shall not be privileged to seek any remedy or maintain any proceeding, directly or indirectly, or to have any such remedy or proceeding sought on the individual's behalf, in (i) any court of the United States, or any State thereof, (ii) any court of any foreign nation, or (iii) any international tribunal." Roosevelt's proclamation also denied access to civil courts, except under such regulations as the Attorney General, with the approval of the Secretary of War, may prescribe. That exception did not appear in the Bush order. The Bush order directs that the trial record be submitted for review and final decision "by me or by the Secretary of Defense if so designated by me for that purpose." The Roosevelt order of 1942 directed that the trial record be transmitted directly to him for action.

The population affected by the Bush order is vastly greater than Roosevelt's 1942 proclamation, which covered "all enemies who have entered upon the territory of the United States as part of an invasion or predatory incursion, or who have entered in order to commit sabotage, espionage, or other hostile or warlike acts." That proclamation applied to eight saboteurs. The Bush order covers any individual "not a United States citizen" who the President determines is or was a member of Al Qaeda, engaged in or assisted in acts of international terrorism injurious to the United States, or knowingly harbored these terrorists. The population of non-U.S. citizens in the United States is approximately 18 million.

On March 21, 2002, the Defense Department released regulations to guide the military tribunals. Instead of the two-thirds majority to convict and sentence in the Bush military order, the two-thirds is retained for conviction, but unanimity is required for the death penalty. Three to seven officers could be appointed to sit on tribunals. For death penalty cases, there would be seven officers. Whereas under the Bush order the trial record would go directly from the tribunal to him or to the Secretary of Defense, the regulations required a review panel appointed by the Secretary of Defense.

CONCLUSION

The Nazi saboteur case represented a dangerous concentration of power in the executive branch. Roosevelt appointed the tribunal and served as the final reviewing authority. "Crimes" related to the law of war came not from the legislative branch, enacted by Congress, but from executive interpretations of international law. Throughout the six weeks of trial by military tribunal and habeas corpus petition to the Supreme Court, Congress was not a participant. The judiciary was largely shut out of the process. The two days of oral argument before the Court were dramatic but hardly a check on the president.

The administration tried the eight Germans in secrecy, but not for the announced purpose of protecting military secrets or safeguarding national security. Secrecy was driven by two factors: to conceal the fact that Dasch had turned himself (and the others) in, and to mete out heavier penalties. The trial could have been conducted openly, with the public and the press invited, without sacrificing any legitimate national interests. On the rare occasions where sensitive data might have been revealed, the courtroom could have been closed for that part of the testimony.

Roosevelt's creation of the military tribunal commission was deeply flawed. It was a mistake to have the Judge Advocate General share prosecutorial duties with the Attorney General. The Judge Advocate General adds integrity to the system of military justice by serving as a reviewing authority, not as a prosecutor. The trial record should never have gone directly to the President. Neither Roosevelt nor any other President is in a position to read a 3,000-page trial transcript with the requisite care and legal judgment.

It was an error for Roosevelt to authorize the tribunal to make its own rules. Procedures need to be agreed to before a trial begins, not after. No confidence can be placed in rules created on the spot, particularly when done in secret. It would have been better for the military tribunal to operate under the procedures set forth in the Articles of War. Those procedures were in place and represented the product of mature thought and careful study over a long period of time. With their statutory base, they would have given congressional sanction to the process and removed the impression of executive arbitrariness.

Roosevelt's proclamation, prohibiting access to civil courts, created a needless confrontation with the Supreme Court. Had Roosevelt created a tribunal and directed it to follow the statutory procedures available in the Articles of War, including an internal review of the record by the Judge Advocate General, then the civil courts would have been in a position to deny jurisdiction to any petition for a *writ of habeas corpus*. Drafting the proclamation as he did, Roosevelt practically compelled the Court to take the case and pretend to exercise an independent review, when all knowledgeable observers knew what the outcome would be.

Assembling the Court in the middle of the summer in emergency session, with briefs hurriedly prepared and read, sent a message of inconsiderateness, not judicial deliberation. Nine hours of oral argument highlighted the lack of preparation. Taking the case directly from the district court, without intervening review by the D.C. Circuit, further underscored the rush to judgment. The petition for certiorari reached the Court a few minutes before it convened, granted cert, and announced its per curiam decision. This hastily drafted *per curiam* was followed by the execution of six of the Germans. Not until almost three months later did the Court manage to issue its full opinion, offering reasons and constitutional analysis.

The reasons and analysis, strained and uninformed in many places, were compromised by the political situation in which the Court found itself. It had to decide without knowing how the secret trial was conducted or how it would turn out. The justices knew that information unavailable to them would be released within a few years, putting the Court's reputation at risk. Nothing in the decision could imply, in any way, that there had been a miscarriage of justice. The customary airing of individual views through concurrences and dissents could not be tolerated.

Stimson had objected to the participation of Biddle and Cramer as prosecutors in 1942. He also disliked the drama of a trial held in the Justice Department. When the need for a military tribunal resurfaced in 1945, he was this time successful in preventing Biddle and Cramer from serving as prosecutors. He saw that the trial was located at Governor's Island, instead of the nation's capital, and he kept Cramer in his statutory role as a reviewing officer with the Judge Advocate General. Stimson raised other objections to the 1942 procedure, such as having the trial record go directly to the President. In 1945, the trial record went first to General Terry and from there to the Judge Advocate General. Instead of having the appointment of the tribunal members and counsel done by the president, as in 1942, those duties were vested in Terry.

The legal mind has a lazy habit of looking for "precedents" to justify what has been done or is about to be done. Little effort is made to scrutinize the precedent to determine whether it was acceptable then or worth repeating now. That something has been done before does not mean it should be done again. There is nothing "apt" about the *Quirin* decision. As Justice Frankfurter later remarked, it "was not a happy precedent." The American legal system would do well not to see its like again.

NOTES

1. William P. Barr and Andrew G. McBride, "Military Justice for Al Qaeda," *Washington Post* November 18, 2001, B7.

2. Transcript, "RG 153, Records of the Office of the Judge Advocate General (Army), Court-Martial Case Files, CM 334178, 1942 German Saboteur Case," National Archives, 541 ("Military Trial").

3. Ibid., 2, 546.

4. Ibid., 677.

5. Francis Biddle, *In Brief Authority* (Garden City: Doubleday, 1962), 328.

6. Ibid.

7. Memorandum for the Assistant Chief of Staff, G-2, June 28, 1942, by Myron C. Cramer, 4; in "German Saboteurs" file, RG 107, Office of the Secretary of War, Stimson "Safe Files," National Archives.

8. Diary of Henry L. Stimson June 28, 1942, Roll 7, 18–29, 131, Manuscript Room, Library of Congress ("Stimson Diary").

9. "Death to Be Sought for 8 Saboteurs," *Washington Post* July 2, 1942, 12.

10. Stimson Diary July 1, 1942, 136.

11. 7 Fed. Reg. 5101 (1942).

12. Biddle, *In Brief Authority*, 331.

13. 7 Fed. Reg. 5103 (1942).

14. Untitled, undated, three-page statement, at 3; Papers of Frank Ross McCoy, Box 79, Manuscript Room, Library of Congress ("McCoy Papers").

15.　"Rules Established by the Military Commission Appointed by Order of the President of 2 July 1942," 3–4; McCoy Papers.

16.　Military Trial, 991.

17.　U.S. Const., Art. I, §8, cl. 10.

18.　Military Trial, 5.

19.　Ibid.

20.　David J. Danelski, "The Saboteurs' Case," 1 J. Sup. Ct. Hist. 61, 68 (1996).

21.　Ex parte Quirin, 47 F. Supp. 431 (D.D.C. 1942).

22.　Stimson Diary, June 29, 1942, 131.

23.　Letters from Attorney General Francis Biddle to Justice James F. Byrnes, December 23, 1941, December 29, 1941, December 30, 1941, January 1, 1942, and January 10, 1942; Special Collections, Papers of James F. Byrnes, Clemson University, S.C.

24.　*Landmark Briefs and Arguments of the Supreme Court of the United States* (Arlington, Va.: University Publications of America, 1975), vol. 39, 343.

25.　Ibid., 557–61.

26.　General Myron C. Cramer, "Military Commissions: Trial of the Eight Saboteurs," 17 Wash. L. Rev. & State Bar J. 247, 253 (1942).

27.　Letter from Harlan Fiske Stone to Bennett Boskey, August 1, 1942; Papers of Harlan Fiske Stone (hereafter "Stone Papers"), Box 69, Manuscript Room, Library of Congress.

28.　Letter from Stone to Frankfurter, September 10, 1942; Felix Frankfurter Papers, Part III, Reel 43, Manuscript Room, Library of Congress (hereafter "Frankfurter Papers").

29.　Ibid., 2.

30.　Ibid.

31.　Ex parte Quirin, 317 U.S. 1, 46–47 (1942).

32.　Alpheus Thomas Mason, "Inter Arma Silent Leges: Chief Justice Stone's Views," 69 Harv. L. Rev. 806, 826 (1956).

33.　William O. Douglas, *The Court Years* (New York: Vintage, 1981), 138–39.

34.　Presumably, Frankfurter sent the document to each justice. I am relying on the copy in the Robert H. Jackson Papers, Library of Congress.

35.　Ex parte Quirin, 317 U.S. 1, 19 (1942).

36.　Ibid., 29.

37.　Ibid., 47.

38.　"Observations on Ex parte Quirin," signed F. B. W.," 1; Frankfurter Papers.

39.　Ibid., 8.

40.　Ibid., 9.

41. "Memorandum Re: *Rosenberg v. United States*, Nos. 111 and 687, October Term 1952," June 4, 1953, 8; Frankfurter Papers, Part I, Reel 70.

42. Michal R. Belknap, "The Supreme Court Goes to War: The Meaning and Implications of the Nazi Saboteur Case," 89 Mil. L. Rev. 59, 83 (1980).

43. Ibid., 95.

44. Michal Belknap, "Frankfurter and the Nazi Saboteurs," *Yearbook 1982*: Sup. Ct. Hist. Soc., 66.

45. David J. Danelski, "The Saboteurs' Case," 1 J. Sup. Ct. Hist. 61 (1996).

46. Ibid., 80.

47. "German Agents, Landed by U-Boat, Seized Here by FBI," *New York Times*, January 2, 1945, 1.

48. Letter of January 7, 1945, from Stimson to Roosevelt, 1-2; RG 107, Records of the Office of the Secretary of War, "German Saboteur" file in Stimson's "Safe File," National Archives.

49. Stimson Diary, January 5, 1945, 18–19, Roll 9, Manuscript Room, Library of Congress.

50. Military Order, 10 Fed. Reg. 548 (1945).

51. "2 Spy Suspects Given to Army for Trial," *New York Times*, January 19, 1945, 14.

52. "Spy Trials Open Today," *New York Times*, February 6, 1945, 5.

53. "Truman Commutes to Life Terms Death Sentences of Two Spies," *New York Times*, June 24, 1945, 1.

Chapter 11

The War on Terrorism and Homeland Security

Presidential and Congressional Challenges

Richard S. Conley

INTRODUCTION

Just a week after the tragic terrorist attacks of September 11, 2001, President George W. Bush used an executive order—the only tool available for swift action—to create a new Office of Homeland Security (OHS). Massive governmental reorganization not only would have required congressional assent but also might have detracted from White House efforts to coordinate federal anti-terrorism programs, particularly given the complexities in reorganization and historical ambivalence toward such executive initiatives on Capitol Hill.[1] Housed in the Executive Office of the President (EOP), OHS provided for a director who serves as an assistant to the president.[2] The same directive also created a Homeland Security Council (HSC).[3] The primary function of the OHS and HSC was to be coordination. Former Pennsylvania governor Tom Ridge, Bush's choice for OHS director, initiated a top-to-bottom review of government counterterrorism programs and worked to promote interagency cooperation.

Initial calls for a reorganization of federal responsibilities came from Congress—*not* the White House. Many legislators, including Senator Joseph Lieberman, critiqued the position of the Homeland Security Director for having no statutory authority.[4] The lack of a congressional mandate, they argued, left Ridge without an independent budget necessary to carry out his duties—and placed him beyond congressional accountability. By June 2002, Bush signed on to the idea of creating a cabinet-level Department of Homeland Security.[5] Congress and the president then moved in the direction of placing nearly 170,000 federal employees under an umbrella Department of Homeland Security.[6] However, by the time members of Congress recessed in the fall to return home to campaign for the November 2002 midterm elections, legislative efforts had stalled. Executive-legislative conflict raged about labor issues and presidential authority over employees of the new department, drawing veto threats from the White House.[7] The president and members of Congress also struggled to determine which functions to transfer from the myriad of agencies with responsibilities for counterterrorism at an estimated cost of $38 billion.[8] Only after the Republicans' stunning victories in the midterm elections did the lame-duck 107th Congress move decisively to pass the reorganization bill in late November 2002.

Bush reversed course and favored a new Department of Homeland Security to gain as much leverage as possible over the structure of congressional legislation. Yet a central question for debate is whether a massive reorganization and consolidation of federal programs is the most appropriate response to terrorist threats. It remains an open question whether programmatic *consolidation* within a single entity, in lieu of centralized policy *coordination* by the White House, will yield greater chances for success.

This chapter assesses organizational options for homeland security with which Congress and the president grappled. The objective is to outline the advantages and disadvantages of several available organizational models and, where appropriate, draw from historical examples of coordination and consolidation efforts. The analysis suggests that Bush and Congress "leapfrogged" from one end of the continuum—a nonstatutory, presidential advisory system—to the other end with plans for a full-fledged reorganization. A model that garnered significant support on Capitol Hill—a terrorism "czar" with coordination responsibilities—might have proven a suitable alternative, at least in the short term. Particularly given the delays in passing Bush's proposal, questions linger about the viability of agency reorganization to secure the home front.

CENTRALIZED COORDINATION, REORGANIZATION, AND HOMELAND SECURITY: ISSUES FOR THE ADMINISTRATIVE PRESIDENCY

Modern presidents have typically preferred to create specialized policy-making structures in the EOP and rely on institutionalized staff.[9] Still, they have sometimes promoted the reorganization of executive departments or the creation of a new department to reassert authority over the bureaucracy or to signal their resolve to address urgent policy issues. But as James P. Pfiffner notes, reorganizations "take up valuable time and must be traded off against other policy priorities. Turf battles must be fought with Congress, the bureaucracy, and interests groups who are all jealous of whatever power they have and will not give it up without a fight."[10] Abortive presidential reorganization efforts include Nixon's "superagencies" approach to domestic programs, Johnson's attempt to create a

Department of Economic Affairs, and Carter's call for a Department of Natural Resources.[11]

Homeland Security and the Coordination-Consolidation Continuum

The debate over the best organizational model for homeland security cuts across these issues. As Figure 11.1 shows, there is a range of organizational possibilities for homeland security. The choices may be arrayed along a continuum that emphasizes either policy coordination or consolidation of functions through reorganization, with implications for congressional oversight and executive independence. The first three boxes in the figure emphasize coordination from the White House with broader executive latitude. On the left-hand side of the figure is a nonstatutory presidential advisor who is "assistant to the president" (Ridge's original charter), has no formal budget authority, and does not require congressional approval. Moving one box to the right is a statutory alternative: Congress would institutionalize OHS within EOP, provide the director with a budget independent of the White House operations budget, and require Senate confirmation of the president's choice for the position. Finally, Congress and the president might instead agree to place one cabinet-level department in charge of homeland security—effectively giving it "lead agency" status to coordinate efforts across the federal government.

The two right-hand side boxes in Figure 11.1 give Congress more oversight over homeland security, at least theoretically, by consolidating federal programs and making appointments to the new agency or department subject to Senate confirmation. Congress can legislate the reorganization of federal counterterrorism and law enforcement programs into an independent federal agency and give the head of the new organization cabinet-level status. Alternatively, Congress may consolidate programs into a fifteenth department of the executive branch—as it did on November 19, 2002.

Each of these options entails significant trade-offs. Many of the options find analogies in past attempts to rationalize policy making, and it is possible to draw

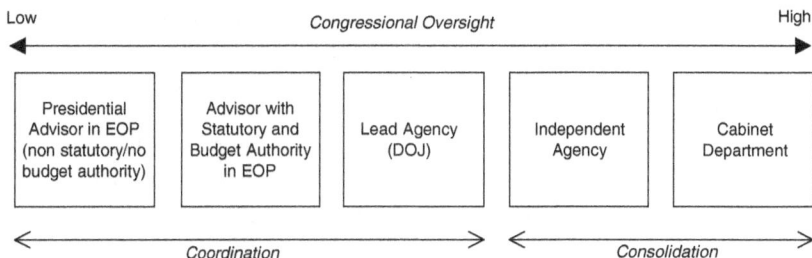

FIGURE 11.1 Homeland Security and Organizational Possibilities.

from those experiences to highlight the advantages and disadvantages of each of the approaches—both in terms of formal structure and informal operation. Let us examine each of the options in turn, beginning with the advisory position into which Tom Ridge was thrust via executive order.

Presidential Advisor?

President Bush's executive order creating OHS and HSC provided for what amounted to a policy coordinating committee in EOP without any permanent status. The director of OHS, Tom Ridge, assumed a position as "assistant to the president" like other counselors who handle various domestic policy matters, liaison with Congress, and such. And like other White House staff who are employed at the president's discretion and do not occupy a statutory advisory position, Ridge's appointment did not require Senate confirmation.

This configuration has several advantages and disadvantages. While Ridge's status gave him a privileged advisory role to President Bush, it shielded him from Congress and limited the OHS budget to discretionary funds from the White House Office budget.[12] Although the National Security Council (NSC) was the explicit model for OHS and HSC, another weakness was Ridge's lack of formal authority over other cabinet departments and agencies, including budgetary review and control. Also absent was an informal pattern of cooperation among entities responsible for homeland security. These concerns came to the fore shortly after Ridge took up his position in October 2001.

Ridge was given the charge, as President Bush stated, to "lead, oversee, and coordinate a comprehensive national strategy to safeguard our country against terrorism and respond to any attacks that may come."[13] On the positive side, as an "executive order coordinator," as Charles Wise puts it, Ridge had the advantage of acting as a neutral broker who is not beholden to the particular interests of any one agency.[14] Furthermore, reporting directly to the president theoretically gave Ridge a lot of clout. Just a few weeks after his appointment, Ridge emphasized that President Bush had mandated that cabinet members "defer to his oversight role" in the OHS. Ridge also accentuated his direct access to the president—just "10, 15 paces away"—noting that he could talk to the president whenever he wished.[15] The perception of Ridge's status vis-à-vis the president can be as, if not more, important than the formal (if ambiguous) functions outlined in Executive Order (E.O.) 13288.[16]

Ridge's position is the focal point for harmonizing homeland security efforts scattered across innumerable agencies (until reorganization takes place). The HSC is the OHS director's primary vehicle for policy coordination. Yet critics are correct to point out that Ridge's success depends on the willingness of others to collaborate and follow his lead. Without any statutory authority, Ridge's "primary power for getting things done is the power of persuasion."[17]

As Ivo Daalder and I. M. Destler explain, while "Ridge and his office have the power to set the agenda, convene meetings, and forge consensus . . . neither Ridge nor anyone on his staff has the authority to tell others what to do—that must come from the acquiescence, if not support, of Ridge's peers themselves."[18]

The HSC, unlike NSC, does not have a similar "culture of cooperation." This is due in part to the fact that NSC is statutory and has been in existence for fifty years.[19] The ambiguity of the OHS charter, which seemingly comprises both advisory and operational functions but has no formal enforcement authority, is reminiscent of the now-defunct National Security Resources Board (NSRB). The NSRB was created as a coordinating committee in the National Security Act of 1947 and was completely reliant on departmental cooperation—and ultimately proved unworkable.[20] The OHS faces an even more daunting task, as Director Ridge must focus on coordination "at the bottom of the Federal government's organizational pyramid"—the agencies at the front lines of law enforcement and tasked with implementing homeland security, including state and local governments.[21]

The first evidence of the severe limits Ridge faced in persuading other agencies and departments to follow his lead came in early 2002. He proposed merging elements of the Border Patrol, Coast Guard, and Customs Service, which would have drawn core entities away from the Departments of Justice, Treasury, Transportation, and Treasury, respectively, and integrated them into a "Federal Border Administration."[22] After the proposal was leaked, the debate predictably descended into the realm of turf warfare. Notwithstanding Ridge's entreaties and arguments that he had the president's backing, the proposal was dismissed rather summarily by the relevant cabinet heads.[23]

Many critiques of the structure of OHS are traceable to the absence of a statutory mandate. Ridge, as director of OHS, lacked substantive budgetary authority in two key ways. First, E.O. 13288 did not empower Ridge to develop a budget for the OHS. Second, the presidential directive did not enable Ridge to formally certify the budget proposals of other entities with homeland security responsibilities that he was to coordinate.[24] As Lindsay and Daalder note, "budgetary control is key to influencing policy, and centralization of responsibility is essential to improving policy."[25] Well-respected Washington insiders, including former Office of Management and Budget Director Leon Panetta, contended that Ridge required explicit budget authority to compel agencies to cooperate with one another and with him.[26]

Finally, Ridge's lack of accountability to Congress spurred calls from members that OHS be institutionalized within EOP through a legislative mandate. Relations between the White House, Ridge, and Capitol Hill became unnecessarily enmeshed in squabbles with partisan overtones in the spring of 2002 over the question of whether Ridge should (or could be compelled to) testify before congressional panels investigating homeland security issues. The Bush White House cast the issue as one of executive privilege between the president and his advisors.[27] Although Ridge eventually worked out compromises with House and Senate panels and briefed members without giving formal testimony, members on both sides of the aisle remained agitated, and none more than the dean of the Senate, Appropriations Chair Robert Byrd of West Virginia.[28]

Statutory Coordinator?

By late spring 2002, Ridge's position grew increasingly untenable. *New York Times* reporter Elizabeth Becker captured the essence of the dilemma:

> ... instead of becoming the preeminent leader of domestic security, Tom Ridge has become a White House adviser with a shrinking mandate, forbidden by the president to testify before Congress to explain his strategy, overruled in White House councils and overshadowed by powerful cabinet members reluctant to cede their turf or their share of the limelight.[29]

Many observers and scholars believed that Ridge's authority and accountability issues could be resolved through congressional action. By giving the OHS permanent status in the EOP with a statutory charter, Ridge and future directors would be able to avoid constitutional struggles over testimony, exercise meaningful control over agency budgets concerned with homeland security, and bolster their coordination role. The establishment of such a national "terrorism czar" was one of the chief recommendations of the Congressional Advisory Panel to Assess Domestic Response Capabilities for Terrorism Involving Weapons of Mass Destruction (the Gilmore Commission") nearly a year before the September 11 terrorist attacks.[30]

Such a statutory line—a White House "czar" for counterterrorism—could have remedied several of the problems of Ridge's position. Congressional legislation creating a permanent position for Ridge in EOP would have brought OHS into conformity with other important White House advisory positions, including the national security advisor and the national economic advisor.[31] A statutory charter also would have solved the dilemma of congressional accountability by making the directorship of OHS subject to Senate confirmation. Finally, a congressional mandate that included the authority for Ridge to certify agency budget submissions would have enabled him to better coordinate counterterrorism programs. Agencies are likely to "sell" programmatic increases under the rubric of homeland security in a restrictive fiscal environment in which surpluses have evaporated.[32] As Jeffrey Birnbaum contends, "the war on terrorism is being used as a ruse to justify all sorts of spending."[33] Substantive budget authority would have enabled Ridge to prioritize and integrate agency proposals with lesser dependence on his personal reputation, skill, and persuasion— though these latter factors would have certainly remained important.

Proponents of a statutory coordinator model can point to similar organizational arrangements—some of which appear more successful than others. In 1943, President Roosevelt created the Office of War Mobilization (OWM) by executive order; Congress later enacted the War Mobilization and Reconversion Act of 1944 that created a statutory Office of War Mobilization and Reconversion (OWMR) with the director subject to Senate confirmation. The OWMR did not have operational responsibilities, maintained a small staff tasked with coordinating a general policy framework, and was widely hailed as effective.[34]

The Office of National Drug Control Policy (ONDCP) is another analogous organizational model in terms of a statutory policy coordinator in the EOP. Created by the Anti-Drug Abuse Act of 1988, the "drug czar" is a cabinet-level position subject to Senate confirmation. The "drug czar's" experiences raised several warning signs for a statutory coordinator of homeland security. Congressional legislation creating the office sought to facilitate the ONDCP director's coordinative role across agencies for drug prevention and law enforcement and circumvent "turf wars" by according him budgetary authority over more than thirty agencies.[35] But much of ONDCP's mission has involved a tug-of-war between Congress and the director about the office's mission—whether the emphasis should be on law enforcement or drug abuse prevention.[36] Several of the ONDCP directors under both Republican and Democratic presidents antagonized members of Congress, supported failed policy initiatives, and were unable to gain control over agency budgets.[37] The combined effect has arguably diminished the drug czar's influence, compounded by the dramatic variation in staffing levels across the Bush and Clinton administrations as the "war on drugs" has received greater or lesser presidential attention.[38] The lesson is that formal budget authority vested in a White House czar cannot stamp out "turf wars," and accountability to Congress does not guarantee smooth relations. Diplomatic skills remain a pivotal variable for relations with Congress and other cabinet heads.

A terrorism czar would likely face many of the same dilemmas as ONDCP in terms of budgetary fragmentation on Capitol Hill. Success in coordinating agency budgets may rest largely in congressional resolve to rationalize the appropriations process. The Gilmore Commission noted a combined total of twenty-five committees responsible for counterterrorism budgets in the House and Senate and recommended integrating efforts into a single committee or several centralized committees to work directly with OHS. However, as Charles R. Wise observes, "Not only is this asking committees that have long exercised jurisdiction to relinquish it in the face of a top national priority at the height of its prominence, it portends a disconnect between programs that are termed 'terrorism programs' and others in the departments and agencies for which the committees are responsible."[39] Notwithstanding congressional reform of the appropriations/authorization process, a terrorism czar in OHS, like the Director of ONDCP, would likely face formidable constraints in coordinating programmatic budgets across agencies, despite formal certification authority in concert with the Office of Management and Budget (OMB).

Lead Agency?

Since the mid-1970s, the Department of Justice (DOJ), because of its role in law enforcement programs, assumed "lead agency" status in combating domestic terrorism.[40] The FBI is the chief responsible agency on this front. The idea is that a department such as Justice can provide a "single focal point in a diffuse landscape of interests and capabilities, thereby enhancing accountability."[41] In 1998, President Clinton issued a directive creating a position for national coordinator for security, infrastructure protection, and counterterrorism within the NSC to assist DOJ with the task of interagency coordination and implementation of counterterrorism measures.[42]

Critics charged that DOJ was poorly positioned to oversee interagency coordination and provide a coherent framework for homeland security. As Thomas Cmar explains, DOJ was "expected to monitor fellow agencies, which created bureaucratic 'turf wars,' made even more intractable because the DOJ had no formal authority by which to hold other agencies accountable."[43] DOJ faced other problems as well. In the wake of the September 11 terrorist attacks, Attorney General John Ashcroft focused much of his attention on an internal reorganization of the department.[44] He spent much time fending off public and congressional criticism that the FBI had not done enough to foresee and thwart the attacks.[45] These circumstances obviously detracted from DOJ's ability to act as the chief coordinative agency for homeland security.

REORGANIZATION

Congress and the president ultimately agreed to unite the multiplicity of anti-terrorism programs that are currently diffused over the federal bureaucratic landscape in a new Department of Homeland Security (DHS) rather than an independent agency. The DHS will be constructed by removing the components of agencies and departments with similar counterterrorism functions— twenty-two in all—and consolidating them. Many elements of President Bush's reorganization proposal, including Ridge's failed effort to consolidate the Customs Service, Border Patrol, and Coast Guard, stemmed from recommendations made by the Hart-Rudman Commission (U.S. Commission on National Security) eight months before the September 11 attacks.[46]

By acquiescing to the idea of agency consolidation, Bush sought to preempt congressional proposals and gain vital leverage over the specifics of any reorganization.[47] In early June 2002, the president proposed amalgamating twenty-two different agencies into a new DHS, with four principle divisions: (1) border and transportation security; (2) emergency preparedness and response; (3) chemical, biological, radiological, and nuclear countermeasures; and (4) information analysis and infrastructure protection. The proposal left the Central Intelligence Agency (CIA) and FBI outside of the new entity's scope.[48] Bush dubbed it "the most extensive reorganization of the federal government since the 1940s."[49]

There are many advantages to the new department. It will be tasked with both coordinative and operational responsibilities, have legal authority lacking in the current OHS directorship in the White House, and, as a permanent institution of the executive branch, will ensure that homeland security is a continuing governmental priority regardless of future presidents' attention to the subject.[50] As Michael O'Hanlon and others, posit, "Assigning clear responsibility for homeland security to a single agency provides clarity in an otherwise diffuse landscape of interests and capabilities."[51]

However, there is no shortage of critiques about the reorganization of homeland security functions. Many emphasize problems of coordination with state and local entities,[52] which the president's proposal may or may not surmount. Moreover, "many institutions and functions that are critical to the task cannot, by their very nature, be included in a consolidated agency,"[53] including such entities as the FBI, the CIA, and agencies in the Defense Department. The DHS will need to coordinate with intelligence authorities with an international scope, including NSC—and lawmakers have not concluded how best to go about this task.[54]

Shuffling offices and agencies may not lead to greater competence. Reorganizations, by their very nature, are disruptive and costly—both in terms of financial and human resources. The development of internal structures and procedures in the new DHS will require time.[55] An ethos of cooperation and a new organizational culture will not take root immediately. Turf wars may continue to overshadow not only internal structures but also interagency coordination efforts for which the new department will be responsible.[56] Critics accentuate the complexity of the undertaking, carefully pointing out, for example, that the Truman-era reforms to which Bush alluded in his proposal produced a variety of unintended consequences and interagency conflicts that took years to overcome.[57] One unintended consequence for the new department may be attrition caused by the uncertainties surrounding reorganization. Key agencies slated for consolidation, including the Coast Guard, the Federal Emergency Management Agency (FEMA), and the Immigration and Naturalization Service (INS), could lose anywhere from a quarter to nearly half of their workforce as employees become eligible for retirement.[58]

Many critics and lawmakers worry that reorganization may only exacerbate redundancy. They can point to past reorganizations, such as the creation of the Department of Defense, to argue that the dysfunctions produced by consolidation—the increased size and new layers of bureaucracy, as well as coordination problems—outweighed the benefits.[59] There is also the question of duplication between the White House and the new department. Tom Ridge is the president's nominee to head DHS. Yet President Bush has suggested that OHS would be retained in the White House after the creation of the department. The exact role of the advisor remains unclear.[60]

Finally, the success of the new DHS is contingent upon the dynamics on Capitol Hill. As the Hart-Rudman report emphasized, the reorganization of federal agencies will require a significant revamping of committee processes in Congress to streamline appropriations, authorizations, and oversight.[61] The situation of agencies in the new DHS necessarily interferes with traditional lines of committee jurisdiction in Congress. Established committees will not cede authority easily. "Turf wars" are not solely limited to the new bureaucracy. Calls for the establishment of select committees or a wholesale reform of the committee system, which has not been attempted since the mid-1970s, have been bogged down in jurisdictional battles.[62] One danger is that jurisdictional disputes, including the diffusion of appropriations responsibility across thirteen congressional committees with responsibility for anti-terrorism programs, threaten to hamstring the new department's operations.

Another danger is that Congress may forfeit the ability to exercise meaningful and authoritative oversight over the DHS and tilt the balance of institutional power toward the White House. In a rush to complete work on the reorganization bill in November 2002, Congress accorded the president extensive latitude to craft the structure of the new DHS. Bush won provisions that afford him broad discretion over hiring and firing decisions, as well as exemptions from public disclosure of the new agency's activities.[63] Civil libertarians' concerns about the new agency's domestic activities can only be addressed through adequate congressional oversight and control.

CONCLUSION

By the spring of 2002, consensus had begun to develop that the "presidential advisor" model was insufficient for the daunting task of coordinating governmental homeland security functions. Similarly, a "lead agency" approach with DOJ at the forefront did not seem workable. Congress and the president thus had two options: the creation of a statutory advisor with a coordinative function, or a large-scale reorganization. The choice of the latter may have come at a price. Precious time was lost. As the president and Senate Democrats squared off over the structure of the bill in the summer and fall of 2002, the federal bureaucracy continued to expand to wage the war on terrorism at home and abroad.[64] The bickering at both ends of Pennsylvania Avenue diverted attention away from interagency coordination.

There were clear-cut benefits to transforming Ridge's position into a statutory coordinator or "czar" in the EOP, particularly in the short term. Had Congress and the president agreed to shore up Ridge's position through a legislative mandate, the White House and Capitol Hill might have accorded themselves more time to reflect about reorganization and alternative structures—and could have done so under less pressure had Ridge's coordinative role been bolstered. As Karen Hult and Charles Walcott note: "agencies frequently find themselves pursuing policies with multiple, ill-defined, and sometimes conflicting goals; relying upon ambiguous or controversial policy technologies; and confronting numerous clients, constituents, and overseers as well as their own panoply of experts."[65] Agencies responsible for homeland security have had to operate without an authoritative, centralizing mechanism for programmatic cooperation and budgetary control, which has complicated their task.

Reorganization will not prove a panacea for the war on terrorism. Reconstituting major governmental functions in the new DHS will take time, patience, and a spirit of cooperation—between the White House and Capitol Hill, between leaders of both parties in Congress, and between the reshuffled agencies. Perhaps the greatest liability for DHS is the high expectations that have been set for it in an environment fraught with uncertainty, a war with Iraq, and continuing terrorist threats against the home front. The risk is that it will be far easier for policy makers, as well as the public, to judge the new agency's failures than its victories. Information on foiled attacks and successful intelligence operations may never see the light of day, and emergency preparedness becomes an issue of public and media attention when counterterrorism measures have already failed—rarely beforehand.

NOTES

1. See Peri E. Arnold, *Making the Managerial Presidency: Comprehensive Reorganization Planning, 1905–1996*, 2nd ed. (Lawrence: University Press of Kansas, 1998).

2. U.S., White House, Executive Order 13288.

3. Members include the president, the vice president, the secretaries of treasury, defense, health and human services, and transportation, the attorney general, the director of the Federal Emergency Management Agency, the director of the Federal Bureau of Investigation, the director of the Central Intelligence Agency, and the director of the Office of Homeland Security.

4. Elizabeth Becker, "A Nation Challenged: Domestic Security; Bush Is Said to Consider a New Security Department," *New York Times*, April 12, 2002, A16.

5. Mike Allen, "Bush Campaigns for Creating Homeland Security Department," *Washington Post*, June 25, 2002, A3.

6. Kathryn Dunn Tenpas and Stephen Hess, "The Bush White House: First Appraisals," *Presidential Studies Quarterly* 32 (2002): 581.

7. Bill Miller and Juliet Eilperin, "Obscure Labor Issues Block Homeland Security Bill," *Washington Post*, September 23, 2002, A8.

8. "Restructuring for Security," *New York Times*, June 13, 2002, A39.

9. Shirley Anne Warshaw, *The Keys to Power: Managing the Presidency* (New York: Longman, 2000), 214–15; Charles Walcott and Karen Hult, *Governing the White House: From Hoover through LBJ* (Lawrence: University of Kansas Press, 1995), chap. 9.

10. James P. Pfiffner, *The Strategic Presidency: Hitting the Ground Running*, 2nd ed. (Lawrence: University of Kansas Press, 1996), 91.

11. On Nixon, see Richard P. Nathan, *The Plot That Failed: Nixon and the Administrative Presidency* (New York: Wiley, 1975); on Johnson and Carter, see Peri E. Arnold, *Making the Managerial Presidency*, chaps. 8 and 10, respectively.

12. Howard C. Relyea, "Homeland Security: The Concept and the Presidential Coordination Office—First Assessment," *Presidential Studies Quarterly* 32 (June 2002): 401.

13. *Weekly Compilation of Presidential Documents* 37 (September 24, 2001): 1349.

14. Charles R. Wise, "Organizing for Homeland Security," A special issue of . . . *Public Administration Review* 62 (March–April 2002): 131–144.

15. August Gribbin, "Ridge Sees a Secure U.S. Homeland; Americans Reassured of Efforts," *Washington Times*, October 19, 2001, A1.

16. Douglas Waller, "A Toothless Tiger?," *Time*, October 15, 2001, 78.

17. James Lindsay and Ivo Daalder, "Whose Job Is It? Organizing the Federal Government for Homeland Security," in *American Politics after September 11*, ed. James M. Lindsay (Cincinnati: Atomic Dog, 2002), 70.

18. Ivo Daalder and I. M. Destler, "Behind America's Front Lines," *Brookings Review* 20 (Summer 2002): 18.

19. Michael O'Hanlon, Peter R. Orszag, Ivo H. Daalder, I. M. Destler, David L. Gunter, Robert E. Litan, and James B. Steinberg, *Protecting the American Homeland: A Preliminary Analysis* (Washington, D.C.: Brookings Institution, 2002), 99; full report at http://www.brook.edu/dybdocroot/fp/projects/homeland/report.html.

20. Anna K. Nelson, "Organizing for War without End: Lessons from the Cold War," *Miller Center Report* 18 (Summer 2002): 21–22.

21. Ivo H. Daalder and I. M. Destler, "Advisors, Czars, and Councils: Organizing for Homeland Security," *The National Interest* (Summer 2002): 3–4.

22. Allison Mitchell, "A Nation Challenged: The Borders; Official Urges Combining Several Agencies to Create One That Protects Borders," *New York Times*, January 12, 2002, A8.

23. John J. Miller, "The Impossible Position of Tom Ridge," *National Review* 43 (June 17, 2002): 35.

24. Thomas Cmar, "Office of Homeland Security," *Harvard Journal on Legislation* 39 (Summer 2002): 455–474.

25. Lindsay and Daalder, "Whose Job Is It?," 70.

26.   Bill Miller, "Ridge Lacks Power To Do His Job, Says Panetta at Hearing; Cabinet Rank, Budget Clout Urged," *Washington Post*, April 18, 2002, A19.

27.   Dana Milbank, "Congress, White House Fight over Ridge Status; Compromise Is Likely on Constitutional Flap," *Washington Post*, March 21, 2001, A33.

28.   Elizabeth Becker, "A Nation Challenged: Domestic Security; Ridge Briefs House Panel, but Discord Is Not Resolved," *New York Times*, April 11, 2002, A23; Bill Miller, "On Homeland Security Front, a Rocky Day on the Hill; Ridge's Briefing Elicits Some Scorn from Sen. Byrd," *Washington Post*, May 3, 2002, A25.

29.   Elizabeth Becker, "Big Visions for Security Post Shrink Amid Political Drama," *New York Times*, May 2, 2002, A1.

30.   Peter Bacque, "Panel Recommends New 'Terrorism Czar'," *Richmond Times-Dispatch*, September 29, 2000, A3; The full text of the Gilmore Commission's several reports is available at http://www.rand.org/nsrd/terrpanel/.

31.   Daalder and Destler, "Behind America's Front Lines," 17.

32.   O'Hanlon et al., *Protecting the American Homeland*, 113.

33.   Jeffrey H. Birnbaum, "The Return of Big Government," *Fortune* 146 (September 16, 2002): 112.

34.   Relyea, "Homeland Security," 402–4.

35.   Michael Isikoff, "Search under Way for a 'Drug Czar'," *Washington Post*, November 17, 1988, A23.

36.   "The Drug Czar's Coherent Legacy," *New York Times*, November 11, 1990, 16.

37.   See Robert Pear, "Drug Policy Debate Turns to Feud between Moynihan and Bennett," *New York Times*, June 18, 1990, A14; Jeffy Seper, "House Answers Bennett Blast with Restored Funds, Gibes," *Washington Times*, June 20, 1990, Michael Isikoff, "Martinez Suffers Setbacks As Drug Control Director; Initiatives Rebuffed As Influence Dwindles," *Washington Post*, February 24, 1992, A1; Jim McGee, "At the Justice Dept., Big Government Keeps Getting Bigger," *Washington Post*, April 5, 1996, A17; Representative Bill McCollum, "War on Drugs Has Fallen Out of National Spotlight," *Roll Call*, June 10, 1996; Paul Bedard, "Attacks on McCaffrey Called Revenge; Caucus Criticism Labeled Personal," *Washington Times*, April 27, 1998, A4.

38.   John Hart, *The Presidential Branch: From Washington to Clinton*, 2nd ed. (Chatham, N.J.: Chatham House, 1995), 94.

39.   Wise, "Organizing for Homeland Security," 135.

40.   For a detailed overview, see Laura K. Donahue, "In the Name of National Security: U.S. Counterterrorist Measures, 1960–2000," BCSIA Discussion Paper 2001–6, John F. Kennedy School of Government, Harvard University, August 2001, http://ksgnotes1.harvard.edu/BCSIA/library.nsf/pubs/ESDP200104.

41.   Daalder and Destler, "Behind America's Front Lines," 17.

42.   O'Hanlon et al., *Protecting the American Homeland*, 101.

43.   Cmar, "Office of Homeland Security," 455–474.

44.   Tom Brune, "The War on Terror: Preparing for Long Battle; Ashcroft Details Plan to Revamp Department," *Newsday*, November 9, 2001, A54.

45.   Noelle Straub and Melanie Fonder, "Ashcroft Silence Exacerbates Hill, White House Tensions," *The Hill*, November 21, 2001, 1; Jonah Goldberg, "Attacks on Ashcroft Are Far Out of Line," *Washington Times*, December 4, 2001, A13.

46.   Hart-Rudman Commission, "Road Map for National Security: Imperative for Change: The Phase III Report of the U.S. Commission on National Security/21st Century," 15, http://www.nssg.gov/PhaseIIIFR.pdf; also see Steven Mufson, "Overhaul of National Security Apparatus Urged; Commission Cites U.S. Vulnerability," *Washington Post*, February 1, 2001, A2; "Turf Tiff: A Crucial Effort to Close U.S. Borders to Terror Is Stymied by Stubborn Cabinet Departments," *Newsday*, January 21, 2002, A18.

47.   Elizabeth Becker, "Bush Is Said to Consider New Security Department," *New York Times*, April 12, 2002, A16; Thomas Oliphant, "Bush's Security Flip-Flop," *Boston Globe*, June 9, 2002, E7.

48.   See Joseph Curl, "Bush Proposes New Security Agency; Asks Hill to Quickly Make Place in Cabinet," *Washington Times*, June 7, 2002, A1.

49.   Quoted in "Traces of Terror; The Plan: 'We Have Concluded That Our Government Must Be Reorganized'," *New York Times*, June 7, 2002, A20.

50.   Wise, "Organizing for Homeland Security," 140.

51.   O'Hanlon et al., *Protecting the American Homeland*, 103.

52.   Daalder and Destler, "Behind America's Front Lines," 17.

53.   Daalder and Destler, "Advisors, Czars, and Councils," 4.

54.   Allison Mitchell, "New Antiterrorism Agency Faces Competing Visions," *New York Times*, June 14, 2002, A27; Curt Anderson, "Access to Intelligence at Homeland Security Main Sticking Point in Congress," *Associated Press*, June 21, 2002.

55.   Cmar, "Office of Homeland Security," 462.

56.   Bob Dart, "Turf Wars Forecast As Agency Created; Harmony May Lie in Giving Attention to Routine Details," *Atlanta Journal-Constitution*, July 19, 2002, 10A.

57.   Fred Hiatt, "Truman's Rose-Colored Reforms," *Washington Post*, July 15, 2002, A17.

58.   Stephen Barr, "A Major Danger for Department of Homeland Security: Retirement," *Washington Post*, June 17, 2002, B2.

59.   Ivan Eland, "Bush Plan Is Just 'Do Something'," *Newsday*, June 10, 2002, A25.

60.   Elizabeth Bumuller and David E. Sanger, "Bush, As Terror Inquiry Swirls, Seeks Cabinet Post on Security," *New York Times*, June 7, 2002, A1.

61.   Morton Kondracke, "Congress Should Heed the Other Warnings in Hart-Rudman Report," *Roll Call*, June 24, 2002, www.rollcall.com/opinion.

62.   Sarah Fritz, "New Department, but Same Old Ways," *St. Petersburg Times*, June 17, 2002, 3A; Mark Preston and Susan Crabtree, "Hill Confronts Reorganization; Turf Battles Erupt over New Dept.," *Roll Call*, June 10, 2002, www.rollcall.com/opinion.

63. Helen Dewar, "Senate Passes Homeland Security Bill," *Washington Post*, November 20, 2002, A1.

64. Edward S. Greenberg, "Will Things Ever Be the Same? The 'War on Terrorism' and the Transformation of American Government," in *American Government in a Changed World*, ed. Dennis L. Dresang (New York: Longman, 2003), 30–31.

65. Karen M. Hult and Charles Walcott, *Governing Public Organizations: Politics, Structures, and Institutional Design* (Pacific Grove, Calif. Brooks/Cole, 1990), 59.

Part 4

The Bush Administration

Chapter 12

The Bush White House

Comparisons with Previous White Houses

Bradley H. Patterson Jr.

The "Bush White House" Defined

The focus of this chapter is the personal staff of the president, what the author calls the "White House staff community," which includes not only the policy elements advising the president, the vice president, and the first lady, together with their detailees, volunteers, and interns, but also the staff of the NSC. Included too are the professional support units that immediately serve the president, including the Military Office, the residence staff, the Secret Service protective details, plus that half of the Office of Administration that directly assists the White House. This chapter touches only briefly on the institutional elements of the Executive Office of the President.

The White House As an Institution

An institution? How could that be said of the White House? Institutions of the federal government are established by statutes, which are either permanent or subject to periodic reauthorization. The duties of institutions are specified in law and, typically, so are their basic internal structures. Federal institutions are headed by officers appointed by the president and with the advice and consent of the Senate; these officers regularly appear before substantive oversight committees of the Congress and testify about their activities; the senior-most persons in such institutions annually come to the appropriations committees of the Congress to defend the institutions' requests for funding. The papers of federal institutions—protected, if needed, by security arrangements—are routinely supplied to congressional committees and, if unclassified, are also subject to Freedom of Information Act lawsuits. The men and women who staff the working levels of federal institutions are career civilian or military employees, with tenure in their positions.

Do these attributes apply to the White House? No. In fact, none of them do. The principal officer in the White House is the president, and the president's duties are set forth or implied by the U.S. Constitution. The basis for the personal presidential staff of modern times, however, is not the Constitution; it is a 1939 presidential executive order.[1] The structure of the White House staff (with only one exception[2]) is governed by no statute; the functions and duties of the various staff elements appear in no law. The appointment of White House staff officers is never made subject to Senate confirmation, and (except in cases of alleged criminality or egregious scandal) the president does not permit them to testify before congressional committees. The funding requests for White House offices are presented and defended to the Appropriations subcommittees not by White House staff officers but by the Director of the Office of Administration. White House papers can and often are denied to Congress pursuant to the doctrine of presidential executive privilege and are not subject to Freedom of Information Act lawsuits. Staff officers do not have tenure in their White House positions (although many civilian and military career men and women are detailed or assigned to the White House from their home departments).

Thus even though the modern White House lacks the accouterments of a typical federal institution, it is an un-institutionalized institution. It *is* an institution because of one quintessential attribute: durability. Statutory bodies can be extinguished by subsequent statutes (e.g., the Office of Economic Opportunity, the Interstate Commerce Commission). Presidential executive orders can be changed by a later stroke of the presidential pen. The White House and its substantive staff have been on the scene for well over sixty years, and it is unthinkable that they would be eliminated. The White House *is* an institution, not of law but of tradition, beginning in 1939. Now, after those six and a half decades, the Bush White House staff stands tall in the executive branch; it is the product, however, of the cumulative decisions and prescriptions of eleven preceding presidents.

White House History and Tradition: Meeting the Needs of the Presidency

At least twenty-nine of the contemporary White House staff units have been present for a half century; some are much older than that. For example, the Executive Clerk (who handles all of the president's official, public papers) originated in 1865; Roosevelt not only appointed his six administrative assistants but added the White House Counsel (everything in the White House has a legal aspect); Truman's administration saw the creation of the NSC staff. It was

Eisenhower who introduced many of the elements now in the modern White House: the Chief of Staff, the Deputy Chief of Staff, the Adviser to the President for National Security Affairs, a strong Legislative Affairs Office, the Office of Intergovernmental Affairs, the Staff Secretary, and the Secretary to the Cabinet. Kennedy brought the vice president (and staff) into the White House neighborhood and created the NSC's Situation Room (which keeps the White House abreast, if needed, of every activity of all of the national security and intelligence agencies). Nixon added the Domestic Council, and by his time the White House had a communications office and a full-time professional advance team. Ford instituted the Office of Political Affairs as a separate unit in the White House. Carter gave his vice president an office suite in the West Wing, invited the first lady to attend cabinet meetings, and created the Office of Administration (OA) in the Executive Office (his E.O. provides that OA "shall, upon request, assist the White House Office in performing its role . . . in direct support of the president").[3] Reagan initiated an office for White House management and administration; George H. W. Bush elevated its head to an Assistant to the President rank. Clinton created the office of the National AIDS Policy Coordinator, charged his vice president with innumerable domestic and foreign policy tasks, and asked the first lady to develop a major domestic policy initiative (health care); she went on to take forty overseas trips, twenty without the president, and she visited eighty-three countries.

Looking back at this history, it is clear that the requirements for conducting an effective presidency have grown. Even before the end of World War II, it was obvious that there had to be a much better meshing of American diplomatic, military, intelligence, economic, and information resources and activities; thus was born the NSC and its staff. Legal issues suffused presidential decision making; a personal White House Counsel was needed. Orderly relations with the Congress were crucial: every program proposed by the president had to be authorized by law, every departmental presidential appointee confirmed, every treaty ratified; the president's personal White House Legislative Affairs Office had to be strengthened. Federal programs were, more and more, being administered by state and local governments; governors, mayors, and county officials therefore had to be consulted and involved in White House policy making—and the Intergovernmental Affairs Office was established. Presidential trips multiplied; the scheduling and advance functions could no longer be handled by ad hoc volunteers. In recent years, presidents never stop campaigning, trumpeting their good deeds; they have made the White House into a theater that is stage-managed by publicity experts. President George H. W. Bush constructed a White House television studio; President Clinton developed a White House Web site (www.whitehouse.gov) and began using the Internet in the "streaming" mode, whereby live audiences from distant cities "meet" with the president. The White House Political Affairs operation is now a central feature of this "permanent campaign." President Clinton's White

House Political Chief, Harold Ickes, wrote the following to Democratic National Committee Chairman Christopher Dodd:

> This confirms the meeting that you and I and Doug Sosnik had on 15 April, 1996, at your office during which it was agreed that all matters dealing with the allocation and expenditure of monies involving the Democratic National Committee ("DNC") including, without limitation, the DNC's operating budget, media budget, coordinated campaign budget, and any other budget or expenditure, and including expenditures and arrangements in connection with state splits, directed donations, and other arrangements whereby monies from fund-raising or other events are to be transferred to or otherwise allocated to state parties or other political entities and including any proposed transfer of budgetary items from DNC related budgets to the Democratic National Convention budget, are subject to the *prior* approval of the White House.[4]

Finally, as presidential staff offices grew in numbers and diversity, it became clear that there had to be coordination and integration of operations within the White House itself—henceforth, the Assistant for Management and Administration and the Chief of Staff. Thus the *institution* of the modern White House has been created, step by step, function by function—not merely to appease political pressures (though pressures there have been), not just to make slots for patronage placements (though political allies are found there), but the elements of the contemporary White House have been established at 1600 Pennsylvania Avenue because they met the needs of the modern chief executive.

Elements of the Contemporary White House Staff

There are 137 separately identifiable offices in the White House, divisible into three categories, as seen in Table 12.1.

Nearly 6,000 men and women work in these 137 offices. None have career tenure at the White House itself, but of this estimated total, only one-third constitute the political cohort that comes in and goes out with each president. The other two-thirds are professionals, and, by tradition, and because of their exceptional skills, they are invited to stay at the White House from administration to administration. Some have served for three and four decades.[6] The presence of this professional group is yet another signal that the White House is an institution with durability and continuity.

The 137 offices in the Bush White House staff exist because, collectively, they are a direct reflection of the requirements of the modern American president—as measured by the twelve presidents since 1939. Not included in that count are

TABLE 12.1
The White House

---

(1) Forty-seven principal policy offices (the Bush additions are shown by asterisks):
- The Vice President
- The First Lady
- The Assistant to the President and Chief of Staff
  (a) The Deputy Chief of Staff for Policy
  (b) The Deputy Chief of Staff for Operations
- The Assistant to the President for National Security Affairs
  (a) The Deputy National Security Advisor
  (b) The Deputy Assistant to the President and Deputy National Security Advisor for International Economic Affairs
  (c) The Deputy Assistant to the President and Deputy National Security Advisor for Combating Terrorism*
  (d) The Executive Secretary of the National Security Council (NSC)
  (e) The Special Assistant to the President and Senior Director for African Affairs
  (f) The Special Assistant to the President and Senior Director for Asian Affairs
  (g) The Special Assistant to the President and Senior Director for Defense Policy and Arms Control
  (h) The Special Assistant to the President and Senior Director for Democracy, Human Rights, and International Operations
  (i) The Special Assistant to the President and Senior Director for European and Eurasian Affairs
  (j) The Special Assistant to the President and Senior Director for Intelligence
  (k) The Special Assistant to the President and Senior Director for International Economic Affairs
  (l) The Senior Associate Counsel to the President and NSC Legal Adviser
  (m) The Special Assistant to the President and Senior Director for the NSC Legislative Affairs
  (n) The Deputy Assistant to the President and Counselor to the National Security Advisor for Communications
  (o) The Special Assistant to the President and Senior Director for Proliferation Strategy, Counterproliferation, and Homeland Defense
  (p) The Special Assistant to the President and Senior Director for Western Hemisphere Affairs
- The Senior Adviser for Policy and Strategy
  (a) The Deputy Assistant to the President and Director of Strategic Initiatives*
  (b) The Deputy Assistant to the President and Director for Intergovernmental Affairs
  (c) The Deputy Assistant to the President and Director of Political Affairs
  (d) The Deputy Assistant to the President and Director of Public Liaison
- The Assistant to the President and Counselor for Communications
  (a) The Special Assistant to the President and Deputy Director of Communications
  (b) The Deputy Assistant to the President and Director of Presidential Speechwriting
  (c) The Special Assistant to the President and Director of Media Affairs
  (d) The Deputy Assistant to the President and Director of Global Communications*
  (e) The Assistant to the President for Homeland Security[5]*
  (f) The Assistant to the President and Counsel to the President
  (g) The Assistant to the President for Domestic Policy
- The Director of the Office of National AIDS Policy

(continued)

TABLE 12.1 (*continued*)
The White House

- The Assistant to the President for Economic Policy and Director, National Economic Council
- The Deputy Assistant to the President and Director of Advance
- The Assistant to the President and Cabinet Secretary
- The Assistant to the President for Legislative Affairs
- The Deputy Assistant to the President for Management and Administration
- The Assistant to the President for Presidential Personnel
- The Assistant to the President and White House Press Secretary
  - (a) The Deputy Assistant to the President and Director of Appointments and Scheduling
  - (b) The Assistant to the President and Staff Secretary
  - (c) The Assistant to the President and Director, USA Freedom Corps Office*
  - (d) The Deputy Assistant to the President and Director of the Office of Faith-Based and Community Initiatives*

(2) Thirty supporting policy offices, including nineteen of the twenty-four elements in the Vice President's staff, nine of the ten units in the First Lady's staff, plus the Presidential Aide and the Oval Office Operations group.

(3) Sixty professional and technical offices, including the Executive Clerk, the Chief Usher, eleven units in the management and administration area, eleven elements in the White House Military Office, twelve in the Correspondence Office, and six in the Secret Service.

---

the lesser units that were established by presidents in the recent past, only to be disestablished by a subsequent president (e.g., the assistant for Consumer Affairs, the Points of Light office).

THE BUSH WHITE HOUSE

A Wholesale Reorganization?

Upon his inaugural, was President Bush bound to continue the elements, structure, and allocation of responsibilities that existed in the White House under his predecessor? No. Could he, therefore, have unscrambled the whole place, sending the vice president and his staff back to the Capitol, telling the first lady just to bake cookies, returning the legal advice function to the attorney general, politics and patronage to the party National Committee, and advance work to the responsibility of locally recruited volunteers, and keeping internal White House coordination (as did Roosevelt, Kennedy, and Carter) in his own hands rather than have a chief of staff? The answer again is, technically and legally, yes, but practically, absolutely not. The genuine need for those functions has become too demanding and the tradition much too ingrained. The "institutionality" of the White House, it turns out, is in fact characterized by some accumulated inflexibilities.

What Did President Bush Do in January 2001?

Bush did not subtract a single one of the principal policy elements that he inherited from President Clinton. He did upgrade two of those offices, strengthened the vice president's staff, reduced the role of the first lady and eliminated one of the units in her office, made some alterations within the NSC group, cut back somewhat the number of volunteers and interns at the White House, and, after September 11, 2001, instituted a dramatically large, new office in his circle of White House assistants.

Communications

The first upgrade was to a White House function that has become a pillar of attention and resources for all of the most recent presidents: the communications domain. President Bush created a new senior post to head this area, an Assistant to the President and Counselor for Communications (Karen Hughes). The existing offices of Communications, Speechwriting, and Media Affairs (and, it is alleged, the Press Secretary) were placed under the Counselor's jurisdiction. By this action, President Bush was clearly underscoring the growing importance—in fact, the all-encompassing priority—of communications/public relations/ "spin" in the environment of the modern presidency.

Politics

The second upgrade was the elevation of the Senior Advisor for Policy (read "politics") and Strategy (Karl Rove) to a prominent position with directive authority over the existing Political Affairs, Intergovernmental Relations, and Public Liaison units. The Senior Advisor has maintained the tight control that the Clinton White House had over not only political strategy but campaign operations as well. Rove's was considerable during Bush's first two years:

> Republicans credit Mr. Rove for planning the strategy for the 2002 election almost from the first day that Mr. Bush became president. . . . White House advisers said he essentially controlled the Republican National Committee from the White House. . . . Mr. Rove's reputation as a powerful and imperious political adviser to Mr. Bush is already well established in Washington. But even those in top Republican political circles said today that they were taken aback by Mr. Rove's relentlessness and gutsiness in sending out the president to races where Democrats were leading—and where Mr. Bush might have been blamed had the Republicans lost.[7]

There were often strings attached to Bush's help, however. Rove micromanaged some races down to details as fine as how long candidates could talk before the president took the stage. A New Jersey Republican official involved in the losing Senate campaign of Doug Forrester described the Rove-Mehlman operation as "relentless."[8] Readers can be assured that the reelection campaign of 2004 had also begun shortly after the 2001 inauguration. In what has now become another continuing tradition, such reelection campaigns are managed tightly and in detail by the White House political staff.

The First Lady

While Laura Bush's functions appeared to have diminished at the outset, with her office at the White House having been switched from the West Wing to the East Wing and her predecessor's Millennium Council having been abolished, the first lady has gradually increased her area of official activities, substituting for the president in giving his Saturday radio address on November 17, 2001, taking a foreign trip by herself (to Europe in May 2002, which included a visit to Prague where she discussed NATO affairs with President Havel), and supervising a staff of at least twenty. This element of White House tradition is still in flux. While the first lady's responsibilities will, for the most part, depend on the personal wishes of the first family, it is clear that a set of expectations has already been built up, and that her role—now and in the future—will not likely return to the Mamie Eisenhower/Pat Nixon model.

The Vice President

The vice president's basic responsibilities are in the Constitution, but beginning with Eisenhower, the modern presidents have built upon that base, adding extra-constitutional duties that appear in no statute but that gradually have hardened into yet another element of the aforementioned White House tradition. The Clinton-Gore relationship became the epitome of that tradition—until the Bush-Cheney duo continued, and in fact expanded it even farther: "Inside the White House, Cheney and his small but powerful staff have emerged as the fulcrum of Bush's foreign policy. . . . Cheney has used his power and authority—unrivaled by that of any vice president in modern times—to help set the course of the administration's War on Terror. . . . He's the single greatest influence on the president."[9]

Vice President Cheney chaired the National Energy Policy Development Group, and his staff of at least seventy-three now includes a Deputy Assistant for Operations, a Director of Homeland Security for the Vice President, a Photo Office, and military aides. Like her predecessor, Mrs. Cheney has an office in the Eisenhower Executive Office Building and a staff to support her (they number at least six; Mrs. Gore had nine).

National Security Affairs

The president consolidated and renamed some of the elements of the NSC but also added a Deputy National Security Advisor for Combating Terrorism and a Special Advisor for Cyberspace Security. Condoleezza Rice's NSC staff of over 200 clearly continues its years' long tradition of coordinating the advice and the paper flow from the members of the president's national security community. Strong voices they are, and the advisors are frequently at odds. Analyzing the fierce internal debate about Iraq, a *Washington Post* staff writer concluded, however:

> The National Security Council structure designed to synthesize differences among Cabinet officials worked effectively. National security adviser Condoleezza Rice, whose authority in dealing with such high-powered players has long been questioned in Washington, was seen across the board as a fair arbiter in presenting all views to Bush. . . . Rice, increasingly seen by the "soft side" of the debate as a valuable honest broker and perhaps even an ally in her discussions with Bush, decided to call each of the involved senior advisers that night to say, 'Look, there really is a decision to be made. " 'Do you have any view that you want to express to the president?' "[10]

There is nothing new about having fierce debates over national security ends and means. What is new are two foreign affairs-related White House traditions. One began with Woodrow Wilson, was expanded under Roosevelt, Truman, and Eisenhower, but has exploded under the most recent presidents: the conduct of personal presidential diplomacy. Not only are there periodic multi-headed international summits, and very frequent one-on-one chief of state meetings—at Camp David or the ranch—but now, constantly, presidents are on the telephone with one another. Occasionally it is "Happy Birthday!" or "How are the wife and kids?" but far more often it is the president personally negotiating the most difficult and contentious issues in American foreign policy. Every one of these contacts requires briefing memoranda in advance, assembled from departmental submissions but squeezed down into succinct prose by the NSC staff. A single week may see fifty or more of such president-to-president telephone calls.

The second growing national security tradition is the president's personal supervision not only of strategy but of tactical operations by U.S. forces. Such supervision is heatedly denied in public but nonetheless occasionally practiced, and of course in secret. Every CIA covert action (e.g., the November 2, 2002, Predator aircraft attack in Yemen) is, by law, preceded by a written presidential "finding"; for such operations; presidential delegation has ended, and with it, "plausible deniability" has disappeared. It is becoming easier and easier for the president and his staff to monitor any and all tactical operations by the explosion of technology that permits the White House to see, hear, communicate with, and control almost every movement happening on a distant battlefield. The NSC's Situation Room can, if the White House wishes, use almost any communication, satellite or drone photo, infrared image, or electronic signal; it is up to the astuteness and skill of the White House NSC staff to make the quintessential judgment calls: how much of this raw data to demand from the national security community, whether and how quickly to bring it to the president's attention without overwhelming both themselves and him, and when, if ever, the White House should intervene.

Mr. Bush's White House vigorously continues these two related traditions in national security affairs; neither he nor his successors will ever go back to the condition idealized by ancient Chinese sage Sun-Tzu: "He will win who has military capacity and is not interfered with by the sovereign."

Special Projects Assistants

President Clinton created six White House offices of a somewhat lesser stature. First among the new posts was the assistant to the president for Y2K conversion (established in anticipation of severe, nationwide, computer-related problems arising from the changeover from dates beginning with "19" to those beginning with "20"). This officer's duties ended with the smooth switch to the new dates in January. Second, Clinton established a Special Envoy to the Americas (appointed to assist in the achievement of a hemispheric "free trade area of the Americas" and in the negotiation of a treaty to bring such an agreement into existence). Third, he created an Office for Environmental Initiatives (earlier called an Office for Climate Change). This unit concentrated on the coordination and development of legislative initiatives for environmental protection in both the domestic and foreign policy spheres. Fourth was the Office for the President's Initiative for One America (an outreach unit to support national and local actions to improve race relations and to emphasize the need to "mend but not end" affirmative action programs). Fifth, a Senior Adviser to the Chief of Staff for Native American Affairs was created, since American Indian tribes enjoy a direct government-to-government relationship with the federal executive, and since issues affecting Indians and Alaska Natives—economic, educational, legal, and financial—cross many departmental boundaries, several presidents have followed Nixon's example of creating a special White House office for leadership and coordination in this area. Sixth, and finally, Clinton established the National AIDS Policy Coordinator (to manage the cross-cutting issues here from different cabinet departments that touch both domestic and international policy and actions).

Like many similar White House "special projects" units created by various past presidents, these six offices reflected both the personal priorities of President Clinton and the political pressures for dramatizing those priorities. Unlike most of the forty-seven principal policy elements listed in the foregoing section, such "special" offices are not endowed with the tradition of continuity; they tend to be temporary. Since a new president brings new priorities, these particular elements of the White House structure can, accordingly, be expected to change when a new chief executive takes charge. President Bush eliminated the first five of the six, just described, and retained the sixth. Then he added four new special support offices of his own: a strategic initiatives unit, reporting directly to the new Senior Adviser for Policy and Strategy; an Office of Faith-Based and Community Initiatives, reflecting President Bush's desire to encourage and increase the social service activities rendered by churches;[11] a White House Freedom Corps Office, to dramatize, enhance, and expand opportunities for volunteer service in the nation, including the Peace Corps and the Corporation for National and Community Service, and using as its instrument a new cabinet committee, the Freedom Corps Council;[12] and an Office of Global Communications, "to coordinate the administration's foreign policy message and supervise America's image abroad" and "to address the question President Bush posed in his speech to Congress the week after the terrorist attacks: 'Why do they hate us?' "[13]

Homeland Security

Within a month after the catastrophic events of September 11, 2001, President Bush created a new, vitally important White House element, the Office of Homeland Security,[14] installing former governor Tom Ridge as director with the rank of Assistant to the President. The language of the executive order gave Ridge no power (only a statute could do that), but its verbs endowed him with much influence. He was to "develop and coordinate the implementation of a comprehensive national strategy;" "coordinate the executive branch's efforts;" "work with the executive departments and agencies;" "identify priorities;" "work with federal, state and local agencies;" "facilitate;" "coordinate and prioritize;" "review and assess the adequacy of;" "strengthen measures;" "develop criteria;" "review plans;" and develop . . . proposals for presidential action . . . for submission to the "Office of Management and Budget." When it came to budget authority, the executive order told Ridge that he could scrutinize "the level and use of funding in departments and agencies for homeland security-related activities and, prior to the [OMB] Director's forwarding of the annual budget submission to the president for transmittal to the Congress, shall certify to the [OMB] Director the funding levels that the Assistant to the President for Homeland Security believes are necessary and appropriate." This constituted an exceptional level of influence, even for a White House office, but, as is true throughout the White House, only the president had the power of decision and action.

In Section 5 of the Executive Order, the president created the Homeland Security Council, a cabinet committee chaired by the president (with the vice president as alternate), to "serve as the mechanism for ensuring coordination of homeland security-related activities of executive departments and agencies and effective development and implementation of homeland security policies." The Assistant to the President for Homeland Security is to be "responsible, at the President's direction, for determining the agenda, ensuring that necessary papers are prepared, and recording Council actions and Presidential decisions."

One year after the initial Homeland Security executive order was promulgated, Ridge was supervising seventeen subordinate offices, in which at least 120 men and women worked; a few were new White House employees, but most were from the cabinet departments. In June 2002, the president submitted to the Congress legislation, which created a Department of Homeland Security. It was enacted in late 2002, transferring many of the employees from the Office of Homeland Security to the new department. The president has announced, however, that the Office of Homeland Security will still remain in the White House:

> Even with the creation of the new Department, there will remain a strong need for a White House Office of Homeland Security. Protecting America from terrorism will remain a multidepartmental issue and will continue to require interagency coordination. Presidents will continue to require the confidential advice of a Homeland Security Advisor, and I intend for the White House Office of Homeland Security and the Homeland Security Council to maintain a strong role in coordinating our government-wide efforts to secure the homeland.[15]

In enacting its fiscal year (FY) 2003 appropriations legislation, the House of Representatives created a specific budgetary account for the White House Office of Homeland Security.[16]

Volunteers and Interns

President Clinton's White House was aided by 1,000 volunteers—men and women, mostly adherents of the president, who rendered free support services one to three days a week, for at least sixteen days a month. Seven hundred fifty people worked in the Correspondence Office. Mr. Bush reduced the volunteer cohort by approximately 200 and also cut in half the number of White House

TABLE 12.2
The Budget Figures for the Policy Elements of the White House Staff (in dollars)

Office Element	FY 2001 (Requested)	FY 2002 (Appropriated)	FY 2003 (Requested)
The President	390,000	450,000	450,000
White House Office	53,288,000	54,165,000	84,550,000
Office of Homeland Security	0	(27,000,000 included in OA amount)	(24,844,000 included in the White House Office amount)
Executive Residence			
• Operating Expenses	10,900,000	11,695,000	12,200,000
• Repair and Restoration	5,510,000	8,625,000	1,200,000
Vice President			
• Salaries	6,673,000	3,925,000	Total of
• Operating Expenses	354,000	318,000	4,400,000
Office of Policy Development*	4,032,000	4,142,000	4,200,000
National Security Council	7,165,000	7,494,000	9,525,000
One-half of the Office of Administration	22,868,000	48,497,500**	35,064,000
Totals	108,180,000	139,837,500	151,589,000

* Domestic Policy, Economic Policy, and AIDS Policy Offices
** Includes one-half of an FY 2002 Emergency Supplemental of $50,400,000)

interns—which had, at one time under Clinton, totaled 1,000 throughout a typical year.

The Budget of the White House

The results of Bush's changes are apparent when one examines the published budget figures for just the policy elements of the White House staff (the president has, by law, been given a raise himself—see Table 12.2). They show $43,408,000—or more than 40 percent—*more* in the published budget for Bush's White House (FY 2003) than the amount from Clinton's final request (FY 2001). As of this writing, the Senate has not yet enacted the FY 2003 appropriations bill for these elements, so the final amounts are not yet known.

Readers should recognize that these published figures do not include the costs of the many employees who are at work in the seven listed White House units. The author's best estimate for the budget of the *entire* White House staff community (as defined at the beginning of this chapter) for Clinton's final year is $730,500,000.[17] If the (unpublished) increased security, Secret Service, and military support costs since the events of September 11, 2001, could be added in, the author's estimate would be that that total figure is now $1 billion.[18]

It seems odd to the author, but it is true that neither the president nor his Office of Administration nor the director of the Office of Management and Budget, nor the General Accounting Office nor the Appropriations Committees of the Congress have, apparently, ever asked for or have tried to put together the costs of the total White House staff community.

Consolidation of Executive Office Accounts

President Bush has proposed an important budgetary and management reform for the Executive Office as a whole: to consolidate its eighteen separately specified budget accounts (including the eight listed in Table 12.2) into a single appropriation. If approved by the Congress, this would give the president the flexibility to transfer funds and personnel throughout the Executive Office to meet the changing and often unexpected needs of the modern presidency without having to importune the Congress to approve each such action by passing a separate piece of legislation.[19]

A CONCLUDING ASSESSMENT

How different, then, is the Bush White House from its predecessor? How much change has there been in structure, size, and function? The answer is, surprisingly little (not speaking of the substance of policy). Has there been an alteration in the growing tradition toward centralization of governance on important issues away from the cabinet departments and into the White House staff? No. Rather, there has been a continuation of that growth, especially in the areas of political management, communications, and national security. The growth of that tradition has, in fact, been buoyed by the exceptional capabilities of the leaders at the top of the Bush White House. In the author's opinion, it is the nation's good fortune that President Bush's White House staff (and many of his cabinet) appointments are men and women of such impressive previous experience in federal office. Vice President Cheney, Secretary of State Colin Powell, Secretary of Defense Donald Rumsfeld, Chief of Staff Andrew Card, National Security Advisor Condoleezza Rice, Legislative Affairs Director Nick Calio, and many others are extraordinarily capable veterans of White House service. From the opening bell of the Bush administration, they needed no coaching about how to discharge their duties, no orientation about how to work effectively in the environment of Washington, no instructions about how to handle differences of opinion—how not to carry their dissents into the public—and they needed no reminders as to who is president.

NOTES

1. A Reorganization Act, effective July 1, 1939, permitted the president to employ six administrative assistants. The White House office itself was created by presidential action, that is, Executive Order 8248 of September 8, 1939. Public Law 95-570 of November 2, 1978, merely allows the president to make his White House office appointments "without regard to any other provision of law" to "perform such official duties as the President may prescribe" and sets limits on the numbers of White House office supergrades.

2. The staff of the National Security Council is authorized by Section 101(c) of the National Security Act of 1947.

3. Executive Order 12028 of December 12, 1977.

4. Senate Committee on Government Affairs, *Investigation of Illegal or Improper Activites in Connection with 1996 Federal Election Campaigns, Final Report*, 105th Congress, 2nd session, 10 March 1999, 1:131.

5. As of this writing, the White House Homeland Security group is composed of seventeen subordinate offices, ten of which are headed by officers with presidentially titled rank. These seventeen are not included in the aforementioned listing because, upon the creation of the Department of Homeland Security, many of these units will become elements of the new department. There will, however, remain in the White House an Office of Homeland Security, but its composition, structure, and staffing are not presently known.

6. Former Executive Clerk Maurice Latta served at the White House for fifty years.

7. Elisabeth Bumiller and David E. Sanger, "Republicans Say Rove Was Mastermind of Big Victory," *New York Times*, November 7, 2002, B-1.

8. Jim VandeHei and Dan Balz, "In GOP Win, a Lesson in Money, Muscle, Planning," *Washington Post*, November 10, 2002, 1. Ken Mehlman is the director of the White House Office of Political Affairs.

9. Glenn Kessler and Peter Slavin, "Cheney Is Fulcrum of Foreign Policy," *Washington Post*, October 13, 2002, 1.

10. Karen de Young, "For Powell, a Long Path to a Victory," *Washington Post*, November 10, 2002, 1.

11. Established by Executive Order 13199 of January 29, 2001.

12. Established by Executive Order 13254 of January 29, 2002.

13. Karen de Young, "Bush to Create Formal Office to Shape U.S. Image Abroad," *Washington Post*, July 30, 2002, 1. This office is now staffed and is listed in the White House telephone book, but the instrument of its establishment, as of this writing, has not yet been formally issued.

14. Established by Executive Order 13228 of October 8, 2001.

15. George W. Bush, "Message to the Congress Transmitting the Proposed Legislation to Create the Department of Homeland Security," *Weekly Compilation of Presidential Documents* 38, no. 25 (June 18, 2002): 1034–38.

16. The bill is H.R. 5120, 107th Congress, 2nd session, enacted July 24, 2002. Senate action is, as of this writing, still pending.

17. Bradley H. Patterson, *The White House Staff: Inside the West Wing and Beyond* (Washington, D.C.: Brookings Institution, 2001), 342–45.

18. For example, while the U.S. Secret Service does not make public either the numbers of its employees who work on the protective details or the associated costs, the overall Secret Service budget went from $826.6 million in FY 2001 to $1.014 billion in FY 2003.

19. The House Appropriations Committee with jurisdiction, the Subcommittee on Treasury, Postal Service, and General Government, has approved a pilot experiment, taking a small step in the direction requested by the president, by providing for the procurement of common goods and services among the Executive Office agencies; as of this writing, the Senate has not yet acted on the FY 2003 appropriations request.

Chapter 13

Vice President Dick Cheney

Trendsetter or Just Your Typical Veep?

Jack Lechelt

INTRODUCTION

George W. Bush, in his pursuit of the presidency, had always wanted Dick Cheney to be his running mate. Unfortunately for Bush, Cheney was not interested at first—but he did take on the task of leading the search for a vice-presidential running mate. Little did Cheney know that by directing the search it would lead right back to him: eventually he acceded to Bush's requests to be the vice-presidential nominee for the 2000 election.[1] It appears, at the midpoint of Bush's presidency, that Cheney is one of Bush's most trusted advisors, and the most influential vice president in the history of the United States.

Far too often, vice-presidential influence, when it has been noticed, is written off as presidential discretion: what the president has given, he can easily take away. While I do not deny the importance of presidential discretion, by ascribing all of Cheney's influence to Bush's personal preferences we ignore other important factors about the office of the vice presidency that have allowed Cheney and his recent predecessors to have had increasing amounts of influence. Cheney is a beneficiary of factors beyond Bush's preferences: in particular, earlier precedents have been established by earlier presidents and vice presidents that have enabled Cheney to walk into an office of stature. Moreover, bureaucratic and institutional aspects of the presidency and the complexity of international and domestic political environment practically mandate that a president utilize his vice president.

DICK CHENEY

Cheney offered George W. Bush a strong résumé, complete with the "insider" Washington experience that Bush so clearly lacked; Cheney has served in many positions of great import: as Chief of Staff to President Ford, Congressman from Wyoming, and Secretary of Defense for Bush's father, President G. H. W. Bush.[2] Unlike previous vice-presidential selections, one can easily see that Bush did not select Cheney because of his electoral vote pull—Cheney's home state of Wyoming has only three electoral votes, which G. H. W. Bush and Robert Dole both easily won in the previous two presidential elections. Moreover, for the Bush/Cheney ticket to have avoided constitutional conflict, Cheney had to reregister as a Wyoming voter, because the Constitution mandates that the president and vice president reside from different states. It is interesting to note, however, that the "outsider/insider experience" balance between president and vice president is hardly new to presidential politics: Bill Clinton, then governor of Arkansas, selected then senator Al Gore, but both were of the same age, politically moderate, and from the South. Also, Ronald Reagan and Jimmy Carter selected Washingtonian insiders as their running mates.

Cheney's Initial Influence

Dick Cheney's influence was evident early, particularly as soon as the Election 2000 Florida fiasco was concluded. The Vice President-elect was placed in charge of the transition, interviewed every cabinet secretary, and turned to many acquaintances in filling important positions. Furthermore, "Mr. Cheney had a direct hand in picking Mr. Bush's Cabinet, especially three of the seven cabinet officers approved . . . by the Senate—Secretary of State Colin L. Powell, Secretary of Defense Donald H. Rumsfeld, and Secretary of Treasury Paul H. O'Neill—all colleagues of his from other administrations."[3] With national security, "an old Cheney loyalist, Stephen Hadley, is deputy national security adviser," and Paul Wolfowitz, deputy to Rumsfeld, is described as a "protégé" of Mr. Cheney.[4]

The Office of the Vice President

Upon taking office, Vice President Cheney was able to surround himself with high-caliber assistants. It is important to recognize that the resources with which he could staff his office were established prior to his arrival, and those resources are impressive. The vice presidency was given a line item in the presidential budget in 1978 with the passage of a law titled "Assistance and Services for the Vice President." The "law authorizes paid staff, including temporary experts and consultants, in order to enable the Vice President to provide assistance to the President in connection with the performance of functions specially assigned to the Vice President by the President in the discharge of executive duties and responsibilities." During the Gore vice presidency, there were

144 people working in his office with a budget of over \$4 million.[5] The suffi-
cient supply of funds and staff offers the vice president an excellent ability to
generally assist the president. More specifically with regard to foreign policy
and national security, "after taking office, Cheney assembled a staff of fourteen
foreign policy specialists, creating what officials say amounts to a mini-
National Security Council. Cheney's office, in effect, is an agile cruiser, able to
maneuver around the lumbering aircraft carriers of the departments of State
and Defense to make its mark." More amazingly, Cheney's foreign policy team
is more highly regarded than the eighty professional staffers of the, NSC. Gore
also had a similar-sized staff, however, Kessler and Slevin state that Gore utilized his foreign policy staff for more specific issues, whereas Cheney "scrapped
any direct operational responsibility in the foreign policy realm."[6]

Generally, beyond specific budgetary amounts or staff numbers, the vice
presidency has increased in stature, which has further helped Cheney's current
status. According to Felzenberg, Cheney is the beneficiary of a more highly
respected office, which has had an improved stature over the past fifty years.
From the creation of the NSC in 1947, and its mandate that the vice president
be a member of the NSC, to President Jimmy Carter's and Vice President
Walter Mondale's establishment of important precedents, the vice presidency
was no longer a means of disposing of public figures.[7] Upon entering office in
1977, Carter established ground rules that aided Mondale's ability to influence
foreign policy. First, on a weekly basis, Carter and Mondale would have a
private lunch together—no aides, cabinet secretaries, or assistants would join
them. Second, the Vice President was included in all paperwork loops: he would
receive whatever documentation the President received or sent out. Third,
Mondale or his staff members were allowed access to all meetings in the White
House. Fourth, Mondale was given an office in the West Wing proximate to
the Oval Office.[8] Finally, Mondale was included in the President's Friday
morning foreign affairs breakfasts, which included the Secretaries of State and
Defense and the NSC advisor. With the exception of the foreign affairs break-
fast, all successive presidents and vice presidents continued these practices.[9]

Even though credit for the current status of the vice presidency should be
shared with Cheney's predecessors, it is easy to see that Cheney has far surpassed
the influence of any of his predecessors. Along with his role in the transition
and his highly regarded foreign policy team, Cheney began his vice presidency
with increased formal authority from President Bush. With every new president, a new directive is put forth detailing the organization of the NSC system;
for President Bush, the system is described in his National Security Presidential
Directive 1 (NSPD1). Clearly, Vice President Cheney is given a much larger
role than any previous vice president in the NSC system, including Vice
President Gore. In NSPD1, the Vice President is specifically granted power to
chair all NSC meetings when the President is not present; moreover, the Vice
President's chief of staff and national security advisor can attend all principal

and deputy committee meetings. Finally, the Vice President is given carte blanche authority to attend any and all NSC meetings.[10]

Cheney's Staff

The Vice President's staff, as mentioned earlier, is both numerous and highly regarded; however, his staff has also meshed well with the President's: Cheney "has . . . integrated the vice presidential staff seamlessly with the presidential staff, allowing the White House to speak with a unified voice as it deals with Congress and the public. . . . Though Bush has ultimate say, Cheney and his aides have been fully integrated into the national security apparatus."[11] Furthermore, Cheney's "aides worked closely with the president's staff [in response to the 9/11 terrorist attacks]. His chief of staff attended most of the A-level meetings at the White House, and two aides—Mary Matalin and Lewis Libby—were given the added title of 'assistant to the president.'"[12] Vice President Al Gore was also able to maintain connections through staff: Gore was "linked to important policy-making structures through members of his staff. For example, Gore's national security aide was a member of the administration's main working group on foreign policy (the deputies' committee), and his long-time Senate chief of staff was named second deputy to the White House chief of staff in May 1993."[13]

CHENEY AND BUSH

As earlier noted, the weekly private lunch between the president and vice president has been in existence since Vice Presidents Rockefeller and Mondale, and they continue with Cheney; however, Cheney's direct and continuous contact with President Bush and the foreign policy process is truly unprecedented. Not only does Cheney dine with Bush once a week and receive daily national security briefings with the President,[14] Cheney "chews over policy at the Pentagon with the president's national security team" on Wednesdays and meets every week with Secretary of State Powell and Secretary of Defense Rumsfeld.[15] Moreover, Bush and Cheney are "together throughout much of the week—at policy briefings, meetings with foreign heads of state, nominee-review sessions, and Cabinet coffees." Even after the terrorist attacks on the United States, when the Vice President was sent to what has been referred to as the "undisclosed location," "bunker," and "cave," Cheney has utilized "state-of-the-art video conferencing facilities to remain completely plugged into decision making."[16] Bumiller, writing for the *New York Times*, claims that Cheney "turned his disappearing act on his head. The more invisible he becomes, the more powerful he seems."[17]

Having a "presence" when decisions are made is not the same as playing a part in the decision making. Here too, however, Cheney is an active player in

Bush's foreign policy process. Actually, the President has been criticized for being too reliant on his assistants—particularly Cheney.[18] Among other things, Cheney has been described as a Chief Executive Officer to Bush's Chairman of the Board, Chief Operating Officer to Bush's CEO, and prime minister to Bush's head of state.[19] Cheney has also been described as the President's "consigliere" and "coach."[20] Many policy positions taken by Bush have Cheney's footprints all over them. This is further realized when one considers that Secretary of State Powell's moderate positions hardly win the day, and that National Security Advisor (NSA) Condoleezza Rice acts more as an honest broker than as a policy advocate.[21]

Generally speaking, Cheney's positions are considered more "hawkish" and have had quite an impact in Bush's White House. More specifically, Cheney "quietly but insistently pressed Mr. Bush to move early on a commitment to build a national missile defense system." Moreover, in Bush's first foreign policy crisis, Cheney "was almost wholly invisible throughout the stand-off with China over the downed U.S. surveillance plane, [however,] the vice president played a crucial role."[22] Along with Powell, Cheney was involved in talks with Chinese officials, hoping to secure the release of the plane's crew.[23]

September 11 Attacks

Of course, Bush's predominant foreign policy focus has been related to the September 11, 2001, terrorist attacks on New York City and Washington. And from the moment of the attacks, Cheney has been an incredibly active participant. After taking to the air on September 11, the President was in constant communication with Cheney, who brought to the President's attention the possible need to shoot down civilian airliners that may be on attack missions.

Within days of the attacks, Cheney was quickly sent off to the "undisclosed location," but he maintained continuous contact with the President and "worked the telephones of world leaders, bringing an experience to the job of coalition building that his boss does not have." Cheney's work for President G. H. W. Bush during the Gulf War of 1991 provided the Vice President with valuable contacts in the post-9/11 response: White House officials claim that "no one else in the administration can replicate the depth and breadth of his connections in the region. Cheney and his staff are routinely on the phone with Arab leaders, an unusual channel in addition to the regular State Department contacts."[24]

Cheney was also seriously involved in America's long-term response to terrorism: the Vice President "recommended to Bush the creation of the Homeland Security Office and suggested Pennsylvania Gov. Thomas J. Ridge as the one to head that office." Prior to the terrorist attacks, Cheney was given the responsibility of assessing the country's preparedness to terrorism, an effort that was "well underway" prior to 9/11. Finally, just prior to the bombing of Afghanistan,

Cheney persuaded Secretary of Defense Rumsfeld to tour the Middle East.[25] The Vice President himself toured the Middle East in March 2002, and while his trip was certainly not a success in its two goals of calming Palestinian-Israeli tension and building support for regime change in Iraq, he made the trip with the President's blessing into a situation that did not offer many opportunities for success.[26]

Iraq

Other areas of foreign policy that were largely shaped by Cheney include the administration's call for Yasser Arafat's removal as the leader of Palestine, which would hopefully open new avenues for peace in the Middle East. Also, "Cheney's office . . . was instrumental in fashioning a statement by Bush on July 12 [2002] encouraging Iranians to get rid of repressive religious leaders."[27]

> The potential war against Iraq is yet another area where Cheney exhibits strong influence: Cheney's impact on the Iraq debate—or his influence on the president—cannot be overstated, officials and experts said. Cheney is involved in key aspects of the planning for Iraq, from the wording of the administration's draft U.N. resolution on resumed weapons inspections to what to do with Iraq if President Saddam Hussein is toppled. In interagency councils, Cheney has been consumed with whether the Iraqi president has obtained weapons of mass destruction, officials say.[28]

Cheney's strongest role in a pending war with Iraq was in making the administration's case to the American people and fellow Republicans who were weary of a unilateral approach to Hussein. Brent Scowcroft (G. H. W. Bush's NSA), James Baker (G. H. W. Bush's secretary of state), and current Republican members of Congress were becoming vocal in their opposition to what appeared to be a determination to "go it alone" in Iraq (albeit with Britain's support), and without congressional approval.[29] The Vice President, speaking before the Veterans of Foreign Wars in Nashville on August 26, 2002, offered a strongly stated argument for regime change in Iraq. Citing Hussein's continuous efforts to acquire weapons of mass destruction (WMD), his willingness to use WMD on his own people, and his continuous disregard for international rules, Cheney claimed "the risks of inaction are far greater than the risk of action."[30] As for the authenticity of Cheney representing the President's preferences, William Kristol was quoted as saying that "when Cheney talks, it's Bush."[31]

Most recently, an excerpt published in the *Washington Post* from Bob Woodward's new book *Bush at War* describes how Colin Powell aggressively worked to convince the President of pursuing multilateral channels in dealing with Iraq.[32] Powell, according to Woodward, was able to persuade Bush that working with the United Nations and forming a coalition was a better option. In Powell's pursuit, he was aided by NSA Condoleezza Rice's performance as an "honest broker" and her determination to ensure that Bush had a wider array of choices. Still, while Powell won the day on such an important topic, the fact that it was such an uphill battle for him and that Cheney has a much easier time in communicating with the President speaks volumes about the influence the Vice President has in the Bush administration. Furthermore, "some officials say that Rice . . . at times is irritated by Cheney's influence, and believes that Cheney's staff roams too freely over the national security council terrain."[33]

Finally, Cheney's role in the Bush White House has been greatly appreciated by foreign officials as well: "foreign officials, including 17 presidents or prime ministers, . . . have learned they must schedule a visit with Cheney as they make their rounds in Washington. A meeting with Cheney is so highly prized that when the vice president recently canceled a meeting with the foreign minister of Kazakhstan because the government had not released a Turkmen dissident, the Kazakh government quickly decided to set the man free."[34]

THE POLITICS OF INFLUENCE

One supposed explanation for Cheney's influence has been saved for last. Presidential scholars and administration insiders have posited that Cheney is highly trusted by Bush because the Vice President has no interest in running for president.[35] First, it is interesting to note that the vice presidency may now be so highly valued by a skilled Washington insider that he need not seek higher office. Second, while Cheney's lack of higher ambition may indeed hold sway with the President, it would seem, in reality, to be a poor reason for granting Cheney more influence. Looking to Cheney's immediate predecessor, Al Gore, one can see both that he had ambitions for higher office and was indeed highly influential in Clinton's foreign policy process. One must keep in mind that the president's and vice president's interests, particularly if the vice president has higher ambitions, are intricately intertwined. A sitting vice president, particularly in the first term, would enhance his own chances for future political success by assisting the current president. One would have a tough time believing that President Carter's electoral loss in 1980 helped Vice President Mondale in 1984. Moreover, a president can rely on an ambitious vice president to offer useful domestic political considerations that more idealistic aides may not appreciate. President Carter utilized just such advice from Vice President Mondale. Zbigniew Brzezinski, President Carter's National Security Advisor, perhaps best states Mondale's importance in Carter's foreign policy: "Mondale's most important substantive contribution was his political judgment. He was a vital political barometer for the President, and Carter respected his opinion on the domestic implications of foreign policy decision making. I also felt that Mondale had a good sense of political timing."[36] Perhaps in the last two years of a second term, when an ambitious vice president is starting to realize that he must actively travel the country, raise funds, and scare off other candidates, one could appreciate a distance between a president and vice president; however, Bush and Cheney are hardly at that phase of their presidency and vice presidency.

CONCLUSIONS

Dick Cheney's active role in President Bush's foreign policy formation is obvious. However, it is also necessary to understand *why* Cheney has been so actively involved in Bush's presidency. Cheney's influence is less a matter of President Bush's personal preferences than it is a result of many other factors.

Three theoretical underpinnings enable us to better understand why Dick Cheney was involved in the Bush foreign policy process. These three factors will also help us understand why the vice presidency in general is more likely to have a larger and continuous role to play in foreign policy. It is important to note that all three factors are interrelated and not mutually exclusive.

Domestic Policy

According to Joseph Pika, there are three places to consider in hopes of better understanding the vice president's increasing role in foreign policy: the Constitution, statutes, and practice and precedents. The Constitution, however, offers little direction for the vice president. In effect, the vice president will perform the duties of the president if the president is unable to do so, and the vice president will preside over the Senate.

Throughout American history, the vice presidency has only marginally been addressed in constitutional amendments. The Twelfth Amendment, Twenty-second Amendment, and the Twenty-fifth Amendment only marginally deal with the vice presidency. The Twelfth Amendment, ratified in 1804, was intended to address the problems of the 1800 presidential election, whereby Thomas Jefferson and Aaron Burr, supposedly on the same ticket, tied in the Electoral College. With ratification of the amendment, the president and vice president would be voted for separately. Alas, it was felt that the Twelfth Amendment would now ensure that only second-rate talents would become vice president: who would knowingly pursue a second-place position?[37] The Twenty-Second Amendment limited a president to serving two terms, which then gave vice presidents a maximum time line in which they would have to wait to begin their own quest. Finally, the Twenty-Fifth Amendment put forth a process in which presidential disability could be addressed. In effect, the Constitution and its amendments provide little guidance for understanding Cheney's role in foreign policy.

Statutory change, like the Constitution, also does not offer much guidance in understanding the vice presidency and its changing role in foreign policy. Paul Kengor hypothesized that the change in the vice president's role came about in large part due to the passage of the National Security Act of 1947 (the Act), which established the National Security Council and included the vice president as a member of the council. Finally, one need not look any further than the Cuban Missile Crisis to find that a president can, more or less, void the Act's intent: President Kennedy created the "Executive Committee" of the NSC (ExCom), which did not include the vice president; furthermore, his closest assistant throughout the affair was his brother Bobby—the attorney general.[38]

According to Pika, the place to look is at practice and precedent: "Practice and precedent have by far been the most important determinants of vice-presidential roles. The development of these roles is a twentieth-century phenomenon."[39] First, the practice of selecting presidents has changed substantially. With control of the campaign now placed in the hands of the candidates, rather than under party control, campaigns have become candidate centered rather than party centered.[40] Weakened ties to political parties have afforded candidates more leeway over their campaigns, and this has led to an increase in the presidential nominee's ability to choose his own vice-presidential running mate.

Further pertinent to Pika's discussion of vice-presidential practices and precedents are four notable changes, which were discussed earlier. By and large, most of these changes were established during the Carter-Mondale term.[41] First, vice presidents now have an office in the West Wing: proximity is power. Second, vice presidents attend the national security briefings that the president receives every morning. Along with the third factor, receiving all of the paperwork that the president sends and receives, the vice president is continually provided with inside information: knowing what the president knows enables the vice president to be actively involved in the policy process. Finally, it has been established that the vice president and president will meet for lunch on a weekly basis without the presence of aides or advisors.

Vice-Presidential Power

Another important component of this discussion comes from Richard Neustadt's *Presidential Power*.[42] In his classic account of the modern presidency, Neustadt presented the concept of vantage points, whereby a president attempts to expand his reach or influence in as many directions as possible. A president can reach farther when he has a trusted assistant who can help fulfill the symbolic needs of the job and can give useful advice from his or her own political experience. Clearly, the president has added vantage points with a vice president who knows which senators to push for passage of a controversial treaty or bill. Along these lines, Cheney was able to maintain useful contacts with Republicans in Congress, which can help maintain support for the President's policies.[43] Moreover, as discussed earlier, presidents are stretched thin: there is no chance that a president can be everywhere at every moment. With a trusted vice president and the glamour and pomp that accompany the second-highest office, the president, in effect, expands his reach.

Bureaucratic Politics

Another important area of theoretical relevance is bureaucratic politics and the notion that certain rules and procedures are in place, making the president's desires to control the bureaucracy difficult at best. Morton Halperin recognized the role that bureaucratic politics would play in foreign policy and felt that the president would have certain options with which to respond to the difficulties of foreign policy leadership; the most relevant concerning the vice president is for the president to adopt or appoint "a special agent who does not have commitments to a particular bureaucratic organization and is free to cut across the concerns of various departments."[44] The vice president is a perfect fit for this role: he has excellent resources (as explained earlier) and the political clout to jump into important foreign policy areas. Paul David, in an article for the *Journal of Politics*, offers a related point: while the president is free to give the vice president additional roles and responsibilities, once those roles are delegated, they are increasingly difficult to take back, hence, the vice presidency increases in importance over time.[45]

Edward Morse also recognized the difficulty that the president would have within the White House due to the aforementioned factors.[46] Rather than a hierarchical chain of command and the importance of cabinet government, issues would become so interrelated that foreign policy would become a function of bureaucratic politics; that is, competition among various professionals in and out of official government positions will attempt to have their preferences reflected in policy. However, Morse also pointed out that the difficulties facing the president were far larger than in-house squabbles, which leads us to the third theoretical point—the changing international environment (and how it relates to domestic policy).

National and International Politics

International and domestic issues are increasingly intermingled; Rosati cites Bayless Manning with coining the term intermestic to describe the growing complexity and intertwining of international and domestic issues.[47] Current economic issues reflect this complexity: any policy that is adopted with regard to the American economy can have an impact far beyond the nation's boundaries. Also, with trade barriers eroding, regulations enacted to protect American workers can result in factories opening overseas where hiring practices and worker safety issues are less regulated. Moreover, as displayed by Robert Putnam and his two-level games, leaders do not simply enter into agreements with a united country behind them: they often must negotiate with many different domestic actors and groups who have their own unique political preferences.[48]

Another development that Morse discussed was the increasing importance of issues that were then considered "low policy," such as trade, economics, and labor. While "high policy" (security and military concerns) will always be important, there is an added complexity in foreign policy with the rise of economic issues. Globalization and the expansion of the free-market system, which brings with it more and larger transnational corporations and international organizations, will mandate that the president utilize any and all resources he has—and the vice president is, again, a perfect resource. Any post-Hussein world will require an expert touch at dealing with Middle East leaders and economic factors that can help create a prosperous future for Iraq. Vice President Cheney has as good a chance as any administration figure to help ensure that the future is brighter than the past.

In conclusion, though Vice President Cheney has surpassed all previous vice presidents in foreign policy influence, he was able to do so based on his predecessors' advances of new practices and precedents. Furthermore, the international environment mandates that the president seek assistance from any and all sources, and the vice presidency is an excellent resource for assistance. There certainly is no guarantee that future vice presidents will be as influential as Vice President Cheney has so far proven to be. But Cheney's activity will put forth new practices and precedents that will increase the chances for a continually enlarged role for the vice presidency, as will the increasingly complex global environment in which presidents and vice presidents must operate.

NOTES

1. Mark Bowden, Ron Hutcheson, and Ken Dilanian, "How Bush Selected Cheney," *Philadelphia Inquirer*, July 26, 2000, A1.

2. See Edward Walsh, "Cheney Leads a Life of Unexpected Turns," *Washington Post*, July 23, 2000, A4.

3. Reuters, "The Vice-President—Savvy Journeyman at No. 2," *The Australian*, January 22, 2001, 9.

4. Dana Milbank, "For Cheney, the Future Is Now," *Washington Post National Weekly Edition*, February 12, 2001, 12; Gerard Baker, "Bush's Constant Friend: Man in the News Dick Cheney: The US Vice-President Keeps a Low Profile but Wields Enormous Influence," *Financial Times*, May 19, 2001, 13.

5. Bradley Patterson, *The White House Staff: Inside the West Wing and Beyond* (Washington, D.C.: Brookings Institution, 2000), 347.

6. Glenn Kessler and Peter Slevin, "Cheney Is Fulcrum of Foreign Policy: In Interagency Fights, His Views Often Prevail," *Washington Post*, October 13, 2002, Barbara Slavin and Susan Page, "Cheney Rewrites Roles in Foreign Policy: Influence 'Unique' for Vice President," *USA Today*, July 29, 2002, 2A.

7. See Paul Kengor, *Wreath Layer or Policy Player?: The Vice President's Role in Foreign Policy* (Lanham, M.: Lexington Books, 2000); Sidney Milkis and Michael Nelson, *The American Presidency: Origins and Development, 1776–1993*, 2d ed. (Washington, D.C.: CQ Press, 1994).

8. Paul Light, *Vice-Presidential Power: Advice and Influence in the White House* (Baltimore: Johns Hopkins University Press, 1984), 151–154.

9. Jimmy Carter, *Keeping Faith: Memoirs of a President* (New York: Bantam Books, 1982). See also Light, *Vice-Presidential Power*, 1984.

10. U.S., White House, *National Security Presidential Directive 1* (2001), http://www.fas.org/irp/offdocs/nspd/nspd-1.html. For Clinton's NSC system, see U.S. White House, *Organization of the National Security Council: Presidential Decision Directive Pdd2* (1993), http://www.fas.org/irp/offdocs/pdd/pdd-2.html.

11. Milbank, "For Cheney, the Future Is Now," 2001, 12.

12. Stephen Hess, *Organizing the Presidency*, 3rd ed. (Washington, D.C.: Brookings Institution, 2002), 171.

13. Joseph Pika, "The Vice Presidency: New Opportunities, Old Constraints," in *The Presidency and the Political System*, ed. Michael Nelson (Washington, D.C.: CQ Press, 2000), 554.

14. Elisabeth Bumiller and David E. Sanger, "Threat of Terrorism Is Shaping the Focus of Bush Presidency," *New York Times*, September 11, 2002, http://nytimes.com.

15. Francine Kiefer, "Behind the Plan, the VP Who's Everywhere." *Christian Science Monitor* (May 18, 2001), 1.

16. See Roland Watson, "Cheney Stays Out of Sight, but He Is Still Calling the Shots," *The Times* October 9, 2001, (London), www.lexis-nexis.com.

17. Elisabeth Bumiller, "Cheney, Shrinking from View, Still Looms Large," *New York Times*, November 30, 2001, http://nytimes.com/2001/11/26/politics/26lett.html.

18. John F. Harris and Dan Balz, "A Well-Oiled Machine: The Bush White House Thrives on Methodical Planning," *Washington Post National Weekly Edition*, March 7, 2001, 6–8.

19. Abraham McLaughlin, "A Vice President-Elect With 'Big Time' Clout," *Christian Science Monitor*, December 20, 2000, 1; Walsh, "Cheney Leads," Gerard Baker, "Bush's Constant Friend: Man in the News Dick Cheney," *Financial Times*, May 19, 2001, 13.

20. Bumiller, "Cheney, Shrinking from View".

21. Slavin and Page, "Cheney Rewrites".

22. Baker, "Bush's Constant Friend".

23. Bill Deans, "Powell Says U.S.-China Ties in Peril," *Atlanta Journal and Constitution*, April 9, 2001, 1A.

24. Watson, "Cheney Stays out of Sight," quote from Slavin and Page, "Cheney Rewrites".

25. Edwin Chen, "Cheney Busy Behind the Scenes: Vice President is kept Hidden for Security Reasons." *Los Angeles Times (*October 12, 2001). http://latimes.com/news/nationworld/wire/sns-worldtrade-cheney-lat.story.

26. Slavin and Page, "Cheney Rewrites," 2002.

27. Ibid.

28. Kessler and Slevin, "Cheney Is Fulcrum".

29. See Jeanne Cummings, "Cheney Rebuke Raps Some Old Colleagues," *Wall Street Journal*, August 28, 2002, A4.

30. U.S., Vice President, *Remarks by the Vice President to the Veterans of Foreign Wars 103rd National Convention*, 2002, http://www.whitehouse.gov/news/releases/2002/08/20020826.html.

31. Elisabeth Bumiller and James Dao, "Eyes on Iraq: Cheney Says Peril of a Nuclear Iraq Justifies Attack," *New York Times*, August 27, 2002, 1.

32. Excerpt from Bob Woodward, *Bush at War* (New York: Simon and Schuster, 2002), 53.

33. Kessler and Slevin, "Cheney Is Fulcrum".

34. Ibid.; see also Slavin and Page, "Cheney Rewrites".

35. See McLaughlin, "A Vice President-Elect," Peter Grier, "Cheney's Vice-Presidential Load Is Heaviest Yet," *Christian Science Monitor*, March 7, 2001, 1; Kiefer, "Kenneth Walsh, "Cheney Out of the Bunker: The Most Powerful V.P. Ever, Now in the Role of a Lifetime," *U.S. News & World Report*, March 25, 2002, 18.

36. Zbigniew Brzezinski, *Power and Principle: Memoirs of the National Security Advisor, 1977–1981* (New York: Farrar Straus Giroux, 1983), 34.

37. See Jules Witcover, *Crapshoot: Rolling the Dice on the Vice Presidency* (New York: Crown, 1992).

38. Even though Johnson was not a part of the ExCom, he "sat in almost all of the key White House meetings." Still, one can easily recognize that Johnson could have been kept out of ExCom meetings. See Graham Allison and Phillip Zelikow, *Essence of Decision: Explaining the Cuban Missile Crisis*, 2d ed. (New York: Longman, 1999).

39. Pika, "The Vice Presidency," 542.

40. James W. Ceaser, *Presidential Selection: Theory and Development* (Princeton: Princeton University Press, 1979).

41. Light, *Vice-Presidential Power*.

42. Richard E. Neustadt, *Presidential Power and the Modern Presidents: The Politics of Leadership from Roosevelt to Reagan* (New York: Free Press, 1990).

43.   On a weekly basis, Cheney dines with Senate Republicans. See Kiefer.

44.   Morton Halperin, *Bureaucratic Politics and Foreign Policy* (Washington, D.C.: Brookings Institution, 1974), 287.

45.   Paul T. David, "The Vice Presidency: Its Institutional Evolution and Contemporary Status," *Journal of Politics*, 29 no. 4 (1967): 721–48.

46.   Edward L. Morse, "The Transformation of Foreign Policies: Modernization, Interdependence, and Externalization," *World Politics* 22 (1970): 371–92.

47.   Jerel Rosati, *The Politics of United States Foreign Policy*, 2d ed. (New York: Harcourt Brace, 1999), 335.

48.   Robert Putnam, "Diplomacy and Domestic Politics: The Logic of Two-Level Games," *International Organization* 42 (1988): 427–60.

Chapter 14

"Comforter in Chief"

The Transformation of First Lady Laura Bush

Robert P. Watson

Introduction

On August 22, 2002, Laura Bush, wife of the forty-third president of the United States, addressed a crowd of teachers, students, and parents in Leander, Texas, to dedicate a new school named in her honor: the Laura Welch Bush Elementary School. The first lady's comments were brief but poignant: "This school bears the name of a person who absolutely loves schools and all the things that happen within these walls—learning, laughing, singing, playing, and something else very important: reading."[1] In a calm Texas drawl, the first lady offered her advice to "practice, practice, practice" and to devote as much time to reading as to watching television in order to become a good reader. Mrs. Bush closed by thanking the teachers for making a difference and donating some of her favorite books to the school's library.

This event not only represents Laura Bush's journey from elementary school teacher to popular first lady with an elementary school named after her but both reflects the first lady's priorities and typifies her style in office in at least four ways: Mrs. Bush is the "education first lady," promoting an array of early childhood education and teaching initiatives; as a former educator and librarian, as well as mother, these are causes that she is ideally suited to embrace and causes that mirror her heartfelt interests; such educational advocacy fits well with President George W. Bush's stated education priorities; and like nearly all of Mrs. Bush's activities, this appearance at the school's dedication was also a "safe" event before a friendly crowd and involved brief, scripted remarks. The first lady is a worthy advocate when speaking about reading, literacy, and education. But throughout her first ladyship, Laura Bush has been notoriously careful not to overextend or venture into politics and policy, even though she has been transformed by the terrorist attacks of September 11,

2001. And in so doing, she appears to have found the right formula for a successful first ladyship.

BESS TRUMAN?

Laura Bush was still a rather anonymous figure during the campaign leading up to the Republican National Convention. At the convention, the prospective first lady delivered an address that was well received and benefited from a tried and trusted formula used by former first ladies: "I know my husband, and he is the right man for the job." The months leading up to the election and later inauguration saw Laura Bush in the standard role of supportive spouse appearing beside her husband, and her public profile remained relatively low compared to that of her predecessor, Hillary Clinton.

In the weeks following the inauguration, a case can be made that Laura Bush was the least visible, least active first lady in recent memory. For better or for worse, she was certainly no Hillary Clinton. Mrs. Bush had neither the political ambitions nor public visibility of her predecessor. As such, she did not attract the criticism that shadowed Mrs. Clinton. Laura Bush also lacked her predecessor's desire to use the office as a means to effect change and her predecessor's record of accomplishment. The new first lady also seemed to lack her mother-in-law's popularity, Nancy Reagan's behind-the-scenes influence, Rosalynn Carter's full plate of goals and activities, Betty Ford's candor and accessibility, Lady Bird Johnson's sense of purpose, Jacqueline Kennedy's magnetic appeal, or even Mamie Eisenhower's sure-handed role in running the social and domestic side of the White House. It is inevitable that presidents—and first ladies—are compared to their predecessors, especially during the first 100 days in office, and Laura Bush came off as white bread in an office that had seen its share of color, controversy, and charisma in recent years. Early polls show that many Americans did not have an opinion of their first lady; they were neither great admirers nor great critics of her.[2] However, they did know what or who she was *not*. Most obviously, she was not Hillary Clinton, which, given the "Hillary fatigue" that existed, ironically served to benefit her. It would appear that the public had had its share of scandal in the White House and was ready for normalcy. And normalcy is what it got. Even though Laura Bush cited Lady Bird Johnson, another Texan, and her own popular mother-in-law, Barbara Bush, as role models, she appeared to be fast on her way to resembling Bess Truman at the outset of her first ladyship.

Bess Truman was certainly not her predecessor, Eleanor Roosevelt, and Mrs. Truman failed to define herself in any significant way or associate herself with a cause or an issue. To a lesser degree, the same can be said of Laura Bush. Like Mrs. Truman, who frequently traveled back to her home in the small town of Independence, Missouri, and went to great lengths to avoid the glare of publicity or the duties associated with the first ladyship, Laura Bush began her first ladyship with a seeming preference for the family ranch in remote Crawford, Texas, over the White House, and she maintained a remarkably low profile at the outset of her husband's presidency.

Laura Bush: Social Advocate

One of the primary means by which first ladies promote themselves, their husbands, and social change is through the advocacy of social causes, commonly referred to as first lady "pet projects."[3] First ladies use their office to champion various issues, typically in a social manner and through nongovernment, nonpolicy measures. Despite the limiting caveats formed by public opinion regarding "proper" roles for first ladies and concerns about power being vested improperly in the wedding band (the first lady is neither elected nor appointed), first ladies have made many meaningful contributions through such social advocacy. Table 14.1 lists the social projects of recent first ladies.

Laura Bush, both before and after the events of 9/11, is not unique in her advocacy of social programs. She is simply the latest in a long line of active presidential spouses. Among her causes are education, reading, and libraries, which are listed in Table 14.2.

TABLE 14.1
Social Projects of Recent First Ladies

First Lady	Project
Hillary Clinton	Child advocacy
Barbara Bush	Literacy
Nancy Reagan	"Just Say No" anti-drug use campaign
Rosalynn Carter	Mental health reform
Betty Ford	Handicapped children
Pat Nixon	Volunteerism
Lady Bird Johnson	Conservation and beautification
Jacqueline Kennedy	Historic preservation of the White House

TABLE 14.2
Laura Bush's Initiatives

Education	Reading
Ready to Read, Ready to Learn	Put Reading First
Teach for America	Healthy Start, Grow Smart
Troops to Teachers	Reach Out and Read
Transition to Teaching	Reading Guide
The New Teacher Project	

One of the projects that Laura Bush has embraced as first lady would seem to be an obvious choice for a former teacher: education. Mrs. Bush's background as a teacher certainly helped her credibility on the issue, and for the most part she has avoided the more sensitive policy debates surrounding education, such as her husband's advocacy of vouchers and standardized testing, preferring to stay with less controversial topics such as improving early childhood education and encouraging individuals to consider a teaching career.

As Table 14.2 indicates, Mrs. Bush has launched several education initiatives. One of these, Troops to Teachers, harnesses the Republican position of supporting the military by encouraging former military personnel to consider a second career as a teacher. This is also a politically safe issue and one that relates to the first lady's general interest in promoting the profession of teaching: "I can't think of a better cause than bringing more teachers into America's schools. Children need our love and support; and they especially need devoted teachers and strong role models."[4] Another of the first lady's educational initiatives is the "Ready to Read, Ready to Learn" program, established in February 2001. The program has three major components: early childhood cognitive development to help children be ready to learn and read when they first enter school; teacher preparation and recruitment, to have well-trained teachers of adequate number in schools with needs; and successful early childhood programs for teachers and parents. In introducing the program, Mrs. Bush reflected on her commitment to reading:

> Some of my fondest memories are of sitting quietly wrapped in my mother's arms, listening to her read to me. Little did I know that she was doing much more than providing comfort and entertainment— she was paving the way for learning and success in school. Unfortunately, not every child is as fortunate as I was. Some children enter school without even knowing the basics, such as the alphabet and counting. For these children, reading and learning can often be a struggle. And it is a struggle that affects every American, because if our children are not able to read, they are not able to lead. Our challenge is to reach these children early and lift them to success. My experiences as a mother and as [an] elementary teacher have taught me that children that are ready to read are ready to learn. As first lady, I will work tirelessly to make sure that every child gains the basic skills to be successful in school and in life.[5]

With the words "As a child, I loved listening to my mother read to me,"[6] Laura Bush has made reading perhaps her most visible project as first lady, both in Texas and in the White House. She advocated everything from family literacy to reading to children to the recognition of authors in an effort to promote reading "from the crib to the classroom." A related program, one dating to her days

TABLE 14.3
White House Conferences on First Lady's Initiatives

White House Conference on Character and Community
White House Conference on Early Childhood Cognitive Development
White House Conference on School Libraries
White House Conference on Preparing Tomorrow's Teachers
White House Conference on Libraries and Museums

as a governor's wife, is the book festival. The success of the Texas Book Festival prompted Mrs. Bush to launch the National Book Festival on September 8, 2001. This was followed by a nationwide National Book Festival on October 12, 2002, featuring state events, authors, and library programs and sponsorship from the likes of AT&T, the *Washington Post*, PBS, and the Library of Congress. The first lady also lends her name to the Laura Bush Foundation for America's Libraries, which provides grants to school libraries across the country to purchase books.[7]

Taking a page from Hillary Clinton's playbook, Laura Bush has co-convened conferences on a variety of subjects (see Table 14.3). For instance, the White House Conference on Character and Community, named to draw support from a wide cross-section of Americans, aimed to link the importance of character to education, although it amounted to little more than another soft political slogan. As chair, the first lady stressed the need to move beyond the "three R's" of education (reading, writing, and 'rithmetic) to include a fourth: responsibility. Noting that children often spend more time with teachers than with their parents, such values as kindness and heroism "can be taught in classrooms and churches, clubs and other places where children gather."[8]

SEPTEMBER 11 AND THE TRANSFORMATION OF LAURA BUSH

On the morning of September 11, 2001, the first lady was on her way to brief the Senate Education Committee about the Summit on Early Childhood Education she helped convene earlier that summer. It was while en route to the office of Senator Ted Kennedy that Mrs. Bush learned that a plane had struck one of the twin towers of the World Trade Center. By the time she met Senator Kennedy at the door of his office, it was apparent that America was under attack. The Senate meeting was cancelled, and one of the first things Laura Bush did was phone her twin daughters. She also phoned her mother for reassurance and received a call from the president, who was in Sarasota, Florida, making an appearance before a group of schoolchildren.

In what might be called a "two first ladies" thesis, the monumental and tragic events surrounding the 9/11 terrorist attacks on the United States transformed Laura Bush. In the days following the attacks, Mrs. Bush appeared on television to calm parents and children, sent letters to elementary, middle, and high school students, and began a dialogue with parents about how to both discuss with and shield their children from the terror facing the nation. She made high-profile appearances at the memorial in Pennsylvania for the victims of the fourth hijacked airliner, with the queen of Jordan in a diplomatic gesture of unity between the United States and the Arab world, and on a variety of television shows, among others. In her public profile and persona, as well as in her apparent commitment to social causes and role as first lady, a different Laura Bush emerged after September 11.

The first lady demonstrated a soothing presence for the nation. She had made unmemorable appearances on behalf of causes prior to September 11, but for the first time in her first ladyship, Laura Bush had found her voice. She mastered the first lady's "velvet glove pulpit"—the social (feminine) and unofficial (the first lady is neither elected nor appointed) version of the presidential "bully pulpit"—and effectively harnessed its power. Like her husband, Mrs. Bush was aided by a "rallying effect,"[9] which saw the nation unite in support of its leaders in a time of crisis. Enjoying an outpouring of public approval, Mrs. Bush's role, image, and approach to the first ladyship were transformed into that of the country's "comforter in chief," using her pulpit to comfort the nation and offer advice to parents on helping their children heal emotional and psychological wounds from terrorist bombing.

Evidence of this transformation in visibility, image, and popularity can be seen in Mrs. Bush's poll numbers. Since 1948, Gallup has been taking polls to determine the most admired women.[10] First ladies have routinely dominated these popularity contests, with most since Eleanor Roosevelt topping the list and several appearing together in the same top ten category. So too has the public been polled regarding the approval of first ladies, although it was not until recent years that these polls were done with any regularity. Table 14.4 indicates Laura Bush's standing as America's most admired woman in the world, and Table 14.5 reveals her high popularity.

Laura Bush's approval rating in mid 2002 reflects the support of seven out of ten Americans. Only one year prior, her approval rating was at 58 percent.[11] Perhaps more telling is that fully 34 percent of the American public had not formed an opinion of its first lady as of the summer prior to the terrorist attacks, after she had been on the job for fully seven months. Similarly, from mid 2001 to mid 2002—after the 9/11 terrorist attacks—Mrs. Bush's negatives dropped from 23 percent to only 8 percent, while her approval is impressively high. Furthermore, polling by the Pew Research Center reveals that the public's perception of Laura Bush after September 11 is not only overwhelmingly positive, but it has broadened into a more sophisticated, a deeper, and a broader image. Similar polls done prior to September 11 found the first lady's image among the public to be rather monolithic: she was described (see Table 14.6) as little more than simply "nice" or "quiet."[12]

TABLE 14.4
Laura Bush's Popularity

Gallup's most admired women poll (2002)	
Laura Bush	12%
Hillary Rodham Clinton	8%
Oprah Winfrey	5%
Barbara Bush	3%
Condoleezza Rice	2%
Margaret Thatcher	1%
Elizabeth Dole	1%
Julia Roberts	1%
Madonna	1%

TABLE 14.5
Laura Bush's Approval Rating

	Total	Rep	Dem	Ind
Approve	69%	85%	60%	67%
Disapprove	8%	3%	13%	7%
Don't know	23%	12%	27%	26%

Note: At midterm (12/2002)

TABLE 14.6
One-Word Description of Laura Bush

Age 18–49		Age 50+	
Men	Women	Men	Women
Honest	Confident	Nice	Lady/Ladylike
Classy	Intelligent	Classy	Intelligent
Caring	Supportive	Concerned	Nice

Clearly, part of the first lady's appeal after 9/11 was the by-product of a "rallying effect." But Mrs. Bush's limited, carefully scripted, and safe role prior to September 11 did not allow the public to develop a deeper impression of her. Well into her first ladyship, she remained an empty vessel waiting to be defined. The patriotic rallying effect appears to have had the unintended consequence of allowing the event to define Mrs. Bush in the public's eyes. It affixed an indelible, emotional, and positive connection between the nation's united response to the tragedy and its first lady. Laura Bush both rose to the occasion and further shaped this connection, as her public appearances increased in number after September 11. Both the messenger and message had changed, although the general approach had not. In her trademark short, scripted appearances before friendly audiences such as the *Oprah Winfrey Show,* Laura Bush spoke directly to the country's fears:

> A lot of the things that we used to complain about, road rage, all of those things, seem very trivial now. Now we know what's really important—the people we love, our country, and to have the chance to tell all the people we love that we love them and to make sure they know that, and to hear it from us every day.[13]

So too did the first lady's projects increase after September 11. For instance, Mrs. Bush began speaking out about the inhumane treatment of women by Afghanistan's Taliban regime, the plight of Afghan children, and the need to support the nation's men and women in uniform. Laura Bush, who had once worried about speaking in public, was delivering national and international radio addresses. Among the many public appearances she made was one as the honorary chair of the "Concert for America," a two-hour commemoration of the 9/11 tragedy, taped at the Kennedy Center on September 9, 2002, and broadcast on the one-year anniversary of the attack. This typified the new, high-profile, symbolic role as comforter assumed by Laura Bush, who, in the wake of 9/11, had emerged as one of the most popular first ladies of all time. On the anniversary of the terrorist attacks, the first lady offered these healing words:

> As we mark the first anniversary of last September's attacks, I hope the Concert for America will allow us to use the arts to soothe our emotions as we remember those whose innocent lives were tragically cut short. I also look forward to an evening to celebrate the unity that makes us all proud to be Americans.[14]

Although her actions and appearances remained rather ceremonial and scripted, she clearly tapped into the public sentiment. As one scholar noted, the country now had "a first lady who's looking like a leader."[15]

WHAT TYPE OF FIRST LADY?

What type of first lady has Laura Bush been during the first two years in office? How is her first ladyship similar and dissimilar to her predecessors? Even though the Constitution is silent on first ladies, and the first ladyship is technically not an office per se, in that she is neither elected nor appointed, it has emerged as an office complete with staff, resources, and an array of roles and duties. As an extraconstitutional development, the first lady's duties are not mandated by statute, but by custom and through the actions of specific first

TABLE 14.7
Duties of the First Lady

Wife and mother
Public figure and celebrity
Nation's social hostess
Symbol of the American woman
White House manager and preservationist
Campaigner
Social advocate and champion of social causes
Presidential spokesperson
Presidential and political party booster
Diplomat
Political and presidential partner

---

ladies a somewhat definable set of roles and responsibilities has come to be identified with the office (see Table 14.7).[16]

Essentially, Laura Bush has performed all of the duties listed in Table 14.7, however, after the 9/11 tragedy, her first ladyship has largely centered on the role of "public figure/celebrity." Through her many social projects, Laura Bush has also fulfilled the duty of "social advocate." Although Mrs. Bush has presided over White House social events, she has not brought new or distinguishing contributions to the duty of "social hostess." Nor has she been particularly active in the capacity of "presidential spokesperson" and "diplomat," as most of her political and international appearances have been social in nature, although she earned rave reviews for her speech at the 2000 Republican National Convention that nominated her husband, and she has traveled abroad.

The first ladyship has evolved to the point whereby it is an institution well equipped to participate in political and policy activities. Indeed, many first ladies have wielded great influence and were among the most popular public figures of their day. The trick for first ladies is to do so without crossing the elusive, shifting line between what constitutes a proper and an improper role for the president's spouse. This is easier said than done, and many first ladies have found themselves on the receiving end of criticism from a fickle public and an unscrupulous political opponent for even the appearance of crossing this line and wielding too much political influence.[17]

Compared to recent first ladies, Laura Bush has not been politically active: she has generally not given the appearance of being comfortable with, much less interested in, power; nor has she given the appearance of participating in the development of policy in her husband's administration. But this is not to say that she has played *no* role in politics and policy. Since September 11, 2001, Mrs. Bush has expanded her public profile and scope of activities to include those that brush up against politics. These include such political gestures as speaking out against the Taliban and terrorists and speaking for the women and children of Afghanistan and families of the victims of terrorism. On November 17, 2001,

Mrs. Bush delivered a radio address from her home in Crawford, Texas, on the subject of the Taliban's mistreatment of women and children:

> The brutal oppression of women is a central goal of the terrorists. . . . Only the terrorists and the Taliban forbid education to women. Only the terrorists and the Taliban threaten to pull out women's fingernails for wearing nail polish. The plight of women and children in Afghanistan is a matter of deliberate human cruelty, carried out by those who seek to intimidate and control.[18]

Mrs. Bush has also testified before Congress twice in the first two years of her first ladyship, once before each chamber. In so doing, she joins such politically active first ladies as Eleanor Roosevelt, who in 1940 was the first to give congressional testimony, Rosalynn Carter, who also testified once before each chamber, and Hillary Clinton, who testified several times.[19] Another activity performed by Mrs. Bush with the potential to involve politics has been international travel, where the first lady visited a U.S. air base in Italy and headed a presidential delegation to the memorial service for the Queen Mother of England. In her first international tour without her husband in May 2002, Mrs. Bush visited the capitals of France, Hungary, and the Czech Republic, accompanied by her then-twenty-year-old daughter, Jenna. During the ten-day tour, the first lady spoke briefly in Paris at a meeting of the OECD on the importance of childhood education and tolerance. In Prague, she spoke to the Afghan people by radio, and she later met with Czech president, Vaclav Havel, but it was not an official visit. At the conclusion of this tour, she joined President Bush in Berlin on May 22, 2002, and together they made official state visits in Germany, Russia, and France before returning to the United States.

The first lady's appearances during these and other international visits were, however, few, cursory, and largely ceremonial. Even though the timing of her solo tour was somewhat early compared to other first ladies, the trip was filled largely with private time, tours of art exhibits, and a token handful of ceremonial appearances, and the first lady's trip to Budapest appears to have been little more than an excuse to visit with her long-time friend, Nancy Brinker, who was given an ambassadorial appointment by George W. Bush. On earlier presidential visits to Europe, Asia, and Latin America, Mrs. Bush had similarly made only token and quick appearances, posing for photo opportunities at cultural sites, cooking noodles in China, and shopping in Italy.[20] Laura Bush's international itinerary remains quite free of political and policy activities, especially when compared to Eleanor Roosevelt's bold visits to soldiers in the field during World War II, Pat Nixon's comments about South Africa's racist policies while on an African tour in 1972, or Hillary Clinton's 1999 criticism of the Tunisian president for his nation's human rights violations and subsequent, infamous Beijing speech on women's rights.

In order to further examine Laura Bush's approach to the office, a few models exist to help scholars compare the different styles of first ladies. One considers the means of influence used to accomplish tasks and goals.[21] Absent any statutory authority or enabling legislation, the first lady has no formal powers, but she has considerable influence. How she wields this influence, however, has varied. Her influence can be seen as deriving from and being used in the political sphere, "pillow" sphere, or public sphere. For instance, the first type of influence stems from her relationship as a political advisor to the president and through various political activities such as testifying before Congress, lobbying for legislation, or heading presidential task forces. "Pillow influence" stems from the special relationship that only the first lady has with the president as his wife. The president might turn to his wife in times of crisis or when faced with a difficult decision, and there are numerous familial and marital manifestations of the presidential marriage that enable the first lady to influence the president to a degree not approachable by paid staffers. Ronald Reagan used to joke about the president living "above the family store," a reference to the fact that the first family lives in the White House, giving first ladies physical proximity to power. When Dwight Eisenhower suffered from health problems during his presidency, it was Mamie Eisenhower who established a quiet room for him to relax and to paint upstairs in the White House. So too did she curtail his work schedule, as did Nancy Reagan and other first ladies, as only they could. Lastly, as a well-known public figure, the first lady has influence simply through her notoriety and ability to marshal public opinion. Simply by appearing on behalf of an issue, the first lady can bring widespread attention to the matter.

Laura Bush has used both the second and third forms of influence. She has often been described as a source of strength in the Bush marriage and has been credited with helping her husband conquer his drinking problem and his "young and irresponsible" past.[22] The president has repeatedly mentioned in public that he owes his success to his wife. Surely in the days after the 9/11 attack, George W. Bush drew strength from his wife's calm confidence and support. So too have Laura Bush's high approval ratings (discussed later) allowed her to use her popularity to promote her social causes, and a large measure of her first ladyship has been outside of the political realm and performed from the point of her public notoriety.

Mrs. Bush has involved herself in politics and policy, at least at the margins. For instance, she has been credited with working behind the scenes to secure funds from U.S. Agency for International Development (USAID) for training women workers in Afghanistan.[23] It has also been suggested that the first lady has been a force in the drafting of education policy in her husband's administration. During a conference she hosted on early childhood education, Secretary of Education Rod Paige stated: "What she brings to the table is the view of an experienced veteran, not only as a teacher and librarian, but as a first lady who actively proposed ideas."[24] In an interview in the teaching newspaper, *Education*

Week, Mrs. Bush dismissed the idea: "I haven't had that much of a role in the actual creating of actual policy. But all my life I've worked on issues that have to do with education."[25] The Bush administration's No Child Left Behind Act offers a possible clue to the first lady's role. The $4 billion program to recruit and train teachers, along with establishing a database of qualified teachers, reflects many of the themes endorsed by the first lady. And Laura Bush is given some credit in securing $30 million for a teacher recruitment program, which she hopes "sends a message about how important it is to encourage people to choose teaching."[26] It is difficult to determine the nature and extent of her influence, but it appears that Laura Bush wields her influence in a far less public manner than, say, Hillary Clinton, and that her influence in policy is minimal and restricted to issues such as education.

Another tool in assessing a first lady's approach to the office is that of the "partnership model."[27] Jimmy and Rosalynn Carter frequently discussed in public their close partnership and collaborations on political endeavors. Many presidential couples spent three, four, or more decades together in marriage, and many were married long before their presidential years. Indeed, unlike the case with many first ladies, presidential aides cannot claim to have known the president well long before his political career began. There is a partnership operating in the White House, as first couples are trusted confidantes and often collaborate on the president's career to the point where it becomes a co-career. This partnership can take many forms: full partnership, partial partnership, behind-the-scenes partnership, a partnership in marriage only, and a nonpartnership, whereby some first couples such as Franklin and Jane Pierce did not work together on Franklin's career and generally did not enjoy a happy or close marriage. Laura Bush's approach to the office has, to a degree, resembled her husband's, and most observers have described the Bush marriage as a close and productive partnership. However, Laura Bush rarely influences her husband on politics or policy, nor do they claim to debate the issues or share a love of politics. Accordingly, her style and the nature of their marriage place her as more of a "behind-the-scenes partner," whereby her influence is felt through more familial and social ways as a trusted, supportive spouse.

As is seen in the example of Laura Bush, there is not a two-dimensional approach to the first ladyship, as is often portrayed in the media. First ladies have generally been portrayed as being *either* politically active or traditional, but not both.[28] First ladies have engaged in both, and some social elements of the office have significant political repercussions. Similarly, there is no one best way to approach the first ladyship, and many have blended approaches to suit their needs. First ladies have enjoyed success and failure from a variety of perspectives and approaches. Laura Bush has not embarked on an active or overtly political course as first lady, but her popularity, successful educational initiatives, and emergence as "comforter in chief" have benefited the Bush presidency. The range and nature of her appearances, speeches, and priorities can be seen in Table 14.8.

TABLE 14.8
Laura Bush's Speeches by Topic

Topic	Number of Speeches
Ceremonies/celebrations	21
International events	16
Reading	15
Arts	14
Authors/library appearances	13
Teaching	11
September 11, 2001, tragedy	10
Public/community service	8
Library/National Book Festival	6
Holidays	6
Early childhood education	4
Memorial services/funerals	3
Historic preservation	2

Note: The number of speeches given, as of November 2002.

HAVING HER CAKE AND EATING IT TOO: FINDING THE RIGHT FORMULA

Laura Bush's calm, studious personality seems to have served her well. As her sister-in-law, Dorothy Bush Koch, has said of her: "She is so comfortable in her own skin. She always does what she feels is right for her and never worries how it is perceived."[29] Laura Bush might possess the right mix of traits and character to satisfy what a rather hard-to-satisfy public feels about its first lady. Given the extensiveness of criticisms leveled against first ladies throughout history, Laura Bush joins a rather elite group of presidential spouses that has been rather immune from criticism, including Edith Roosevelt, Grace Coolidge, and Mamie Eisenhower.[30] Beyond the usual flattering stories found in "women's magazines," even the news media has put on "kid gloves" in treating Mrs. Bush in a remarkably kind and positive manner.

When the first lady commented on NBC's *Today Show* before the inauguration that she supported the Supreme Court's view of permitting women the right to choose, she was not criticized for it. Indeed, it was scarcely given coverage, whereas first ladies such as Rosalynn Carter, Betty Ford, and Hillary Clinton were attacked in public for similar comments. When students at UCLA protested an invitation extended by their campus for Laura Bush to speak at commencement, citing her "shallow credentials," the story was not a story.[31] Yet when nearly the same event faced First Lady Barbara Bush over a commencement address in 1990 at Wellesley College, the media devoted considerable coverage to it. At the 2000 Republican National Convention, Laura Bush took the proverbial "swing" at her husband's opponent, Al Gore, while issuing a direct challenge to Democrats on the issue of education when she said in response to Gore's practice of spending the night at the homes of teachers while campaigning: "Well, George spends every night with a teacher." Not only was the line well received, but Laura Bush avoided criticism from the public, press, or Democrats for an attack—albeit a good-natured one—that would have landed her predecessors in hot water. Demonstrating her remarkable immunity from criticism and a shifting standard by the media, Laura Bush went on to joke without reprisal that she was not going to be like Mrs. Clinton, because she would not run for the Senate from New York. Furthermore, at least three staff members in the Office of the First Lady—chief of staff, director of projects, and director of communication—attend White House briefings and meetings,[32] yet neither the press nor the opposition party has cried foul, which was not the case with the activities of Hillary Clinton's staff or Rosalynn Carter's decision to attend cabinet meetings and to schedule business breakfasts or luncheons with her husband. So too has Laura Bush fund-raised for the Republican Party, but little was made of her actions. Her predecessors were taken to task for similar actions and, having "entered the political fray," were considered fair game for critics.

What Laura Bush has succeeded in doing in her first two years in office is finding the right formula for a successful first ladyship, something that has eluded nearly every one of her predecessors. Among the interesting facets of the transformation of Laura Bush have been her ability to sustain her high popularity, her ability to avoid criticism, and her ability to carve out a role that allows her "to have her cake and eat it too," whereas her predecessors were "damned if they do, and damned if they don't." When she chooses to be less active, she seems to benefit from the perception that she is a traditional spouse disinterested in politics. When she chooses to be more active, she is seen as doing so for noble purposes. Short, scripted appearances are applauded as meaningful. Questions are either avoided or "lobbed" as easy-to-hit "softballs".

The defining elements of Mrs. Bush's successful formula include the following: (1) *Starting slow and gradually expanding the role*. Mrs. Bush has become increasingly active and visible, slowly expanding the scope of her activities yet being careful not to involve herself in politics and policy. The September 11 tragedy certainly helped—if not propelled—her to expand her role to parallel the rise in her approval ratings, and do so "under the radar"; (2) *Avoiding giving the appearance of wanting power or being interested in politics* (something not done by Hillary Clinton). The public is more likely to grant one the benefit of the doubt and an expanded role if one does not appear to desire it; (3) *Restricting her activities to the public and "pillow" spheres of influence*. At the midpoint of her first ladyship, Laura Bush had emerged as an active and a successful social advocate, but she has done so by focusing on *social* appearances and avoiding public policy solutions and the political questions surrounding the issue; (4) *Picking the right projects and causes* that complement her husband's agenda (education reform, War on Terror) reflects her true interests and personal experiences, which are feminine and noncontroversial (the unifying theme among her projects is how they impact children—reading books to children, early childhood education, the condition of Afghan children); (5) *Making safe, highly scripted appearances before friendly crowds.* Laura Bush's comments are almost always quite brief and heavily scripted with little room for question and answer sessions. Many of the first lady's appearances and activities seem almost excessively cautious and trite. For instance, during what was supposed to be a working event, a Teach for America program in San Francisco featured gushing recollections by the first lady and others of former teachers: "I remember my teacher"; "She was the best teacher I ever had, because she was the happiest teacher I ever had"; "She taught me to read"; and so on.[33] During an appearance at a fund-raiser for the Utopia Rescue Ranch, Mrs. Bush's remarks included the following:

> Like any pet owner, I worry about the dogs when I travel without them. I've heard that some dogs will wait at the window or door for their owners to return. So I make sure they have enough treats to keep them happily occupied . . . and that someone is around to give them plenty of fresh air and sunshine. When I'm not around, I know the dogs are in good hands. They're generally well-behaved dogs. When the President and I are home together, the dogs are always nearby. We take turns exercising them on the South Lawn.[34]

Conclusion

Laura Bush's style reveals the lessons of previous first ladyships. She is neither Hillary Clinton nor her famous mother-in-law, Barbara Bush, but she is somewhere between the two in her approach to the office. She is active but not too active; she supports important issues but in a social sense rather than through policy initiatives; and she maintains the aura of a traditional spouse disinterested in politics, policy, and publicity while making meaningful contributions to her husband's presidency and enjoying enormous popularity. Much like her husband, Laura Bush's style is built around safe, short, and highly scripted appearances and events, carefully cultivated to promote just the right image. So too has she benefited—like her husband—from generally low expectations about her performance and public speaking. And, like her husband, she has generally exceeded them and improved as a communicator. Her efforts have earned praise from the press and public alike, giving Laura Bush a remarkable first two years in her first ladyship. Indeed, she has emerged as one of the least criticized first ladies in history. It remains to be seen whether she has been too safe, has squandered opportunities to put her immense popularity to work, or has conducted what has amounted to little more than a continuous approval campaign.

Laura Bush differs in her approach from her recent predecessors in the office and is hard to "pigeon-hole." In a way, the former schoolteacher's successful formula for being first lady has borrowed from the lessons of her predecessors. From Bess Truman to America's most admired woman, Laura Bush has been able to have her cake and eat it too. There is little doubt that she has emerged in the wake of the 9/11 tragedy as the nation's "comforter in chief." In her words, spoken to grieving families who lost loved ones in the terrorist attacks:

> The burden is greatest, however, for the families—like those of you who are without those lost. America is learning the names, but you know the people. And you are the ones they thought of in the last moments of life. You are the ones they called, and prayed to see again, and the ones they loved.
>
> One of last Tuesday's victims, in his final message to his family, said that he loved them and would see them again. That brave man was a witness for the greatest hope of all—the hope that unites us now. You grieve today, and the hurt will not soon go away. But love is real, and it is forever, just as the love you share with your loved ones is forever.[35]

NOTES

1. See www.whitehouse.gov/news/releases/2002/08/20020822-5.html.

2. See www.gallup.com for polls on the First Lady.

3. Robert P. Watson, *The Presidents' Wives: Reassessing the Office of First Lady* (Boulder: Lynne Rienner, 2000).

4. Mrs. Bush's remarks were made at the Teach for America event in San Francisco and can be found at www.whitehouse.gov/news/releases/2002/06/20020612-8.html.

5. Laura Bush provided the foreword for the *Ready to Ready, Ready to Learn* program, September 6, 2002. It can be found at www.whitehouse.gov/firstlady/news-speeches/releases/print/read-booklet.html.

6. See www.whitehouse.gov/firstlady/initiatives/education.

7. The Laura Bush Foundation for America's Libraries is part of the Community Foundation for the National Capital Region. It is a 501(c)(3) nonprofit that makes grants to school libraries across the United States to purchase books, and it raises money through a leadership council of the foundation. Laura Bush serves as the honorary chair, although she is not active in the organization. For more information, see www.laurabushfoundation.org/foundation.html.

8. See www.whitehouse.gov/news/releases.2002/06/20020619-29.html, June 19, 2002.

9. It is common for a president facing a crisis, particularly a national security crisis, to enjoy a significant bump in support from the public, known as a "rallying effect." This was certainly the case for George W. Bush, who experienced a jump of over thirty points in approval ratings immediately after the September 11, 2001, terrorist attack.

10. Laura McQuillan, "Bush Dominates Most-Admired Poll," USA Today.com, December 26, 2001. See also, www.gallup.com for its most-admired polls, taken since 1948.

11. See "Laura Bush's Changing Image: No Longer Just 'Nice': No One Dislikes Her!" the Pew Research Center, July 2, 2002, www.people-press.org/reports/display.php3?reportid=158.

12. Ibid.; see the Pew Research Center.

13. Laura Bush appeared on television on the *Oprah Winfrey Show* on September 6, 2002. See www.oprah.com/tows/pastshows/tows_past_20010918_b.jhtml.

14. See www.whitehouse.gov/news/releases/2002/07/20020724-2.html.

15. Robin Gerber, "A First Lady Who's Looking Like a Leader," Newsday.com, August 12, 2001. This program is offered by the James MacGregor Burns Academy of Leadership at the University of Maryland. See www.academy.umd.edu/aboutus/news/articles/08-12-01.html.

16. For further information on the evolution of the First Lady's role, see Watson, *The Presidents' Wives*, 69–92.

17. Ibid., 34–40.

18. Laura Bush delivered a radio address on November 17, 2001. See www.whitehouse.gov/news/releases/2001/11/20011117.html.

19. Colton C. Campbell and Sean McCluskie, "First Ladies and Legislative Activism," in *American First Ladies*, ed. Robert P. Watson (Pasadena, Calif.: Salem Press, 2001), 386–93.

20. Sandra Sobieraj, "Laura Bush on First Solo International Trip," May 13, 2002, www.compuserve.com/news/story.jsp?floc=mm7-news&sc=1151&idq=/ff/story/.

21. The "3 Ps" model is discussed in Watson, *The Presidents' Wives*, 99–101.

22. Sobieraj, "Laura Bush," www.compuserve.com/news/story.

23. Joetta L. Sack, "Laura Bush: A Teacher in the (White) House," *Education Week*, August 8, 2001, www.edweek.org/ew/ew_printstory.cfm?slug = 43laura.h20.

24. Ibid.

25. Ibid.

26. Gerber, "A First Lady," 2.

27. See Watson, *The Presidents' Wives*, 137–143.

28. Ibid., 161–162.

29. Lois Romana, "Say Hi to . . . Laura: The New First Lady Brings a Quiet but Determined Style to Center Stage," *Detroit News*, January 26, 2001, www.detnews.com/2001/features/0101/27/c01-180005.html.

30. See Watson, *The Presidents' Wives*, 34–40.

31. The UCLA student protest is discussed in *The Daily Bruin*, February 20, 2002, www.uwire.com/content/topnews022002003.html.

32. See Gerber, "A First Lady," 2.

33. See the remarks by Mrs. Bush at the Teach for America event in San Francisco, www.whitehouse.gov/news/releases/2002/06/20020612-8.html.

34. See www.whitehouse.gov/news/releases/2002/05/2w20529-1.html.

35. See www.whitehouse.gov/news/releases/2001/09/20010917-19.html.

Conclusion

Robert P. Watson, Tom Lansford, and Bryan Hilliard

THE PRESIDENCY OF GEORGE W. BUSH AT MIDTERM

The first two years of George W. Bush's presidency included its share of high points and low points, a few notable successes among an otherwise mediocre record of legislative achievement, and the grave challenges of terrorist attacks, the subsequent United States'-led War on Terror, and a sluggish economy. At midterm, the report card on the Bush presidency is mixed. Indeed, one's perception of Bush's performance might be, as the old saying suggests, a by-product of where one sits (and how one sees the issues). This book, as is the case with this concluding assessment, includes a rich variety of viewpoints and an early effort to offer a balanced, fair, and accurate evaluation of the Bush presidency.

The "first 100 days" of a presidency are often used as a period to begin assessing presidential performance.[1] Known as the "honeymoon period," presidents typically enjoy higher levels of public support and some leeway from Congress and the media during these initial, important days in office. From the media's perspective, presidential scandals and personal character lead the coverage of the White House. As such, these issues mark a logical place to begin the evaluation. George W. Bush's first 100 days were far from impressive. The president achieved no significant legislative victory during this period of time, backed out of his pledge to reduce carbon dioxide emissions, and mishandled several high-profile environmental and energy issues. Most notable among them, the president appeared to be too eager to cut environmental programs and clean water quality standards but simultaneously and zealously promoted oil drilling in ANWR.

This is only part of the picture, but Bush's detractors would note that the aforementioned missteps were reinforced when a White House energy task force, headed by Vice President Dick Cheney, endorsed an obviously pro-oil, anti-environment energy agenda. Not only did this anger environmentalists and conservationists, but when the story broke that Cheney's energy task force was comprised of oil executives who met behind closed doors to draft policy, ethical questions were raised. Further, it did not help the vice president that he had only recently stepped down as the head of Haliburton, an energy and oil-drilling corporation, pocketing a cool $20 million in cash and $10 million in company stock. The General Accounting Office (GAO) for the first time in history moved to have the vice president investigated in relation to the work of his task force. However, Cheney stonewalled its requests for public records. The inquiries by the GAO and the vice president's refusal to cooperate dragged on until the midterm, before the watchdog agency abandoned its would-be investigation in a whimper. All the while the president was largely absent from the discussion. No charges were brought, the media lost interest in the story, and the public appeared disinterested in possible wrongdoings; the administration survived unscathed its first potentially scandalous ethical dilemma.

When a string of high-profile corporate scandals emerged a year later, in mid 2002, the administration's close ties with some of the very industries under fire, such as Enron, produced further questions about Bush's own record as a former oil executive who appeared to profit enormously while his company failed. Both the president and vice president found their former business dealings under review, as records indicated that they had benefitted from campaign donations from businesses and executives involved in the ethical scandals. Cheney also had the bad judgment to host a fund-raiser for corporate leaders at the vice-presidential residence. However, little would come from the matter. The administration had to jettison SEC Commissioner Harvey Pitt, but it did so discreetly, as the 2002 election results came in very favorably for the Republican Party. Again, the Bush presidency would come through an ethical dilemma unscathed, in noticeable contrast to many previous administrations, and would ultimately enjoy a rather scandal-free first two years.

At 100 days, Bush's critics alleged that his true conservative colors were apparent. At the outset of his administration, the president had inherited a Senate split evenly among Democrats and Republicans, with his own party controlling the leadership post and the vice-presidential tie-breaker vote. However, shortly after the 100-day mark, Republican Jim Jeffords of Vermont left the party to become an Independent. His alignment with the Democrats gave them a one-seat advantage in the Senate, thereby jeopardizing Bush's ability to count on Senate passage of his legislative agenda. Several of Bush's initiatives and nominees grinded to a halt in the Senate, and the president was forced to scale back an already spartan agenda. In June 2001, the media reported that Bush and fellow Republicans had treated Jeffords unprofessionally, and, at about the same time, prominent Republicans in the chamber, such as Olympia Snowe of Maine and John McCain of Arizona, called for more moderation in the party and a new approach to executive-legislative relations.

In his initial months in office, President Bush also angered U.S. allies and internationalists over his unilateral actions in foreign policy. These included criticisms of the United Nations, banning aid to international organizations offering abortion services and counseling, and backing out of the Kyoto Treaty on global warming. Critics who suggested that Bush was disinterested in consulting—much less working with—allies on international matters used the president's unscripted comments as ammunition. Bush often confused the facts and appeared unknowledgeable about international affairs, such as when he mistakenly reversed long-standing policy on Taiwan and China by advocating U.S. military support for Taiwan. Such political bungles, an apparent disinterest in either the nuances of diplomacy or the details of public policy, and long vacations at the Bush ranch in Crawford, Texas, resulted in an image of a president only marginally comfortable with the office and only marginally engaged in the task of governing. This was reinforced by the president's lack of live news conferences and inaccessibility to reporters.

Those in the president's party would take a different view of his presidency, however. After a slow start, a few key incidents served to spark a rebound by the president. Ironically, the initial incident would come on the international front, where Bush had received so much criticism. In April 2001, a Chinese fighter jet collided with a U.S. Navy surveillance plane, forcing it down on Chinese soil. After China held the U.S. crew against its will, Bush was seen by the American public as standing firm on his demand that the fliers be released. When the crew was released unharmed, public opinion praised the president's success. Bush's "Lone Ranger" approach to foreign policy was balanced by a newly emerging view that he was a mature leader capable of handling a crisis.

The following month, Bush worked hard to build bipartisan and broad public support for his tax cuts. It worked. In late May 2001, the president was rewarded with the passage of sizeable tax cuts, the centerpiece of his economic stimulus package. Even though his tax cuts failed to improve the economy in the short run, the president's handling of the economy was not the liability it might otherwise have been. Perhaps learning a lesson from his father's presidency, George W. Bush spoke often and openly about the poor economy. He was effective in addressing the nation about the need for cutting taxes and in making his case that the money belonged back in the hands of citizens rather than with government. Rather than avoid the problem or deny the existence of a sluggish economy, Bush managed to both politically downplay expectations and demonstrate genuine concern about the country's economic situation. Using simple and direct statements, the president assured Americans that he understood the problem and was working to remedy it. Bush also passed a watered-down version of his educational package—the "Leave No Child Behind Act" —showing that he could deliver on one of his main campaign promises. Again, before the fall recess, the House of Representatives passed the president's energy bill containing oil drilling in ANWR. Although he could not muster enough votes in the Senate, Bush stood his ground on the issue and managed to keep oil drilling and energy in the forefront of public debate.

The first eight months of the Bush presidency were largely defined by the weak economy. No single legislative triumph or foreign policy misstep stood out among the public. Bush's approval rating held unspectacularly but respectfully at just over 50 percent. The president was fortunate enough—fairly or unfairly— not to be held accountable by the public for the nation's economic woes, and he was generally applauded for his tax cut attempt to stimulate the economy. However, with tax cuts and a sagging economy, the nation watched the new budget surplus erode back to the deficit column where it had been since 1969.

TABLE 1
Pre-and Post-9/11 Approval

Poll	Pre-9/11		Post-9/11	
	Approval	Disapproval	Approval	Disapproval
CBS/NYT	50	38	84	9
Newsweek	50	31	82	11
ABC/WP	55	41	86	12
CNN/USA/Gallup	51	39	86	10

Note: Poll numbers just prior to 9/11 and just after 9/11.

Nevertheless, Bush was credited by a majority of Americans as a leader taking the country in the right direction.

And then, on September 11, 2001, terrorists hijacked four U.S. commercial aircrafts, crashing two into the twin towers of the World Trade Center—which collapsed into rubble, killing thousands—one into the Pentagon and the final one into a field in western Pennsylvania, presumably diverted from another devastating public target.

Public Opinion

The terrorist attacks made Bush a war president. As such, nearly everything about his presidency changed after September 11, 2001, giving rise to what can be seen as the two presidencies of George W. Bush: pre-9/11 and post-9/11. In the wake of the terrorist strikes, the president seemed to find a new purpose in the war. And the public responded. He was more engaged, more visible, and far more popular. The most obvious difference in the post-9/11 presidency was Bush's extraordinarily high approval ratings. The president's approval rating went from a mediocre 50-plus percent before the tragedy to a high of 90 percent after the terrorist strikes of 2001. This remarkable change in public approval can be seen in Table 1.

Presidents pay attention to public opinion polls, if for no other reason than that journalists, politicians, and the public read them. Approval ratings assess the public's impression of the president by asking such questions as "Do you approve or disapprove of the way President Bush is handling his job?" or "What is your overall opinion of President Bush? Is it favorable or unfavorable?" Most recent administrations have vested considerable effort into building or main-taining high approval ratings, and the Bush team is no exception. High approval ratings translate into an advantage in governing. Generally, members of the president's own party are likely to express approval, while the opposite is true of those of the opposing party. Yet, as is seen in Table 2, Bush was able to sustain

TABLE 2
Bush's Approval Ratings

Poll	Aver. %	High %	Low %
CBS/NYT	71.6	90	50
Newsweek	73.4	88	52
ABC/WP	73.6	92	55
CNN/USA/Gallup	70.5	90	51

Note: Represents Bush's approval, 01/20/01–12/02.

impressively high and bipartisan approval ratings in the period after September 11, 2001.

It is not unusual for presidents to receive broad-based public support during times of crisis. Known as a "rallying effect," the public moves beyond partisan differences and supports the president, uniting behind him as the symbolic leader of the nation when it might not otherwise do so.[2] Such "positivity bias" reflects a perception of the president as a hero. This often happens during the initial "honeymoon" period, or after a national security crisis. For example, the approval rate at the outset of a presidential term is typically higher than the percentage of the popular vote that a president carries. Bill Clinton won the 1992 election with only 43 percent of the popular vote, but he enjoyed approval ratings in the 50s when taking office in 1993. The same rallying effect can be seen during other wars, such as the Persian Gulf War of 1991, when George W. Bush's father, George H. W. Bush, saw his approval ratings grow by twenty and then thirty points.

However, such approval is generally a false measure of real approval. When approval forms as a result of a rallying effect, it is often short term and bound by the event that occasioned it. As such, in Bush's case, this statement is only partially true. His support would go only as far as the War on Terror. Bush was able to enjoy widespread support for a full year after the initial 9/11 bombing, and he continued to be popular through the midterm. Yet, as could be predicted, the approval did not translate into broad support for a number of his policies, and it eroded gradually in late 2003, almost to the point where it began just prior to the 9/11 tragedy.

Regardless, a nearly forty-point jump in approval occurred after the terrorist strikes in 2001. This transformed the president, allowing him to use his popularity to build further support for his vision on how a war against terrorism should be fought. In the months after the bombing of the World Trade Center and the Pentagon, the president was remarkably successful in establishing public support for U.S. military strikes against Afghanistan, on the grounds that the radical Islamic regime of the Taliban had both harbored and supported terrorism, principally Osama Bin-Laden, the suspected mastermind behind the terrorist attacks against the United States. Bush was also victorious in gaining support from both the Congress and the United Nations in the form of resolutions supporting his actions. The president initially opposed the creation of an independent commission to investigate intelligence lapses before 9/11, fought against federalizing airport security, and delayed action on a homeland security agency—all issues that would eventually be popular components of the War on Terror. Ironically, Bush's popularity did not help him in preventing these developments from moving forward; it only delayed their passage. Yet he was so popular that he was not criticized for opposing or delaying these programs and ultimately received credit for all of them. In fact, as is evident in Table 3, Bush's average approval rating measured over the first two years of his presidency was higher than that for any other president since such polls were taken.

Another example of the transformation of the president after the terrorist attacks was that the president became much more visible and appeared far more engaged in decision making. The eminent scholar, James MacGregor Burns, notes the existence of what he refers to as "transformational leadership"—the ability of a key event to spark a response by a president and a president's ability to lead and govern in extraordinary times.[3] Such a statement was not used to describe George W. Bush's presidency prior to 9/11, but similar descriptions were commonplace in the months following the terrorist attacks. Transformed, Bush made several highly public and popular appearances, including one at the site of the former twin towers in New York City, prayed for the victims at the National Cathedral, and rallied a shocked nation to the cause of fighting terrorism. The United States received the well wishes and support of governments and people nearly worldwide. NATO evoked Article 5, declaring an attack on one member to be an attack on all signatory nations. European criticism of Bush's

TABLE 3
Presidential Approval Ratings

President	Aver. %	High %	Low %
G.W. Bush	72	90	50
Clinton	54	73	37
G. Bush	61	89	29
Reagan	53	65	35
Carter	45	74	28
Ford	47	71	37
Nixon	49	67	24
Johnson	55	79	35
Kennedy	70	83	56
Eisenhower	65	79	48

Note: Represents Bush's approval, CBS/NYT and Newsweek Polls, 01/20/01–12/02. Adapted from James Pfiffner, *The Modern Presidency*, 3rd. ed. (Bedford/St. Martin's Press, 2000).

unilateralism was replaced by a show of sympathy and solidarity. The president embraced a new sense of internationalism and purpose, and he was transformed.

Legislative Record and Policy Priorities

George W. Bush campaigned on the pledge to move beyond partisan bickering and politics as usual, holding up his record of working with Democrats while serving as governor of Texas. This pledge was often repeated during the campaign and in his inaugural address. Early on in his presidency, Bush fulfilled the promise by attending retreats for Democrats in the Senate and House in February 2001. Bush also entered the White House with a scaled-down legislative agenda, symptomatic of either his bipartisanship or Reaganesque leadership style. Much like Ronald Reagan before him, only a few key items were placed on the table by Bush. These included tax cuts, the creation of faith-based initiatives (public funds for religious organizations performing social services), standardized testing in schools, and military preparedness in the form of more military spending, pay raises for armed forces personnel, and a new missile defense system, ala Reagan's Strategic Defense Initiative, or "Star Wars" program. Unlike Jimmy Carter or Bill Clinton, who attempted to advance countless major and minor legislative items and were unsuccessful, the new Bush administration wisely organized around these few issues. This incremental approach and his bipartisan gestures appeared to guarantee success.

However, the results were mixed. The president's campaign pledge to bring a bipartisan approach to the deep divisions plaguing Washington came up short, as partisan bickering actually increased during the first eight months of 2001,[4] and the moderate-centrist image that he tried to fashion during the campaign as a "compassionate conservative" did not translate into 2001. Bush's one notable legislative success involved building public support for his tax cuts, an effort aided by two factors. A sudden and seemingly unsuspected endorsement of Bush's plan by respected Federal Reserve Board Chair Alan Greenspan countered Democrats' assertion that the tax cuts would disproportionately benefit the wealthy, hurt the poor by requiring cuts in social programs, and threaten the budget surplus and solvency of Social Security and Medicare. Bush also helped himself in a masterful speech in February 2001 before a joint session of Congress, where he politicized the tax cuts by selling his $1.6 trillion plan as a compromise between Democrats who wanted less cuts or no cuts and Republicans who wanted more cuts. The president's argument that he was simply giving the budget surplus back to the taxpayers because it was their money resonated well with the public and ensured the eventual passage of the plan.

The lean legislative agenda of the Bush administration otherwise produced only a minimal legislative record. At the midterm of his presidency, George W. Bush could point to few substantive legislative successes aside from his tax cuts.

TABLE 4
Total Public Laws Passed

President	Years (Congress)	Number of bills
G. W. Bush*	107 (2001–2003)	236
Clinton	106 (1999–2001)	580
Clinton	105 (1997–1999)	394
Clinton	104 (1995–1997)	333
Clinton*	103 (1993–1995)	465
G. Bush	102 (1991–1993)	590
G. Bush*	101 (1989–1991)	650
Reagan	100 (1987–1989)	713
Reagan	99 (1985–1987)	666
Reagan	98 (1983–1985)	623
Reagan*	97 (1981–1983)	473
Carter	96 (1979–1981)	614
Carter*	95 (1977–1979)	633
Ford	94 (1975–1977)	588
Nixon/Ford	93 (1973–1975)	650

Note: * = President's first term.

As Table 4 indicates, few bills were passed by the 107th Congress. In fact, Bush signed the fewest number of laws of any recent administration. While this number is telling, it must be balanced against the trend in the past few congresses to group together into massive or omnibus bills what might have been separate bills. Relatedly, Bush did not campaign in 2000 as a foreign policy candidate. Indeed, his primary campaign themes involved such domestic issues as education, tax cuts, and personal issues as his integrity, bipartisanship, and fiscal discipline. As such, it is ironic that his greatest success—his leadership after 9/11—came courtesy of an international event. But with the exception of the War on Terror and his bold victory in securing passage of his UN resolution, Bush's first two years produced few accomplishments internationally. Table 5 reveals that fewer treaties were sponsored by the Bush administration during 2001 and 2002 than any other recent administration.

There was a notable lack of legislative accomplishment by Bush up to the midterm, in spite of or perhaps because of the War on Terror. On the one hand, one might expect the president to use his high approval—especially approval ratings that were nearly unprecedented—to aggressively forward his legislative agenda, taking advantage of the opportunity to earn passage of his programs. This was the case with such presidents as Theodore Roosevelt and Franklin D. Roosevelt, both of whom were very popular and very willing to use that popularity to advance a bewildering array of initiatives. On the other hand, to attempt to do so might have the effect of jeopardizing the president's high approval. This is especially the case if the approval was the result of a rallying effect. The national security crisis—and not the fundamental support in the

TABLE 5
Total Treaties

President	Senate (Years)	Number of treaties
G. W. Bush*	107 (2001–2003)	17
Clinton	106 (1999–2001)	49
Clinton	105 (1997–1999)	58
Clinton	104 (1995–1997)	36
Clinton*	103 (1993–1995)	39
G. Bush	102 (1991–1993)	41
G. Bush*	101 (1989–1991)	22
Reagan	100 (1987–1989)	22
Reagan	99 (1985–1987)	31
Reagan	98 (1983–1985)	32
Reagan*	97 (1981–1983)	28
Carter	96 (1979–1981)	61
Carter*	95 (1977–1979)	26
Ford	94 (1975–1977)	28
Nixon/Ford	93 (1973–1975)	37
Nixon	92 (1971–1973)	35
Nixon*	91 (1969–1971)	25
L. B. Johnson	90 (1967–1969)	28

Note: Number of treaties submitted to Senate; * = president's first term.

president's basic agenda—was the reason for the high approval. As such, the approval might erode while trying to gain passage of sticky domestic issues seemingly unrelated to the crisis at hand. Moreover, a president involved in a national security crisis might either not have the resources to tackle *both* the war and domestic problems, or might seek to avoid difficult domestic matters to not jeopardize his ability to conduct a war.

This did not deter Abraham Lincoln, Woodrow Wilson, or FDR, all of whom addressed a number of sensitive and day-to-day domestic matters during times of war. Whether or not George W. Bush neglected the domestic front during the War on Terror or whether he wisely focused his energies on the more pressing problem (war) is open to debate. His critics might allege that he has been rather inactive on the home front, and not risking his high approval on such issues as the economy, environment, education, and energy is a blemish on his war record. Bush's supporters might suggest that he is only biding his time or did not neglect the home front. Such issues are sure to invite heated debate and expend political capital. Another argument for Bush's limited agenda and apparent inactivity on many seemingly pressing problems is that as a conservative his success has been in refraining from, or restraining unnecessary, government activism. Bush does not favor a strong role for the federal government. As such, rather than undertake federal initiatives to address the problems facing the country, Bush preferred a course that would allow communities, faith-based organizations, and private individuals to take the lead.

TABLE 6
Presidential Vetoes

President	Total	Overridden
G. W. Bush	0	0
Clinton	20	1
G. Bush	46	1
Reagan	78	9
Carter	31	2
Ford	66	12
Nixon	43	7
L. B. Johnson	30	0
Kennedy	21	0
Eisenhower	181	2
Truman	250	12
F. D. Roosevelt	635	9

The existence of a divided Congress, with the House controlled by the Republican Party and the Senate controlled by the Democratic Party for much of his first two years in office, might be used as an argument to both attempt to move ahead boldly (the House can already be counted on for support) or move ahead cautiously (deals must be struck with the Senate). Another factor to consider in attempting to explain Bush's minimal legislative record is that he was able to get virtually whatever he wanted from Congress, especially after 9/11. Bush did not have to exercise the veto in two years. This might be taken as an example that he has been reluctant to use it. But a more accurate explanation is that he did not *have* to use it. Measures disagreeable to him did not make it to his desk. Table 6 shows the use of the veto by recent presidents.

Another way to assess Bush's policy priorities is to examine his radio addresses, speeches, and other public actions to see which topics were emphasized. The Appendix of this book contains a list of Bush's proclamations, executive orders, and radio addresses. From them it is apparent that his legislative agenda through the midterm was comprised of a handful of issues. For instance, aside from symbolic ceremonies and holidays, Bush has championed only a few basic issues, including building support for the War on Terror, changing the regime in Iraq, promoting Christian principles, cutting taxes, and encouraging the nation to work together to improve the economy. This is seen in the Appendix and in Table 7, which lists the topics of Bush's radio addresses.

Administration

Presidential transitions are always complicated and critical. The president-elect has ten or eleven weeks from the time of the November election to the inauguration

TABLE 7
Bush's Radio Addresses by Topic

Topic	Number of addresses
Ceremony/Holiday	13
Economy	12
War on Terror	11fi
Education	6
Iraq	6
Accomplishments/Agenda	5
Taxes	5
Budget	4
Welfare/Medicare/Health Care	4
Energy	3

Note: Partial address or joint topic calculated as fi address.

on January 20 to screen thousands of potential nominees for hundreds of appointments requiring Senate confirmation and hundreds not requiring such approval. The administration must prepare both its position on the issues and assemble its team to implement the president's agenda, all the while considering a host of factors from the diversity of its appointments, to potential ethical problems that might be encountered with a nominee, to the competence and loyalty of the new team, to the preferences of the Senate. George W. Bush faced another challenge: his transition was "truncated" due to the contested November election, giving him even less time for the transition. However, Bush's shortened transition was considered one of the better transitions producing one of the most capable White House staffs.[5] David Gergen, former presidential aide and respected political commentator, deemed Bush's transition the most "disciplined and focused" in years.[6]

Bush was far less engaged in the staffing decisions than some other presidents such as Bill Clinton or Jimmy Carter. However, he appointed a capable and an experienced team to run the transition. Dick Cheney, who headed Bush's transition, had been part of the process during the Nixon, Ford, and Reagan transitions as well as Bush's father's transition. The Bush team began the process while the 2000 election was still unresolved, and it made the first nominations as soon as the election controversy ended.

During the first session of the 107th Congress (2001), Bush submitted a total of 310 nominations to the Senate, with seven pending from the previous administration, producing a total of 317 nominees. The seven from the Clinton administration were withdrawn, two of Bush's own had to be withdrawn, thirty-five were returned at the August 2001 recess, and forty-one were pending at the end of the first session of the 107th Congress. Yet Bush was able to get 231 appointees confirmed, and he made three recess appointments, which, if

TABLE 8
Appointments at 100 Days

Organization	G.W. Bush Jobs/Nomin./Confirm.	Clinton Jobs/Nomin./Confirm.	Reagan Jobs/Nomin/.Confirm.
Departments	330/112/24	325/130/39	253/116/65
Agencies	94/11/2	101/12/4	99/13/5
EOP	25/8/3	26/9/5	14/4/4
Total	449/131/29	472/151/48	366/133/74

Note: EOP = Executive Office of the President; Jobs = Total jobs requiring appointment; Nomin. = Total nominations made; Confirm. = Total confirmations approved.

unconfirmed, expire after the close of the next session of the Congress.[7] Overall, Bush was successful in getting his team both assembled and confirmed. The average number of days to confirm Bush's executive appointments was only thirty-six, which is a normal time frame. Compared to Clinton and Reagan, for instance, Bush was somewhat slower to nominate appointees and have them confirmed.

At the 100-day mark (see Table 8), Reagan made 36 percent of his executive nominations, while Clinton made 33 percent, and Bush made 30 percent. At 100 days, Reagan had 20 percent of his nominees confirmed, Clinton 10 percent, and Bush only 6 percent. Such executive nominations include the cabinet/executive departments, independent agencies, boards and commissions, and the Executive Office of the President. The process requires background checks by the FBI, which lengthen the time. For nonexecutive or lower-level appointments, Reagan had made roughly 81 percent of his nominations by the 100-day mark, Clinton 42 percent, and Bush 44 percent.[8] Yet given Bush's shortened transition, the numbers are justifiable and reflect a reasonably efficient and effective transition.

Table 9 lists Bush's cabinet confirmations. The only two cabinet nominees to draw fire were Attorney General-designee John Ashcroft and Labor Secretary-designee Linda Chavez. Chavez was forced to withdraw her name when ethical questions about her past emerged. She was successfully replaced by Elaine Chao. Ashcroft was opposed by a number of civil rights and women's groups for an alleged record of opposition to such groups. Still, Ashcroft and all of Bush's nominees were approved by the Senate, with most confirmed on the first day. Table 10 provides a comparison with other recent administrations, pointing to an average transition and confirmation record for Bush. Table 11 offers an overall confirmation record by department, showing the relative ease with which Bush's team was confirmed. The only two departments experiencing rejections and delays in confirmations were the Justice Department and the Treasury Department.

TABLE 9
Bush's Cabinet Confirmations

Cabinet	Announced	Confirmed
Agriculture	12/20/00	1/20/01
Commerce	12/20/00	1/20/01
Defense	12/28/00	1/20/01
Education	12/29/00	1/20/01
Energy	1/2/01	1/20/01
HHS	12/29/00	1/24/01
HUD	12/20/00	1/23/01
Interior	12/29/00	1/30/01
Justice	12/22/00	2/1/01
Labor	1/11/01	1/29/01
State	12/15/00	1/20/01
Transportation	1/2/01	1/24/01
Treasury	12/20/00	1/20/01
Vets Affairs	12/29/00	1/23/01

TABLE 10
Comparison with Other Presidential Cabinet Confirmations

Dep't.	Clinton announce-confirm	Reagan announce-confirm	Carter announce-confirm	Nixon announce-confirm
Agr.	12/24/92–01/21/93	12/23/80–01/22/81	12/20/76–01/20/77	12/11/68–01/20/69
Comm.	12/19/92–01/21/93	12/11/80–01/22/81	12/20/76–01/20/77	12/11/68–01/20/69
Def.	12/22/92–01/20/93	12/11/80–01/20/81	12/21/76–01/20/77	12/11/68–01/20/69
Educ.	12/21/92–01/21/93	01/07/81–01/22/81	N/A	N/A
Ener.	12/21/92–01/21/93	12/22/80–01/22/81	12/23/76–09/01/77	N/A
HHS	12/11/92–01/21/93	12/11/80–01/21/81	12/23/76–01/24/77	12/11/68–01/20/69
HUD	12/17/92–01/21/93	12/22/80–01/22/81	12/21/76–01/20/77	12/11/68–01/20/69
Inter.	12/24/92–01/21/93	12/22/80–01/22/81	12/18/76–01/20/77	12/11/68–01/20/69
Just.	12/24/92–02/11/93	12/11/80–01/22/81	12/20/76–01/25/77	12/11/68–01/20/69
Labor	12/11/92–01/21/93	12/16/80–02/03/81	12/21/76–01/20/77	12/11/68–01/20/69
State	12/22/92–01/20/93	12/16/80–01/21/81	12/03/76–01/20/77	12/11/68–01/20/69
Trans.	12/24/92–01/21/93	12/11/80–01/22/81	12/14/76–01/20/77	12/11/68–01/20/69
Treas.	12/10/92–01/20/93	12/11/80–01/21/81	12/14/76–01/20/77	12/11/68–01/20/69
Vet.	12/17/92–01/21/93	N/A	N/A	N/A

President Bush has also been credited for assembling a diverse team. While it is not as diverse as that of his predecessor, Bill Clinton, it is far more diverse than other Republican administrations, including at the cabinet level three women and five ethnic minorities (see Table 12). A complete list of Bush's judicial, ambassadorial, and other appointments appears in the Appendix.

TABLE 11
Profile of Bush's Success in Appointments

Department	Confirmed	Returned	Withdrawn	Average number of days for confirmation
Agriculture	12	4	0	25
Commerce	22	1	0	41
Defense	44	3	1	33
Education	11	1	0	37
Energy	11	1	0	31
HHS	11	2	0	47
HUD	9	1	0	30
Interior	9	1	0	44
Justice	23	7	0	48
Labor	12	2	0	25
State	30	6	0	26
Transport.	13	4	0	34
Treasury	15	3	0	60
Vets Affairs	9	0	0	30

TABLE 12
Female Appointments

President	Years	Cabinet appts.		Total appts.	
		Appts.	Women	Appts.	Women
G. W. Bush	2001–2002	14	3 (21.4%)	1079	219 (20.2%)
Clinton	1993–2001	29	12 (41.4%)	2160	592 (27.4%)
G. Bush	1989–1993	17	3 (17.6%)	903	181 (20.0%)
Reagan	1981–1989	33	3 (9.1%)	2349	277 (11.8%)
Carter	1977–1981	21	4 (19.0%)	919	124 (13.5%)
Ford	1974–1977	12	1 (8.3%)	250	35 (14.0%)
Nixon	1969–1974	31	0 (0.0%)	625	25 (4.0%)

GRADING THE PRESIDENT AT MIDTERM

It is not an easy task to evaluate a president, much less attempt an assessment and a grade at midterm. In the words of presidential scholar and rater James P. Pfiffner, "as a scholar I know that ranking and rating the presidents is not very rigorous and does not necessarily tell us what we would like to know, nevertheless I find it irresistible." Pfiffner goes on to maintain that the discussion produced by ratings is useful in considering what determines successful and unsuccessful presidents and what we look for in a leader. He concludes: "Despite the many legitimate reservations that scholars have about ranking presidents . . . it is a useful exercise."[9]

A group of thirty scholars assembled at a conference on November 22 and 23, 2002, at the Gulf Coast Campus of the University of Southern Mississippi to evaluate and grade the Bush presidency. The graders included a wide array of

TABLE 13
Bush's Grade by Scholars

Grade	Category	Mean	Range
B−/C+	Overall	2.52	A−/F
C	Foreign policy	2.11	A−/F
C−	Domestic policy	1.58	B/F
B−	Relations/Congress	2.64	A−/C−
B	Leadership	3.00	A/D
C	Integrity	2.15	A/F
C+	Ethics	2.20	A/F
B	War on Terror	2.99	B+/C+
B	Appointments/Staff	3.11	A/B−
C−	Economy	1.77	C/F

Note: Thirty scholars of the presidency were asked to offer a letter grade (plus and minus grades were permitted) for President Bush at the midterm of his presidency. Twenty scholars participated in the grading. The scores were averaged (mean) to determine a grade.

scholars reflecting a balance of perspectives and viewpoints, all of whom were informed months in advance of the assignment to grade President Bush.[10] Table 13 reveals the grades, which include an overall grade and grades on specific issues. All grades were considered in determining the average (mean) grade for each category.

The grades varied considerably, with the diversity of grades—Bush received grades ranging from nearly "A" to "F" for many categories—more indicative of the results than any consensus grade that might have emerged. Indeed, the task produced considerable disagreement, and the rationale offered for each grade also ranged from the very positive to the very critical. Excerpts from scholars performing the grading representative of the types of rationale used to explain the grading follow.

Overall

- "Bush has been successful when embodying the head of state role and less successful when acting as head of government."
- "The president much better represents the American public's concerns than he is given credit for."
- "... especially since 9/11, Bush has proven his ability to mold public opinion on the most important issues. His personal popularity remains quite high, as does his handling of the office."
- "Bush exerted strong presidential leadership immediately following 9/11 as commander in chief. . . he has not followed it up in the long run. He did not seize the moment and take advantage of the opportunity to promote long-lasting . . . changes."

- "Bush will be remembered for his response to the terrorist attacks of 9/11. His action was strong, swift, and successful."
- "The president's knack for framing choices in stark terms has served him well in handling the War on Terror, but it has not served him well in explaining to the American people his positions on stem cell research, corporate scandals, global warming, or . . ."
- Bush has been skillful in either bringing the public to support his positions, or at least in preventing open opposition. His media relations have been superb, given the favorable media treatment that he receives."

Foreign Policy

- "The administration for the first eight months largely ignored foreign policy issues, except in a narrow U.S.-first, go-it-alone way."
- "Actions since 9/11 have to some degree squandered the goodwill that did occur after the attacks. The "for-us" or "against-us" orientation seems not only overly simple but also very limiting for future foreign policy actions."
- "Bush has improved relations with such important countries as Britain, Russia, China, Taiwan, Pakistan, India, Mexico, Columbia, and countries around the Russian periphery."
- ". . . too little consultation with other nations, and too much unilateralism. It has alienated France and Germany, downplayed NATO, ignored the UN, been somewhat inconsistent."
- . . .the president has earned praise for his quick military victory in Afghanistan. . . . However, the most visible blotch on Bush's handling of U.S. foreign policy has been his inability to define U.S. policy objectives following 9/11."
- "Bush is accused of being unilateral, but that is simply because he strenuously pushes what he perceives as American interests . . . but he has not done enough to reach out to allies."
- "Bush's simplistic unilateral approach to foreign policy has strengthened the resolve of our potential adversaries and offended our traditional allies."

Domestic Policy

- ". . . a partisan, conservative Republican agenda."
- "Neither recession nor corporate scandal nor the rise in the percentage of the population without health insurance has stimulated significant policy action from the White House."
- "Bush is making the Democrats respond to him."

- "Bush has not provided a clear-cut position on several important issues and has significantly faltered in leading others."
- "The Bush agenda for domestic policy was primarily to cut taxes, and he proceeded to get Congress to do this. However, in so doing he unbalanced the budget . . . and [since] has not seemed interested in domestic affairs, or had much of a policy. . ."
- "From the counterproductiveness of environmental policy changes to indifference on voting reform to rather simple and inconsistent rhetoric on stem cell research, the president has not provided any compelling vision."
- "Bush was effective in getting Congress to pass the measures of his limited agenda but ignores more fundamental problems of a rising national debt, the environment, and the growing discrepancy in the incomes of the rich and poor."

Relations with Congress

- "Despite continuing as president his campaign rhetoric of bipartisanship, Bush has emerged as the most partisan president in recent memory."
- "The administration has been relatively effective in using whatever necessary means to get Congress to approve its actions but [this is counteracted by] the methods of doing so."
- "The Bush administration has been inconsistent in dealing with Capitol Hill, especially the Democrats, sometimes accommodating (education) and sometimes unduly antagonistic and ham-handed (homeland security)."
- "Notwithstanding Bush's well-intentioned efforts to make inroads with moderate Democrats, . . . officials in his administration have by no means behaved in a uniformly bipartisan manner."
- "Bush has shown he can work with Democrats and produce substantive policy achievements."
- ". . . he has not built a coalition for support in the same manner as Ronald Reagan."
- "The president has become reasonably effective in dealing with Congress, especially in view of the extreme nature of some of his proposals. He has appeared to modify the cavalier attitude that brought about a shift in control of the Senate to Democrats [in 2001]."

Leadership

- "When presented with a clear enemy like Al Qaeda or Saddam Hussein, Bush has shown an ability to connect with the American people and manage the media. But absent a clear good versus evil dynamic, he has had difficulty transcending his support among Republicans."

- "I judge leadership not just in terms of response to specific events. . . . In terms of immediate response to 9/11, Bush showed leadership . . . but in wartime, all previous presidents have asked for . . . sacrifice. Bush has asked nothing but cosmetic kinds of actions and essentially no sacrifice while continuing to increase benefits disproportionately for those at the top."
- ". . . high grade on effectiveness of media strategy."
- "Bush appears to have strong, solid support from his fellow Republicans."
- ". . . his bull-horn speech in NYC was exactly what the country wanted."
- ". . . rallied the nation and the world behind his war on terrorism . . . however, Bush himself has not shown enough leadership in dealing with the economic malaise."
- "The best way to rate any president's leadership skills is by evaluating how he performs in response to unanticipated crises . . . Bush had to deal with perhaps the gravest threat to America . . . since the Japanese assault on Pearl Harbor. . . . He performed admirably in the aftermath of [9/11]."

Integrity

- "Bush clearly gets high marks for integrity compared with his predecessor."
- "If integrity means being honest on underlying personal and political values, I would give Bush an A. But, the willingness . . . to use war and "patriotic" actions against Democrats suggests to me some basic questions of integrity. . . . In addition, the extremely pronounced secrecy orientation of the Bush administration is troubling and raises serious questions about integrity."
- ". . . honest, straight-shooting approach to politics has been a welcome change in Washington."
- "Bush combines Andrew Jackson-like commonness with Reagan-like political symbolism to form a refreshing style. His man-of-the-people style causes one to even forget he is a member of the Bush family dynasty."
- ". . . an ability to reach across the aisle."
- "Bush is probably the least conflicted president since Truman. However, the principles on which Bush bases his integrity (loyalty, being a good sport and a team player) are limited in nature."

Ethics

- "There have been no serious repercussions to the economic scandals."
- "George W. Bush and his administration have been notably scandal free."
- "Bush's penchant for secrecy may prove his undoing (. . . the drunk driving "October surprise" . . . Bush should have announced that a year before!). Further, he does not seem comfortable with disagreement, and this has made it difficult for him to referee conflicts within his own administration, and limited his contact with a . . . fractious Congress."
- "Bush has worked to restore the authority of the presidency that had suffered damage from recent court decisions."
- "Bush has taken positions opposite to those upon which he campaigned, adopted policies that in some cases are the same as those he condemned in the Clinton administration, and supports his vice president's unique claim of executive privilege on matters of public policy."

War on Terror

- "Bush's response to the terrorist attacks of 9/11 . . . merit high marks. The Taliban has been rendered toothless, and Al Qaeda has been severely weakened."
- "Determined to take whatever action is necessary to safeguard American economic, military, and political interests at home and abroad, Bush has demonstrated the will to make commitments on behalf of those interests unilaterally if necessary but also multilaterally whenever possible."
- "It doesn't make American citizens more secure to alienate half the world."
- "The strong and accurate sense of the president that the United States must provide leadership in the War on Terror is counterbalanced by his administration's excessive willingness . . . to go it alone at any and all costs."

Appointments/Staff

- ". . . appointees to the White House, cabinet, and other officials have almost without exception been people of the highest ethical standards."
- "The individual integrity of the Big Three of his cabinet—Powell, Rice, Rumsfeld—is laudable."
- "The president's inner circle in foreign policy is precisely the group that should be fighting the War on Terror . . . but, ideological factors,

rather than subject matter knowledge and experience, [seem] to have carried the day in the filling of other positions."

Economy

- "On corporate responsibility, the Bush administration came late and awkwardly, given the corporate histories of the president and vice president. In addition, the efforts seemingly favored by the president . . . have been largely rhetorical, with efforts now to undercut even those actions."
- ". . . he needs a more coherent plan for dealing with the troubled economy."
- "Much of the current economic weakness is not the fault of the Bush administration . . . nevertheless, the Bush administration has been lax in promoting economic reform and economic programs to stimulate the economy."
- "Bush inherited a weak economy that has worsened after [9/11]. The increase in spending on defense and law enforcement as a result . . . has returned the federal government to deficit spending."
- "Bush's efforts to reinvigorate the economy have produced mixed results."
- "The economy seems to be of secondary concern to promoting the wealth of individuals."
- "The size of the tax cut . . . was justifiable, but it did not rationalize the tax code and was not part of an overall economic policy."

Other attempts to grade the administration at midterm were undertaken by the *National Journal* and the Harris-Zogby Poll. The *National Journal* offers a report card on the Bush cabinet and senior advisors, listed in Table 14, while the poll in Table 15 reveals approval ratings for Bush's advisors. A number of the cabinet officers were rated in the "B" range, consistent with the "B" grade assigned to Bush's staff in Table 13.

Arguably, one of the president's biggest victories was the surprising 2002 midterm election. Historically, the president's party has done poorly during midterm or "off-year" elections. Yet Bush boldly, and against conventional wisdom and history, campaigned for his party's candidates in several states. The president, not known to be a vigorous campaigner, appeared in several states and campaigned harder than he did during the 2000 race. Moreover, Bush nationalized the election, making it a mandate on his leadership of the War on Terror. With both the House and Senate at stake, Bush helped his party regain control of the Senate and extend its margin as the majority party in the House, making it the first time in history that a president's party has taken control of

TABLE 14
Report Card by National Journal

Grade	Staff member (Department)
A	Colin Powell (State)
A−	John Ashcroft (Justice)
A−	Donald Evans (Commerce)
A−	Anthony Principi (Veterans Affairs)
B+	Donald Rumsfeld (Defense)
B	Spencer Abraham (Energy)
B	Daniels (OMB)
B	Norman Mineta (Transportation)
B	Tommy Thompson (HHS)
B	Zoellick (USTR)
B−	Elaine Chao (Labor)
B−	Gale Norton (Interior)
C+	Mel Martinez (HUD)
C+	George Tenet (CIA)
C	Roderick Paige (Education)
C−	Christie Todd Whitman (EPA)
D	Paul O'Neill (Treasury)
D	Ann Veneman (Agriculture)

Note: "Grading the Cabinet," National Journal
(January 14, 2003). See http://www.npr.org/
display_pages/features/feature_934659.html.

TABLE 15
Bush Staff Approval

"How would you rate the job [name] is doing?" Cabinet member	Positive	Negative
Colin Powell	74%	21%
Donald Rumsfeld	59%	30%
John Ashcroft	51%	33%

"Do you have a favorable or an unfavorable opinion of the following people?"

Staff	Very fav.	Somewhat Fav	Somewhat Unfav.	Very unfav.	?
C. Powell	52%	38%	2%	2%	5%
D. Cheney	23%	38%	11%	16%	12%
D. Rumsfeld	18%	27%	10%	10%	35%
J. Ashcroft	14%	27%	10%	14%	31%

Note: Harris-Zogby Poll (January 4–6, 2003); N = 1,001 likely voters. See
http://nationaljournal.com/members/polltrack/2003/national/03cabinet.htm.

both chambers of the Congress in a midterm election, only the third time in a century a sitting president's party picked up seats in the midterm, and the first time in a half century that the Republicans controlled both houses. Even though the economy was weak—something that usually spells defeat for the sitting president—Bush was able to keep the economy and other domestic problems off the radar map, while keeping the public focused on the war. It was truly a historic election and one that perhaps finally gave Bush the mandate that eluded him after the controversial election that put him in office.

A FINAL WORD: HINDSIGHT AND HISTORY

Bush concluded the midterm of his presidential term by being voted over-whelmingly as the "most admired man" in Gallup's long-running poll (see Table 16). For whatever shortcomings this poll has, especially for the serious effort to assess presidential performance, it nonetheless reflects Bush's consider-able popularity, resulting from the terrorist attacks of 2001 and Bush's subsequent handling of the War on Terror.

Two years is an eternity in politics, and at the time of this writing, a lot has happened since the midterm and a lot will continue to happen in the remain-der of Bush's presidency. There is no crystal ball when it comes to predicting presidential performance, and even the most cautious effort at evaluating per-formance is not guaranteed to hold true. The midterm is just that—halfway into one's term. But it is helpful to start the process of thinking about how and why we evaluate presidents, as it is beneficial to commence what will be a long-running attempt to assess the presidency of George W. Bush, one that will last

TABLE 16
Most Admired Man/Woman (2002)

Top 10 Most Admired Men		Top 10 Most Admired Women	
1. George W. Bush	28%	1. Hillary Clinton	7%
2. Jimmy Carter	9%	2. Oprah Winfrey	6%
3. Colin Powell	4%	3. Laura Bush	6%
4. Pope John Paul II	3%	4. Barbara Bush	3%
5. Bill Clinton	3%	5. Margaret Thatcher	3%
6. Rev. Billy Graham	2%	6. Jennifer Lopez	2%
7. Nelson Mandela	1%	7. Elizabeth Dole	2%
8. Al Gore	1%	8. Condoleezza Rice	2%
9. Ronald Reagan	1%	9. Maya Angelou	1%
10. Denzel Washington	1%	10. Madeleine Albright	1%

Note: "George W. Bush Is 2002's Most Admired Man, No Consensus on Most Admired Woman," Gallup News Service (December 27, 2002). See http://www.gallup.com/poll/releases/pr021227.asp?version=.

long after his time in office. Indeed, a compelling argument exists for why we should evaluate presidents, and an equally compelling argument exists for beginning the process early. This period of time includes the "100 days" often used to formulate an initial assessment about the newly elected president. Such major decisions as staffing the administration, establishing the presidential agenda, delivering the first State of the Union address, and other items all set the course for the presidency and help assess what type of president George W. Bush will be for the remainder of his term and, ultimately, what type of president he was.

At the time of this writing, it remains to be seen how Bush's first two years will impact his remaining time in office, and how the Bush presidency will impact the country. In determining George W. Bush's eventual standing among the presidents, scholars with the benefit of hindsight will one day factor in such questions as: Did Bush get reelected? Did he leave the office and country stronger than when he entered office? Did his policies and appointments succeed and leave positive, lasting impact long after his presidency ended?

Bush's presidency, in particular, was noteworthy through the midterm, as there appeared to be two different presidencies—one before 9/11 and one after 9/11. The momentous tragedy of the terrorist attacks on the World Trade Center and Pentagon forever changed the country and the presidency, and they occurred on Bush's watch. Bush commenced a difficult and new kind of war. All the while, Bush faced an economic crisis after the prosperous nineties. So too was it the first presidency of the new century and new millennium, and one of the most controversial presidential elections in history. It will truly be fascinating to learn how this presidency turns out, and this assessment will hopefully assist in understanding the many questions that scholars and citizens alike will have about the forty-third president.

NOTES

1. For an assessment of the first 100 days, see John Frendreis, Raymond Tatalovich, and Jon Schaff, "Predicting Legislative Output in the First One-Hundred Days, 1897–1995," *Political Research Quarterly* 54 (December 2001): 853–70. For arguably the most dramatic first 100 days (FDR), see Arthur M. Schlesinger Jr., *The Age of Roosevelt: The Coming of the New Deal* (Boston: Houghton Mifflin, 1958).

2. For a discussion of the rallying effect, see George C. Edwards III and Tami Swenson, "Who Rallies?," *Journal of Politics* 59 (February 1997): 200–12. For a discussion of it in regard to war presidents, see John E. Mueller, *War, Presidents, and Public Opinion* (New York: Wiley & Sons, 1970).

3. James MacGregor Burns, *Leadership* (New York: Harper & Row, 1978).

4. Congressional Quarterly's roll call and party unity reports revealed an increase in partisanship under George W. Bush.

5. Nearly all of the thirty scholars participating in the conference "Assessing the Presidency of George W. Bush," held at the University of Southern Mississippi-Gulf Coast on November 22 and 23, 2002, agreed that Bush's transition was one of the best. For further information, see chapter 12 by Bradley Patterson in this book. For information on "truncated transitions," see Joseph A. Pika, John Anthony Maltese, and Norman C. Thomas, *The Politics of the Presidency*, 5th ed. (Washington, D.C.: CQ Press, 2001).

6. David Gergen's comments on Bush's transition were made during his March 9, 2001, comments on ABC. See www.abcnews.com.

7. The president can make appointments when Congress is on recess, however, such recess appointments expire at the end of the congressional term unless they are confirmed by the Senate before then. Bush made a few recess appointments in the fall of 2001.

8. See Rogelio Garcia, Nominations and Confirmations to Policy Positions in the First 100 Days of the George W. Bush, William J. Clinton, and Ronald W. Reagan Administrations, Congressional Research Service Report, July 17, 2001; Henry B. Hogue, Presidential Appointments to Full-Time Positions in Executive Departments during the 107th Congress, 2001–2002, Congressional Research Service Report, April 1, 2002; Henry B. Hogue, Presidential Appointments to Full-Time Positions in Independent and Other Agencies during the 107th Congress, Congressional Research Service Report, June 5, 2002.

9. James P. Pfiffner, "Ranking the Presidents: Continuity and Volatility," *White House Studies* 3, no.1 (2003): (23–34).

10. A total of thirty scholars attended the "Assessing the Presidency of George W. Bush" conference held at the University of Southern Mississippi-Gulf Coast on November 22 and 23, 2002. A total of twenty participated in the grading. All were notified months in advance and asked to provide an overall grade for President Bush and grades for various categories (domestic policy, foreign policy, relations with Congress, etc.). The twenty scholars represent a wide array of viewpoints, and every effort was made to produce a fair and an accurate assessment.

Appendix

Executive Orders by President Bush

Date	Executive Order
12/19/02	half-day closing of federal agencies/departments on 12/24/02
12/12/02	equal protection of laws for faith-based organizations
12/12/02	responsibilities for agencies vis-à-vis faith-based initiatives
12/11/02	President's Commission on the U.S. Postal Service
11/20/02	delegating authority under Trade Act of 2002
11/15/02	undocumented aliens in Caribbean
10/07/02	establish Board of Inquiry on disputes affecting maritime industry
09/18/02	environment and transportation infrastructure reviews
08/29/02	amend EO on regulations for safeguarding vessels, harbors, ports
08/13/02	proper consideration of small entities in agency rule making
07/09/02	establishment of Corporate Fraud Task Force
07/03/02	expedited naturalization EO
07/03/02	Taliban
06/20/02	EO details unavailable
06/20/02	President's Council on Physical Fitness and Sports
06/20/02	promoting fitness
06/06/02	amending EO on air traffic performance
04/29/02	President's New Freedom Commission on Mental Health
04/12/02	amending Manual for Courts Martial
03/21/02	Homeland Security Council

03/19/02	providing order of succession in EPA
02/12/02	advisors for historically black colleges/universities
02/07/02	amending EO on President's Commission on Excellence in Education
01/30/02	establish USA Freedom Corps
01/17/02	amending EO 13223
01/07/02	exclusions from Federal Labor-Management Relations
12/28/01	eleven EOs on succession of federal agencies/cabinets
12/27/01	normal trade relations treatment
12/21/01	Council of Europe in Respect of the Group of States against Corruption
12/20/01	establish Emergency Board
12/14/01	Afghanistan combat zone
12/06/01	closing federal agencies on 12/24/01
11/28/01	establish President's Council on Bioethics
11/27/01	waive dual compensation provisions for CIA
11/16/01	national emergency construction authority
11/13/01	military
11/09/01	citizen preparedness in War on Terror
10/22/01	Department of Health and Human Services
10/16/01	critical infrastructure protection
10/12/01	Educational Excellence for Hispanic Americans Commission
10/08/01	establish Office of Homeland Security
10/03/01	Excellence in Special Education
10/01/01	continuance of federal advisory committees
10/01/01	President's Council of Advisors on Science and Technology
09/24/01	terrorist financing
09/14/01	ready reserves to active duty
08/17/01	export control regulations
07/31/01	energy efficient standby power devices
07/02/01	information unavailable
06/20/01	21st Century Workforce Initiative
06/19/01	Community-Based Alternatives for Individuals with Disabilities
06/06/01	amending EO 13125
06/01/01	information unavailable
05/28/01	Task Force to Improve Health Care Delivery for Our Nation's Veterans
05/23/01	prohibit importation of rough diamonds from Sierra Leone
05/18/01	regulations on energy supply
05/18/01	expedite energy-related projects
05/02/01	Commission to Strengthen Social Security
04/30/01	Task Force on Puerto Rico's Status
04/06/01	amend EO 13202

04/05/01	amend EO 10000
04/04/01	terminate emergency authority for export controls
03/09/01	establish Emergency Board
02/21/01	preserving open competition in government contractor's labor relations
02/21/01	notifying employees of rights concerning paying union dues
02/21/01	revoke EO on nondisplacement of qualified workers
02/21/01	labor-management partnerships
02/12/01	Information Technology Advisory Board
01/29/01	agency responsibilities on faith-based initiatives
01/29/01	establish White House Office of Faith-Based and Community Initiatives

Public Radio Addresses by President Bush

Date	*Topic*
12/14/02	unemployment benefits
12/07/02	Iraq
11/30/02	Thanksgiving
11/23/02	foreign affairs
11/16/02	Department of Homeland Security
11/09/02	UN Resolution on war
11/02/02	judicial branch
10/26/02	health care
10/19/02	[no topic]
10/12/02	[no topic]
10/05/02	Iraqi threat
09/28/02	Iraqi threat
09/21/02	Department of Homeland Security
09/14/02	Saddam Hussein
09/07/02	homeland security
08/31/02	USA Freedom Corps
08/24/02	forest management
08/17/02	economy
08/10/02	Economic Forum
08/03/02	president's accomplishments
07/27/02	corporate corruption
07/20/02	economic security
07/13/02	national priorities
07/06/02	nation's independence
06/29/02	corporate corruption
06/22/02	Fitness Challenge

06/15/02	home ownership
06/08/02	terrorism
06/01/02	U.S. Military Academy graduation
05/25/02	president's trip to Europe
05/18/02	Medicare
05/11/02	welfare reform
05/04/02	Cinco de Mayo
04/27/02	economy
04/20/02	terrorism
04/13/02	tax relief
04/06/02	Middle East
03/30/02	Easter
03/23/02	foreign relations
03/16/02	Afghanistan children
03/09/02	economy
03/02/02	public schools
02/23/02	energy security
02/16/02	president's trip to Asia
02/09/02	Black History Month
02/02/02	pensions
01/26/02	president's priorities
01/19/02	Dr. Martin Luther King Jr.
01/12/02	economy
01/05/02	economy
12/29/01	year in review
12/25/01	Christmas
12/22/01	economy/terrorism
12/15/01	economy
12/08/01	economy
12/01/01	economy
11/24/01	Thanksgiving
11/17/01	violence against women
11/10/01	War on Terror
11/03/01	anthrax
10/27/01	War on Terror
10/20/01	terrorism
10/13/01	economy
10/06/01	Aid to Afghanistan
09/29/01	War on Terror
09/22/01	economy
09/15/01	response to terrorism
09/08/01	education
09/01/01	education

08/25/01   budget
08/18/01   Faith-Based and Community Initiatives
08/11/01   stem cell research
08/04/01   Medicaid
07/28/01   American with Disabilities Act
07/21/01   G-7/8 Summit
07/14/01   Medicare
07/07/01   education
06/30/01   military
06/23/01   Patients' Bill of Rights
06/16/01   Father's Day
06/09/01   home ownership
06/02/01   tax plan
05/26/01   Memorial Day
05/19/01   energy plan
05/12/01   energy plan
05/05/01   Cinco de Mayo
04/28/01   first 100 days
04/21/01   democracy in Western Hemisphere
04/14/01   Easter
04/07/01   education/tax reform
03/31/01   children
03/24/01   budget
03/17/01   tax relief
03/10/01   tax relief
03/03/01   tax relief/budget
02/24/01   budget
02/17/01   tax relief/education
02/10/01   national security
02/03/01   tax relief
01/27/01   education

Proclamations Issued by President Bush

Date   *Proclamation*
01/17/03   Martin Luther King Jr. Day
01/17/03   modify rules to NAFTA
01/15/03   Religious Freedom Day
01/14/03   National Sanctity of Life Day
01/13/03   centennial of Korean immigration to United States
01/13/03   modify duty-free trade
01/02/03   National Mentoring Month

12/31/02	New Year's message
12/16/02	Wright Brothers Day
12/09/02	Human Rights Day/Week
12/06/02	Pearl Harbor Remembrance Day
12/03/02	Drunk and Drugged Driving Prevention Month
11/29/02	World's AIDS Day
11/22/02	National Family Week
11/14/02	modify Caribbean Basin Economic Recovery Act
11/14/02	America Recycles Day
11/09/02	World Freedom Day
11/08/02	Employer Support of Guard and Reserve Week
11/06/02	Veteran's Day
11/05/02	centennial of West Wing of White House
11/01/02	National Hospice Month
11/01/02	National Adoption Month
11/01/02	American Indian Heritage Month
10/31/02	Andean Trade Promotion and Drug Eradication Act
10/31/02	Diabetes Month
10/31/02	Alzheimer's Awareness Month
10/29/02	Family Caregivers Month
10/23/02	UN Day
10/18/02	Character Counts Week
10/18/02	Forest Products Week
10/18/02	Year of Clean Water
10/11/02	National School Lunch Week
10/11/02	White Cane Safety Day
10/11/02	National Cystic Fibrosis Awareness Week
10/10/02	Columbus Day
10/10/02	Gen. Pulaski Memorial Day
10/08/02	Leif Erikson Day
10/05/02	German-American Day
10/05/02	Fire Prevention Week
10/05/02	Child Health Day
10/01/02	National Breast Cancer Awareness Month
10/01/02	National Domestic Violence Awareness Month
10/01/02	National Disability Employment Awareness Month
09/29/02	Gold Star Mother's Day
09/23/02	Family Day
09/23/02	Minority Enterprise Development Week
09/19/02	National POW/MIA Recognition Day
09/16/02	Citizenship Day and Constitution Week
09/14/02	Nationally Historically Black Colleges and Universities Week
09/14/02	National Farm Safety and Health Week

09/14/02	National Hispanic Heritage Month
09/05/02	National Alcohol and Drug Addiction Recovery Month
09/04/02	Patriots' Day
08/31/02	National Days of Prayer and Remembrance
08/30/02	National Ovarian Cancer Awareness Month
08/28/02	agreement on imports of line pipe, Trade Act
08/28/02	modify duty-free treatment for Argentina
08/24/02	Women's Equality Day
08/16/02	National Health Center Week
08/14/02	National Airborne Day
07/29/02	Bicentennial of U.S. Patent and Trademark Office
07/26/02	National Korean War Veterans Armistice Day
07/26/02	Parent's Day
07/26/02	anniversary of Americans with Disabilities Act
07/17/02	Captive Nations Week
07/04/02	trade proclamation
07/01/02	Lewis and Clark Bicentennial
06/28/02	Independence Day proclamation
06/14/02	Father's Day
06/13/02	Flag Day
06/07/02	Great Outdoors Week
06/05/02	National Child's Day
06/04/02	National Homeowners Month
05/31/02	Black Music Month
05/31/02	National Fishing and Boating Week
05/21/02	Prayer for Peace, Memorial Day
05/21/02	National Missing Children's Day
05/21/02	National Maritime Day
05/17/02	World Trade Week proclamation
05/17/02	National Safe Boating Week
05/16/02	Armed Forces Day
05/13/02	National Hurricane Awareness Week
05/10/02	Police Week
05/10/02	National Defense Transportation Day
05/09/02	Mother's Day
05/06/02	National Tourism Week
05/06/02	Small Business Week
05/03/02	restore nondiscriminatory trade treatment to products of Afghanistan
05/02/02	National Charter Schools Week
05/02/02	Loyalty Day
05/02/02	Asian/Pacific American Heritage Month
05/02/02	Older Americans Month

05/01/02	Law Day
04/26/02	National Day of Prayer proclamation
04/23/02	National Park Week proclamation
04/19/02	National Organ and Tissue Donor Awareness Week
04/19/02	National Volunteer Week
04/18/02	National Crime Victim's Rights Week
04/17/02	death of Byron White proclamation
04/12/02	Jewish Heritage Week
04/12/02	Pan American Day
04/10/02	National DARE Day
04/04/02	National Former Prisoner of War Recognition Day
04/01/02	Cancer Control Month
04/01/02	National Child Abuse Prevention Month
03/25/02	Greek Independence Day
03/25/02	National Bone and Joint Decade proclamation
03/25/02	Education and Sharing Day
03/14/02	National Poison Prevention Week proclamation
03/11/02	West Point Bicentennial Day proclamation
03/06/02	Women's History Month proclamation
03/05/02	steel products proclamation
03/04/02	Save Your Vision Week proclamation
03/04/02	Irish-American Heritage Month proclamation
03/04/02	American Red Cross Month
03/04/02	National Colorectal Cancer Awareness Month
02/27/02	continuance of Cuba National Emergency Notice
02/22/02	Zimbabwe proclamation
02/04/02	National African American History Month proclamation
02/02/02	American Hearth Month proclamation
01/18/02	National Mentoring Month
01/18/02	Martin Luther King Jr. Holiday
01/18/02	National Sanctity of Human Life Day
01/16/02	Religious Freedom Day
12/27/01	trade relations EO
12/20/01	Christmas message
12/13/01	Wright Brothers Day
12/09/01	Human Rights Day/Week
12/07/01	Pearl Harbor Remembrance Day
11/30/01	Drunk and Drugged Driving Prevention Month
11/30/01	World's AIDS Day
11/30/01	National Hospice Month proclamation
11/30/01	National Diabetes Month
11/21/01	imports of steel proclamation
11/21/01	National Family Week

11/16/01   Day of Thanksgiving
11/15/02   America Recycles Day proclamation
11/14/01   imports of lamb proclamation
11/13/01   National Farm-City Week proclamation
11/12/01   National American Indian Heritage Month proclamation
11/09/01   Chronic Obstructive Pulmonary Disease Month proclamation
11/09/01   National Alcohol and Drug Addiction Recovery Month pro-
           clamation
11/09/01   National Family Caregivers Month
11/09/01   National Alzheimer's Disease Awareness Month proclamation
11/09/01   World Freedom Day
11/09/01   Employer Support of Guard and Reserve Week
11/05/01   National Adoption Month proclamation
11/01/01   National Prostrate Cancer Awareness Month proclamation
10/30/01   Veteran's Day proclamation
10/24/01   UN Day proclamation
10/24/01   National Red Ribbon Week for a Drug-Free America proclamation
10/23/01   National Character Counts Week proclamation
10/19/01   National Forest Products Week proclamation
10/15/01   White Cane Safety Day proclamation
10/15/01   National School Lunch Week proclamation
10/10/01   Gen. Pulaski Memorial Day proclamation
1/20/01–10/1/01

President Bush's Judicial Appointments

Name	Office	Announced	Nominated
J. R. Adams	district ct (OH)	10/10/02	pending
L. M. Africk	district ct (LA)	01/23/02	04/17/02
P. Anderson	district ct (CA)	01/23/02	04/25/02
M. C. Armijo	district ct (NM)	08/02/01	11/06/01
H. E. Autrey	district ct (MO)	03/22/02	08/01/02
J. D. Bates	district ct (DC)	06/20/01	12/11/01
M. M. Baylson	district ct (PA)	01/23/02	04/30/02
R. R. Beistline	district ct (AK)	11/08/01	03/12/02
R. E. Blackburn	district ct (CO)	09/10/01	02/26/02
L. J. Block	ct of fed claims	08/02/01	10/02/02
J. E. Boasberg	superior ct	05/13/02	08/01/02
K. O. Bodre	district ct (AL)	08/02/01	11/06/01
G. L. Bower	U.S. tax ct	09/13/02	pending
T. W. Boyle	4th circuit ct	05/09/01	pending
S. G. Braden	U.S. claims ct	05/01/02	pending

J. D. Breen	district ct (TN)	10/10/02	pending
D. L. Bunning	district ct (KY)	08/12/01	02/14/02
D. C. Bury	district ct (AZ)	09/10/01	03/15/02
J. S. Bybee	9th circuit ct	05/22/02	pending
K. K. Caldwell	district ct (KY)	08/02/01	10/23/01
L. S. Camp	district ct (NE)	05/19/01	10/23/01
C. J. Carney	district ct (CA)	10/10/02	pending
P. G. Cassell	district ct (UT)	05/19/01	05/13/02
R. F. Cebull	district ct (MT)	05/18/01	07/20/01
D. S. Cercone	district ct (PA)	03/22/02	08/01/02
S. R. Chesler	district ct (NJ)	01/23/02	pending
E. P. Christian	assoc judge	04/04/01	05/24/01
J. J. Clark	assoc judge	11/29/01	03/13/02
R. H. Clark	district ct (TX)	01/23/02	10/02/02
E. B. Clement	5th circuit ct	05/09/01	11/13/01
R. B. Clifton	9th circuit ct	06/22/01	07/18/02
R. M. Colloton	district ct (IA)	08/01/02	pending
C. C. Conner	district ct (PA)	02/28/02	07/26/02
J. F. Conti	district ct (PA)	01/23/02	07/29/02
D. L. Cook	6th circuit ct	05/09/01	pending
T. J. Corrigan	district ct (FL)	05/22/02	09/12/02
F. L. Cramer	U.S. tax ct	11/29/01	pending
R. R. Crane	district ct (TX)	09/21/01	03/18/02
L. D. Davis	district ct (PA)	01/23/02	04/18/02
L. E. Davis	district ct (TX)	01/23/02	05/09/02
J. C. Dever	district ct (NC)	05/22/02	pending
R. E. Dorr	district ct (MO)	03/22/02	08/01/02
C. V. Eagan	district ct (OK)	08/02/01	10/23/01
K. D. Engelhardt	district ct (LA)	08/02/01	12/11/01
M. C. England	district ct (CA)	03/22/02	08/01/02
C. E. Erdmann	armed forces	08/01/02	pending
R. R. Erickson	district ct (ND)	09/12/02	pending
M. A. Estrada	DC circuit ct	05/09/01	pending
S. J. Feurstein	district ct (NY)	07/25/02	pending
S. P. Friot	district ct (OK)	08/02/01	11/06/01
G. L. Frost	district ct (OH)	08/01/02	pending
M. E. Fuller	district ct (AL)	08/01/02	pending
J. K. Gardner	district ct (PA)	04/22/02	10/02/02
J. S. Gibbons	6th circuit ct	10/05/01	07/29/02
D. C. Godbey	district ct (TX)	01/23/02	08/01/02
C. V. S. Granade	district ct (AL)	08/02/01	pending
R. L. Gregory	4th circuit ct	05/09/01	07/20/01
W. C. Griesbach	district ct (WI)	01/23/02	04/25/02

R. A. Griffin	6th circuit ct	06/26/02	pending
J. E. Gritzner	district ct (IA)	07/10/01	02/14/02
S. E. Haddon	distict ct (MT)	05/18/01	07/20/01
A. S. Hanen	district ct (TX)	01/23/02	pending
H. L. Hartz	10th circuit ct	06/21/01	12/06/01
J. L. Heaton	district ct (OK)	08/02/01	12/06/01
L. R. Hicks	district ct (NV)	08/02/01	11/05/01
S. M. Hicks	district ct (LA)	09/12/02	pending
R. J. Holwell	district ct (NY)	08/11/02	pending
M. B. Horn	fed claims ct	08/01/01	pending
D. L. Hovland	district ct (ND)	06/26/02	pending
J. R. Howard	1st circuit ct	08/02/01	04/23/02
H. E. Hudson	district ct (VA)	01/23/02	08/01/02
W. P. Johnson	district ct (WV)	08/02/01	12/13/01
J. E. Jones	district ct (PA)	02/28/02	07/29/02
K. A. Jordan	district ct (DE)	07/25/02	pending
C. K. Jorgenson	district ct (AZ)	09/10/01	02/26/02
R. A. Junell	district ct (TX)	07/18/02	pending
B. E. Kasold	vet claims	03/21/02	pending
J. E. Kinkeade	district ct (TX)	07/18/02	pending
R. G. Klausner	district ct (CA)	07/18/02	pending
M. S. Krieger	district ct (CO)	09/10/01	01/25/02
R. B. Kugler	district ct (NJ)	08/01/02	pending
C. B. Kuhl	9th circuit ct	06/22/01	pending
J. E. Lancaster	district ct (MN)	01/23/02	04/25/02
A. G. Lance	vet claims	09/24/02	pending
C. D. Land	district ct (GA)	09/21/01	12/13/01
L. Leibovitz	superior ct	05/14/01	08/03/01
R. J. Leon	DC circuit ct	09/10/01	02/14/02
C. F. Lettow	fed claims ct	08/01/01	pending
J. L. Linares	district ct (NJ)	08/01/02	pending
T. L. Ludington	district ct (MI)	09/12/02	pending
A. M. Ludlum	district ct (TX)	07/11/02	pending
J. C. Mahan	district ct (NV)	09/10/01	01/25/02
K. A. Marra	district ct (FL)	01/23/02	09/09/02
J. E. Martinez	district ct (FL)	01/23/02	09/13/02
P. R. Martinez	district ct (TX)	10/05/01	pending
W. J. Martini	district ct (NJ)	01/23/02	pending
F. J. Martone	district ct (AZ)	09/10/01	12/13/01
S. H. Mays	district ct (TN)	01/23/02	05/09/02
M. W. McConnell	10th circuit ct	05/09/01	pending
D. W. McKeague	6th circuit ct	11/18/01	pending
T. F. McVerry	district ct (PA)	01/23/02	09/03/02

M. J. Melloy	8th circuit ct	07/10/01	02/11/02
M. P. Mills	district ct (MS)	07/10/01	10/12/01
S. B. Neilson	6th circuit ct	11/08/01	pending
T. L. O'Brien	10th circuit ct	08/02/01	pending
S. J. Otero	district ct (CA)	07/18/02	pending
P. R. Owen	5th circuit ct	05/09/01	pending
B. D. Parker	2nd circuit ct	05/09/01	10/12/01
J. H. Payne	district ct (OK)	08/02/01	10/23/01
T. W. Phillips	district ct (TN)	06/26/02	pending
C. W. Pickering	5th circuit	06/25/01	pending
S. Prost	fed circuit	05/21/01	09/21/01
W. D. Quarles	district ct (MD)	09/12/02	pending
R. Raggi	2nd circuit ct	05/01/02	09/20/02
L. R. Reade	district ct (IA)	06/26/02	pending
D. C. Reeves	district ct (KY)	08/02/01	12/06/01
R. R. Rigsby	superior ct	03/04/02	07/26/02
W. J. Riley	8th circuit ct	05/23/01	08/03/01
J. G. Roberts	DC circuit ct	05/09/01	pending
J. A. Robinson	district ct (KS)	09/10/01	12/11/01
J. M. Rogers	6th circuit ct	12/19/01	pending
F. W. Rohlfing	district ct (HI)	01/23/02	pending
T. M. Rose	district ct (OH)	01/23/02	05/09/02
M. A. Ross	superior ct	04/04/01	05/24/01
C. A. Royal	district ct (GA)	10/05/01	12/20/01
C. M. Rufe	district ct (PA)	01/23/02	04/30/02
H. W. Saad	6th circuit ct	11/08/01	pending
F. F. Saddler	superior ct	06/11/02	pending
T. J. Savage	district ct (PA)	03/22/02	08/01/02
A. J. Schwab	district ct (PA)	01/23/02	09/13/02
D. W. Shedd	4th circuit ct	05/19/01	pending
D. B. Smith	3rd circuit ct	09/08/01	07/31/02
L. R. Smith	8th circuit ct	05/22/01	07/15/02
W. E. Smith	district ct (RI)	07/18/02	pending
A. J. St. Eve	district ct (IL)	03/22/02	08/01/02
T. C. Stanceu	U.S. ct of intl. trade	12/19/01	pending
W. H. Steele	11th circuit ct	10/05/01	pending
J. Sutton	6th circuit ct	05/19/01	pending
T. M. Tymkovich	10th circuit ct	05/25/01	pending
T. A. Varlan	district ct (TN)	10/10/02	pending
O. F. Vincent	superior ct	08/03/01	11/15/01
J. F. Walter	district ct (CA)	01/23/02	04/25/02
R. B. Walton	DC district ct	06/20/01	09/21/01
T. B. Wells	U.S. tax ct	09/10/01	10/02/01

J. S. White	district ct (CA)	07/25/02	pending
M. E. C. Williams	fed claims ct	06/24/01	pending
F. L. Wolfson	district ct (NJ)	08/01/02	pending
V. J. Wolski	U.S. claims ct	09/12/02	pending
T. L. Wooten	district ct (SC)	06/18/01	11/18/01
J. C. Zainey	district ct (LA)	10/10/01	02/11/02

President Bush's Ambassadorial Appointments

Name	Office	Announced	Nominated
G. L. Argyros	Amb to Spain	04/25/01	11/15/01
R. L. Austin	Amb to Trinidad	08/27/01	09/26/01
H. H. Baker	Amb to Japan	03/26/01	05/23/01
R. L. Baltimore	Amb to Oman	05/04/02	10/02/02
V. M. Battle	Amb to Lebanon	05/09/01	08/03/01
R. M. Bell	Special envoy	05/05/02	08/01/02
S. A. Bernstein	Amb to Denmark	04/25/01	08/01/01
R. D. Blackwill	Amb to India	03/21/01	07/10/01
J. W. Blaney	Amb to Liberia	05/14/02	08/01/02
J. R. Blankenship	Amb to Bahamas	03/26/01	11/15/01
C. G. Bond	Amb to Bosnia	07/11/01	09/26/01
R. L. Boyce	Amb to Indonesia	08/07/01	09/26/01
S. F. Brauer	Amb to Belgium	04/20/01	05/25/01
A. E. Brazeal	Amb to Ethiopia	05/10/02	10/02/02
M. G. Brennan	Amb to Zambia	05/04/02	10/02/02
N. G. Brinker	Amb to Hungary	05/23/01	08/03/01
W. L. Brown	Amb to Austria	10/02/01	11/15/01
W. R. Brownfield	Amb to Chile	09/05/01	01/25/02
R. F. Burghardt	Amb to Vietnam	08/22/01	11/15/01
L. E. Butler	Amb to Macedonia	02/22/02	03/20/02
B. E. Carlson	Amb to Latvia	05/26/01	10/30/01
P. Cellucci	Amb to Canada	02/13/01	04/05/01
P. R. Chaveas	Amb to Sierra Leone	06/21/01	07/12/01
G. B. Christy	Amb to Brunei	05/10/02	pending
D. R. Coats	Amb to Germany	04/12/01	08/03/01
S. M. Cobb	Amb to Jamaica	04/04/01	08/01/01
J. J. Danilovich	Amb to Costa Rica	06/19/01	09/26/01
J. R. Dawson	Amb to Peru	05/6/02	pending
J. M. DeThomas	Amb to Estonia	05/16/01	10/30/01
C. W. Dell	Amb to Angola	06/20/01	08/03/01
L. M. Dinger	Amb to Micronesia	08/22/01	11/15/01
R. J. Egan	Amb to Ireland	03/14/01	08/03/01

W. S. Farish	Amb to UK	03/05/01	07/10/01
R. P. J. Finn	Amb to Afghanistan	03/01/02	03/20/02
R. F. Freeman	Amb to Belize	04/12/01	08/01/01
J. I. Gadsden	Amb to Iceland	06/05/02	10/02/02
A. O. Garza	Amb to Mexico	07/16/02	pending
A. H. Gioia	Amb to Malta	04/04/01	07/10/01
E. W. Gnehm	Amb to Jordan	07/22/01	08/03/01
D. N. Greenlee	Amb to Bolivia	09/05/02	pending
M. E. Guest	Amb to Romania	06/07/01	08/01/01
J. R. Hamilton	Amb to Guatemala	06/05/02	pending
J. V. Hanford	Amb at large	09/26/01	01/25/02
D. A. Hartwick	Amb to Laos	05/23/01	07/10/01
C. A. Heimbold	Amb to Sweden	04/13/01	08/01/01
H. H. Hertell	Amb to Domin Repub	05/02/01	09/26/01
J. A. Holnes	Amb to Burkina Faso	06/13/02	10/02/02
J. A. Hooks	Amb to Rep Congo	06/11/01	07/12/01
D. J. Hrinak	Amb to Brazil	07/17/01	01/25/02
T. C. Hubbard	Amb to Korea	05/23/01	08/01/01
F. P. Huddle	Amb to Tajikistan	06/22/01	09/26/01
V. J. Huddleston	Amb to Mali	06/04/02	10/02/02
J. Huggins	Amb to Botswana	08/02/02	pending
M. T. Huhtala	Amb to Malaysia	07/16/01	08/01/01
E. J. Hull	Amb to Yemen	05/03/01	08/03/01
C. R. Hume	Amb to South Africa	10/02/01	10/30/01
D. N. Johnson	Amb to Thailand	10/25/01	11/15/01
D. C. Johnson	Amb to Cape Verde	05/14/02	10/02/02
E. L. Johnson	Rep to UN	10/09/01	11/15/01
W. J. Hybl	Rep to UN	08/20/01	11/15/01
R. H. Jones	Amb to Kuwait	04/24/01	08/03/01
R. W. Jordan	Amb to Saudi Arabia	07/12/01	10/03/01
T. H. Kattouf	Amb to Syria	05/16/01	8/03/01
J. F. Keane	Amb to Paraguay	09/03/02	pending
L. E. F. Kennedy	Amb to Turkmenistan	06/07/01	09/14/01
P. F. Kennedy	Rep to UN	06/06/01	09/14/01
K. A. Kenney	Amb to Ecuador	05/10/01	08/01/02
M. Klosson	Amb to Cyprus	05/05/02	08/01/02
J. J. Kolker	Amb to Uganda	05/04/02	10/02/02
D. C. Kurtzer	Amb to Israel	05/25/01	07/10/01
F. L. Lavin	Amb to Singapore	06/11/01	08/01/01
H. H. Leach	Amb to France	03/26/01	07/10/01
R. G. Loftis	Amb to Lesotho	07/03/01	08/03/01
D. L. Lyon	Amb to Fiji	06/25/02	pending
M. E. Malinowski	Amb to Nepal	07/03/01	09/26/01

N. C. Marcus	Rep to UN	10/09/01	11/15/01
G. D. T. Mathieu	Amb to Niger	06/04/02	10/02/02
D. J. McConnell	Amb to Eritrea	04/23/01	07/12/01
J. C. McDonald	Amb to Gambia	06/14/01	09/26/01
M. B. McElveen-Hunter	Amb to Finland	04/25/01	10/30/01
J. D. McGee	Amb to Swaziland	10/17/01	01/25/02
K. J. McGuire	Amb to Namibia	08/13/01	09/26/01
M. K. McMillion	Amb to Rwanda	08/23/01	10/30/01
R. M. Miles	Amb to Georgia	01/24/02	03/20/02
T. J. Miller	Amb to Greece	06/07/01	08/01/01
K. E. Moley	Rep to UN	08/03/01	09/26/01
W. D. Montgomery	Amb to Yugoslavia	10/10/01	11/15/01
B. C. Moore	Amb to Nicaragua	05/10/02	08/01/02
K. P. Moorefield	Amb to Gabon	11/01/01	01/25/02
L. C. Napper	Amb to Kazakhstan	06/22/01	08/01/01
W. L. Nesbitt	Amb to Madagascar	09/25/01	10/30/01
R. E. Neumann	Amb to Bahrain	07/20/01	09/14/01
R. J. Nicholson	Amb to Holy See	04/16/01	080/1/01
J. D. Nigroponte	Rep to UN	03/06/01	09/14/01
R. F. Noriega	Perm Rep	05/31/01	08/01/01
J. D. Ong	Amb to Norway	08/10/01	01/25/02
J. M. Ordway	Amb to Armenia	06/26/01	10/30/01
J. N. Palmer	Amb to Portugal	04/12/01	10/30/01
L. L. Palmer	Amb to Honduras	06/05/02	08/01/02
J. W. Pardew	Amb to Bulgaria	02/07/02	03/20/02
E. N. Phillips	Amb to Barbados	07/18/01	01/25/02
N. J. Powell	Amb to Pakistan	06/25/02	08/01/02
J. Price	Amb to Mauritius	05/18/01	01/25/02
P. R. Prosper	Amb at large	03/21/01	07/11/01
M. E. Quinn	Amb to Qatar	05/16/01	08/03/01
C. T. Randt	Amb to China	04/30/01	07/10/01
C. A. Ray	Amb to Cambodia	07/07/02	pending
G. J. Rees	Amb to East Timor	09/03/02	pending
A. Render	Amb to Cote d'Ivoire	05/16/01	09/26/01
M. Reynolds	Amb to Switzerland	04/26/01	08/01/01
F. J. Ricciardone	Amb to Philippines	11/14/01	02/04/02
R. A. Roth	Amb to Senegal	06/18/02	pending
R. V. Royall	Amb to Tanzania	07/11/01	10/30/01
R. R. Sanders	Amb to Congo	09/05/02	pending
E. R. Sauerbrey	Status of Women	06/17/02	pending
J. T. Schieffer	Amb to Australia	06/07/01	07/27/01
R. A. Schnabel	EU	08/29/01	09/26/01
M. F. Sembler	Amb to Italy	07/27/01	11/15/01

C. S. Shapiro	Amb to Venezuela	10/09/01	01/25/02
M. R. Sharpless	Amb to CAR	07/02/01	09/26/01
M. J. Silverstein	Amb to Uruguay	06/19/01	08/03/01
S. A. Siv	Rep to UN	10/12/01	11/09/01
P. H. Smith	Amb to Moldova	08/02/01	09/26/01
C. M. Sobel	Amb to Netherlands	10/02/01	10/30/01
G. M. Staples	Amb to Cameroon	07/02/01	07/12/01
C. Stapleton	Amb to Czech Rep	04/06/01	08/03/01
J. G. Sullivan	Amb to Zimbabwe	06/15/01	08/03/01
C. J. Swindells	Amb to New Zealand	04/25/01	07/10/01
P. Terpeluk	Amb to Luxenberg	01/24/02	03/20/02
M. D. Tutwiler	Amb to Morocco	03/22/01	07/10/01
A. R. Vershbow	Amb to Russia	05/01/01	07/10/01
M. M. Wahba	Amb to UAE	05/16/01	09/14/01
R. B. Walkley	Amb to Guinea	05/14/01	09/16/01
L. E. Watt	Amb to Panama	06/27/02	pending
R. N. Weiser	Amb to Slovak Rep	05/04/01	11/15/01
C. B. Welch	Amb to Egypt	04/27/01	07/10/01
R. S. Williamson	Rep to UN	10/04/01	110/9/01
M. C. Yates	Amb to Ghana	10/16/02	pending
J. H. Yellin	Amb to Burundi	05/06/02	08/01/02
J. Young	Amb to Slovenia	06/19/01	08/03/01

About the Contributors

Douglas M. Brattebo, Ph.D., is Assistant Professor of Political Science at the U.S. Naval Academy, where he teaches Honors Introduction to American Government, The American Presidency and the Executive Branch, and a Seminar on the Democratic Peace. In May 2002, he won the Naval Academy's campuswide Apgar Award for Teaching Excellence.

Richard S. Conley, Ph.D., is Assistant Professor of Political Science at the University of Florida. His research on presidential-congressional relations has appeared in *American Politics Research, Political Research Quarterly, Polity, Presidential Studies Quarterly*, and *White House Studies*. His most recent book is *Reassessing the Reagan Presidency* (University Press of America, 2003).

Laura Coppeto is a student majoring in political science at Villanova University. After graduation she will pursue an advanced degree in public policy with a concentration on education policy. She is a member of the National Society for Collegiate Scholars.

Byron W. Daynes, Ph.D., is Professor of Political Science at Brigham Young University. His more than fifty articles and book reviews in the field of political science have appeared in *Women and Politics, Congress and the Presidency, Presidential Studies Quarterly*, and *The American Political Science Review*. Daynes is co-author and/or co-editor of twelve books. His most recent (with Glen Sussman and Jonathan West) is *American Politics and the Environment* (Longman, 2002).

Chris J. Dolan, Ph.D., is Assistant Professor of Political Science at the University of Central Florida. His research on the American presidency focuses on economic policy making, White House staffing and organization, presidential decision making, and the politics of American foreign relations. He is currently writing a book on presidential power and the National Economic Council, and his work has appeared in *Congress and the Presidency, White House Studies, Politics and Policy,* and *International Politics.*

Louis Fisher, Ph.D., is Senior Specialist in Separation of Powers at the Congressional Research Service/Library of Congress. An award-winning author of fifteen books, he has published 300 articles in edited books, law reviews, political science journals, encyclopedias, magazines, and newspapers. His specialties include war powers, constitutional law, the presidency, and executive-legislative relations. Fisher has been invited to testify before congressional committees thirty-eight times.

Bryan Hilliard, Ph.D., is Assistant Professor of Philosophy at New England College. He is director of the Frank Maria Center for International Politics and Ethics and serves on the editorial boards of *The International Journal of Politics and Ethics* and *White House Studies.* His research interests are focused in the areas of physician-assisted death, managed care ethics, bioethics and constitutional law, and political leadership. He has been published in *Journal of Integrative Studies, White House Studies, JONA's Healthcare Law, Ethics, and Regulation,* and *Cambridge Quarterly of Health Care Ethics.* Hilliard is currently working on a book on the connections between U.S. Supreme Court decisions and medical ethics.

Bill Kirtley, Ph.D., is Professor of Government and Economics at Central Texas College. He also teaches on U.S. Naval vessels traveling around the world. He is currently researching and writing a book on Oregon's Death With Dignity Act.

Tom Lansford, Ph.D., is Associate Professor of Political Science at the University of Southern Mississippi-Gulf Coast and a Fellow of the Frank Maria Center for International Politics and Ethics. Lansford is a member of the governing board of the National Social Science Association, the editorial board of the journal *White House Studies,* and the book review editor for *The International Journal of Politics and Ethics.* He has published articles in journals such as *Defense Analysis, The Journal of Conflict Studies, European Security, International Studies, Security Dialogue,* and *Strategic Studies.* Lansford is the author of a number of books. His most recent book is *All for One: NATO: Terrorism and the United States* (Ashgate, 2002).

Jack Lechelt is completing his dissertation for the Ph.D. in the Department of Government and International Studies at the University of South Carolina. He has authored numerous scholarly publications. His research interests include the presidency, vice presidency, and foreign policy.

Robert Maranto, Ph.D., teaches political science and public administration at Villanova University in Pennsylvania. In collaboration with others, he has published numerous scholarly articles and books, including *School Choice in the Real World* (Westview, 2001) and *Radical Reform of the Civil Service* (Lexington, 2001).

Bradley H. Patterson Jr. is one of the nation's most recognized experts on the organization and functioning of the modern White House staff. He served fourteen years on the White House staff for presidents Eisenhower, Nixon, and Ford, is a retired federal career executive who worked with the Department of State, Department of Treasury, and Peace Corps, and is a veteran of the Brookings Institution. Patterson is past president of the American Society for Public Administration and Senior Fellow of the National Academy of Public Administration. His most recent book is the award-winning *The White House Staff: Inside the West Wing and Beyond* (Brookings Institution, 2000).

W. W. "Bill" Riggs, retired Marine Corps officer and Ph.D., is Assistant Professor of Political Science and Public Administration at Texas A&M International University in Laredo. His research interests include the politics of the "colonias" and communitarianism.

Glen Sussman, Ph.D., is Associate Professor and Chair of the Political Science Department at Old Dominion University. He is the author of three books and over fifty articles, book chapters, and scholarly papers. His research focus is the American presidency, environmental politics and policy, and citizen participation.

Cameron G. Thies, Ph.D., is Assistant Professor of Political Science at Louisiana State University. His research interests include theoretical and methodological issues related to the study of international relations and foreign policy. His work has appeared in the *European Journal of International Relations, International Interactions, International Studies Perspectives, Political Psychology*, and *Comparative Political Studies*.

Robert P. Watson, Ph.D., is Associate Professor of Political Science at Florida Atlantic University and founding editor of the journal *White House Studies*. He is the author, editor, or co-editor of twenty books and has published over 100 scholarly articles, chapters, and essays. Watson has been interviewed by CNN, MSNBC, *USA Today*, and many other media outlets, appeared on C-SPAN's *Book TV*, was a guest for CNN.com's coverage of the 2001 presidential inauguration, directed the first-ever "Report to the First Lady," which was presented to the White House in 2001, and served as a visiting scholar at numerous universities and historic presidential sites and libraries.

Index

www.ingramcontent.com/pod-product-compliance
Lightning Source LLC
Chambersburg PA
CBHW020339270326
41926CB00007B/237

* 9 7 8 0 7 9 1 4 6 1 3 4 1 *